PROBLEMS OF RELIGION

AN INTRODUCTORY SURVEY

BY

DURANT DRAKE

A.M. (HARVARD), PH.D. (COLUMBIA)

Professor of Philosophy at Vassar College
Author of Problems of Conduct

GREENWOOD PRESS, PUBLISHERS
NEW YORK   1968

COPYRIGHT, 1916, BY DURANT DRAKE

Reprinted with permission of the
Houghton Mifflin Company

First Greenwood reprinting, 1968

LIBRARY OF CONGRESS catalogue card number: 68-19268

PRINTED IN THE UNITED STATES OF AMERICA

BL
48
D7

TO MY WIFE

WHOSE LIFE REVEALS THE SECRET OF RELIGION
FAR BETTER THAN ALL MY WORDS

PREFACE

THIS book, like its predecessor, *Problems of Conduct*, represents a course of lectures given for several years to undergraduates of Wesleyan University. It is hoped that these lectures in printed form will be useful, not only for other college classes, but for the general reading public that is interested in the great and vital problems of religion. Their aim is to give a rapid survey of the field, such that the man who is confused by the chaos of opinions on these matters, and himself but little able to judge between conflicting statements, may here get his bearings and see his way to stable belief and energetic action. In so limited a space it will not be possible to attempt an adequate presentation of the arguments for each view advanced or a rebuttal of the infinitely numerous and shifting arguments by which the various current doctrines seek to justify themselves. All that can be done is to offer the results of the best scholarly work in the wide field covered, and thereby to present a general perspective of those truths, some old and some but recently acquired, which bear practically on our religion.

The carefully chosen lists of readings appended to each chapter, together with the more specific references in the footnotes, will serve — for those who are interested enough to pursue any topic further — as a check upon the author's conclusions and an initiation into the further aspects of the several problems. Practically all of this selected literature is in English, and is readable, as well as worth reading. The hopelessly antiquated literature is not cited, except occasionally, where it seems necessary for the sake of fairness in presenting both sides of a long controverted matter. The literature that indulges in rhetoric rather than in solid argument is also omitted, and all that range of books once useful but now stranded by the onrushing tides of criticism. Such names as Edwards, Emmons, Hodge, on the one hand, and Strauss, Renan, Ingersoll, on the other, are absent; but whatever of their thought survives in contemporary discussion will be found represented in the more recent works referred to. The ideal of justice to all legitimate opinions has been kept in mind, but has not precluded the attempt to present as clearly as possible whatever conclusions seem to the author warranted by our present-day knowledge.

There are two fires between which the critical writer on religion stands. On the one side, his historical investigations and scientific attitude inevitably seem cold and unfriendly to him whose personal belief is, necessarily, treated as one of many forms of possible religious belief, springing originally, as all have, out of superstition and error, and developed largely through the forces of prejudice and emotion. From the other side come the murmurs of those who, standing outside of these beliefs, and feeling no pull of longing or loyalty toward them, feel an impatience at so much concern with what appears to them a mere conglomerate of preposterous and visionary ideas. In the introductory chapter that follows, I have essayed to defend what, fortunately, for most readers will now in these more tolerant times need no defense, an attitude toward religion that is both warm, sympathetic, reverent — and critical, open-eyed, resolute to follow the truth wherever it lead.

Parts of this book, in manuscript, have been read by Dr. Percy W. Long, of Harvard University, Professor Clayton R. Bowen, of the Meadville Theological School, President Albert Parker Fitch, of Andover Theological Seminary,

Professor J. W. Hewitt, of Wesleyan University, Professor C. B. Hedrick and W. P. Ladd, of the Berkeley Divinity School, and Professor D. C. Macintosh, of the Yale School of Religion. In an earlier form it was read, with sympathetic and illuminating comment, by that leader and inspirer of us all, William James. To all of these I render grateful acknowledgment; and to two others whose written and spoken words have been of the utmost service to me — Professor George Santayana, formerly of Harvard University, and Professor Dickinson S. Miller, of the General Theological School, New York. To none of these, however, must any responsibility be attributed for the opinions which I here espouse.

My thanks are due to the editors of the *American Journal of Theology*, the *Biblical World*, the *Monist*, and the *International Journal of Ethics* for permission to reprint various sentences and portions of chapters which have appeared as a part of earlier essays in these periodicals.

DURANT DRAKE.

CONTENTS

INTRODUCTORY 1
    The importance of the study of religion.
    The need of a critical attitude toward religion.

PART I. HISTORICAL

CHAPTER I. THE ORIGINS OF RELIGION 9
    The sources of primitive religious ideas and practices: —
      I. The precarious situation of primitive man.
     II. The spontaneous attribution of life and will to inanimate objects.
    III. Dreams and the mystery of death.
    IV. Abnormal and mysterious experiences.
     V. Reflection upon the origin of things.
    VI. Man's need of deliverance from himself.

CHAPTER II. GREEK AND ROMAN RELIGION . . . 20
    In what striking ways did religion develop in Greece?
    What is the permanent significance of the classic Greek religion?
    What were the main currents in Roman religion?

CHAPTER III. BUDDHISM AND ZOROASTRIANISM . . 36
    What was the soil from which Buddhism grew?
    What was the nature of Buddha's mission?
    What were the striking aspects of his teaching?
    What was the subsequent history of Buddhism?
    What was the essence of Zoroastrianism?

CHAPTER IV. THE HEBREW RELIGION 49
    How did the Hebrew monotheism arise?
    What are the striking features of the religion of the prophets and psalmists?
    How did the Messianic hope arise?

CHAPTER V. JESUS THE CHRIST 63
    What are the sources of our knowledge of the life of Christ?
    What were the salient events of his life?

What were the striking features of his personality?
What were the striking features of his teaching?

CHAPTER VI. PAUL AND THE FOUNDING OF THE CHURCH — 82
How did the Christian Church originate?
What are the salient facts of Paul's life and personality?
What was the gist of Paul's teaching?

CHAPTER VII. EARLY CHRISTIANITY 96
What were the causes of the triumph of Christianity?
Under what influences did the Church evolve her creeds?
What was the origin of the conceptions of
    I. The Atonement?
    II. The Trinity?
    III. Heaven, Hell, and Purgatory?

CHAPTER VIII. LATER CHRISTIANITY; MOHAMMEDANISM — 113
By what process did the Roman Church become dominant?
What was the significance of the Reformation?
What have been the subsequent tendencies of Christianity?
What are the essential features of Mohammedanism?

SUMMARY OF PART I 128
What has been the trend of religious evolution?

PART II. PSYCHOLOGICAL

CHAPTER IX. THE GOD OF EXPERIENCE 135
How does God appear in human experience?
    I. God in nature.
    II. God in our hearts — the Holy Spirit.
    III. God in Christ.
What is the nature of God as thus revealed?

CHAPTER X. SACRIFICE AND SIN 151
What is the history of the concepts of sacrifice and sin?
What are their dangers?
What is their permanent value?
The doctrine of Original Sin.

CONTENTS

CHAPTER XI. SALVATION, CONVERSION, AND ATONEMENT 166
What is the meaning of salvation?
What is the meaning and value of conversion?
The doctrine of the Atonement.

CHAPTER XII. FAITH AND PRAYER 180
What is the nature and value of faith?
What has been the evolution of prayer?
What is the function and value of prayer?

CHAPTER XIII. RELIGIOUS LOVE AND PEACE . . . 197
The spirit of love and service in religion.
Religious peace.
Mysticism and Christian Science.

CHAPTER XIV. THE ESSENCE OF RELIGION . . . 213
How shall we determine the essence of religion?
What is the relation of religion to theology?
What is the relation of religion to morality?
What is the essential nature of religion?

CHAPTER XV. THE CHRISTIAN RELIGION 229
Is Christianity the true religion?
The Gospel of Christ.
The Gospel about Christ.
The Christian life and Christian creeds.
Who is the true Christian?

SUMMARY OF PART II 243
What function does religion have in the life of man?

PART III. PHILOSOPHICAL

CHAPTER XVI. THEOLOGICAL METHOD AND THE SCIENTIFIC SPIRIT 249
The three methods of theology:—
  I. Authority.
  II. *A priori* reasoning.
  III. The scientific method.
The opposition of the Church to the scientific spirit.

CONTENTS

CHAPTER XVII. THE INTERPRETATION OF THE BIBLE   264
    How did the conception develop of the inerrancy of the Bible?
    What facts have altered our conception of the Bible?
    Is the Bible inspired, the Word of God, authoritative?
    Wherein consists the greatness of the Bible?

CHAPTER XVIII. MIRACLES 280
    What considerations have weakened the belief in miracles?
    Of what value is the belief in miracles?
    What should be our attitude toward miracles?

CHAPTER XIX. CREATION AND DESIGN 295
    Can we draw theological inferences from
        I. The sheer existence of the universe?
        II. The existence of certain classes of facts?
        III. Marks of design or purpose?

CHAPTER XX. THE INTERPRETATION OF RELIGIOUS EXPERIENCE 312
    What cautions should be observed in interpreting religious experience?
        I. The voice of conscience.
        II. Conversion.
        III. Faith-healing.
        IV. Mysticism and intuition.

CHAPTER XXI. PRAGMATIC ARGUMENTS 332
    Can we trust a belief:
        I. Because its untruth would be intolerable?
        II. Because our hearts vouch for it?
        III. Because it "works"?

CHAPTER XXII. THE COUNTER-ATTACK UPON SCIENCE   351
    Is reason untrustworthy because the product of blind forces?
    Is science based upon unproved and self-contradictory postulates?
    Is science based upon purely subjective data?
    Is science restricted in its scope?

CHAPTER XXIII. THE PROBLEM OF EVIL 366
    Can evil be conceived as a partial view of the good?
    Is evil necessary for character-building?
    Is evil necessary at a stage in the evolution of humanity?
    Is evil the result of man's perverse use of his free will?
    Is evil to be attributed to God at all?

CONTENTS

CHAPTER XXIV. IMMORTALITY 383
  The evolution of the belief in a future life.
  What considerations make against the belief?
  What are the leading arguments for the belief?

CHAPTER XXV. THE VENTURE OF FAITH 397
  Which is the higher ideal, loyal belief or impartial investigation?
  Should we accept or reject beliefs of whose evidence we are uncertain?
  May non-evidential motives properly influence belief?

SUMMARY OF PART III 412
  What is the present status of theology?

INDEX 417

PROBLEMS OF RELIGION

INTRODUCTORY

The importance of the study of religion

(1) PRACTICALLY, if not absolutely, all known races of men have been in some sense or degree religious; and to many of them religion has been the most vital of all matters. Hence, the study of this great tract of human interest is essential for all who would comprehend what the life of man historically has been. And Christianity, the faith, confessed or potential, of the great majority of the probable readers of this book, deserves particular attention — just as school geographies properly lay special stress upon the topography of the State in which they are to be used, or historical curricula upon the history and traditions of the fatherland. But, indeed, objectively considered, if we may judge by its results achieved and its evident vitality and promise, Christianity is the greatest of all religions, and bids fair to be more and more the dominant religion of the world. The purely scientific interest in religious phenomena, and particularly in Christian experience, should, then, be at least as great as that in any other field open to our research.

(2) But more than this. Religion is a very precious possession, and a study of it should attract those who feel the lack in their own lives of its comfort and inspiration. There is in most men a great reservoir of potentiality of the religious life; not wholly suffocated by material interests, not quite choked by the increase of knowledge and the crumbling of antique doctrines, it awaits the spreading of a com-

prehension of the possibilities of religious living apart from discredited dogmas, to flood society with renewed enthusiasm and power. A study of religion is practically of supreme importance when it can tap this latent spirituality and lead to an espousal of the religious life.

(3) Again, it is important for those who are disturbed in their faith, who are groping for light, or clinging desperately to doctrines they cannot whole-heartedly believe because they cannot see how to get along without them; for those who have lost their childhood's creed and turned their backs to religion because that creed represented the only religion they knew. Something to clarify the clouded minds of such men and women, religious in their hearts but confused in their outlook and paralyzed in their worship, — some way of harmonizing the conflicting ideals that beset them, — should come from a careful study of facts as they are.

(4) Even those who are happy in a dogmatic slumber, but through their dogmatism are retarding the influence of religion in the world, and making it harder for others to find peace and religious fellowship, may be urged for the general good to question their presuppositions and look at religion with greater detachment from prejudice and desire. Only by willingness to criticize our own beliefs and confess our individual bias can we hope to approach to anything like a mutual understanding and working agreement.

(5) Finally, a realization of the dynamic in religion should be a summons to those who are not helping in the work Christianity has to do in the world; should reënlist the interest of the earnest, intelligent, able men and women who have in such numbers abandoned the churches. Their help is needed, badly needed, to free the Church from those outgrown conceptions that once aided, but now hamper her; to win for her again the full respect of the thinking world; and to keep her through these bewildering changes infused

with such earnest idealism that she may be the power for righteousness of which the world, with its permanent temptation to selfishness and lust and greed, stands now, as always, in need.

The need of a critical attitude toward religion

Truth is not the only good in life; nor is criticism, however valid, necessarily desirable. The religious spirit, in whatever fantastic garb it be clothed, and however irrational the doctrines by which it seek to justify itself, is more beautiful and valuable than any accuracy of knowledge; and it were better to leave those doctrines uncriticized — if that were possible — than to weaken or maim that spirit. But there are definite and important reasons why a scientific attitude toward religious dogmas has become our imperative duty.

(1) The insistence upon irrational views interferes badly with the spread of accurate knowledge; and, more than that, the spirit of dogmatism, the reluctance to criticize and reconsider beliefs in the light of observation and experiment, stifles that free and impartial study of evidence which has been the greatest contribution of the physical sciences to civilization. As will be shown in chapter XVI, historic religion — and notably Christianity — has been a very disastrous barrier to intellectual progress. For this reason, then, we must be willing to scrutinize critically our deepest beliefs, because we want the truth; and we cannot be sure that we have the truth, that we are not, instead, standing in the way of enlightenment, unless we seriously undertake so to do.

(2) But for the sake of our eventual assurance and peace, we must purge our religion of its superstition and error. For however we may cover our eyes and our ears, the truths that are being taught by archæologists and anthropologists, by historians and naturalists, are likely sooner or later to trickle

into our consciousness and torture us with misgivings. And when a man whose religion has been based upon unwarranted postulates or intertwined with illusory assurances finds that he has been in so far deceived, he is apt to lose his faith entirely and drift into skepticism and despair. It does not pay, in the long run, to found our hopes upon what the best thought of the age disproves or renders doubtful.

(3) And finally, for the sake of the religion itself that we love, and its future in the world, we must submit it to the surgical operations of criticism. Nine tenths of the attacks upon Christianity are directed against the unessential and untrue accretions that are really separable from its inner kernel of living truth. Thus, our faith has become to some a derision and a laughing-stock, and by others has been cast impatiently aside, simply because the churches have stood in the way of that surgical work which alone can save it — and must save it before it is too late. Pious ignorance hurts the cause of religion almost as much as worldliness and sin; no cause can be safely guarded by an organization or a spirit of dogmatism that ignores facts and turns its back upon probabilities. And it is precisely because the battle with worldliness and sin is so desperately hard and long that religion must rid itself of its impediments, must strip for the struggle. It is entirely needless that so many of our finest should be alienated from the Church; but unless we accept the situation, excise the vulnerable portions of our creeds, and adjust our doctrines to the demands of the contemporary intellect, these men and women are bound to drift in greater and greater numbers away from the Church, and, very often, away from the precious truths of which she is the appointed teacher and custodian.

It was the vivid realization of this situation that drew Matthew Arnold into writing critically of religion; and his essays, though superseded in many matters by the work and thought of later scholars, are a notable example of reverent attempt to prune the luxuriant growths of religion, and by pruning to save it. There were those who expostulated with him, saying, as he tells us, "Why meddle with religion at all? Why run the risk of breaking a tie which it is so hard to join again?" And he replies: "The risk is not to be run lightly, and one is not always to attack people's illusions about religion merely because illusions they are. But at the present moment two things about the Christian religion must surely be clear to anybody with eyes in his head. One is, that men cannot do without it; the other, that they cannot do with it as it is." [1]

Matthew Arnold was regarded in his day as a dangerous heretic; but to-day there are very many in the churches who realize as keenly the need in which our religion stands of revision and restatement. Dean Farrar, for example, writes: "He who helps to disencumber Christianity from dubious or false accretions is rendering to it a service which may be more urgently necessary than if he composed a book of evidences." It is only imposture that has need to fear the light; and the Church ought not merely to admit the truth reluctantly, step by step, but to take the lead in seeking the truth, whatever time-honored arguments or even precious assurances it may have to discard.

It is not pride of knowledge, then, or a scientific dogmatism, that demands a revision of our religious ideas, but a realization that there is much error in our traditional conceptions, and that the truth alone ultimately serves. The results of such a revisory work will by many be stigmatized as iconoclastic, as irreligious, as mischievous. The world's progress has always been accompanied by such cries. But

[1] Preface to *God and the Bible*. This preface, and that to *Literature and Dogma*, admirably state the point here insisted upon.

the world does progress, and if we are to keep our religion abreast of it we must air our beliefs in all currents of modern thought, we must question them freely, we must express the results of our reflection fearlessly and openly. To be afraid to think or to speak out our thoughts would be to stifle religion and bring about inevitable decay. And then, what seems daring and subversive to-day will be taken for granted to-morrow; as Arnold says, "The freethinking of one age is the commonplace of the next."

But, after all, it does not rest with us to decide whether religion shall be criticized or no. Destructive criticism has long been abroad, criticism that fails to do justice to the truths it discards, that throws away the kernel with the husk. This anti-religious propaganda is having its ill effects upon the religious spirit of the age. To save religion itself — or so much of it as is true and worthy our allegiance — demands our efforts. And to accomplish a just and adequate reconstruction we need first to go through the purgatorial fires of criticism. Religion must be solidly based on fact; unless it is willing to look science and history in the face and adjust itself to their results, it cannot long continue to live.

Yet let us throughout remember that to live the religious life is more important than to understand the truth about religion; and while willing ourselves to sacrifice whatever may be required to the attainment of that truth, let us, wherever we have to do with what has inspired and comforted men, walk reverently and with unshod feet; for the ground whereon we tread is holy ground.

PART I
HISTORICAL

CHAPTER I

THE ORIGINS OF RELIGION

RELIGION, as we view it historically, is a complex composite, woven of many strands that stretch back into the remote past. Our task in this chapter is to trace some of the more important of these sources, and give a rapid pen-picture of the mental attitudes of primitive man that combined to make him religious.

The sources of primitive religious ideas and practices

I. The precarious situation of primitive man. When man, scarcely yet more than a brute, begins to think about his needs and to strive consciously for those ends toward which blind instinct has hitherto driven him, he finds himself in a precarious and uncertain situation. He rears a rude shelter — the storm batters it, the winds shake it, the lightning threatens to destroy it; he plants a few seeds to insure himself food — the sun scorches them and the drought spoils the fruit of his labors; the tempest buffets him, the thunder terrifies him — he realizes his helplessness before these powers that are so much greater than he, and on whose kindly aid he is dependent for his prosperity, nay, his very existence.

Lucretius observes that men "much more keenly in evil days turn their minds to religion." [1] And, indeed, that robust old atheist elsewhere confesses, "Who is there whose mind does not shrink into itself with fear of the gods, whose limbs do not creep with terror when the parched earth rocks under the terrible blast of the thunderbolt, and the roaring sound

[1] *De Rerum Natura*, III, 53.

sweeps across the heavens? . . . Or when the full fury of the wild wind scours the sea and drives across its expanse the commander with his brave legions and his elephants, does he not in prayer seek peace with the gods?"[1] Thus it was commonly repeated in antiquity that fear made the gods; fear, and, we may add, hope; that despair of man at his own frail faculties that cries out to some one, to any one, for help. When it is fear of his fellow man, or of the brutes, he is not without means of self-protection; but when his apprehension is of those physical forces by which he is surrounded, which so often menace his welfare and his life, he knows not how to save himself. Ignorant for the most part as yet how to meet these dangers by physical means, and under the need of doing something to ward off the evil, he cries out, he gesticulates, he commands, he beseeches these Powers not to harm him.[2]

All this is prior to any definite formulation of the idea of a god or spirit; it is mere spontaneous psychological reaction. Magic, — the attempt to coerce the surrounding Powers by incantations and mysterious rites, — prayers, sacrifices for appeasement, vows — all such activities antedated articulate belief; it was in his quieter and more reflective moments, no doubt, and as an explanation and justification of these instinctive acts, that primitive man attained to a definite and steady belief in quasi-human Beings behind the blessings and catastrophes that befell him. Indeed, among many savage races but lately studied, there has been no real personalizing

[1] *De Rerum Natura*, v, 1210.

[2] Animals also may whine and tremble in the presence of danger. But man alone, with his dawning self-consciousness, remembers the danger, reflects upon it, *realizes* the precariousness of his situation and his dependence upon the Powers about him. It is man's faculty of imagination, constructive thought, and auto-suggestion, his ability to react to unperceived and merely imagined objects, that develops out of these otherwise transitory and vague moods a permanent, if flickering, conception of superhuman Powers besetting him.

of nature-forces. We have in the Algonkin "manitou" and the Melanesian "mana" a mysterious potency, a vital power, recognized in things, to be reckoned with and dealt with cautiously, but not clearly personal. Of the aborigines of Australia we are told by various observers that they offer no sacrifices or prayers to any personal Beings. But "even though they appeal to no spirits in their ceremonies, these ceremonies do express valuational attitudes of a definitely religious character." [1] That cultural stage characterized by vague fears of the supernatural, when man was as yet hardly conscious of the fact of personality in himself, and so hardly postulating personality of natural forces, has been termed by recent writers the pre-animistic stage.[2]

II. The spontaneous attribution of life and will to inanimate objects. As man's mental life became more acute, there was an inevitable tendency toward the genuine personification of the powers of nature. William James tells us [3] how irresistibly he was dominated by the impulse to think of the great San Francisco earthquake — which he felt at Palo Alto — as a living being. It was The Earthquake; it stole into his room, it shook him as a terrier shakes a rat; it exulted in its power. He reports, further, that practically every one experienced a similar psychological reaction, even those who, like him, were most accustomed to scientific concepts and abstract analysis. It is, thus, only our sophistication and intellectual maturity that prevent us from feeling all natural forces, or at least the violent and dangerous ones, as endowed with personality. So an English writer, describing his own experience as a boy: "Sitting on the hillside when the hot season was coming near its end he saw the

---

[1] King, p. 171, footnote. Throughout this book, works named in the bibliography at the close of a chapter will be referred to in the footnotes of that chapter by the author's name only.

[2] See Marett, chaps. I, IV.

[3] "The Earthquake," in *Memories and Studies*.

thunderstorms come across the hills. From far away they came, black shadows in the distance, and the thunder like far-off surf upon the shore. Nearer they would grow and nearer, passing from ridge to ridge, their long white skirts trailing upon the mountain-sides, until they came right overhead and the lightning flashed blindingly, while the thunder roared in great trumpet tones that shuddered through the gorges. The man watched them and he saw how gods were born. It was Thor come back again — Thor with his hammer, Thor with his giant voice. Thus were born the gods. Thor and Odin, Balder, God of the Summer Sun, Apollo and Vulcan, Ahriman and Ormuz, night and day." [1]

We must remember that all those physical events, the intricate causes of which our modern science explores, are to the savage pure mystery, inexplicable and arbitrary. Having no idea of natural causation, as we now understand it, he instinctively regards all the moving objects about him after the nearest analogy he has, his own life. When they harm him he ascribes to them the feelings he has when he injures another; when they favor him he imagines them kindly disposed; by a naïve and natural fallacy he reads into them his own emotions and thinks of their activity, now beneficent, now baneful, as caused by intermittently friendly and malicious impulses such as he finds in his own heart. The burning, warming sun, the portentous and muttering thunderhead, the broad, majestic river that brings fertility or flood

---

[1] H. Fielding Hall, *The Hearts of Men*, p. 72. Cf. Gilbert Murray, *Four Stages of Greek Religion*, p. 25: "The process of making winds and rivers into anthropomorphic gods is, for the most part, not the result of using the imagination with special vigour. It is the result of not doing so. The wind is obviously alive; any fool can see that. Being alive, it blows; how? why, naturally; just as you and I blow. It knocks things down, it shouts and dances. It whispers and talks. And, unless we are going to make a great effort of the imagination and try to realize, like a scientific man, just what really happens, we naturally assume that it does these things in the normal way, in the only way we know."

to his soil, the treacherous, rushing winds — these are all living beings to him, beings greater and more powerful than he; they are his gods.[1]

III. Dreams and the mystery of death. Another source of the belief in spirits is the inability of primitive men to realize the fact of death. Having no comprehension of the actual relations of mind and body, or of the hopeless finality, for our mundane experience, of death, they are slow to grasp the fact that he who was greatly honored or feared but the other day is now utterly non-existent and without power for their weal or woe. Do not men lie as still when heavy with sleep, or in a drunken stupor, when stunned or fainting or in an epileptic trance? Yet these still live, for they return to action. Moreover, in one's own dreams has one not left one's body lying still and traveled afar, unseen and unheard by others? Perhaps, then, while this hero's body is lying as if in sleep, the real person that feels and acts, inside of the body, has but left it lying here and is still about, continuing a sort of dream life, wherefrom he may perchance still help or harm the living. If his personality was powerful and made a deep impression upon men, they will still see him and talk with him in dreams; the nervous and emotional will fancy they see him as ghost or apparition while awake; these rumors, quickly magnified as they spread, will leave no doubt in the minds of those who feared or revered him. Ought he not, then, to be propitiated, to be besought for help? If an untoward misfortune befalls the tribe, perhaps he is angry at being so soon forgotten; if good fortune comes, perhaps it was his unseen assistance. The tribe unites in offering him sacrifices, he becomes a tribal god.

In a society where patriarchal authority or the power of the chieftain was strong, — as was the case very generally through a long period of early human history, — the worship

[1] See, for examples, E. B. Tylor, *Primitive Culture*.

of ancestors or tribal chiefs, thought of as still continuing some sort of a shadowy existence, was almost inevitable. Some students [1] have gone so far as to conclude that all the gods were originally human heroes, glorified by the apotheosis of time. There is no doubt that many have thus come into suppositious existence, for the process has been carried on into historic times, in the deification of prophets and seers and kings. Moreover, the spirit of a deceased chieftain might be thought to abide on some remote mountain-peak, whence he sent showers or thunderbolts upon his people; and hence Beings generally regarded as nature-gods might readily have sprung from this other source. Crop- and wine-gods may have arisen from the custom of bringing food and drink to the graves of the dead.[2] But the personification of natural forces is also so instinctive a process that there seems little doubt of the reality of both sources of the conception of gods. Among some peoples nature-gods seem to predominate, among others — as still in China — ancestor- or chief-worship is more prominent. But in China there is the worship of Heaven, and in Rome there were the Manes, amid a host of nature-gods; almost everywhere the two strands mingle in a way difficult or impossible now to disentangle.

IV. Abnormal and mysterious experiences. Those are the two principal sources of the conception of gods — the animation of physical objects and the ascription of continued life to the dead. But every mysterious experience no doubt aided the growth of such beliefs. The uncanny phenomena of clairvoyance and hypnotism, photisms and auditory hallucinations, multiple personality and automatisms — all those curious experiences that have filled the lives of saints

[1] For example, Herbert Spencer and Grant Allen.
[2] For concrete instances of the "making of a god" in such wise, see J. E. Harrison, *Prolegomena to the Study of Greek Religion*, chap. VII.

and nowadays fill the treatises on abnormal psychology — were not unknown to the savage, and no doubt increased his sense of an unseen world about him. By many primitive peoples these abnormal experiences were actually cultivated and assumed considerable importance. We have in historic times the well-known Greek oracles, the early Hebrew prophets, the Mohammedan dervishes, the Shamans of Siberia, practicing automatic utterance; we have the clairvoyant Witch of Endor consulted by Saul, and the Cumæan Sibyl with her vision of the future.

The fact is, once the general conception of unseen quasi-human Beings becomes generally accepted, anything may give rise to a new one. So the Arabs have their djinns and demons, the Irish their "little people"; and elves, satyrs, fauns, mermaids, and a thousand other imagined beings, dance about the world, in addition to the larger and more important Powers. Once originated, anyhow and anywhere, such fancies grow and spread like gossip. Primitive man has little critical faculty or basis of experience from which to judge any tale he may be told; whatever plays upon his emotions, his fears, and his hopes — the terrifying, the comforting, the awe-inspiring — is readily accepted and tenaciously held by his mind. For that matter, almost up to the present time every village had its ghost stories; and the more backward localities, though restrained by their allegiance to Christianity from developing a worship of gods, were full of fairies, banshees, apparitions, and superstitions. The rapid spread of the belief in witchcraft even among the educated, only a few generations ago, shows further how naturally credulous is the human mind, and how reluctant to banish beliefs, however irrational, that appeal to the imagination and emotions.[1]

---

[1] For the "abnormal" element in primitive religion, see Pratt, chap. III, sec. 3; Lang, chaps. IV–VII.

V. Reflection upon the origin of things. Further, as man, with his developing reflective power, came to reason concerning the origin of things in general, — all the great world that he could not have made himself, so vast is it and wonderful, — he naturally conjectured that some greater Being, supremely powerful and intelligent, was its creator. Imaginative men would invent tales of how the world came into existence, as well as explanations in terms of superhuman activity for all that seemed mysterious and inexplicable. Best known to us, of course, are the two accounts given, respectively, in the first two chapters of Genesis. But these are only variant forms of legends far older, and common, in one shape or another, to many primitive peoples. Children to-day, at a certain stage of mental awakening, are apt to puzzle over the problem of origins, and to work out by themselves some fantastic or plausible solution. The creator-god is likely, however, to be rather remote and intangible, and unless identified, as by the Hebrews, with the intimate tribal god, to have little real significance for the practical religious life.[1]

VI. Man's need of deliverance from himself. These supernatural figures are, moreover, only the framework of religion; its rites, its practices, its laws of conduct, its attitudes of heart and will, are from the earliest times the real content of religion, as a phase of human life. The gods of mankind have been not only quasi-physical Powers supposed to inhabit the earth or the heavens, they have also been actual moral forces, speaking in men's conscience, warning them from sin, enjoining upon them practices and ideals of life which to some extent have actually guided their action. Primitive man has, to be sure, no comprehension whatever of the rational grounds of right conduct; he feels only the vague inner impulse to certain acts, or the pressure of the

[1] See Lang, p. 199; Leuba, p. 96 *f.*

community-will. But the condition of success in his life, indeed, of life at all, is the superposition of moral obligations upon those immediate animal impulses which uncontrolled would give him but a brutish and brief existence. He is in need of repressing some of his most powerful impulses for more ultimate ends, and of submitting his personal will to those larger loyalties which make social life possible. He can only dimly understand these necessities, but he can feel their force; and as they often cross his immediate wishes, and are easily transgressed, penalties are early enforced by the tribe to insure obedience to them, and they are commanded by those in authority together with the rites and duties which are to be performed to the tribal god.[1] What more natural than that these moral duties should also be thought of as duties to the god, and the inner voice of conscience interpreted as his commands to the individual? The felt authority of the moral law seems to give an additional testimony to the existence of the god whose will it is supposed to be, and the belief in the god lends its prestige and awe to the moral obligations. Thus, as men emerge more and more from their animal state and formulate ideals of life, they usually express their service to the ideal in terms of service to some god.

Religion, we have said, owes its origin in part to the need of deliverance from the menace of the powers of nature. But man early feels the need of a further deliverance, a deliverance from himself; from his restlessness and cross-purposes, from the weight of selfishness and sin. The pleasures which he seeks too often turn to ashes in his hands, the passions that lure him on leave him dissatisfied, he is the victim of his own impulses and longings, often impotent to attain his ends and without any lasting satisfaction for his

[1] For an account of the origin of morality, see my *Problems of Conduct*, chaps. I–III.

bewildered heart. In a happy environment, as among the Greeks, he may live in the moment and turn away from this reflective depression; but when life presses hard upon him he finds himself lonely and weary and heavy-laden. To what, to whom, shall he turn for safety, for guidance, for any lasting joy and peace?

The usual means of deliverance that occurred to man was an appeal to those superhuman Powers by which he so readily believed himself surrounded. Some god became to him a savior not only from outward harm, but from inward confusion and unrest; in his service he found the depersonalizing and unifying principle which could give his life dignity and peace. Uncultivated man is unable to grasp readily the abstract conception of a life free from personal desires, a life of self-forgetting service; but he finds this life, which alone can lift the human heart permanently above internal discord and personal fears, in the concrete conception of loyalty to his god.

Religion, it is clear, has its historic roots in the great welter of primitive superstition; for this reason it has become discredited in many eyes. But this is a hasty deduction. It often happens that beliefs originating in misunderstanding and false reasoning turn out to have, after all, the profoundest truth in them. Few of our most assured beliefs can afford to boast of their lineage; reason tests, but seldom originates.[1] So we need not look askance at the great gods of mankind because they have emerged from a confused host of imaginary supernatural Beings cf little or no religious value. Religion is something that has come *out* of this chaos; and its value, now that we have it, is independent of its source. It is important to bear in mind that a

[1] Cf. what I have said of the humble origin of morality in *Problems of Conduct*, pp. 173–74.

supernatural Being is not, *ipso facto*, a god; it is "only when he enters into some stated relation with men, or rather with some community of men." [1] It is not until superstition is infused with moral, or spiritual, values that it becomes worthy of the name religion.

C. H. Toy, *Introduction to the History of Religions* (with bibliographies). I. King, *Development of Religion*. A. Menzies, *History of Religion*, pt. I. S. Reinach, *Orpheus, A History of Religions, Introduction*. R. R. Marett, *Threshold of Religion*. G. Galloway, *Philosophy of Religion*, pp. 88–131. L. T. Hobhouse, *Morals in Evolution*, pt. II, chap. I. E. S. Ames, *Psychology of Religious Experience*, pt. II. J. B. Pratt, *Psychology of Religious Belief*, chap. III. D. G. Brinton, *Religions of Primitive Peoples*. F. B. Jevons, *Introduction to the History of Religion*. J. H. Leuba, *Psychological Study of Religion*, pt. II. A. Lang, *Making of Religion*. E. Clodd, *Animism*. H. Spencer, *Descriptive Sociology; Principles of Sociology*, vol. I, chaps. VIII–XVII. G. Allen, *Evolution of the Idea of God*. A. Sabatier, *Outlines of a Philosophy of Religion*, bk. I., chap. I. W. Bousset, *What is Religion*, chap. II. *American Journal of Religious Psychology*, vol. 2, pp. 12, 57. *Schaff-Herzog Encyclopedia of Religious Knowledge*, art. Comparative Religion.

[1] W. R. Smith, *Religion of the Semites*, p. 112.

CHAPTER II

GREEK AND ROMAN RELIGION

THE peoples of Christendom for a long time treated all the non-Christian religions as simply "heathen" and therefore unworthy of anything but disproof and contempt. Later, a few came to investigate with some curiosity and tolerance their queer customs and outlandish names. Only recently have they sought to look at them from the inside, to get at what they meant to those who believed and practised them, and see if there be not in them some inspiration for us too, some lesson which we can incorporate into our own faith and practice. It is in this friendlier and more sympathetic spirit that we would approach them.[1]

As our space is limited, we can only touch upon one or two of the many forms which religion assumed as the race became civilized; and then, in somewhat greater detail, we will recount the history of the Hebrew-Christian religion,

---

[1] This spirit was well expressed by an old and little-known writer, Maximus of Tyre: "God himself . . . is unnamable by any lawgiver, unutterable by any voice, not to be seen by any eye. But we, being unable to apprehend his essence, use the help of sounds and names and pictures . . . yearning for the knowledge of Him . . . like earthly lovers, [who are] happy in the sight of anything that wakens the memory of the beloved. . . . If a Greek is stirred to the remembrance of God by the art of Pheidias, an Egyptian by paying worship to animals, another man by a river, another by fire, I have no anger for their divergences; only let them know, let them love, let them remember." (Quoted by Murray, p. 98, more fully.) To this we may add Emerson's "The religions we call false were once true. They also were affirmations of the conscience, correcting the evil customs of their times." ("Character," in *Lectures and Biographies*.)

Cf. also, on the study of ancient religions, *American Journal of Philology*, vol. 29, p. 156.

which has become, through a dramatic series of events, the dominant faith of the world. But we must not fail to speak of that beautiful Hellenic religion which, though utterly vanished from the earth in its literal acceptation, has furnished and still furnishes such inspiration for art, for literature, and for life, that it is fitly called " the mother-tongue of the imagination." [1]

In what striking ways did religion develop in Greece?

(1) Prior to the conquest of Greece by the Aryan invaders of the second millennium B.C., there had been a civilization in some respects brilliant among the pre-Hellenic inhabitants of the peninsula; this age is now generally termed the Mycenæan or Ægean Age. Of its religion our knowledge is uncertain; but it included many elements that persisted, like the people themselves, and mingled with the religion of the conquering race. Through all the classic period we find traces of popular beliefs and rites, festivals and sacrifices, whose origin dates far back before the Hellenic (or Achæan) invasions. But it is not those survivals that most interest us, or such elements in the superimposed religion as were similar; it is rather the differentiating characteristics of the Olympian religion, those powerful gods that came down from the north with the invaders and made their home, according to common belief, upon Mount Olympus. These gods of the " buccaneer kings " of the age of the migrations — the Heroic Age, as we have been accustomed to call it — were themselves at that time little more than " a gang of conquering chieftains," the reflection in the skies of their worshipers. But as the Achæans mingled with the indigenous peoples and became more civilized, these " savage old Olympians " [2] turned gentler too; splendid, aristocratic

[1] G. Santayana, *Poetry and Religion*, p. 56.
[2] These phrases are from Murray.

figures as they remained, they dominated the dawning culture of Hellas, giving to it a common religion, far cleaner and more wholesome, freer from debasing superstitions, from obscene and bloody rites, than the native cults which it assimilated or superseded.

(2) The lordly Olympians were at the outset chiefly or wholly personifications of natural forces; Zeus, for example, was the same sky-god that we find in the Sanskrit Dyaus and the Roman Jove. But the popular imagination of this singularly imaginative race, and the bards in whom it abounded, delighted in weaving stories about them, refining out much of the cruelty of nature's ways that clings hard to nature-gods, until they created the glorious company of the Homeric pantheon, and, finally, the Zeus of Æschylus and Pheidias, the Hermes of Praxiteles, the Aphrodite of Melos — still, as she stands, armless and on alien soil, the highest human conception of queenly womanhood. Already, in the earliest extant literature of the Hellenes, their gods are half-detached from their natural sources and endowed with human emotions and purposes apart from those which might have been read into observed events. The needs of the people had seized upon myths once purely natural, found types of human fortunes in them, and developed in them new meanings. Poets and story-tellers, with their love of the dramatic and the picturesque, had projected their own impulses into these beings so vividly real to them, and had woven about them many adventures, plausible because human-like, but no longer a mere interpretation of phenomena. Thus, the gods, sharing human passions and sorrows, were brought nearer to men, and their enlarged powers and greater perfection became a more adequate picture of man's aspirations and ideals. And thus many of the tales of the gods, when collated and systematized in the latter days — as, notably, by Hesiod — had

little relevance left to the life of nature, the original nucleus of transparent myth having been engulfed by the new interest which had attached to them.

Mythology is the product of the poetic faculty working upon that primitive and instinctive animism or spiritism which is also, and earlier, the material for religion. The conduct-reaction upon it, together with the feelings of reverence, awe, worship, and the like, constitute religion; the playful, detached, imaginative attitude toward it produces mythology.[1] In classic Greece the poetic and artistic results overshadow for us the more serious development. And it is, within limits, true that "the less seriously the gods are taken, the more luxuriantly does mythology flourish"; it was frowned upon by the pious, and must not be taken as an adequate expression of the religion that existed by its side. Yet the development and expurgation that were made, instinctively, perhaps, by the humanity and refinement of the Ionian bards, and consciously by the later philosopher-poets, influenced the religion itself profoundly, and helped to make it superior to the other religions of the ancient world in certain respects which we shall be ready, in a moment, to note.

(3) This Olympian religion, which left such a deep impress upon the literature and art of classic Greece, was never, however, the whole of Greek religion. The mystery-worship of Eleusis, and the Orphic brotherhoods, which came into prominence in the seventh century B.C., and were probably a revival or outgrowth of pre-Olympian cults, maintained a vigorous life long after the Olympians had vanished, yielding finally only to the Christian conquest, although their outward expressions — initiation ceremonies, lustrations, sacrifices, processions, pæans, and mystic

[1] For the nature of mythology, see *Encyclopædia Britannica, ad loc.* Santayana, chap. IV.

plays — have vanished far more completely than the temples and statues and poetry of the Olympians.[1] But they were never the normal and universal possession of the people. They were mystic brotherhoods, spreading by conscious propaganda, promising a deeper and more spiritual life, a penetration into the inner secrets of being, and salvation after death. They reveal to us a widespread hunger for a more personal religion, an individual communion with God, which was to receive its eventual satisfaction in Christianity. They present us with the earliest example of a religion set free from local and political limitations, and conceived, at least in germ, as a universal and voluntary brotherhood — with no dogma, indeed, but with a sense of deepened insight, a purified will, and a larger hope. These mystic brotherhoods did not antagonize the state religion, but supplemented it for the more spiritual-minded, and helped to pave the way for the Christian revolution.[2]

(4) Beginning about the sixth century B.C., and reaching its culmination in the fourth, a great wave of philosophic interest swept over the cultured classes of Hellas. As in the case of the earlier refining of the Olympian religion, the movement seems to have begun with the Ionians, the Greeks who had crossed the Ægean, and reached its climax in Athens. For the first time in recorded human history a truly scientific spirit arose, and men questioned every hitherto accepted belief. Xenophanes ridiculed the irrationality of the popular religious conceptions, and pointed out their immoral aspects. Other thinkers, divesting themselves of their preconceptions, began to construct original pictures of the cosmos. A general decline of naïve beliefs en-

[1] It is true, however, that some of them survive in altered form in Christianity.

[2] *Encyclopædia Britannica*, arts. *Mystery, Orpheus, Mithras*. F. Cumont, *The Mysteries of Mithra, Oriental Religions in Roman Paganism*. Harrison, chaps. IX–XII. *Monist*, vol. 11, p. 87.

sued. The troops of anthropomorphic gods, with the rather childish — if often poetic — tales that clung to them, began to seem absurd; and the idea of a unitary purpose in things, a reason or ideal that was working itself out in the world, was suggested. Already Zeus — the roof of sky that bends over all — had become, in the popular mythology, the father and chief of the gods; and the name came to be often used to signify the One Great Power behind all appearances. A fragment of Æschylus runs, " Zeus is the ether, Zeus the earth, Zeus the heaven, Zeus the universe and whatever is beyond the universe." In Plato's *Phædo* we can glimpse the crystallization of the great thought that the universe forms a single moral order. Platonists and Stoics developed this vaguely monotheistic or pantheistic doctrine, with its call to trust in the outcome of events, its consolation and hope, far greater than that which the current polytheism could offer. It did not originate in the right way to catch the heart as the Christian monotheism did; it was too speculative, too remote, impersonal, and man-made, to become popular; and so it remained the philosophy of the few rather than the religion of the many. But it had an important part in making monotheism more natural and thus paving the way for the acceptance of Christianity.[1]

(5) The philosophic movement of Greece gave the deathblow to the Olympian religion, but did not replace it in the hearts of the people. A stern Stoicism brought comfort to many, indeed; and an Epicurean skepticism spread among the upper classes. But the masses turned rather with a revulsion which often accompanies an age of enlightenment, toward all sorts of wild superstitions. Cults of Oriental origin became prominent, with their extravagant and morbid conceptions. Despair at the failure of the old free city-states, a loss of trust in reason and organized effort, — in

[1] See J. Adam, *Religious Teachers of Greece.*

all that had made the glory of Hellas, now overwhelmed by political catastrophes, — a reaching-out for personal salvation, for ecstasies and spiritual exaltations, for something new to cling to, something greater to hope for, mark the final stage of Greek religion. Professor Murray, repeating a phrase of Professor Bury's, calls this phase a "loss of nerve." Through it the new star of Christianity was slowly rising.

What is the permanent significance of the classic Greek religion?

Many as were the phases of religion in Greece, it is the classic, the Olympian, religion that has left the deepest stamp upon civilization. Never so profound or so tender as Christianity or Buddhism, it yet has a lesson and charm for us in the sense of kinship with nature, the fearless, buoyant attitude toward life, the self-forgetting loyalty, and the spirit of moderation and freedom from excess that breathe through its mythology and are witnessed in its history. That the lovely Greek pantheon is an elaboration and blossoming-out of those primitive personifications of nature which were the common stock of the Aryan races is seen by a comparison with early Sanskrit literature. In the Vedas we meet with a poetic naturalism similar in many respects to that of the Greeks. But that branch of the Aryan race that migrated to the plains of India was dragged down by the struggle for existence, and its religion lost its original spontaneity and cheerfulness, until it was finally overshadowed and absorbed by a religion of renunciation and redemption. The Greeks, on the other hand, favorably situated in a smiling land, temperamentally lighthearted and politically free,[1] developed their religion on

[1] Free, that is, from alien domination, and from the sort of crushing despotism that prevailed so largely farther east. Of course they were constantly conquering one another; but there was a large element of free political activity down to the Macedonian conquest.

natural and wholesome lines. With their keen and sympathetic observation of nature, their exuberant imagination, and their healthy love of living, their gods came to express the wondrousness of natural phenomena, and the nobility and glory of free, dignified, loyal, happy human life. Of this spirit we have in Greek literature and art the ripe and perfect expression, a priceless possession to all who love nature in her many aspects, and retain, or love, the youthful and unsubdued attitude toward life.

(1) Judaism and Christianity set little importance by nature; their emphasis has been upon inward things; they have looked back, to past events, and forward, to future salvation, but very slightly at the immediate natural environment. And the modern man is apt to think of nature as the mere material for his labors, obdurate and resistant to his will. The Greeks, on the other hand, lived consciously in the presence of natural forces. The earth was to them a kindly mother, who brought forth many rich and beautiful gifts for men; the various crises in her life, the changing seasons, the growth of the corn and the vine, awakened their interest and gave opportunity for many a festival and rite. There was Persephone, carried away by Pluto to the underworld while plucking flowers in the field, but permitted, because of the sorrow of her mother, to return for two thirds of each year to the bright sunshine. What a happy allegory of the life of nature, with its annual death and its assured reappearance in the spring! And how near to us all do such allegories bring that life, of which our own is, after all, but a fragment and offshoot!

So to the Homeric bards the dawn was a rosy maid arising from the couch of night, the winds were shepherds of the fleecy clouds; and over all this manifold terrestrial life, father of all, was the open sky — *sublime hoc candens quod invocant omnes Jovem*. To hear the whispering of dryads in the murmur of trees, the laughter of naiads in the ripple of brooks, to give all these living, moving things names and think of them as akin to human life, to tell of such commonplace phases of nature in these poetic and romantic terms, was to find in them a new wonder and a new delight. This intimate communion with nature, so real to the heart of Hellas, and so alien to our modern religion, is left to be the perpetually recurrent theme of poets and artists, the invaluable bequest of a singularly gifted and imaginative people to our rather drab and utilitarian age.

(2) But it is not merely the love of nature and of outdoor adventure that we find in the Homeric religion, it is something finer and nobler that most endears it to us; it is the splendid fearlessness, the manly, undaunted attitude toward life that rings through it — that spirit that, without any belief that "all is for the best," without any hopes of heaven, found life, when nobly lived, full of zest and well worth the living.[1] To the Greeks, as to all men, pain was pain, sorrow and separation and death were real, and not to be mitigated by reflection. But they did not let them spoil the joys which they found or the ardor with which they followed their ideals.[2]

The Homeric religion was, on the whole, light-hearted;

---

[1] This is not true of all the Greek poets. Euripides, e.g., is a good deal of a pessimist.

[2] Cf. William James, *Varieties of Religious Experience*, p. 87: "The Greeks and Romans [did not have] any such desire to save the credit of the universe as to make them insist, as so many of us insist, that what immediately appears as evil must be 'good in the making,' or something equally ingenious. Good was good, and bad just bad, for the earlier Greeks. They neither denied the ills of nature, — Walt Whitman's verse, 'What is called good is perfect and what is called bad is just as perfect,' would have been mere silliness to them, — nor did they, in order to escape from those ills, invent 'another and a better world' of the imagination, in which, along with the ills, the innocent goods of sense would also find no place. This integrity of the instinctive reactions, this freedom from all moral sophistry and strain, gives a pathetic dignity to ancient pagan feeling."

the gods were generally kindly, except when specially provoked, the religious festivals occasions of gladness and feasting, dance and song — rather strikingly different from our drab and somber Sabbaths.[1] Chesterton, who, in spite of his (rather dubious) orthodoxy, is more pagan than Christian in spirit, would infuse gayety into our holy days. But whatever we may say to that, we can admire the spirit immortalized in Odysseus and his hardy mariners —

> "Souls . . .
> That ever with a frolic welcome took
> The thunder and the sunshine, and opposed
> Free hearts, free foreheads."

(3) Another marked aspect of the Olympian religion was its *sōphrosynē*, its freedom from excesses of superstition or rite; it expressed and defended the enlightenment, intelligence, reasonableness, and order of Hellas, against the dark background of brutality and barbarism that ringed it about. There was in it a dignity and restraint, a distrust of brute power and unbridled passion, expressed in the motto Μηδὲν ἄγαν, and called by us the classic spirit. The Hellenes waged no religious wars, never spurned the gods of other peoples and trampled upon them as the fanatical Hebrews and the Christians did. They sought a calm and sympathetic wisdom; the tales that grew up about their gods mingle with their poetic interpretation of nature the embodiment of the Greek ideal of manhood and womanhood — that ideal of ripe physical perfection and all-round development which the Greek statues and the noblest Greeks themselves so adequately embodied.

[1] Of course there is another side to the picture. Some even of the Ionian rites and ceremonies were gloomy. Some of them were bloody and barbarous, in spite of what I say in the following paragraph. In short, all religions were more alike than in our love for sharp contrasts we are apt to suppose. But I am purposely emphasizing those aspects of the Olympian religion that constitute its *differentia*.

(4) But there was a more earnest side to Greek religion — its family piety and civic patriotism. To the Athenian the goddess Athene was the visible symbol of his beloved and beautiful city. Euripides makes Theseus cry out to his men when the Thebans pressed them hard, "O sons of Athens! if ye cannot stay this stubborn spear of the men sprung from the dragon's teeth, the cause of Pallas is overthrown." Loyalty to the goddess "stood for the ideal of tempered and disciplined courage devoted to patriotic ends";[1] like loyalty to the flag or sovereign to-day, it was a symbolic and imaginative way of expressing the important duty of patriotism, which drew men together, gave them something great and self-transcending to live for, and enabled the Greek cities to attain to a high level of civilization. One who reads the biographies of Plutarch, who sees there what splendid devotion this civic religion bred, what glory it gave to life, who hears of the Spartan lads, from their childhood living for the larger life of which they were a part, not only ready, if necessary, to die for their country, but undergoing a daily discipline and self-denial for her, can never speak of this highest form of the pagan religion without reverence and wistful regret.

The habit of self-examination and a vigorous pursuit of personal righteousness are our inalienable inheritance from Judaism; the spirit of love and compassion, together with much more, from Christianity. But to all this we may do well to add that natural courage and buoyancy of heart that we find among the Greeks, and that seems, together with the love of nature, the spirit of *sōphrosynē*, and the inculcation of patriotism, to be somewhat lacking in the Hebrew and Christian Scriptures.

Of course it would be foolish to imagine that this spirit

[1] Farnell, *Higher Aspects*, pp. 80, 81.

possessed all of those early Greeks, as it would be to suppose that the spirit of Christ possesses all the inhabitants of Christendom. But as there is a certain spirit of inward aspiration, of self-forgetting love and compassion, which we call the Christian spirit, never completely realized — except in the Christ of Christian belief — but coming to flower here and there in some saint, and found in a degree in many an obscure and humble life, so the spirit which we find here and there in the best Greek literature and biography, and more strikingly and prevalently there than anywhere else, may fittingly be called the Greek spirit.[1]

What were the main currents in Roman religion?

(1) The old Roman religion — called by later tradition, after the name of a mythical king, the Religion of Numa — was, like the temper of the people, less exuberant and imaginative, more serious and prosaic, than that of the Greeks. At first scarcely more than an agricultural religion, concerned with the safety and fertility of crops and herds, and of their human owners, it became, perhaps through Etruscan influence, a strong civic religion, consolidating the clanspeople and keeping them loyal to the little state. The Romans were, like the Hellenes, a branch of what is generally called the Aryan race; like them they were invaders, pushing themselves into a country already occupied. But their religion was far more primitive than that of their cousins. Their gods were simply the natural Powers about them, not as yet clearly anthropomorphic, and so with no mutual relationships, no detachment from the physical processes themselves. The Romans seem to have

[1] Or, if any one prefers, the Homeric or Olympian spirit. The reader must bear in mind that I have been dwelling upon but one particular phase of the enormously varied and confused religious life of Greece — the phase of which the Homeric poems and the best Greek architecture and sculpture are the immortal expression.

had no theological or metaphysical curiosity; they were content to know nothing of their gods but their visible activity. Their interest was rather practical; and their religion consisted of a great mass of ancient observances, deemed necessary to keep these Powers assuaged. In Professor Carter's phrase, it was a " science of propitiating the right Power on the right occasion "; and the priest was the expert, the " legal adviser " in these practices.[1] We miss the picturesque pantheon of the Greeks, the poetry and charm and intimate friendliness of their gods; but there is a devoutness, an " earnest sobriety," a scrupulousness about the old family worship, and its expanded form, the state religion of adult Rome, that help explain the greatness to which Rome attained. The most prominent of the early gods were Vesta (the hearth) and the Lares and Penates (the protectors of the little holdings, of the house and its stores); later it was Jupiter Optimus Maximus, like the Jewish Jehovah a sky-god seen in storms and lightning, and the patron of the growing nation.

This nature-religion remained very real to the Romans during the period of their waxing power, long after the Greeks had lapsed into skepticism and Oriental excesses. Polybius, writing in the second century B.C., says, " The most important superiority which the Roman state shows, it seems to me, lies in their religious faith; for I take it that that scrupulous fear of the gods that other peoples are being rather ashamed of is just what holds together the Roman state."[2] Ennius sums it up in his splendid line —

"*Moribus antiquis stat res Romana virisque.*"

It was this civic religion that made Rome what it was, and, decaying, let her empire also decay. From the legendary " pious Æneas " (pious, in that his reverence for the

[1] *Religion of Numa*, p. 70.   [2] VI, 56.

traditions of his country and his endeavor to perpetuate them formed the dominating purpose of his life) through the long roll of devoted citizens during the republic and early empire, until luxury and debauchery sapped their integrity and simplicity of heart, the religion of the Romans was a thing of power and majesty, a religion that gave a meaning, an inspiration, and a joy to life. It is easy to point out its failures and its superstitious side; it is more profitable to consider what sort of men, at its best, it bred.

(2) Rome, however, with her expanding power, became too enlightened, too broadened, too sophisticated to retain her simple faith; the traders from Magna Græcia introduced the more interesting Greek gods, and these *di novensides*, "newly settled gods," gradually displaced the more shadowy *di indigetes*, the "indigenous gods." Presently Greek literature and art and mythology poured in upon the people and fascinated them with their brilliancy and beauty. So far as possible the two sets of gods were synthesized; some superficial resemblance led to the identification of Athene with Minerva, Artemis with Diana, Hera with Juno, Ares with Mars, and so on [1] — the result being a practical displacement of the native cult by the Hellenic, disguised and modified by the retention of the old names and many of the old rites.

In many ways this Hellenization of Rome was of extreme advantage to her; but it made inevitably for a loss of the old sobriety and depth of faith. Greece already took her religion very lightly; and the spirit of skepticism and unrest spread rapidly in Rome. The more the galaxy of temples grew, the greater the number of cults introduced, the more elaborate the festivals and the more intoxicating the orgies of the semi-Oriental cults, the less religion really affected

[1] The equation of Zeus with Jupiter was really valid; the two names come from the same root.

the conduct of the people. The old religion had had, indeed, its repressive and cramping aspect, and the lightening of its yoke was not altogether an evil. Lucretius, who exulted in the decline of faith, described the earlier time as one in which "human life lay foully crushed to earth under the weight of religion," and declared that it was better " to be able to look at all things with a mind at peace." [1] But the waning of belief meant a decline of piety and a spread of laxity in morals. Virgil tells us,[2] "Right and wrong are confounded; so many wars the world around, so many forms of wrong"; and Horace is witness to a state of cynical pleasure-seeking far removed from the simple and virtuous, if rude, ancestral tradition.

Augustus attempted to restore the old state religion to something of its older and purer form; but he could not dislodge the Greek and Oriental cults or inject a genuine faith into the repetition of ancient rites. The old primitive nature-worship had lost its reality, the new and spectacular worships had no deep roots in the people's hearts. As times went from bad to worse, the confusion grew greater; delirious orgies of sensuous Eastern cults, the Phrygian Magna Mater, Egyptian Isis and Osiris, and the noble Persian Mithras, sought to satisfy that heart-hunger, that growing sense of sin and craving for salvation, which were to find their eventual satisfaction only in Christianity — Christianity, which would have made no appeal to the West in the old days, but was admirably fitted to meet the needs of the confused, wicked, and weary world of the Empire.

G. Murray, *Four Stages of Greek Religion*. A. Fairbanks, *Handbook of Greek Religion*. L. R. Farnell, *Cults of the Greek States; Higher Aspects of the Greek Religion*. G. F. Moore, *History of Religions*, chaps. XVII–XX. A. Menzies, *History of Religion*, chaps. XIV, XVI. S. Reinach, *Orpheus*, chap. III, sec. 1.   P. V. N.

---

[1] *De Rerum Natura*, I, 62; v, 1194.   [2] *Georgics*, I, 505–6.

Myers, *History as Past Ethics*, chaps. x–xi. G. Santayana, *Poetry and Religion*, chap. iii; also in *New World*, vol. 8, p. 401. L. Campbell, *Religion in Greek Literature*. G. L. Dickinson, *Greek View of Life*, chap. i. J. Adam, *Religious Teachers of Greece*. W. Pater, *A Study of Dionysus, the Myth of Demeter and Persephone* (in *Greek Studies*). J. E. Harrison, *Prolegomena to the Study of Greek Religion; Religion of Ancient Greece*.

W. W. Fowler, *Religious Experience of the Roman People*. J. B. Carter, *Religion of Numa; Religious Life of Ancient Rome*, chaps. i–iii. A. Menzies, *op. cit.*, chap. xvii. G. F. Moore, *op. cit.*, chaps. xxi–xxii. Reinach, *op. cit.*, chap. iii, sec. ii. T. H. Glover, *Conflict of Religions in the Early Roman Empire*, chap. i. W. Pater, *Marius the Epicurean*. G. Hodges, *The Early Church*, chap. i.

CHAPTER III

BUDDHISM AND ZOROASTRIANISM

What was the soil from which Buddhism grew?

VERY different from the free and hearty life of the Greeks was the existence of the natives of India. A crowded population, a burning sun, fever and pestilence, wild beasts and poisonous reptiles, made life a continual struggle, and bred that sense of world-weariness that makes effort seem futile and paralyzes progress. The caste system kept the masses submerged; the luxury of the few jostled against the poverty of the many, from whom sorrow and pain were never far away. The meaninglessness and burden of life were only intensified by the widespread belief in transmigration, — a reincarnation of souls in form after form, with no aim, no advance, no goal, — to be dreaded, but hardly to be escaped. A pessimistic view of life and a longing for relief, rest, salvation from sorrow and sin are the background against which Buddhism stands with its welcome message of release and inner peace.

It had not always been so in India. The early Aryan invaders, coming down from the Persian highlands, seem to have been a robust and normally happy folk, whose religion consisted largely in the recitation of hymns of praise to their nature-gods. Their sacred books, the Vedas, contain these hymns, — which reveal an already highly developed poetic skill,[1] — together with legends, speculations,

---

[1] The date of the earliest of the Vedic books is much in doubt. But conservative scholars surmise that it may be around 2000 B.C. See Bloomfield, lect. I.

laws, and precepts. The gods are for the most part kindly disposed, although there is little intimacy with them, little of that intermingling of gods and men that we find on Hellenic soil, or of the close fatherly love that characterizes the Hebrew Jehovah. In fact, these Aryan nature-gods, who in Greece were so thoroughly humanized, remain in India much more " transparent," i.e., more clearly impersonations of natural forces; so that the process by which their incipient personalities faded out into the engulfing Brahma, the Universal Spirit, the One Reality, was comparatively easy. "Polytheism is decadent even in the hymns of the Rig-Veda themselves. It shows signs of going to seed for philosophy." [1]

It is impossible now to trace the process by which the gods lost what personality they had and were merged into the Brahma, or Atman, the One Cosmic Breath, Self, Power, Being.[2] The process doubtless covered many hundreds of years, and was the result of the philosophic spirit at work upon the naïve nature-worship, a realization of the essential unity of Nature beneath her manifold and often discordant phases. Again, where the doctrine of transmigration came from we cannot say; it has cropped up in many lands, though it has nowhere else so obsessed a people as in India. But, at any rate, we find the pantheism, the belief in transmigration, and the pessimism in the Upanishads and Brahmanas; they seem indelibly stamped, to this day, upon the Hindu people. To escape from the evils of life has been their *summum bonum;* and to the Brahman this escape, this salvation, can come only through the realization by the individual of his essential identity with the One Great Being, the World-Soul, the Divine Life that contains no evil.

[1] Bloomfield, p. 230.
[2] On this, consult, besides the books cited at the end of the chapter, J. Wedgwood, *The Moral Ideal,* chap. II.

All else than this life is Maya, illusion, mere nothingness, and cannot matter.[1] With this intuition there supervenes upon the soul a great and holy calm which lifts it forever above the accidents of life. Fastings and observances, self-mortification, and a sort of auto-hypnosis lead to the goal, which is a killing-off of the life of impulse, passion, and desire, a submergence of self in the Infinite.

What was the nature of Buddha's mission?

Against such a background stands the life of Gautama, the Buddha. Born a prince, in the eastern valley of the Ganges, surrounded by luxury and wealth, with health and power at his command, he early recognized the futility of these material things for lasting satisfaction. When he awoke to realize the miseries of the poor and the weak, his heart yearned toward them, and he felt that neither rich nor poor had learned how rightly to live. At the age of twenty-nine he renounced his position and adopted — like St. Francis, centuries after him, and like Tolstoy in our own times — the life of poverty, which is the life of the people. Thus he set forth on his long quest for a way of relief for himself and his people; and seeking for years, with pure heart and passionate longing, he finally came to see that only in renunciation, in the abandonment of personal desires, in inward purity and loving service, could that relief be found. He gathered about him a group of mendicant disciples and went about teaching his great Secret until his peaceful death at an advanced age — some time in the earlier part of the fifth century B.C. The way of life that he taught has been the religion of more men and women than any other faith of historic times.

It was in the simplicity and spirituality of his message

---

[1] This is precisely the note of Christian Science, and of the modern Transcendental philosophy, which borrowed from Hinduism.

that its power lay. He was, like Christ, no reformer of outward conditions; he became early convinced that salvation lay not in any abundance of material goods. But the ideals of the Brahmanic priests were as empty as the worldly aims of the nobles and princes; not in fastings or bodily asceticism, in trances and ecstasies, not in rites or ceremonies or prayers to the gods, was peace to be found, not in speculation or in dogma. The solution of life was rather an inward change; the Way lay open to all, without regard to learning, to possessions, to caste or race. Brahmanism was at once too subtle, too philosophical, and too formal, too exacting in its requirements. Few could rise to the realization of the unreality of life and find peace in mystic union with Brahma; few could carry out the elaborate program of observances, or find lasting satisfaction therein. When Buddha was asked concerning the nature of the self, the cosmos, and the future life, he refused to answer; "because these inquiries have nothing to do with things as they are, with the realities we know; they are not concerned with the Law of Life; they do not make for religious conduct; they do not conduce to the absence of lust, to freedom from passion, to right effort, to the higher insight, to inward peace." [1]

The Buddha's teaching was not, indeed, free from supernatural conceptions; growing up in the atmosphere of Brahmanism, as Christ did in that of Judaism, he could no more than Christ fail to reflect the ideas of his time. But they only outwardly affect his religion. The conception of transmigration he adopted from contemporary belief; it was to a certain extent the vehicle of his teaching (as the expectation of a coming Kingdom of God was the vehicle of Christ's teaching), but was not really essential to it. Buddhism is distinctly and explicitly a way of life, a way to salvation, to emancipation from sin and sorrow in this world, and is jus-

[1] Quoted by J. Estlin Carpenter, *New World*, vol. 1, p. 90.

tified by its results without consideration of a future existence. Nor did that expectation of reincarnation add the element of consolation; the future life was not thought of as a sudden transition to a state of bliss; and unless the weight of sorrow could be removed by a change of heart in this life it would not be less in the next. The Nirvana that was longed for and looked forward to was the extinction of all restlessness and selfish desire, the perfect self-surrender and peace — an ideal perfectly natural to this life and inhering in its needs. So this strange dread of reincarnation, which is implied in much of the Buddha's teaching, did not materially influence the way of life he taught or add to the value of his message.

There is no belief in Providence in Buddhism; man must work out his own salvation in a world of law. Buddha may never have questioned the existence of gods; but he found them of no religious importance. He taught a means of deliverance which requires no belief in superhuman Powers and asks no help of them. In its pure and unadulterated form, Buddhism is one of the least superstitious and irrational of human religions. It teaches that salvation and peace are inward things, that the soul can be freed from the dominion of the body's ills, that happiness is to be found not in changing outer things but in changing ourselves.

What were the striking aspects of Buddha's teaching?

(1) Buddhism is not a virile religion, like the Greek or the Hebraic-Christian religion; there is a shadow over it, a sadness, and a sense of the vanity of worldly desires. Hence it is often called a pessimistic religion. But we must remember the environment into which it came; it did not bring sadness into life, it found it there; it does not invent, it acknowledges it. In this it is a far profounder and more adequate religion than that of the Greeks, which did not

grapple with sorrow or seriously regard it. Buddhism, like Christianity some centuries later, brought a message to the weary, the troubled, the sick at heart. It is essentially a religion of deliverance.

(2) The solution, the salvation, that Buddhism offers is a purely subjective one. There is no theodicy, no attempt to explain and justify the existence of evil, only a message of how to escape it. The cause of our suffering lies in the fact that our hearts are set upon objective things; the remedy lies in ceasing to care about them and learning to care only about what lies within our power, our own attitude of heart and will.

"The treasure thus laid up is secure, and passes not away;
Though he leave the fleeting riches of this world, this a man takes with him,
A treasure that no wrong of others, and no thief, can steal." [1]

The close parallelism between these verses and the familiar saying of the Gospels will be noted by all readers. Like Christ, five hundred years after, Buddha called men to the life of renunciation, the life " ungrasping among those who grasp." Like Christ, and Paul and Luther, he swept away outward observances and demanded an inward change of heart as alone essential.

(3) Buddhism emphasizes the importance of each moment's act. The saying, "Whatsoever a man soweth, that shall he also reap," is closely paralleled in its scriptures; by an inexorable sequence of cause and effect we make our own future; each act and thought moulds us, makes us what we are to be, decides our future. In particular, it is forbidden to take life; the orthodox Buddhist will kill no animal, for food or in self-defense. It is forbidden to drink intoxicating liquors; Buddhism has been a bulwark against alcoholism. Sexual offenses, lying, and stealing are the other cardinal sins. The importance of watchfulness over our faults,

[1] Quoted by Rhys-Davids, *Buddhism*, p. 127.

meditation on holy matters, and continual re-consecration is never to be forgotten.

(4) Duty is thus sternly emphasized. But equally prominent is the teaching of compassion and love. The Buddha was filled with tenderness toward all living things, and taught his disciples to be kind to animals, hospitable to strangers, and at peace with one another. "Never in this world," he said, "does hatred cease by hatred; hatred ceases by love." And Buddhists have kept truer to this teaching than Christians have to the similar commands of Christ. They have not persecuted their fellow men, established inquisitions, or set forth on crusades. In Burma, where the faith has been kept purest, it has bred a singularly gentle and peaceable folk, who call all men and all beasts their brothers, who give gladly, because it is sweet to give, and forgive heartily, because it is best to forgive.

> "Let us live happily, then, not hating those who hate us!
> Let us live free from hatred among men who hate.
>
> "Let a man overcome anger by kindness, evil by good;
> Let him conquer the stingy by a gift, the liar by truth." [1]

It is easy to point out defects in Buddhism. It has not energized its converts, being rather a sedative than a stimulant. It has not sought to redeem the social order, contenting itself with pointing out a way of escape from a hopelessly evil world. It is lacking in the Hebrew-Christian (or Zoroastrian) sense of the cosmic significance of morality, and the enthusiasm of enlisting in a divine war against sin and sorrow which is bound in the end to triumph. It taught, long before Christianity, the need of self-surrender and love; but it does not espouse them with the joyous *abandon* of the true Christian saints. Such wisdom of unworldliness as Buddha — and as Christ too — taught easily paralyzes

[1] From the Dhamma-pada.

activity; and Buddhism did not have the good fortune to be taken up, as Christianity was, by peoples whose native energy should balance its unworldly teaching. We find in Buddhism a renunciation of things that are vital and important in life. But we can forgive this cramping of the spirit when we see what a priceless comfort and blessing it has been to millions of its adherents. If it has not let loose the latent energies of men as Christianity has, — or is this because the Oriental is not so easily aroused to energetic action? — it is at least free from many of the faults that have marred the history of Christianity, from its arid and bitter controversies, and its militant intolerance. "Surely this is a simple faith . . . and to know that it is a beautiful faith you have but to look at its believers and be sure. If a people be contented in their faith, if they love it and exalt it, and are never ashamed of it, and if it exalts them and makes them happy, what greater testimony can you have than that?"[1]

Christianity and Buddhism are at heart in many ways akin; and we need not be disloyal Christians to reverence him who was first to find the way of peace for man, who first taught in immortal words the need of self-surrender and of charity, and whose own life was one of spotless purity, dignity, and peace.

What was the subsequent history of Buddhism?

Buddha, like Christ, left no written teachings; his disciples wrote down from memory what they could recall, and to this were quickly added all sorts of semi-legendary traditions. A sacred literature thus arose, and a scripture-canon was formed, as with the Christian Testament — varying in its contents in the different countries to which Buddhism spread. The Buddha soon became a supernatural

[1] H. Fielding Hall, p. 50.

figure who had come to earth to share the lot of men, and with whom personal communion could be had. As, later, in the case of Christ, legends of miraculous birth and many wonders grew up around his memory and were devoutly believed. Indeed, the similarity between the lives of these two, the world's greatest religious teachers, and between the beliefs of subsequent ages about them, is in many ways striking. Gautama the Buddha (or Enlightened) and Jesus the Christ (or Anointed), both men of rarely pure and compassionate nature, both inheriting the conceptions by means of which they taught, but infusing them with new inwardness and freeing them from formalism and observance, both holding out to men a way to salvation and peace, found that Way in its fundamental aspects identical. The two gospels, so much alike at the outset, were received in very different soil and met with a very different fate, Christ's teaching being taken up by the Græco-Roman world, while Buddha's spread among the gentler but more stagnant Orientals; so that the existing systems which go by their names are now widely different from each other. But the original teaching of both transcended these limitations of time and place; both were in essence the message of a better way of life, but little affected by speculation and involving allegiance to no creed. The Way of both teachers was the Way of love and purity and self-surrender. Both teachers inspired great personal loyalty and soon came to be thought of as semi-divine, as coming from heaven to save men; of both were many miracles and marvels told, and with the teaching of both was incorporated a mass of contemporary and subsequent speculation.

As in the case of Christianity, councils were held after Buddha's death to determine the rules and doctrines of the new order. Schisms arose; but the Way spread, and was adopted about 250 B.C. by the ruler Asoka, the Constantine of Buddhism. For a while intense missionary activity prevailed, the period of expansion lasting until the seventh century A.D. Then Buddhism was almost exterminated in India by the Mohammedan invasion and the renaissance of the older Hindu religion. In Ceylon, in Burma, Siam, and Tibet it is still the dominant faith; while in China and Japan, where the masses are nominally Buddhists, it has been more or less fused with the native religions. It is now again on the increase in India; and various propagandist movements have recently been organized there and in Japan — among them a Young Men's Buddhist Association, modeled after the Young Men's Christian Association.

The question as to the future of Buddhism — which still probably outnumbers Christianity — is of great interest. Professor Rhys-Davids declares it probable that Buddhism will again become a great power in the East. If so, in what form — the later supernaturalistic or the primitive simple gospel — it would be hard to forecast. How much vitality the religion has, how well it can adapt itself to the truths of modern knowledge and absorb the contributions of other faiths — and whether, therefore, it will permanently share the world with Christianity and whatever other religions stand the test of time — only the future will show.[1]

What was the essence of Zoroastrianism?

A few words must suffice for one other great Aryan faith, before we turn to the Semitic religions. Zoroastrianism was a reform of the old Persian religion, as Buddhism was of the Hindu and Christianity of the Hebrew religion. The ancient Persians were cousins of the old Aryan Hindus, and their

[1] For the question as to the future of Buddhism, see *New World*, vol. 1, p. 89. For discussions of contemporary religious tendencies in India, see J. N. Farquhar, *Modern Religious Movements in India*; *New World*, vol. 1, p. 601; vol. 9, p. 451; *American Journal of Theology*, vol. 5, p. 217; vol. 13, p. 589.

gods were closely similar to the Vedic gods. But instead of becoming enervated and depressed like the dwellers in the hot and fever-swept Ganges valley, they remained a vigorous and virile people, filled, indeed, with a sense of the omnipresence of struggle, but of a struggle that was glorious, challenging, and assured of ultimate victory. Zoroaster, who lived, apparently, not long before the time of Buddha,[1] was, like him, a reformer of great zeal and spirituality, very practical in his teachings, although more speculative in his bent. The Bible that contains his teachings, the Avesta (commonly called Zend-Avesta), is rather closely similar to the Vedas in language and in many of its conceptions. But an entirely different stamp has been put upon it, an entirely new direction given.[2] The old pantheon is not abolished, but is subordinated to two central figures, Ahura-Mazda (Ormuzd) and Angro-Mainyu (Ahriman), the Good God and the Bad God, who, with their subordinate spirits, have opposed each other from the beginning of time, and are the source, respectively, of all the good and bad in the world.

In Zoroastrianism, then, the universal polytheism of primitive religions has become a sharp dualism; the sense of vivid contrast and of struggle permeates its thought and practice. Fertile land *versus* desert, light *versus* darkness, day *versus* night, joy *versus* pain, order *versus* chaos, truth *versus* error, goodness *versus* sin, life *versus* death — the universe is divided between the two great Powers, and its history is the history of their age-long struggle. In particu-

---

[1] His date remains uncertain. Indeed, there have been many who have deemed him a wholly mythical figure. But the tendency nowadays is to accept his historicity and the traditions that place him in the seventh century B.C., or a little earlier. Cf. Professor G. F. Moore, "No serious student any longer doubts that Zoroaster was an historical person."

[2] It is interesting to note in passing that the good god Deva of the Hindu religion has become a demon in Zoroastrianism. One suspects that to be because the Deva-worshipers rejected Zoroastrianism.

lar, the soul of man is the scene of conflict. By every pure thought and good deed he forwards the cause of Ormuzd, by every weakness and sin he aids the powers of darkness. No man liveth unto himself alone; the whole cosmic system of which he is a fragment gains or loses with his moral victories and defeats — while the future life of the individual is determined by his guilt or merit here. The final decisive conflict is not far away, wherein Ahriman and all his cohorts will be routed, after which the reign of universal righteousness and peace will prevail.

Thus, instead of renunciation and peace, Zoroaster taught the need of effort and reform; the evil in the world was to be not passively endured, but actively fought and banished; its presence was due not merely to our weakness and folly, but to an Evil Principle which we must all join in opposing, until it is finally overcome and human life is redeemed. There was rather little of ceremony in the religion, no temples or statues of the gods; but sacred fires were kept burning on the hilltops in honor of the great god whose loyal soldiers men must be. A bit of this sacred fire was carried to India by the Parsees who fled before the Mohammedan invasion, which in Persia, as in so many lands, wiped out the indigenous religion. In the region about Bombay they still hold to a faith which is a development of their ancestral Iranian cult. But in Persia itself the old faith is as dead as are the Olympian gods of Greece.

M. Bloomfield, *Religion of the Veda*. A. Barth, *Religions of India*. E. W. Hopkins, *Religions of India*. P. D. C. de la Saussaye, *Manual of the Science of Religion*, chaps. LVIII–LXXXIII. G. F. Moore, *History of Religions*, chaps. XI–XIV. A. Menzies, *History of Religion*, chaps. XVIII–XX. T. W. Rhys-Davids, *Buddhism; Buddhist India; Dialogues of the Buddha*. R. S. Copleston, *Buddhism, Primitive and Present*. P. Carus, *Gospel of Buddha*. Sir Edwin Arnold, *The Light of Asia* (poem). H. E. Warren, *Buddhism in Translations*. M. Müller, ed., *Sacred Books of the East*, vol. X.

H. Hackmann, *Buddhism as a Religion*. H. F. Hall, *The Soul of a People*. P. V. N. Myers, *History as Past Ethics*, chap. VII. M. Monier-Williams, *Brahmanism and Hinduism*. *Hibbert Journal*, vol. I, p. 465. *Hastings' Encyclopædia*, *Schaff-Herzog Encyclopædia*, and *Encyclopædia Britannica*, ad. loc.

A. V. W. Jackson, *Zoroaster*. J. H. Moulton, *Early Zoroastrianism*. *Encyclopædia Britannica*, and *Schaff-Herzog Encyclopædia*, ad. loc. G. F. Moore, *op. cit.*, chap. XV. S. Reinach, *Orpheus*, chap. II, sec. II. E. Rindtorff, *Religion des Zarathushtra*. J. Milne, *Faiths of the World*, pp. 91-121. J. Wedgwood, *The Moral Ideal*, chap. III.

CHAPTER IV

THE HEBREW RELIGION

We must now turn our attention to that dramatic series of events that in an obscure corner of the Mediterranean coast developed a religion which has become the most important in the world's history. Christianity is a development of Judaism; so, indeed, is Mohammedanism. All three have shown extraordinary vigor and vitality, so that the Aryan religions have steadily fallen away before the Semitic. But no one of these three would have existed, at least in its actual form, but for the peculiar history of that handful of tribes that formed the small but patriotic Jewish nation.[1]

How did the Hebrew monotheism arise?

In the earliest days of the Jewish people that extant documents allow us to reproduce with any assurance,[2] we find them a loose aggregation of nomadic tribes, closely

---

[1] For Hebrew history see C. F. Kent, *History of the Hebrew People; History of the Jewish People.* C. H. Cornill, *History of the People of Israel.* H. P. Smith, *Old Testament History. Encyclopædia Britannica.*

[2] See H. T. Fowler's *History of the Literature of Ancient Israel.* Our main source is, of course, the Old Testament itself. See S. R. Driver's or C. H. Cornill's or J. E. MacFadyen's *Introduction to the Old Testament.* The best editions of the Bible for historical study are: C. F. Kent's *Students' Old Testament* (the most accurate and up-to-date translation into English yet available, the books arranged partly in chronological and partly in topical order, introductions and textual footnotes, in six large volumes); P. Haupt, ed., *Polychrome Bible* (a new and admirable English version, with excellent explanatory notes; the different documents distinguished by differently colored backgrounds on the pages. Unfortunately publication has been stopped for financial reasons, with only a few volumes available);

akin in manners and religion to the less civilized of their Semitic cousins. In or about the thirteenth century B.C. they fought their way into the land of Canaan and merged with the earlier inhabitants, who were also a Semitic people, far more advanced in civilization and far less austere in their morals and religion. The Hebrew nation that emerged was thus of a mixed race, heir to the peaceful arts of the agricultural and city-dwelling Canaanites, but stamped with the purer and more ascetic ideals of desert life. An alert and ambitious people they were, with intense racial pride; a small nation, indeed, politically insignificant, and never very broad in their interests, but possessed with a belief in their own destiny. Their aspirations, at first largely political and worldly, became chastened by the rough handling of their stronger neighbors until they came to embody, in their noblest representatives, an enthusiasm for spiritual perfection and a regenerated moral order on earth — the future Kingdom of God.

The early Jews were as polytheistic as their neighbors; [1]

The New Century Bible (Frowde, New York); a series of small duodecimo volumes, using the R.V. text, with excellent introductions and explanatory footnotes: the best complete edition for students, in spite of the inferiority of the R.V. text to the more recent translations); *The Bible for Home and School* (The Macmillan Company. A similar edition, of about equal excellence, as yet only partially published — fourteen Bible books at date of writing, 1914; R.V. text); R. S. Moulton, ed., *The Modern Reader's Bible* (R.V. text; the books somewhat rearranged, and their material printed in modern literary form, without the confusing conventional division into chapters and verses. The one-volume edition, which is handiest, has the chapter- and verse-numbers in the margin. Literary introductions and notes. Excellent for the general reader; perhaps the most palatable form; but not adapted for historical study. The arrangement is rather arbitrary and not always based on solid critical grounds).

Of the texts in common use, the R.V. (English Revised Version of 1881) is far more accurate than the A.V. ("Authorized" Version of 1611); the S.V. (American Standard Version of 1901), still more accurate; the S.V. is gradually supplanting the others. It retains the Elizabethan English as far as possible.

[1] Their very name for God — Elohim — was originally a plural.

THE HEBREW RELIGION

it was only gradually that their particular tribal patron Jehovah [1] overshadowed the others and became their One God. Many Biblical passages refer to the worship of other gods before, and indeed long after, the introduction of Jehovah-worship — for Moses' attempt, similar to that of Mohammed, eighteen centuries or more afterward, to simplify his people's religion into a monolatry, was much less successful; although continued by the great prophets, it was not finally triumphant until after the political ruin of the nation. In the oldest of the Biblical decalogues, which no doubt most nearly represents the laws of Moses, the commandment is clear, "Thou shalt worship [henceforth] no other god; for Jehovah, whose name is Jealous, is a jealous god." [2] And in the older strata of the composite Biblical history we find signs of the preëminence given to Jehovah in the early post-Mosaic days — as in the ancient song preserved to us in Exod. 15:2–21, wherein we read: —

"I will sing unto Jehovah, for he hath triumphed gloriously, ...
He is our God, and we will praise him, ...
Jehovah is a warrior, Jehovah is his name, ...
Who is like unto thee, Jehovah, among the gods?"

But all through the days of the Hebrew state we read of the worship of many other gods proceeding side by side with

---

[1] The name was almost certainly "Jahveh" (pronounced Yahwáy), "Jehovah" resulting from a mistaken insertion of the vowels of the word "Adonai" into the JHVH which the old vowel-less Hebrew texts contained. But I retain here the familiar, if inaccurate, form "Jehovah." The rendering "the Lord," in the older English Bibles, has no justification. The Jews, being forbidden to pronounce the name of their God, substituted this word "Adonai" for it when reading aloud in the synagogue service. The vowels of this word were written in, to remind the reader to use it. The translators of the Greek version (LXX) used the word Κύριος, the equivalent of Adonai; and the English translators rendered it Lord.

[2] Exod. 34:14. The narrative which contains this decalogue (one of the J passages) was written about the ninth century B.C., i.e., about four hundred years after the time of Moses. But the decalogue, in approximately the same words, may date from Moses. The later decalogues — e.g., the familiar one in Exod. 20 — repeat the same commandment.

that of Jehovah. Joshua, we are told, begged his people, in an eloquent speech, to renounce their other gods, making the plea, so often used in later times, that it was Jehovah — Moses' God — who had led them out of the bondage in Egypt — an episode in their early tribal life which later generations continued to look back upon with a peculiar horror. "Now therefore put away, said he, the strange gods which are among you, and incline your hearts unto Jehovah." [1] But in spite of the repeated denunciations of the Jehovah-enthusiasts, monotheism, so meager, so alien to the universal practice of antiquity, made slow headway; even as late as Ezekiel we find the complaint that the people still serve other gods, — "Ye pollute yourselves with all your idols even unto this day," — and the final exasperated cry, "As for you, O house of Israel, thus saith Jehovah: Go ye, serve ye every one his idols, and hereafter also, if ye will not hearken unto me; but pollute ye my holy name no more with your gifts." [2] Among these early gods were the Teraphim, images of ancestors (the Manes of the Romans); and this ancestor-worship survived long after the settlement in Canaan.[3] Animals were worshiped also — the calf (or bull), the serpent,[4] and the local Baals, or agricultural gods of the Canaanites. The Old Testament books, compiled late in Jewish history, tend to hush up this earlier polytheism; but the actual situation is easy to read between the lines.

As for Jehovah, he was, it seems, originally a storm-god of Mount Sinai. The etymology of the name is obscure; but a conjecture as good as any is that it meant "he who fells" — referring to the thunderbolts, which, as in the case of

[1] Joshua 24. Cf. also Gen. 35 : 2, 4.
[2] Ezek. 20. Cf. also chap. 23.
[3] Cf. Gen. 31:19, 30–35. Deut. 26:14. Judges 18:20. 1. Sam. 19:13, 16. Hos. 3:4. Jer. 16:7.
[4] Cf. Exod. 32:4. 1 Kings 12:28. 2 Kings 18:4.

THE HEBREW RELIGION

Zeus and Jupiter, were his weapons. Various Biblical allusions show us that his home was long thought to be in the South;[1] and many passages connect him with clouds and thunder and rain.[2] He was, apparently, the god of the Midianites, among whom Moses had lived before he assumed the leadership of his people. There, according to tradition, Moses found him worshiped; there, after the flight from Egypt, he bound the people to him by a solemn covenant, at the foot of the sacred mountain, Sinai, where he dwelt;[3] and there he instructed them, following the counsel of his Midianite father-in-law, in " the statutes of Jehovah, and his laws."[4] On one occasion, at least, his Midianite wife knew better than he what Jehovah required.[5] From this testimony, and because of other indications,[6] there is strong reason for believing the tradition of two of the three Biblical documents[7] when they tell us that Jehovah was introduced to the Hebrews by Moses.

At any rate, whatever historical value there may be in these accounts, and whether or not the Jews adopted the worship of Jehovah from the inhabitants of the Mount Sinai region, they early came to look upon him as their especial god, their patron and protector against the tribes

[1] Cf. Hab. 3: 3–7. Judges 5: 4–5. 1 Kings 19: 8 *ff*. Deut. 3: 2.
[2] Cf. Ps. 29: 3–7; 18: 7–14; 68: 7–9, 33–35.
[3] Cf. Exod. 3 and 19. Jehovah speaks to Moses "out of the mountain."
[4] Exod. 18: 16. [5] Exod. 4: 24–26.
[6] Among other indications are these: The name Jehovah is not found in compounds before the time of Moses; the earliest prophets do not refer to the dealings of Jehovah with the pre-Mosaic patriarchs; the Midianites were long friends of Israel — Jael was one; and the fact suggested by the Cain story, that the Kenites (= Midianites) bore the mark (tattoo) of Jehovah (their ancestral god) upon them.
[7] E and P (cf., e.g., Exod. 3: 15; 6: 2). The J document, has Jehovah worshiped by the Hebrews from the beginning. But in view of the strong convergence of evidence to the contrary, we must reject this tradition in favor of that held in common by E and P. Besides, it is easy to see how the J tradition would arise, and much harder to conceive the emergence of the E and P tradition if J were right.

with whom they were at war. He was still but one of many gods whom they also honored, but through the supremacy of those who particularly worshiped him, he came to be the chief god; and, as always, among barbarous peoples in a precarious situation, the chief bond of union between the various Jewish tribes. We read that he had his especial habitation in a sort of wooden chest called the Ark, carried by his people with great pomp and ceremony, that he might fight for them and give them his protection and favor.

Had all gone smoothly in Jewish history, the Jews might have remained as polytheistic as their contemporaries. They were not, indeed, nature-lovers, not imaginative or sympathetic, and would never have created a poetic mythology; they were intensely serious and practical by temperament, and the only gods for which they had much use were those that they invoked to help them in battle. But they frequently lost in battle, and had all they could do to maintain their existence. Many were, no doubt, the appeals from this or that band to invoke more zealously this or that god; but the Jehovah worshipers carried the day. There arose a sect that insisted that Jehovah alone could save them. They pointed to the escape from Egyptian bondage, under Moses, who worshiped Jehovah; and all the victories since that time they referred to Jehovah's help, their defeats to their defection from him to other gods and his consequent anger. Jehovah was most powerful; by loyalty to him alone could they be successful.[1] Instead of treating the other gods with the usual tolerance and good-fellowship, the Jehovists demanded the exclusive worship of their god; Jehovah was a jealous god, and would have no other gods beside him. Joining stern moral requirements with this demand, they gave to this Jehovah-worship the prestige of moral supe-

[1] Cf., e.g., Deut. 1: 30; 4: 3-4; 5: 6-9; 6: 14-15. Ps. 44: 5-7. 1 Kings 16: 30-33; 18: 17-21. Hos. 11: 1-7.

THE HEBREW RELIGION

riority. Gradually the other cults were assimilated or stamped out; by the reform of Josiah (*ca.* 621 B.C.) Jehovah-worship became the only legal religion.[1]

As time went on, and Egyptians and Assyrians threatened the integrity of their little kingdom, priests and prophets preached more and more vehemently the need of devotion to Jehovah and to his commandments. Finally, as the hope of safety became dimmer and despair began to enter the hearts of the people, a conviction came to certain of the prophets that their danger lay not in the weakness of their god before the stronger gods of rival nations, but in his wrath at his own people for their disobedience. Unless repentance were instant, they proclaimed, he might use these nations for their chastisement; for he was a stern god and required loyalty to his laws. Never was the necessity of justice and purity preached more passionately than by these patriotic and earnest prophets of Israel, who trusted in Jehovah to save them from their enemies, but felt that he required of them clean hands and a pure heart.

Jehovah did not save them. But so dominant had this conviction of the prophets become that when finally the Jews were conquered and their leading men carried into exile, a strong party held to the belief that he had not been overcome, but had punished them for their sins. This belief grew during the Exile. A purified remnant of Jehovah's people, purged of their sins, were to return and finally establish a kingdom based on that pure and moral worship which he demanded. So, at the actual return of the pious minority to Palestine, the Jehovah-worshipers were more completely in power than ever, and their insistence on morality more scrupulous.

Through this thought, that Jehovah had used other na-

[1] The book of Deuteronomy, written in all probability shortly before this date, was the official code legalized at that time.

tions for his purpose of punishing the Jews, came the conviction that he was not merely one of many gods, but the One Universal God; other gods were declared not only unworthy of their allegiance, but actually unreal and nonexistent. As the Jews grew from a collection of tribes to a flourishing kingdom, Jehovah was more and more invested with royal attributes; by the unknown prophet of the Exile (Is. 40–66) he was extolled as creator and ruler of the earth. Still more important, as attention was concentrated more and more on moral ideals, the conception of Jehovah became ennobled until he grew from just such a capricious, and at times bloodthirsty, tyrant as most contemporary deities were, to that just and merciful God that Christianity a little later proclaimed to the world.

What are the striking features of the religion of the prophets and psalmists?

Wherein was this Hebrew religion, at its best, superior to its contemporaries? Why was the Jehovah-cult of the Jews better than, say, the Moabite Chemosh-cult? Simply because it was more moral, more spiritual. Jehovah, at first principally useful in their eyes as a god of battles,[1] came to be the embodiment of their conscience. "Thus saith Jehovah," said the prophets, regarding their moral intuitions as his commands, and so as august and binding. The demand for exclusive allegiance to Jehovah meant practically a single-minded, whole-hearted devotion to righteousness. Even the cut-and-dried formalism of the post-exilic religion, that seems to us, as indeed it largely was, very petty and devitalized, meant to the devout a daily, unquestioning, faithful following of the Divine will. The Old Testament

[1] Cf. such passages as: "Through thee will we push down our enemies; through thy name will we tread them under that rise up against us.... Thou hast saved us from our enemies, and hast put them to shame that hated us" (Ps. 44: 5–7).

pictures vividly the increasing moralization of the Jewish religion. The prophets — who in early times were dervishes similar to those of many Semitic peoples, and notably of the later Mohammedans — became in Israel preachers of righteousness, a group of unsurpassed moral teachers, who, instead of abandoning the popular religion, as the Greek seers did, incorporated their new ideals into it, developed and ennobled it with their insight, and thus remain, next to Jesus, the chief religious inspiration of the Western world.

The Jews, of all early peoples, cared the most for right conduct; their Scriptures, taken over by Christianity, are infused with this passionate interest. It is to this, above all other influences, that we of the modern world owe that ingrained hatred of sin, so foreign to the pagan world, which has helped the readers of the Bible through all these centuries to conquer their passions and rise above a brutish life. Other religions have an equal or greater share of miracles and marvels, of rites and ceremonies; but they lack the spiritual fire. It is this that gave Judaism its sublimity, its preëminence over contemporary cults, and now, transmitted to Christianity, makes the latter most worthy of our allegiance.

We may, more specifically, mention three aspects of this Hebrew devotion to righteousness: —

(1) It was, first and foremost, an ideal for the nation as a nation, a high conception of public morality, of God-fearing politics, of social justice. Prophets arose, under the stress of national suspense and agony, who denounced in ringing terms the oppression by the rich, the injustice and gluttony and lust of Jehovah's faithless people. These are the men who made Israel's religion great, — Elijah, standing up against a murderous king and demanding justice in the name of Jehovah;[1] Amos, proclaiming to the self-satisfied and astonished people that punishment would fall upon them

[1] 1 Kings 21.

"because they have sold righteous men to pay a petty debt, because they trample on the heads of the poor, and miscarry justice for the humble";[1] Hosea, rebuking his fellows "because there is no truth, nor mercy, nor knowledge of God in the land. There is nought but swearing and breaking faith, and killing, and stealing, and committing adultery."[2] "Cease to do evil," cried the great Isaiah, "learn to do well; seek justice, relieve the oppressed, defend the fatherless, plead for the widow."[3] In the humaneness of its provisions the Jewish code was far in advance of contemporary legislation;[4] and the prophets looked forward ardently to a purged and transformed social order, wherein righteousness should rule in every relation of man to man. It was not merely the individual, but the national life that must be regenerated. For it is through righteousness, they held, that a nation lives and through the rottenness of sin that it perishes.

(2) The crushing of the Jewish state put, for the time, a quietus upon these collective aspirations, concentrating attention upon personal purity and individual salvation — wherein was both a loss and a gain. But, indeed, the civic religion of the earlier prophets was a matter not of outward forms, but of an indwelling spirit. "For I desire mercy," said the prophets, speaking in the name of Jehovah, "mercy, and not sacrifice; and the knowledge of God more than burnt offerings."[5] "I hate, I despise your feasts, and I will take no delight in your solemn assemblies. Take thou away from me the noise of thy songs; I will not hear the melody of thy viols. But let justice roll down as waters,

[1] Amos 2:7. Cf. also 3:9–10; 4:1–2; 5:15; 6:1–7; 8:4–7.
[2] Hosea 4:12. Cf. also 7:1–7; 12:7–8.
[3] Isa. 1:16–17. Cf. also 1:21–28; 3:14–26; 5:8–13; 10:1–2. Mic. 2:1–2.
[4] See, e.g., Exod. 23:11–12. Lev. 19:9–18, 33–36; 25:13–55. Deut. 23:15–16; 24:10–22.
[5] Hos. 6:6.

THE HEBREW RELIGION

righteousness as a mighty stream." [1] "Trample my courts no more, bring no more vain oblations. I cannot endure wickedness coupled with worship. . . . Your hands are full of blood. Wash you, make you clean; put away the evil of your doings from before mine eyes." [2]

The unknown writers of the psalms were equally possessed with this sense of the need of inward purity; the value of "a broken and a contrite heart" — a heart that knows its own weakness and sin and loathes it — a thought repugnant to paganism — had never elsewhere been expressed as by them. The Greeks and Romans exalted the manly virtues — honor, integrity, temperance, courage, and patriotism; but one would search long to find in their literature aspirations such as these: " Have mercy on me, O God. . . . Wash me thoroughly from mine iniquity, and cleanse me from my sin. For I acknowledge my transgressions, and my sin is ever before me. . . . Behold, thou desirest truth in the inward parts; . . . Purge me with hyssop and I shall be clean; wash me and I shall be whiter than snow. . . . Create in me a clean heart, O God, and renew a right spirit within me. Who can understand his errors? Cleanse thou me from secret faults. . . . Let the words of my mouth and the meditations of my heart be acceptable in thy sight." [3]

(3) Another noteworthy fact is that to the noblest Jews this imperious summons to righteousness was not a burden and a yoke, but a happiness above all others. "It is joy to the righteous to do righteousness." [4] The psalmists burst forth into rhapsodic celebrations of this joy: " Blessed is the man whose delight is in Jehovah's law." "I will delight myself in thy commandments, which I have loved. Unless thy law had been my delight, I should have perished."

---

[1] Amos 5: 21–24.
[2] Isa. 1: 12–16. Cf. also Ps. 40: 6; 50: 7–23; 51: 16–17. Joel 2: 13.
[3] Ps. 51: 1–10; 19: 12–14.   [4] Prov. 21: 15.

"The daughters of Judah rejoiced because of thy statutes, O Jehovah." "Oh, how I love thy law! it is my meditation all the day.... Thy testimonies are the rejoicing of my heart."[1]

In short, righteousness is the great word of Judaism; the sense of its importance, the enthusiasm and joy in it that accepts it not as a necessity, but as a glorious privilege, is the great contribution of the Jews to the world.[2]

How did the Messianic hope arise?

But this devotion to moral ideals was by no means all of their religion; there was also the hope of Jehovah's help. Through all their misfortunes they clung to the faith that he would in his own time confound their foes and vindicate the trust of the faithful. As they realized more and more their weakness and the might of their enemies, they came more and more to picture this overturn as accomplished by a striking and dramatic cataclysm. When this should be accomplished, these proud and powerful neighbors of theirs

[1] Ps. 1: 1–2; 119: 47, 92, 97, 111; 97: 8.
[2] Cf. Rauschenbusch, p. 4: "The fundamental conviction of the prophets, which distinguished them from the ordinary religious life of their day, was the conviction that God demands righteousness and demands nothing but righteousness."
And Matthew Arnold, *Literature and Dogma*, pp. 50, 326: "As long as the world lasts, all who want to make progress in righteousness will come to Israel for inspiration, as to the people who have had the sense for righteousness most glowing and strongest; and in hearing and reading the words Israel has uttered for us, carers for conduct will find a glow and a force they could find nowhere else.... Other nations had something of this idea, but they were not *possessed* with it; and to feel it enough to make the world feel it, it was necessary to be possessed with it."
Arnold should have said, however, "come to the Bible for inspiration," rather than "to Israel." Probably not one in ten, or one in a hundred, in Israel ever had this passion for righteousness. The Bible writers are of those few. As in describing the "Greek" spirit I warned the reader that such a spirit actually possessed but few of the Greeks, so the "Hebraic" spirit possessed numerically few Hebrews. But in both cases it was the few that counted in influencing the world's life.

THE HEBREW RELIGION

were to be cast into darkness, and Jehovah would reign on earth over the faithful remnant of his people, giving them the final reward of their fidelity, which they pictured in very material terms, as an earthly kingdom, with earthly pleasures, a glorification of Israel before the world.[1]

Many elements in their situation contributed to these pathetic popular hopes — their outward impotence under the galling yoke of their oppressors; their dogged belief in Jehovah's power; the memory of the golden age of David behind them, now idealized, and a constant spur to their ambitions; their lack of belief in a life after death. But some leader there must be, appointed by Jehovah, to establish this Divine Kingdom — some messiah [2] consecrated to the task of freeing the people and realizing for them their divine destiny. Some thought of him as a conqueror like David, a great military leader, who would put to rout their enemies and establish a world-wide rule. Others pictured him rather as a supernatural figure, to come on the clouds of heaven and judge the nations by the strength of Jehovah's right arm — Israel simply awaiting in passive prayer this miraculous deliverance. Still others, and the noblest of the Jews, held that the people must first be transformed in their hearts and worthy of so great a salvation; only when they were faithful and pure enough would Jehovah manifest his power, and inaugurate the reign of peace and universal prosperity.[3]

[1] See, e.g., Isa. chaps. 9, 11, 30: 18 f., 40, 60, 65: 17 f., 66: 18 f. Mic. 4, 7: 7 f. Amos 9: 14 f., Zeph. 3: 8 f., Jer. 23: 3 f., 30: 18 f. Ezek. 34: 11 f., 37: 21 f.

[2] The word "messiah" (translated in Greek into the word "christ") meant "anointed." Kings, prophets, and priests were anointed for their special work in the service of God; a messiah was, then, a man consecrated to some divine work. And The Messiah was to be The Man consecrated by God to this greatest of all tasks, of bringing in the Kingdom of God.

[3] See W. D. E. Oesterley, *Evolution of the Messianic Idea.* E. C. A. Riehm, *Messianic Prophecy.* F. J. Delitzch, *Messianic Prophecies in Historical Succession.* C. F. Kent, *Sermons, Epistles, and Apocalypses of Israel's Prophets,* pp. 39-48. G. S. Goodspeed, *Israel's Messianic Hope.*

All of these variant dreams were gradually accepted by the piety of the people as authoritative. Attempts to reconcile them were, of course, hopeless; but different groups pinned their faith to different aspects of the picture — while many, of course, were skeptical altogether. When and where and how should appear this Messiah? This prophet and that was looked to eagerly, but the Great Event came not yet; and the people, intense with expectation, exhorted by their prophets to repent of their sins before it should be too late to have a part in the New Order, chafing under their bondage, awaited their hero and savior. Orthodox Jews still await Him; liberal Jews have long ago become disillusioned and given up the fantastic hope.[1] But at the time when that hope was most intense, a small band, mostly of Galilean peasants, believed they had found this Messiah, this Christ, in the person of a young prophet named Jesus.

J. P. Peters, *Religion of the Hebrews*. H. P. Smith, *Religion of Israel*. R. L. Ottley, *Religion of Israel*. W. E. Addis, *Hebrew Religion*. A. Loisy, *Religion of Israel*. K. Marti, *Religion of the Old Testament*. A. Duff, *Theology and Ethics of the Hebrews*. J. C. Todd, *Politics and Religion in Ancient Israel*. L. B. Paton, *Primitive Religion of Israel*. K. Budde, *Religion of Israel to the Exile*. T. K. Cheyne, *Jewish Religion after the Exile; The Two Religions of Israel*. C. Cornill, *Prophets of Israel*. W. R. Smith, *Prophets of Israel*. L. W. Batten, *The Hebrew Prophet*. M. Buttenwieser, *Prophets of Israel*. G. Santayana, *Reason in Religion*, chap. v. S. Reinach, *Orpheus*, chap. vii. W. Rauschenbusch, *Christianity and the Social Crisis*, chap. i. *New World*, vol. 4, p. 98. *Biblical World*, vol. 42, pp. 234, 305, 373; vol. 43, p. 44. Kautsch, in *Hastings' Bible Dictionary*, extra volume, p. 612.

---

[1] For the present status of the Jewish religion see *New World*, vol. 4, p. 601.

For the period between the Testaments, see C. H. Toy's *Judaism and Christianity*. W. Fairweather, *Background of the Gospels*. R. H. Charles, *Religious Development between the Old and New Testaments*.

CHAPTER V

JESUS THE CHRIST

What are the sources of our knowledge of the life of Christ?

In studying the history of the founding of Christianity, as in the case of all religious history written by the believers themselves, we must beware of accepting at its face value whatever is told us by the narrators. As notably in the traditions of their own history that the Jews treasured in their sacred books, so in the Christian tradition legendary material has crept in, and events have been unconsciously colored and warped in accordance with later religious conceptions. If we honestly desire to know what can now be known of the Great Teacher whose name has become, to us of "Christendom," synonymous with virtue itself, we must be willing to look through the veil of mist which the religious veneration of centuries has drawn about him and study the records that remain to us of his life as we would study those of any other great religious leader — Buddha, Confucius, St. Francis — sifting the historical from the legendary, allowing for the evident bias of biographers, and deducing only what can legitimately be deduced from the confused and scanty material we have to draw upon.

At the outset we must face the fact that outside of a small band of followers, mostly illiterate fisher- and peasant-folk, Christ made no impression upon his times. His public career lasted probably not over a year and a half, and was spent, except for the last few days or weeks, in the out-of-the-way province of Galilee. To the priests and Jewish upper classes, as to the Roman officials, that brief and humble career was not distinguishably different from those of the numerous other contemporary reformers and agitators. The outside references to Christ — brief allusions by the Jewish historian Josephus (by many considered spurious) and the Roman authors Tacitus, Suetonius, and Pliny — are scarcely enough even to testify to the fact of his existence, since they doubtless merely accept the belief of the early Christians in a historic Jesus who was crucified by Pontius Pilate. But the witness of Paul, our earliest source, is quite enough to guarantee his historicity; for Paul, though he never knew Jesus in the flesh, must have talked, a very few years after his death, with many who had known him well. He tells us, in his few extant letters, nothing to speak of about the earthly life of Jesus; but he is witness to the extraordinary impression that Jesus had made upon his little circle of disciples. And fortunately there is material enough in the three Synoptic Gospels to enable the skilled historian to reconstruct with considerable assurance the historic figure of Jesus and the main events of his public life. Such a reconstruction has been made, with infinite pains and loving care, by the coöperative efforts of many modern scholars. Except for a few mooted points — and principally those affected by dogmatic considerations — there is now a pretty general agreement among reliable historians as to the probable facts of his career and the cardinal points of his teaching.

Besides the Synoptic Gospels there are some fragments of non-canonical narratives; these, however, are mostly late and of very dubious authenticity; at best they add little of importance to the picture. The Fourth Gospel is now generally conceded to be later than the Synoptics, and rather theological than historic in its interest. Written to set forth the view of the author [1] as to the nature and mission of

[1] The author's name may have been John; but (*pace* some conservative scholars who still cling to the traditional view) he was certainly not the

JESUS THE CHRIST

Christ, it is valuable in showing the tendencies of early Christian theology, for its intrinsic charm and sweetness, and for its insight into the meaning that Christ's life had and was to have for his followers. But it is of little value in helping us to get an idea of the real Jesus as he lived and taught on earth. The book was probably not intended to be taken as a literal record of events, but as a dramatic picture illustrating and explaining the author's conception of Jesus as the Logos (Word) or Earthly Manifestation of God. The literary device, by which speeches and acts are attributed to Christ in accordance with what the author conceived that he might have said and done, was not uncommon or considered illegitimate in those days. Indeed, it was the common practice of ancient historians.

We are thrown back, then, upon the three Synoptic Gospels, as, practically speaking, our only source. The first and third of these were composed by combining the Mark biography (itself evidently a compilation of traditions rather than a first-hand narrative) with a collection of Sayings of Christ (together with certain other scattering material, particularly in the Third Gospel). The collection of Sayings, which tradition attributes to the Apostle Matthew (whence his name has become attached to the Gospel that makes greatest use of it) exists now only as it has been incorporated into our Gospels. As they stand, "Mark" dates from 70–75 A.D., "Matthew" and "Luke" from five to twenty years later. That is to say, the earliest extant document recording the facts of Christ's life and teaching dates from about forty or forty-five years after his death. The repetition of its incidents in the parallel narratives of the other Gospels is of no corroborative value, since the authors

disciple. See E. F. Scott, *The Fourth Gospel, its Purpose and Theology.* J. Warschauer, *The Problem of the Fourth Gospel.* B. W. Bacon, *The Fourth Gospel in Research and Debate.*

simply copied from Mark. No one of the Gospels was written by a personal friend of Christ or eyewitness of the events of his life.[1]

What were the salient events in his life?

Jesus was the oldest of at least seven brothers and sisters.[2] Wherever he may have been born,[3] he was brought up, as a carpenter, or house-builder, at Nazareth in Galilee, and known all his life as a Nazarene. Of his youth we know practically nothing, save that he must have become deeply versed in his national Scriptures and filled with the expecta-

---

[1] It is needless to point out that forty years is long enough for the legendary element to have grown to any length. Witness Bonaventura's life of St. Francis, dating likewise from forty years after that Saint's death, and replete with marvel and miracle. Parallel cases could be cited from every field of religious history.

See P. Wernle, *Sources of Our Knowledge of the Life of Jesus*. V. H. Stanton, *The Gospels as Historical Documents*. F. C. Burkitt, *Earliest Sources for the Life of Jesus; The Gospel History and its Transmission*. E. F. Scott, *The Apologetic of the New Testament*.

The best Introductions to the New Testament in English are those of G. A. Jülicher, B. W. Bacon, J. Moffatt, G. B. Gray, and A. S. Peake. The translation of the New Testament by J. Moffatt (3d ed., 1914) is perhaps the best to date. The *Twentieth Century New Testament* (F. H. Revell Company) and R. F. Weymouth's *Modern Speech New Testament* are versions in modern colloquial English, useful in clarifying obscure sayings. See further the remarks on editions of the Bible on pp. 49–50. A good Harmony of the Gospels is useful in making it easier to trace the development of the tradition from Gospel to Gospel; J. M. Thompson's *Synoptic Gospels* is the best to date.

[2] Mark 6:3.

[3] The birth- and infancy-stories with which the First and Third Gospels are now prefaced are later than the bulk of those Gospels; together with the resurrection-stories at the end, they are called by scholars The Outer Envelope. See Holtzmann, chap. IV; Réville in *New World*, vol. 1, p. 695 (also in his *Vie de Jésus*, unfortunately not translated). For the question of the virgin birth see P. Lobstein, *Virgin Birth of Christ*. J. E. Carpenter, *Bible in the Ninteenth Century*, pp. 480–97. O. Pfleiderer, *Primitive Christianity*, Eng. tr., vol. II, pp. 504–10; also *American Journal of Theology*, vol. 10, p. 1.

tion of the imminent fulfillment of the hope of Israel.¹ At the age of about thirty he was attracted by the vigorous preaching of another young man named John, who had drawn quite a following about him and was called "The Baptist" (or "Baptizer"), from a rite of purification from their sins which he enjoined upon his disciples. John was a striking figure, a reincarnation of the old spirit of the prophets, forceful, ascetic, severe in his denunciations of the sins and injustices of the people, solemn in his warning that they must not count on their descent from Abraham to insure them participation in the speedily coming Messianic Kingdom; only those who were found worthy would be admitted, and immediate repentance was imperative. Jesus was among those who submitted to his rite of baptism;² and, according to the tradition, it was at that moment that he became conscious of his mission. John was soon thereafter thrown into prison, and presently executed, by the ruler of the country. But Jesus took up the rôle of prophet, with the summons he had heard on the Baptist's lips, "Repent ye, for the Kingdom of God is at hand!"³

By the vigor of his preaching and the force and charm of his personality, Jesus quickly attracted attention and gathered disciples about him, as John had done. Moreover, he soon found himself possessed in a remarkable degree of the power to work what we should call faith-cures, and was surrounded by an eager crowd of health-seekers. In his own home, Nazareth, he was, indeed, received with jeers; and the narrator tells us frankly that he was unable to perform many cures there because of their lack of faith. But in the lakeside towns, some miles away, he created quite a stir; and

¹ The incident recorded in Luke 2: 41–52 illustrates, if it is historical, his early interest in religion.
² Jesus seems never to have administered baptism; but the earliest disciples did. See E. F. Scott, *Beginnings of the Church*, chap. VII.
³ Mark 1: 14. Matt. 4: 17.

there most of his preaching was done. Jesus himself seems to have sought to avoid too much healing activity, whether because it tended to bring him, like John, too dangerously into Herod's notice, or simply because it interfered with the preaching which he had more at heart. The burden of his message was the call to repentance, and his favorite method the illustration in incomparable parables of the inner qualities necessary to insure participation in the imminently approaching Kingdom.

Outwardly, then, he seemed a prophet like John, though of a gentler and more spiritual nature.[1] But in his own heart he came to believe himself, it is impossible now to be sure when or how,[2] the long-awaited Messiah; or rather the Messiah-elect, who in God's own time would be endowed with supernatural power to bring in the New Age.[3] At first he told no one of this secret belief in his own destiny. But when Peter, the most ardent and impulsive of his followers, expressed the same conviction, he did not deny it, enjoining silence, however, upon his disciples until "his time should come." [4] Meanwhile he was content to pass from village to village, winning as many as he could from their heedlessness

[1] It is significant that the people took him for John *redivivus*. "Who do men say that I am? And they told him, saying, John the Baptist; and others Elijah; and others, One of the prophets." Mark 8: 28.

[2] The tradition puts his "Messianic conviction" at the time of the Baptism. But many scholars believe that it took possession of him only later, at the height of his success, in connection with his inevitable recognition of his mental and spiritual supremacy over his fellows.

[3] This by no means implied that he equaled or identified himself with God. It is needless to point to such verses as Mark 10: 18, "Why callest thou me good? None is good save One, even God"; it suffices to realize what the Jewish conception of the Messiah was — a more or less glorified and supernaturally endowed figure, but absolutely distinct from God himself. The question of the divinity of Christ will be discussed below, on p. 142 ff.

The Greek word $\chi\rho\iota\sigma\tau\acute{o}\varsigma$, by the way, which has been transliterated into our *Christ*, means *he-who-is-to-be-anointed* — i.e., the *Messiah-elect* — rather than one who is now playing the part of Messiah.

[4] Mark 8: 29-30.

and sin, teaching them the Way of life that he believed to be in harmony with God's will, and awaiting in perfect faith the time when he should be called upon to play his glorious Messianic rôle.

The first flush of his success, however, soon paled. The scribes were offended from the beginning because he assumed their rôle of authoritative interpreter of the Scriptures, while scorning their minute and hair-splitting casuistry. The Pharisees, the orthodox of their day, were scandalized because he refused to keep the proper fasts, to observe the Sabbath punctiliously, to refrain from eating with the "unclean." Their distrust and hatred of Jesus were quickly matched by his fearless and outspoken rebukes of their hypocrisy and self-righteousness; and the rupture thus brought about grew steadily greater. There are indications in the Gospel narrative that many of his temporary adherents deserted him, and that at times he was even forced to flee the country by the threats made against him. The Galilean mission bade fair to dwindle into insignificance; and when he finally left his home-country and "set his face steadfastly to Jerusalem," — well aware of the fate that probably awaited him at the capital, — it was with a bitter denunciation of the hard-heartedness and unbelief of the towns where his preaching career had been spent.[1] Something more dramatic must be done; matters must be brought to a head, the crisis evoked — and that could only be at the holy city; — "I must go on my way ... for it cannot be that a prophet perish out of Jerusalem."[2]

It is possible that Jesus expected, when he went to Jerusalem, at the time of the feast of the Passover, that Jehovah would intervene there dramatically to vindicate him by investing him with the Messianic powers. But there are indications that he had already become convinced that he must

[1] Matt. 11: 20–24.   [2] Luke 13: 33.

first suffer and die, and was only then to come, from heaven, in the spectacular manner of the popular expectation. For this he could find Scriptural warrant. The descriptions of the "suffering servant" of Jehovah,[1] although originally referring to the people of Israel as a whole, were currently taken as prophetic descriptions of the coming Messiah, and were doubtless applied by Jesus to himself. He could take these predictions of a "man of sorrows" as referring to the preliminary phase of his appearance, and so harmonize them with the glorified pictures of the triumphant Messiah to be found elsewhere in the Scriptures. Thus by his rejection and death should the humble and faithful be clearly separated from the hard-hearted and unbelieving, and all the Scripture be fulfilled.[2] At any rate, he did not falter. His first act was to drive out from the Temple, with the aid, probably, of his little band of loyal followers, the money-changers and sellers of sacrificial animals, who, to his mind, were shockingly out of place within the sacred precincts. And it was, in all probability, this impetuous act, incurring, as it must have incurred, the anger of the priests and all maintainers of the established order, that actually brought about his death.

From that moment the Jewish authorities sought for an unimpeachable excuse for putting Jesus out of the way. He had, however, doubtless awakened considerable popular interest in the city; and they hesitated to incur any widespread resentment. But before many days one of his intimate circle of disciples himself gave them their handle. Become skeptical, probably, of Jesus' pretensions, and with that, of course, angry at his presumption, or possibly with a blind trust in them and an impatience to bring on the dénouement, Judas betrayed his secret claim to the Messiah-

---

[1] See Isa. 42: 1–9; 49: 1–6; 50: 4–9; 52: 13; 53: 12.
[2] Cf. Matt. 26: 56.

ship to the priests.¹ Such blasphemy deserved death. He was arrested, brought before the council, and asked pointblank if he was the Messiah. He answered, " I am. And ye shall very soon see the Son of Man sitting at the right hand of power and coming on the clouds of heaven." ² To the priests — indeed to any one save the few who had come thoroughly under the spell of his personality — such an assertion on the part of a humble and unknown Galilean was the most impudent and outrageous sacrilege. The crowd turned against him; and he was hustled off, amid jeers and insults, to an ignominious fate. We are told of his agony of spirit in the garden where he was arrested, and can guess the bitter doubt that found utterance in the despairing cry from the cross, "My God, my God, why hast thou forsaken me!" ³ But he conquered his weakness, bowed to the Divine plan, and met his death serenely, a martyr to his faith in his own destiny. Surely the pathos of human blindness and blunder was never more tragically exemplified than at this moment when the leaders of the Jewish people misprized and sentenced to death, in the flush of his early manhood, the noblest and rarest of their sons, the man of whom a centurion, standing by at the end, in the late afternoon of that April day, and catching his last words, "Father, into thy hands I commend my spirit," is reported to have said, "Truly this man was son of a god!" ⁴

¹ This seems the most probable explanation of the "betrayal." The information of Judas would not have been necessary to disclose his whereabouts, since he was teaching daily in public, and could easily be followed to his sleeping-place.

² Mark 14: 62. Matt. 26: 64. The phrase translated in the older versions "henceforth," or "hereafter" (ἀπ' ἄρτι), means rather "soon," or "presently." This prediction is in consonance with a number of other reported sayings of Jesus.

³ Mark 15: 34.

⁴ Or "a Divine Hero" — i.e., one of the innumerable divine or semidivine beings whose existence the pagan mind accepted. This reported

What were the striking features of Christ's personality?

Of the resurrection-faith — that startling conviction that thrilled the little band of believers and became the cornerstone of a new community — we shall presently speak. But with the closing-in of Good Friday night the curtain fell on the life-work of him who is generally conceded to be the greatest of earth's saints and seers.[1] Such as we have sketched them, or not far different, we must conceive the main facts of his life to have been — a brief flash of light in a dark and confused age. But this is not all the story. To the world of the past nineteen centuries that life has been the type of human excellence, the ideal and pattern of the life of the spirit. And it is fitting that so it should be. For more significant than the outward course of his young life, so tragically cut short, is the secret of his personality, which has so steadily dominated the religious consciousness of men.

But the historic Jesus that emerges to our view as the result of the modern historical study of the Gospels is a very different figure from the effeminate Christ of mediæval art or the misty God-man of traditional dogma. It is rather a dominating and grippingly human personality — strong, fearless, stern, passionate in exhortation and rebuke; and yet with a rare purity and sweetness, a penetrating faith in sinful men, and a boundless love. The longer one lingers over the Gospel narratives, the more one comes to comprehend the remarkable personal impression which he made upon the

remark of the Roman soldier has nothing, of course, to do with the much later theological belief suggested to the modern reader by its usual English rendering, "the Son of God." Luke 23: 46. Mark 15: 37–39.

[1] For appreciations of Christ's personality on the part of those who have no belief in his supernatural character, see, e.g., J. S. Mill, *Theism*, pt. v. Matthew Arnold, *Literature and Dogma*, chap. III. Emerson, "Divinity School Address" (in *Nature, Addresses, and Lectures*). E. Renan, *Life of Jesus*, chap. 28.

hearts of those who knew him well and the heroic devotion which he aroused.

(1) Perhaps his most marked trait was his eagerness to save the lost, his yearning sympathy for all who might be brought to repent and live the better life. He mingled gladly with sinners and outcasts, not to rebuke them or to weep over them, but joining heartily in their merriment, sitting with them at table, and summoning them gently to their heritage in the Kingdom. Little children were brought to him to be blessed, and the sick flocked to him to be healed. For all who were humble and open-hearted, who hungered and thirsted after righteousness, however far they might be from grace by any conventional standards, he had a tender compassion, a wide and forgiving love. "O Jerusalem, Jerusalem, which killeth the prophets, and stoneth them that are sent unto thee! how often would I have gathered thy children together, even as a hen gathereth her chickens under her wings, and ye would not." [1] Of a young man we are told, "And Jesus, looking upon him, loved him." [2]

(2) In spite of his freedom from asceticism and formality, his readiness to mingle with ordinary unpretending and sinful people, he lived himself a life of stainless personal purity. Through his absolute allegiance to the will of God as he conceived it, — expressed in the famous utterance, "Not my will but thine be done," and kept aglow in his heart by long hours of solitary prayer, — he was able to reject every temptation to ease or personal aggrandizement, and, in spite of his sensitive nature and frail physique,[3] to keep unflinchingly in the path of his duty, even when it led to a torturing and undeserved death. The verdict of his disciples was that he

[1] Matt. 23:37. [2] Mark 10:21.
[3] This is clearly shown by the fact that he was unable to carry his own cross (or the transverse beam of it), as was usually done by the condemned; and by his quick death — strong men being able to stand the pain of crucifixion for many hours, or even several days.

was "not one that cannot be touched with the feeling of our infirmities; but one that hath been in all points tempted like as we are, yet without sin." [1]

(3) Naturally of a happy and peaceful disposition, — see how the breath of the Galilean spring breathes through his earlier utterances, — he blazed into anger when confronted with hypocrisy and self-righteousness, with the selfish and scheming orthodoxy of the scribes and Pharisees. In sharpest contrast with his pity for the downcast and erring is his sternness with the hard-hearted and callous. He did not hesitate, when necessary, to use physical violence to end evil practices; witness the episode of the cleansing of the Temple. "Think not," he said, "that I came to bring peace on the earth; I came to bring not peace, but a sword!" No wonder the people took him for Elijah or John the Baptist. [2]

(4) His insight into human nature, his direct, straightforward perception of moral truths, together with his natural talent for expression, gave him a felicity of utterance which has never been surpassed. Capable upon occasion of subtle argumentation, overflowing now and then into genial humor, biting irony, or flash of wit, but in general homely in his language, and free from the useless verbiage of the schools, keen and quick at epigram and paradox, with a gift at simile and parable, his sayings remain to-day among the most memorable — many of us would say the most memorable — of the spiritual teachings of all times. Free from all servitude to the orthodoxy of his day, following always his own vision, and calling to his disciples, "Why of yourselves judge ye not what is right?" [3] his words must have been of rare stimulating power. He uttered few truths, if any, that

---

[1] Heb. 4: 15.

[2] See, for instances of his fierce and scornful invective, Matt. 11: 20-24; 10: 12-15; 10: 33-37. Mark 10: 25. Luke 6: 24-25. Matt. 23.

[3] Luke 12: 57.

had not been expressed before; but in the clarity, terseness, and limpid simplicity of his phrasing, rid as it is of so much that repels or mars the vision in the utterances of earlier and later teachers, we have reason enough to understand how his auditors "wondered at the words of grace which proceeded out of his mouth." [1]

What were the striking features of his teaching?

Every great teacher must express his insight in the language and conceptions of his time and people — else he will not be understood, and will have no influence. Jesus was a Jew [2] of nineteen centuries ago, preaching to men whose minds were steeped in a very peculiar and local *Weltanschauung*, scarcely intelligible to us save by considerable historical study. His mind was, of course, moulded by the environment in which he grew up, and his concepts were those of his countrymen in the first few decades of our era. To understand him, therefore, we must take into account the meaning that his words would have for his auditors, and

[1] Luke 4: 22. Cf. W. Bousset, *What is Religion?* p. 217: "The Jewish Rabbis had, indeed, said all that Jesus said; but, unfortunately, they said so much else besides. . . . The classic is always the simple."

[2] The Galileans were, to be sure, of mixed race; and it is possible — if that possibility is of any comfort to any one with anti-Semitic prejudices! — that his ancestry was partly Aryan. But, indeed, the Jews are among the finest of human stocks.

The Davidic genealogies in Matthew and Luke are of no historic value, as is shown by the fact that they contradict each other hopelessly. (And both, by the way, purporting to derive Jesus' descent from David through Joseph, are utterly at variance with the virgin-birth idea, which rejects Joseph as Jesus' father.) If there had been in possession of the family a record of descent from David, another and mistaken genealogy could hardly have obtained circulation. The two variant genealogies were, of course, the product of the prior conviction that the Messiah *must* come, as the prophets had predicted, from the line of David. But Jesus himself publicly confuted that idea (Mark 12: 35–37), showing that he did not base his belief in his Messiahship on such grounds. And for us the question whether he was or was not descended from that idolized adventurer-king has no particular interest.

not read into them our twentieth-century ideas. To apply his teachings to our needs we shall, indeed, have, to some extent, to translate them into our current terms and modes of thought; and when we have done that, we shall find them of perennial inspiration. To a large extent the problems of men then are their problems now; in its essential import the teaching of the great seers is never outdated. And this is in unusual degree the case with Jesus. For he was no social reformer,[1] he was a reformer of the heart; and while outward conditions change so rapidly as to make the political and social revolutionist of one era a mere historical object of reverence for the next, the spiritual prophet speaks to the common needs of men through all the ages. But, on the other hand, to get a correct historical view of his teaching, we must see him in his setting, take what he says in the sense in which his disciples must have understood it, and not try to explain away what is alien to our modern thought, or what time has proved untrue.

(1) The background of Christ's teaching was the imminent approach of the Messianic era — the Kingdom of God on earth, and the consequent necessity for immediate repentance. Only the pure in heart, the faithful followers of Jehovah, were to have part in this kingdom; the wicked were to be cast into "outer darkness, where there is wailing and gnashing of teeth." The Judgment Day was at hand; the wheat was to be separated from the tares, and the new age of universal righteousness and peace was to be ushered in.

The appearance of the Messiah, with his dramatic installation of the New Order of things, so eagerly awaited by the people, might be at any moment; and only the righteous should have part in it. "Be ye ready, for in such an hour as

[1] In view of some contemporary writing about Christ it may be well to insist upon this point. See, for an effective elaboration of it, *Biblical World*, vol. 42, p. 26.

ye think not the Son of man cometh. Verily I say unto you, this generation shall not pass away till all be fulfilled."[1] Later piety, disappointed in its expectations, construed these promises in a metaphorical sense, to mean an inner coming in the hearts of men; obviously they could not long continue to take literally prophecies that had not been fulfilled. But every student is forced to admit that Christ's immediate predecessors and successors expected the establishment of an outward kingdom, and meant literally what they said; and all the ingenuity of theologians, reading our ideas back into Christ's words, cannot make them fit the metaphorical interpretation. Nor can we consider them interpolations; the Gospels are too full of them. The only passage that gave much plausibility to the traditional interpretation, "The Kingdom of God is within you," is almost certainly a mistranslation. It reads properly, "The Kingdom of God cometh not with observation [i.e., not so gradually that you can watch it coming], but behold! the Kingdom of God is [all of a sudden] in the midst of you!"[2] In this suddenness with which it should come lay the point of the repeated exhortations to be ready, to watch, to repent before it was too late. Certainly, if Christ put an esoteric meaning into his words, he utterly failed to convey his altered meaning to his disciples; and it is fundamentally inconsistent with the sincerity and straightforwardness of his nature that in such an important matter he should have used words in one sense which his listeners were bound to understand in another. We are bound, therefore, to conclude that Jesus shared the belief of his countrymen in an outward and vis-

[1] Matt. 24: 34, 42–44; 25: 13. Luke 12: 40; 21: 32, 36.

[2] Luke 17: 20–21. The correct translation is given in the margin of the Revised Version. The Greek preposition is, by itself, ambiguous. But the verses following, with their emphasis upon the suddenness of the coming, corroborate this interpretation. And Jesus is speaking to his opponents, the Pharisees; the Kingdom was surely not within *them*.

ible change, a New Era to be established by God, there in Judea, in the imminent future.[1]

That Jesus should have shared this delusion, and especially that he should have believed himself the One destined by God to play the rôle of Messiah, may seem strange to us, with our long perspective by which to discount the pathetically sanguine hopes of the long-suffering Jews. But after all, there was a deeper truth in his dream of a coming Golden Age and his own part in its establishment than any of his contemporaries could know. Though its coming be far more removed than he thought, the time will yet come when God's will shall prevail on earth; and in the bringing-on of that consummation he will be seen to have, in truth, played the master-rôle. And even without his conception of the Kingdom, and his Messiahship, the essence of his teaching would have been the same. It was not a mere interim-morality; it was a description of the ideal life of the coming millennial era, which he urged men to adopt now, so as to be ready and prepare the way for that glorious consummation. Even if others were still living the old life of sin, this little band could be already living by the eternal ideals. Jesus taught this Way of life for the same reason that other religious leaders have taught similar ideals — because it approved itself to his heart and proved itself in his experience the way of solution for life's perplexities and sorrows. Other motives than the impending Judgment-Day he often gives;[2] and there can

[1] The so-called eschatological school — Weiss, Schweitzer, Tyrrell, Burkitt, Streeter, *et al.*, have done good service in emphasizing this side of Jesus' teaching. For corroboration of the point of view here taken, any of these may be consulted. See also H. L. Jackson, *Eschatology of Jesus*. E. von Dobschütz, *Eschatology of the Gospels*. *Hibbert Journal*, vol. 10, p. 83. M. Jones, *The New Testament in the Twentieth Century*, bk. I, chap. VI. E. F. Scott, *The Kingdom and the Messiah*. A. Schweitzer, *The Mystery of the Kingdom of God*.

[2] For example, "That ye may be sons of your Father who is in heaven"; "For no man can serve two masters ... God and mammon"; "For where your treasure is, there will your heart be also."

be no doubt that his passionate earnestness and love of men would have expressed itself in fundamentally the same ideals, whatever the hopes had been that determined their particular form and phrasing.

(2) The Jewish Jehovah, Lord of Hosts, was in his conception the loving Father whom one or two of the prophets had pictured; the Father, for his thought, not only of the nation but of each individual. The word Abba, Father, so often on his lips, was long repeated by his disciples. The first commandment was to love God; and his life was spent in the constant sense of companionship with him. Every event was ordered by his will; "not a sparrow shall fall on the ground without your Father." To his anxious, fearful friends he cries out, "O ye of little faith!" "Your heavenly Father knoweth that ye have need of these things." This sense of the love of God has been of unspeakable comfort to millions of believers, as it must have been to him; and by many it has been called the main element in his teaching. Certainly it was constantly in the background of his thought.

(3) Of his practical teaching the keynote was charity, compassion, the beauty of boundless forgiveness and unlimited love. The inimitable parables of the Good Samaritan and the Prodigal Son, of the Ninety and Nine, and the Lost Piece of Silver,[1] are the most famous of all lessons on the law of love. Those who were to inherit the Kingdom were those to whom the Messiah might say: "I was an hungered and ye gave me meat; I was thirsty and ye gave me drink; I was a stranger and ye took me in, naked and ye clothed me; I was sick and ye visited me, I was in prison and ye came unto me. . . . Inasmuch as ye have done it unto one of the least of these my brethren ye have done it unto me."[2] The great moral commandment, according to Jesus, is to "love thy neighbor as thyself." Men must not allow them-

[1] Luke 10: 30–37; 14: 8–22. Matt. 18: 12–14.   [2] Matt. 25: 35–40.

selves to be angry with one another; they are to interrupt even a sacrifice to be reconciled; they are to forgive one another not only seven times but "seventy times seven times"; they are not to judge others, but — "cast out first the beam that is in thine own eye." "Blessed are the merciful" and "the peacemakers," he said, and bade men love even their enemies. When they made a feast they were to invite not their rich neighbors, who could requite their favor, but "the poor, the maimed. the lame, the blind . . . because they have not wherewith to recompense thee." His method with sinners was not that of sternness, but the awakening of the better nature in them; his heart went out to them and he had compassion on them. "The Son of man came to save that which was lost," he said; and of the repentant harlot who anointed his feet, "Her sins, which are many, are forgiven; for she loved much." At the end, on the cross, in the agony of death, he uttered those immortal words: "Father, forgive them, they know not what they do."

(4) Next to the love and compassion in Jesus' teaching we are struck by its purity, its unworldliness, and spiritual aspiration. "A man's life," we are told, "consisteth not in the abundance of things which he possesseth," but is an inward thing. All worldly pleasures and lusts that choke the higher life must be given up. Men must become simple-hearted as children; "of such is the Kingdom of Heaven," he said, pointing to the little ones they brought him to bless. The purity must be genuine and inward, not a mere observance of the letter of the law. "Hear ye all of you and understand," he proclaimed; "there is nothing from without the man that going into him can defile him; but the things which proceed out of the man are those that defile the man." But this was in no spirit of laxity. On the contrary, he enjoined upon his disciples that their righteousness "exceed the righteousness of the scribes and Pharisees." They must not

only not commit murder, but not even be angry with their brothers; not only refrain from adultery, but from looking at a woman lustfully; love not only their neighbors, but their enemies. They must pluck out an eye or cut off a hand that stood in the way of their duty; they must seek first the Kingdom of Heaven, and be content with nothing less than perfection.

These are the things that make Jesus a great spiritual teacher — his constant emphasis on the spirit of love and forgiveness, his intense aspiration for perfection and readiness to thrust aside anything that stood in the way, the directness with which he probed to the bottom of the heart and demanded not only the outward form of goodness, but purity of thought and motive. He required no allegiance to any creed, he enjoined no observances on his followers, he founded no organization; he taught a Way of life, a way through which millions of his followers, of many races and constantly varying forms of belief, have come to inward harmony, purity, and peace.

O. Holtzmann, *Life of Jesus*. A. Neumann, *Jesus*. W. Bousset, *Jesus*. A. Réville, *Vie de Jésus*. G. H. Gilbert, *Jesus*. J. Warschauer, *Jesus, Seven Questions*. A. Schweitzer, *Quest of the Historical Jesus*. S. J. Case, *Historicity of Jesus*. C. F. Kent, *Life and Teachings of Jesus*. C. G. Montefiore, *Religious Teachings of Jesus*. J. E. Carpenter, *The Historical Jesus and the Theological Christ*. B. H. Streeter, *The Historic Christ*, in *Foundations* (The Macmillan Company, 1913). M. Jones, *The New Testament in the Twentieth Century*, pt. I, chaps. II–IV. G. B. Foster, *Finality of the Christian Religion*, chaps. VIII–IX. W. Rauschenbusch, *Christianity and the Social Crisis*, chap. II. T. R. Glover, *Conflict of Religions in the Early Roman Empire*, chap. IV. S. Reinach, *Orpheus*, chap. VIII, secs. 1–41. H. C. King, *Ethics of Jesus*. B. W. Bacon, *Christianity Old and New*, IV. H. Sturt, *Idea of a Free Church*, chap. V. Weinel and Widgery, *Jesus in the Nineteenth Century and After*. *Hibbert Journal*, vol. 5, p. 136; vol. 10, p. 766. *American Journal of Theology*, vol. 18, p. 225. *Biblical World*, vol. 43, pp. 75, 238.

CHAPTER VI

PAUL AND THE FOUNDING OF THE CHURCH

How did the Christian Church originate?

NATURALLY enough, in spite of Christ's specific assurances, his disciples were upset at his execution and scattered, in alarm for their own safety.[1] Then they waited in intense expectation for the speedy return which he had promised. It seems to have been Peter, ardent and impetuous, first to hail Jesus as Messiah, who now first had the experience which to him at least was convincing proof that Jesus was still living and about to fulfill his promise of a glorious advent from the heavens. Peter had lost his nerve at his Master's arrest, had denied that he knew him, and fled to his Galilean home. But Jesus had rested his hopes in him not in vain — "Simon, Simon, behold, Satan asked to have thee ... but I made supplication for thee, that thy faith fail not; and do thou, when once thou hast turned again, stablish thy brethren." [2] So there, amid the scenes that so poignantly spoke to his heart of the beloved Master, there came to him we know not what experience; there, at any rate, the resurrection-faith, which rested originally upon Christ's promise, received its first corroboration.[3]

Paul, who is by many years our earliest witness, mentions, after the "appearance" to Peter, one "to the Twelve," then "to above five hundred brethren at once," then "to

[1] Cf. Mark 14: 27–28. 16: 7. Matt. 26: 32; 28: 7–10. There are other indications.

[2] Luke 22: 31–32.

[3] Paul puts the appearance to Peter first. And there are many other indications.

James," then "to all the apostles," "and last of all he appeared to me also."[1] Of none of these other "appearances" have we any description; of his own experience, which he includes with the others as of the same nature, these are his only further words — "It was the good pleasure of God to reveal his Son in me, that I might preach him among the Gentiles"; and "Have I not seen Jesus our Lord?"[2] But the three descriptions of Paul's experience in Luke, though they may date from as much as sixty years after the event, and are, indeed, in several particulars flatly contradictory to one another, are no doubt correct in their general picture of the scene.[3] It is quite possible that all or some of the other experiences may have been described in the original ending of Mark's Gospel, long since lost. But we can now be certain of little beyond the fact that a few of the faithful were assured that Jesus had been "revealed in them," and that the conviction rapidly spread; so that, as Tacitus says, the propaganda, temporarily repressed, burst forth again.[4]

[1] The word ὤφθη ("appeared") was never used of one man in the body meeting another. Jesus never "appeared" to any one before his death. The word was used for visions of super-earthly Beings. Angels "appeared" in dreams, etc.

[2] 1 Cor. 15: 5–8. Gal. 1: 11–17. 1 Cor. 9: 1.

[3] Acts 9: 1–9; 22: 5–13; 26: 12–20. Luke is a rather unreliable historian, as we see by comparing so many of his accounts with Paul's briefer, but of course vastly more reliable, — because first-hand, — statements.

The scene in Acts, chap. 2, though it is certainly in many respects unhistorical (e.g., Luke quite misconceives the phenomenon of "speaking with tongues," whose real nature we can clearly apprehend in Paul's letters. And the setting of the scene in Jerusalem, in line with his view as to the seat of the earliest church, in contradiction to the convergence of evidence that the early propaganda was in Galilee, throws suspicion upon the whole story), may be an echo of Paul's "appearance" "to above five hundred brethren at once." Such collective visions, ecstasies, or inspirations, are not uncommon in religious history.

[4] *Repressaque in præsens exitiabilis superstitio rursum erumpebat.* (Annals, xv, 44.)

The stories at the end of our Gospels are so late in origin, so confused and mutually contradictory, so out of line with Paul's allusions and with all

The new faith, communicated from the little band of ecstatic believers in Galilee, spread here and there throughout Judea, and into the surrounding regions where scattered communities of Jews were awaiting the good news of the Messiah's coming. It was in Antioch, we are told, that they were first called Christians. In the tenth chapter of "Matthew" we have, apparently, a picture of that early itinerant preaching. The missionaries went not to the Gentiles, but "to the lost sheep of the house of Israel." They took no gold or silver in their purses, but trusted to charity for their support, while they spread the glorious tidings that the Messiah had actually appeared, in the person of Jesus, had suffered and died, but had burst the bonds of Sheol and was soon to come on the clouds of heaven to establish the Kingdom. When they were persecuted for their blasphemy in one city, they fled to the next, relying on the Master's promise that they should not have gone through the cities of Israel before he would come.[1] Peter was the head of the band;[2] and his

inherent plausibility, that they must be pretty completely discounted. Paul shows no knowledge of an empty tomb; Christ's resurrection, in his thought, is an emergence of his spirit "from the region of the dead" ($\dot{\epsilon}\kappa$ $\nu\epsilon\kappa\rho\hat{\omega}\nu$) — a spiritual resurrection such as he expected for all the faithful, not a reanimation of the body and rising from the grave. Indeed, the whole discussion in 1 Cor. 15 is aimed against those who understood the Resurrection to mean a raising of the dead body — the belief, in embryo, which the Gospel stories represent. Moreover, it is noteworthy that Paul asserts that the Twelve were at one with him in his ideas on these matters (1 Cor. 15:11). Jesus himself had never predicted the emergence of his body from the grave. We must be on guard, in reading the words of Jesus and Paul, against reading back into them the later ideas embodied in the Gospel endings.

The completest and most scholarly discussion of these matters in any language, to date, is C. R. Bowen's *Resurrection in the New Testament*. See further, K. Lake, *The Historical Evidence for the Resurrection of Jesus Christ*. A. Réville, in *New World*, vol. 3, p. 498. *Monist*, vol. 11, pp. 1, 361. *American Journal of Theology*, vol. 13, p. 169. *American Journal of Religious Psychology*, vol. 1, p. 30.

[1] Matt. 10:5-23.

[2] It is noteworthy that Paul, after his conversion, went to consult Peter — and did not deem it necessary to see any others of the Twelve. (Gal. 1:18-19.)

preaching may be fairly well recorded in the passage: "Ye men of Israel, hear these words: Jesus of Nazareth, a man approved of God unto you by mighty works and wonders and signs . . . this Jesus did God raise up, whereof we all are witnesses. Being therefore by the right hand of God exalted, and having received of the Father the promise of the holy spirit, he hath poured forth this that ye see and hear. . . . Repent ye, and be baptized in the name of Jesus, the Christ, unto the remission of your sins; and ye shall receive the gift of the holy spirit." [1] Eagerly they went from house to house, "preaching the Kingdom of God, and teaching concerning the Lord Jesus, the Christ." [2]

What are the salient facts of Paul's life and personality?

An insignificant Jewish sect the Christians would have remained, dwindling gradually from vanishing hopes, had not a second religious genius arisen at just the right moment to transform the new faith from a variation of Judaism into a universal religion. Christ had freed the Jewish religion from its incubus of legalism, making it thus potentially universal — as one or two of the prophets had done before him; he had even intimated that outsiders might be admitted to the Kingdom. But the time had been short; his preaching, and that of his disciples, was to the Jews alone. The Græco-Roman world had scarcely heard of this obscure Messianic propaganda until Paul took it up, colored it with his marked individuality, and spread it north and west. At his death a chain of Christian communities extended across the Empire from Jerusalem to Rome.[3]

---

[1] Acts 2:22:38.   [2] Acts 28:31.
[3] Paul was, indeed, only one of many laborers. We think of him as the man who did the work primarily because some of his letters chanced to be preserved, and because the author of Acts emphasizes his part. But he was, no doubt, the most brilliant and important of the missionaries to the Gentiles.

Approximately of an age with Jesus, Paul was a man of very different stamp. Born "a Pharisee, a son of Pharisees," in the Greek city of Tarsus, he unites in his mental outlook the two conflicting currents of Hebraism and Hellenism. "I advanced in the Jews' religion," he tells us,[1] "beyond many of mine own age among my countrymen, being more exceedingly zealous for the traditions of my fathers." But he thought in Greek, and had some conversance with Greek philosophy. Brought up in a profligate city of mixed population, his view of the natural life of men is pessimistic and tinged with the world-weariness of contemporary Roman society — in striking contrast to the village atmosphere and wholesome buoyancy of Jesus' early preaching. Impetuous, headlong, self-reliant, obstinate, fearless, wrestling with strong passions, and acknowledging his own infirmities,[2] he lacks the Master's divine sweetness and poise. His extant letters are noticeably dissimilar in style from the recorded sayings of Jesus; they reflect the subtleties of his theological training, and lack the Great Teacher's simplicity and naturalness. Yet, in spite of his darker temperament, his broader training, his more complex and confused outlook upon life, Paul came to be possessed by the same serene and gentle spirit, which he humbly confessed to be not of his own origination, but the spirit of Christ living again in him.[3]

The crisis in his career came at the age of about thirty-five, a few years after the death of Jesus. He had come to Jerusalem too late to see him in the flesh, and learned of him at first only through the prejudiced reports of his Pharisaic brethren. The little band of disciples in the capital added to their blasphemy, in giving the sacred Messianic title to an unknown provincial peasant, the insult of glorying in his ignominious and accursed death by crucifixion, and the infidelity of laxity in obeying the traditions of Jewish ortho-

[1] Gal. 1:14.   [2] Cf. Rom. 7:7-25.   [3] Cf., e.g., Gal. 2:20.

doxy. Joining ardently in their persecution, Paul's better nature must have been deeply affected by witnessing their heroism and faith — as his physical being shuddered at the sight of Stephen's blood and agonizing death. He presumably investigated the new cult more or less, and must have been impressed by the nobility of Jesus' sayings, as by the radiant assurance of the believers — an assurance and peace and self-mastery which he, in his long struggle with himself under the Law, had never attained. So that, while he continued obstinately in his persecution, it was "kicking against the pricks." In this unstrung and inwardly divided condition, fresh from participation in the martyrdom of Stephen, in the heat and glare and fatigue of midday journeying, just outside of Damascus, he had the vision which determined his whole future life. God then and there, as he always believed, "revealed his Son in him," giving him thereby the summons to believe on Jesus and to take up the missionary work, which he in fact took up with zeal and prosecuted through all dangers and tribulations till it brought him, in his turn, to a martyr's death.[1]

[1] The important question whether Paul's experience (uncertain in its exact nature, but undoubted in its general purport) is explicable in physical and psychological terms — that is, came as the natural result of the influences playing upon his peculiar and rather pathological temperament, according to ascertainable laws — cannot be settled by the historian. It involves the whole question of the supernatural, and must be left, together with the question of the origin of the resurrection-faith, and the questions concerning the many visions and miracles recorded in the Bible and elsewhere, to solution, if at all, by the general considerations to be discussed in chapter XVIII. If we believe at all in the continued life of Christ, it is not difficult to conceive of some means, whether telepathic or more ordinary, or perhaps some channel not yet known to us, whereby he may have touched and kindled the mind of Paul — and the minds of many disciples before and since. On the other hand, psychology has done so much in recent years to bring within the domain of the natural the realm of visions and voices, and the like, that we cannot say that all of these experiences, so indubitably objective to those who have them, may not be ultimately shown to be purely subjective. Paul, as we know from his own pen, was subject to

The essence of Paul's conversion was his conviction that Jesus was, indeed, the awaited Messiah. Back to Jerusalem he eventually went, to confer with the heads of the Christian community and learn what he could of Jesus.[1] He seldom referred, however, — we judge from his letters, — to Christ's words or to the events of his earthly life, save to the Last Supper and the Crucifixion, which came to have for him a symbolic meaning. Frankly, he found little material in the humble earthly career of the Master for his propaganda; what he did was rather to keep his eyes fixed upon the conception of the Messiah which had been formed in him by his Jewish training, with the simple but all-important change that this Messiah had appeared for a brief preliminary sojourn upon earth, had returned to heaven, and was about to descend again for the great Day of Judgment. Paul always regarded his own gospel as directly inspired by the risen Christ, and felt no need of limiting himself to a repetition of the preaching of the earthly Jesus or of the Twelve. He was, no doubt, far better educated than they, and highly individual in his ideas. He carved out his own path, and stuck to it until he had moulded the future of the nascent religion along the lines of his own profound and daring genius.

For fifteen years or so he preached in the villages of Syria and Cilicia, to the Jewish residents mostly, but also to such Gentiles as had come somewhat under the influence of Jewish thought and would listen. Of the latter he did not require obedience to the intricate requirements of the Law — an obedience which they would doubtless never have given.

visions and trances; and his experience must certainly be judged side by side with the many thousands of similar experiences of Christian and non-Christian saints.

For discussion of Paul's conversion, see B. W. Bacon's *Story of St. Paul*, *ad loc.*, and *American Journal of Religious Psychology*, vol. 1, p. 143.

[1] Not till after three years, however, and then but for a fortnight, conferring with two apostles only. So he vigorously asserts in Gal. 1: 15-18.

This laxity aroused a protest from the stricter Jewish Christians, which resulted in Paul's finally being summoned to Jerusalem to explain. But he had had time to accomplish results; the same gifts of the Spirit which attested the truth of the preaching of the Twelve had appeared among his converts. The apostles were impressed, and granted him official permission to convert the Gentiles without requiring obedience to the Law. Later, in Antioch, a sharp difference of opinion arose on a related point, and Paul broke with Peter and the other pillar-apostles — a breach which weighed heavily on his spirit, so that he ever after looked wistfully forward to its healing, while, at the same time, he refused to back down or compromise.[1] Paul alone had heard the call of the great world outside of Jewry — the call symbolized in the "Come over and help us" of the Man of Macedonia of his dream; in his vision Christianity was already a bigger thing than Judaism had ever been or could become. And he well knew that the intolerable and needless burden of the Law must be definitely laid aside if the faith was to capture the hearts of the wider circle of needy men and women toward whom he yearned.

He turned his face westward then; and the next half-dozen years of his life were spent in incessant preaching tours, through Asia Minor and the Balkan Peninsula, with his headquarters for long at Corinth and Ephesus. Finally he determined to penetrate to Rome itself, where others had already started a church, and on beyond to Spain. But first he would take to the apostles at Jerusalem, as a peace-offering, a great contribution of alms for the poor there from his

[1] The question at Jerusalem had been, May Gentiles become Christians without obeying the Jewish law? The decision had been, Yes. The question at Antioch was, Are these Gentile Christians "clean," so that Jewish Christians may eat and associate with them? Paul said, Yes; James said, No. Peter first sided with Paul, but was won over, together with Barnabas, by James.

infant churches. He made his way to Jerusalem; and what the reception of his offering was we are not informed. But we learn that he was set upon by the Jews, in whose eyes he was an arch-traitor, was tried by the local Roman official, appealed to Cæsar, and was sent to the Rome of his dreams as a prisoner. There he had relative freedom for a year or two to preach, — though under constant guard, — but finally came to trial, and, according to tradition, was executed, at the age of sixty or a little over, — leaving behind him a group of churches growing yearly in numbers, and eight or ten hasty but precious letters, which have carried the fire of his eager and indomitable spirit down through the Church of nineteen centuries.

What was the gist of Paul's teaching?

There is much in Paul's letters, we must confess, which is obscure, and not a little that is grotesque, alien to our modern thought, and even repellent. Most or all of this is due to the survival in his thoughts of pre-Christian conceptions; the ingenious rabbinical arguments of contemporary Jewish theology, blending with the expression of his own first-hand and glowing Christian experience, have caused endless trouble to the devout ever since.[1] His love of theorizing, never systematic, but always positive and dogmatic, is largely responsible for the creedal yoke which the Church has so long borne. Christ's teaching had been almost exclusively practical; Christian theology has rested rather upon Paul's very hasty and occasional utterances. Paul was not really a

---

[1] Cf. the quibbling in Gal. 3: 16; the argument is as absurd in the original as in English. And the superstitious survivals in 1 Cor. 11: 7, 10. (To understand the latter verse, see Gen. 6: 1–4.) Far-fetched and absurd exegesis of the Scriptures, in true rabbinical style, is common: cf. Gal. 4: 21–31. 2 Cor. 3: 12–15. 1 Cor. 9: 8–11; 10: 1–11. Rom. 9: 22–25. His belief in the preëxistence of the Messiah, and his vivid portrayal of the coming Judgment Day, are contemporary Jewish elements; etc., etc.

PAUL AND THE FOUNDING OF THE CHURCH 91

great thinker; his merit lies rather in his eloquent and personal expression of the new spirit, the redeemed and spiritual life, which had replaced in him the restless and vacillating life of his youth, and in the practical work which he accomplished. His theorizing is highly polemical and pragmatic, determined and developed by the exigencies of the controversies into which he was forced,[1] and by no means self-consistent or central in his teaching. Yet, by one of the ironies of history, these concepts, and this very language, have determined in a remarkable degree the whole course of modern theology.

It is easy enough, however, to separate the gold from the dross; and it is gold of fine quality. We will summarize the most significant notes in Paul's teaching: —

(1) The core of it was the profound doctrine of Salvation by Faith. In his own experience he had learned the futility of the Law, its powerlessness to quicken the inner springs of conduct; all his youth he had battled in vain with his passionate nature in the attempt to keep true to its innumerable prescriptions. But in the ardor of his new faith he found himself able to rise above his sins; the communion with Christ, which was so real to him, filled him with a new spirit, made him over from a carnal to a spiritual man, so that, overcoming evil with good, as he phrased it, he no longer cared for the fleshly things that had once held him down. This saving faith was not an assent of the intellect, it was an allegiance of the heart, a full and happy loyalty, that made the endless injunctions of Jewish casuistry seem needless and petty. Moreover, the Master himself had cared little for these outward rules and conformities and had preached a gospel of

---

[1] His insistence on faith, e.g., was a necessary counter to the zeal of the Jewish Christians for the Law. The exalted Christology of Colossians and Ephesians (which many students think, however, to be not genuinely Pauline) was a counter to the Gnostic depreciation of Christ's position.

freedom. And the Gentiles to whom Paul preached would never accept the yoke of the Law; the simpler way was that to which all the practical needs of his mission drew him. So it is natural that he should have felt a rush of scorn for all that older religious machinery, and bidden his converts "stand fast in the freedom wherewith Christ hath set us free, and not be entangled again in the yoke of bondage." As he had found the power of a better life born in him at his conversion, had felt himself saved, cleansed from his burden of sin, and endowed with a new spirit, so — there being nothing peculiarly Jewish in the experience — they might hope, by opening their hearts to Christ's spirit and letting it dominate them, to rise into the redeemed life and become heirs of the promises.[1]

(2) This was no invitation to laxity. On the contrary, it involved a complete renunciation of the unregenerate life; when Christ lived in the believer he would no longer care for the lusts of the flesh. To Paul, Christ's death had a deep symbolic meaning; the preaching of the Cross was, practically, an invitation to die to the old life and rise with Christ to the new. Instead of the Hellenic ideals of culture and moderation, which had proved ineffective against the temptations to cruelty and lust, Paul demanded an absolute turnabout. "Be not fashioned according to this world," he wrote, "but be ye transformed by the renewing of your mind . . . always bearing about in the body the dying of Jesus, that the life also of Jesus may be manifested in our body." "Put to death, therefore, your earthly impulses — fornication, uncleanness, passion, evil desire, and covetousness . . . anger, wrath, malice, railing, shameful speaking out of your mouth; lie not to one another; seeing that ye have put off the old man with his doings and have put on the new

[1] For further discussion of salvation by faith, see below, pp. 172–73; 180–86.

man." "Abhor that which is evil, cleave to that which is good."[1]

(3) But with all this stern and high summons to men there is mingled the *caritas*, the tender, ministering love, which he owned as Christ's work in him and so memorably eulogized in the poetic phrases of 1 Cor. 13. He is usually very patient with his weak and troublesome flock, admonishing them gently, and picturing for them the beauty of the life of mutual helpfulness and affection. "Bear ye one another's burdens," he wrote, "and so fulfill the law of Christ." "In love of the brethren be tenderly affectioned one to another . . . bless them that persecute you, bless and curse not. . . . Render to no man evil for evil . . . but if thine enemy hunger, feed him; if he thirst, give him to drink." "Let no man seek his own, but each his neighbor's good." "For the whole law is fulfilled in one word, even in this: Thou shalt love thy neighbor as thyself." "Put on, therefore, as God's elect, holy and beloved, a heart of compassion, kindness, humility, meekness, long-suffering; forbearing one another, and forgiving each other, if any man have a complaint against any; even as the Lord forgave you, so also do ye. And above all these things put on love, which is the bond of perfectness." "For even as we have many members in one body, and all the members have not the same office; so we, who are many, are one body in Christ and severally members one of another."[2]

(4) The regeneration and peace of the believers were but the pledge and foretaste of the glorious life in the Messianic era about to open. This present world was soon "coming to nought," the new age at hand, wherein "each shall receive his reward according to his own labor." "The time is short,

---

[1] Rom. 12:2. 2 Cor. 4:10. Col. 3:5-10. Rom. 12:9.
[2] Gal. 6:2. Rom. 12:10-20. 1 Cor. 10:24. Gal. 5:14. Col. 3:12-14. Rom. 12:4-5.

brethren; meanwhile, let those that have wives live as though they had none; those that weep as though they wept not; those that rejoice as though they rejoiced not; those that buy as though they possessed not; and those that use the good things of the world, let them use them sparingly; for this manner of world soon passeth away." "Now we see as in a mirror, darkly; but then, face to face." "We shall not all die, but we shall all be transformed, in a moment, in the twinkling of an eye, at the last trumpet-call; for the trumpet will sound, and the dead will rise incorruptible, and we shall be transformed." "We that are left alive unto the coming of the Lord shall by no means precede those that have died. For the Lord himself shall descend from heaven, with a shout, with the voice of the archangel, and with the trumpet of God; and those that have died in the faith shall first rise; then we who are still alive shall together with them be caught up into the clouds, to meet the Lord in the air; and so shall we forevermore be with the Lord." "But concerning the exact time, brethren, you have no need that aught be written you. For you know perfectly that the day of the Lord is to come like a thief in the night. When they are saying, Peace and safety, then sudden destruction is to come upon them, as travail upon a woman with child; and they shall in no wise escape. But ye, brethren, are not in darkness, that that day should overtake you like a thief; . . . so then . . . let us watch and be sober." And later in his ministry, "Salvation is now nearer us than when we first believed. The night is far spent and the day is at hand." [1]

This pathetic hope of a supernaturally transformed earthly life, derived from contemporary Jewish anticipations, and shared, evidently, by Jesus himself, was destined,

[1] 1 Cor. 2:6; 3:8; 7:29-31; 13:12; 15:51-52. 1 Thess. 4:15 to 5:8. Rom. 13:11-12.

in the nature of things, soon to pass away — or rather to be transformed into the hope of future life in an unseen heavenly realm. But the eagerness and consolation of this primitive Christian hope can hardly be imagined by us, in our soberer world. Naïve and illusory as it was, it gave an immense stimulus to that life of faith, that new dedication of the soul, that crucifixion of the fleshly life and happy espousal of the Christ-life, which made Paul's little churches the source of so much that is best in our modern life.

H. Weinel, *St. Paul, the Man and His Work*. W. Wrede, *Paul*. A. Schweitzer, *Paul and His Interpreters*. J. Moffatt, *Paul and Paulinism*. C. Clemen, *Paulus*. B. W. Bacon, *Story of St. Paul; Founding of the Church*. A. Sabatier, *Apostle Paul*. P. Gardner, *Religious Experience of St. Paul*. A. Deissmann, *St. Paul*. E. R. Wood, *Life and Ministry of Paul*. C. C. Everett, *Gospel of Paul*. M. Arnold, *St. Paul and Protestantism*. J. R. Cohn, *St. Paul in the Light of Modern Research*. K. Lake, *Earlier Epistles of St. Paul*. C. von Weizsäcker, *Apostolic Age*, vol. I, p. 79 *f.* R. Scott, *Pauline Epistles*. S. Reinach, *Orpheus*, chap. VIII, secs. 42–69. *Hibbert Journal*, vol. 10, p. 45. *American Journal of Theology*, vol. 14, p. 361. *New World*, vol. 8, p. 111; vol. 9, p. 49. *Constructive Quarterly*, vol. 1, p. 163. *Biblical World*, vol. 44, p. 375.

CHAPTER VII

EARLY CHRISTIANITY

What were the causes of the triumph of Christianity?

THE times were ripe for the new faith. The old pagan religions had waned and were taken lightly or openly disbelieved. The Roman Empire was corrupt to the core; the virtue and austerity that made Rome what it was had given way to extremes of bestiality and lust. A loss of hope in human effort, a despair of the natural sources of happiness, a revulsion from the wantonness of the age, led to a lapse of patriotism and a hunger for individual salvation, for some supernatural personal assurance and guidance. The best men found a modicum of happiness in fleeing from the world and living a life of Stoic self-containment. Just as among the Hindus, centuries before, the need was for a religion of deliverance. Any number of salvation-cults were introduced; none was so simple, so full of hope, so beautiful in the pure and brotherly life of its adherents, as this Christianity that Paul and his followers taught. It caught men's imaginations and spread with marvellous rapidity.

(1) The sweetness of consolation that it offered needs no comment. The great loving Father-God had sent his Anointed One to earth to announce his plan for men; a glorious future awaited them if they would but believe and trust in him; this Divine Man had suffered, just as they had to suffer; all was intended and right and paved the way to a great consummation. A new value was at once added to life; its accidents became unimportant in the light of the future. Christ, the Good Shepherd, came closer to the heart than the

Jewish Jehovah, and far closer than the cold and impersonal God of Greek philosophy, — offering a more intimate personal relationship and a more assured hope in the beyond.

(2) Linked with this great hope, and its witness, was the New Life, which was itself a redemption from the vanity and sin of the existing order. Instead of self-assertion and pride of power, which were virtues to the ancients, the new teaching enjoined patience, humility, purity, simplicity of heart — a spirit almost new to the pagan world. The primitive church was an intimate brotherhood, caring for the poor and the weak in its membership, and including women in its regard, — as the cult of Mithras, which bade fair to be its most dangerous rival, did not.[1]

(3) Christianity also had an advantage in its attachment to a definite historic person. Mithras, and the other gods that competed for popular favor, were mythical beings whose reality it was possible for the sophisticated to doubt; Christ had but lately been seen on earth, as any one could prove. And all the historic background of the Old Testament, which Christianity took over, helped to give it an atmosphere of actuality lacking to the other Oriental cults. "It had its roots in a national faith, moulded by the trials and passions of a singularly religious people; that connection with Judaism gave Christianity a foothold in history ... which it was a true instinct in the Church never to abandon."[2]

[1] For illustrations of the spirit of primitive Christianity cf. Lucian (*De Morte Peregrini*, 13): Christians "spare no expense" in assisting one another, "for their first legislator had persuaded them to believe that they were all brethren of one another." And Aristides (*Apology*, 15): "The Christians ... honor father and mother and show kindness to their neighbors. ... If they hear that one of them is imprisoned or oppressed on account of the name of their Messiah, all of them care for his necessity; and if it is possible to redeem him, they set him free. And if any one among them is poor and needy, and they have no spare food, they fast two or three days in order to supply him with the needed food."
See E. A. Edghill, *The Spirit of Power*, *passim*. Scott, chap. VI.

[2] G. Santayana, *Poetry and Religion*, p. 82.

(4) Finally, in the energy and skill of her propaganda the Christian Church outstripped her rivals. She, almost alone, developed a close and effective organization; she alone of the real religions developed an elaborate philosophy and fed the intellects as well as the hearts of her converts. The old pagan religions had not been proselyters; men grew up in them as a matter of course, and seldom sought to convert those whose allegiance naturally belonged elsewhere. Before the vigorous missionary zeal of the Christians they made the resistance only of passive distrust or physical persecution. So, in an age of intellectual ferment, the acute polemic of the Church fathers, and their ingenious theologies, were effective; while in an age of heart-hunger, their earnest and well organized missionary campaigns made startlingly rapid headway.

It is small wonder, then, if, with the great hope they possessed, and the self-forgetting brotherliness of their life, which was its own reward, these Christians went about with radiant faces and rejoicing hearts, drawing gradually to their fold those that labored and were heavy laden, seeking for the rest that Christ had promised to those who followed him. "The consciousness of new loves, new duties, fresh consolations, and luminous unutterable hopes accompanied them wherever they went. They stopped willingly in the midst of their business for recollection, like men in love. . . . Nothing in this world remained without reference to the other, nor was anything done save for a supernatural end." [1]

Under what influences did the Church evolve her creeds?

It was, of course, not without many struggles, internal and external, that Christianity in its eventual form became dominant. The Jewish Christians bitterly opposed the admission

[1] G. Santayana, *Poetry and Religion*, pp. 86–87.

of Gentiles to their church, and Paul and his followers worked between the fires of Jewish-Christian opposition and pagan skepticism. The Gentiles soon so outnumbered the Jews in the new church that the former difficulty settled itself; in 70 A.D., by the destruction of Jerusalem, the Jewish nation practically ceased to exist, and the intransigent Jewish-Christians came to be considered heretics, under the disparaging name of Nazarenes.

The resistance of paganism was, of course, much more obstinate; and the struggle lasted for centuries. Intermittently persecuted by the State, but flourishing all the more through the faith and blood of its martyrs, the new cult grew so steadily that by the fourth century its adoption as the state religion of the fast disintegrating Roman empire became politically expedient. Constantine's conversion was doubtless more an act of statesmanship than of religious conviction. The old Roman religion could no longer command general allegiance; amid the multitude of sects there was only this one that gave promise of becoming a genuinely uniting force. Christianity could not be repressed, the various forms of paganism might be; herein lay a new possibility for the unification of the Empire.[1] A little later the pure and noble Emperor Julian made a last desperate attempt to stem the rising tide of Christianity and put the dying religion of his fathers on its feet again. But his few months' reign — spent chiefly in the incessant wars of the times — made little impression; and after this final protest the dominance of Christianity was never really in question.

The pagan opposition to Christianity had not been, however, so sharp as might be supposed. The new religion assimilated, as it spread, many of the former beliefs and practices

[1] In a letter to Alexander, Bishop of Alexandria, he states that his motive was to establish throughout the Empire "some one definite and complete form of religious worship."

of the people; and its gradually forming doctrines assumed shapes not unfamiliar in many of their aspects. The conception, for example, of an incarnated God, dying and rising again, whose body and blood were tasted by the devout believers, resembled closely various prevalent and popular beliefs. During the centuries wherein Christian belief was still fluid and developing simultaneously in many different directions, those variations that were most in line with the antecedent beliefs of the people naturally attracted their sympathy and tended to win the day. Moreover, Jesus was a Jew; the Greek- and Latin-speaking peoples might translate and repeat his words, but to them they inevitably had different meanings and lent themselves to another set of ideas. Habits of thought and religious practices are not easily transformed; and if the pagan world was Christianized, so also was Christianity paganized. It may be doubted, indeed, whether "orthodox" Christianity is not more Greek than Hebraic in spirit and form; certainly on its theoretical side it reflects the conceptions of the Græco-Roman world that accepted, and in accepting moulded after its own ways of thinking, the still Jewish beliefs of the apostles.[1]

[1] Grant Showerman (*American Journal of Philology*, vol. 29, p. 156) calls primitive Christianity an "agency for the ingathering of universal religious experience, and modern Christianity the heir to the riches of all the ages."

Cf. J. T. Shotwell (*The Religious Revolution of Today*, p. 45): "We must not forget that Christianity was not all Christian; that it never has been so. It is, and was from the first, drawn from all antiquity, and preserves for us things that were sacred untold ages before there was a temple at Jerusalem. It was a new consecration of consecrated things. However revolutionary it seemed, it kept as much of the old régime as could be applied in the new."

And Grant Allen (*Evolution of the Idea of God*, pp. 227, 389): "At the moment when the Empire was cosmopolitanizing the world, Christianity began to cosmopolitanize religion, by taking into itself whatever was central, common, and universal in the worship of the peoples among whom it originated. . . . Christianity triumphed because it united in itself all the most vital elements of all the religions then current in the world, with little that was local, national, or distasteful."

See also G. Friedlander, *Hellenism and Christianity*. H. A. A. Kennedy,

EARLY CHRISTIANITY

This process of absorption and universalization could not, to be sure, go on too rapidly without evoking violent revivals of the purer Christian spirit. Montanism — the name given to a conservative reaction breaking out in the middle of the second century — fought the growing Hellenic tendencies in the Church and sought to turn it back to its more primitive and Jewish forms, particularly cultivating the "gifts of the spirit" and the naïve belief in the imminent return of Christ to earth. And if it failed to check the inevitable drift, on the other hand the Hellenization of Christianity failed to eliminate all the naïve and legendary elements of the religion and mould it into a completely rationalized system. The prevailing tendency was that which retained much of the Hebraic background and spirit — a *via media* between the opposing forces.[1]

The fluidity and individualism of early Christianity received its first decisive check at the Council of Nicæa, which drew up, in 325 A.D., under the domination of the just-converted Emperor Constantine, the first authoritative Chris-

St. Paul and the Mystery Religions. S. J. Case, *Evolution of Early Christianity*, chap. IX. M. Jones, *The New Testament in the Twentieth Century*, bk. I, chap. VII. H. Delahaye, *Legends of the Saints*, chap. VI. *Monist*, vol. 12, p. 416 *ff*.

[1] The Gnostic movement, termed by Harnack the "over-acute Hellenization of Christianity," should perhaps be mentioned here. But recent scholarship holds that Gnosticism was not primarily an attempt to reconcile Christianity with Greek thought. It was rather a pre-Christian mystery-religion, deriving partly from Greek and partly from Oriental sources, which incorporated into its system the historical Saviour Jesus, reverenced Paul, and became a quasi-Christian sect, while retaining anti-Christian ideas, such as a decided dualism. The Gnostics for the most part rejected the Old Testament and the Jewish element in Christianity. They believed in post-apostolic revelation to a succession of prophets, whence their superior insight, revelation, knowledge ($\gamma\nu\tilde{\omega}\sigma\iota s$). They first (probably) imported the sacramental idea into Christian circles; and through the opposition which they aroused they provoked the Church into a firmer organization and unification of creed. The best known Gnostics were Marcion and Valentinus, who flourished in the second century. See Bousset in *Encyclopædia Britannica* (11th ed.), *Gnosticism*.

tian creed. Up to the promulgation of this Nicene creed each church had had its own baptismal formulas; and such creeds as had been formulated were neither long nor of general acceptance. Constantine was probably not deeply religious by temperament, but he was a good administrator; having decided to make Christianity the state religion, he wished its doctrine more exactly determined.[1] And there seemed an immediate necessity for some exercise of authority, in view of the violent disputes current on all sorts of major and minor points of doctrine. It was only after long and bitter controversy that the decision swung as it did. And although later creeds show considerable change of conviction, it is difficult to overestimate the effect upon the subsequent course of Christian thought of the conceptions which through the prestige of this imperial church council were now imposed upon the Church.[2]

The Athanasian Creed, so called, is considerably later than the Nicene, dating probably from the sixth century. These, and the other creeds, bear the stamp of the particular controversies which were then raging. In an age when the centrifugal forces within the Church were great, and the attacks upon it from without multitudinous and acute, it was a perhaps justifiable instinct of self-preservation that led it to this hard and fast definition of its position. But the result was an arrested development, the formation of a

[1] Responsible as he partly was for this petrification of theology and imposition of a creedal yoke, he nevertheless gave some sound advice to the disputatious bishops. In the letter already quoted he writes, "My advice is, neither to ask nor answer questions which, instead of being scriptural, are the mere sport of idleness or an exercise of ability; at best keep them to yourselves and do not publish them. You agree in fundamentals."

[2] The so-called Apostles' Creed was considerably earlier in formulation, but does not occur in its present form before 750 A.D., and was never an official creed, like the Nicene and later creeds. Its earliest forms date, perhaps, from about 150 A.D. But the tradition ascribing its origin to the apostles is quite late and without foundation. Cf. Harnack in *Nineteenth Century*, vol. 34, p. 158; and the encyclopædias.

crust of dogma, representing the conceptions of that intellectually keen and subtle but egregiously unscientific age, which has nearly choked the modern church and is still costing heavy effort to burst.

Two historic movements, then, united in Christianity. On the one hand, the deep religious fervor of the Jews, freed by Christ from what was local and unessential, and translated by Paul into terms intelligible to the outer world; on the other, the great intellectual movement of Greece, the metaphysical conceptions that had been developing from Plato and Aristotle into Neo-Platonism and Stoicism. The Hebraic element brought undeniably much that persisted and leavened society. Yet when men trained in contemporary philosophy sought to grasp and explain the mysteries of the new faith, — which the Church insisted should be accepted first and understood, if possible, afterwards, — they wandered far from the original gospel. The transition from the then current Greek speculation to Christian theology — as from pagan to Catholic ritual — was hardly as violent as the change from the faith and teaching of Christ to the body of doctrine that grew up about his name.

For one thing, the symbolism so common in the Jewish writings was a stumbling-block to the pagan mind; and many a metaphor and trope was taken literally and crystallized into doctrine: as, for example, when the words of Christ to his disciples calling the wine and bread, by a natural and pathetic figure, his blood and body, became hardened into the extraordinary dogma of transubstantiation.[1] In such manner did the Aryan speculative temper make strange work of the Hebraic parables and intuitions! All sorts of ingenious subterfuges sought to reconcile the resultant inconsistencies, and many conflicting theologies competed with one another for dominance. Council after council debated

[1] For the probable meaning of Christ's words, see Scott, chap. VIII.

the points at issue, the majority vote ruled, and all other doctrines than those accepted were dubbed heresy. So grew up the body of Christian theology, widely different, in its ultimate form, from the Christianity of Paul, and still further, of course, from the religion of Jesus.

Yet the Christianization of the Græco-Roman world wrought a great change. Speculative tendencies continued with little change of direction, popular conceptions and observances were absorbed; but underneath all this the spiritual earnestness and purity and love of Jesus and his followers were finding their way into the world. A new ideal of life was set before the mind, far vistas of sympathy and mercy and self-surrender replaced the pagan ideal of self-assertion; and through all the mutations of theology the Christian life still glowed in the hearts of men and beckoned them onward.

What was the origin of the conceptions of

I. *The Atonement?*

Among the conceptions slowly crystallized by the impingement of Greek thought upon the primitive Christian experiences and hopes was that of the Atonement. That a new and redeemed life was possible to men through a mystic union with Christ had been the fundamental note of Paul's teaching. As Adam had plunged the whole human race into sin, so Christ had rescued them; he was the Second Adam, the Saviour of men. Thus could Jewish Messianism be interpreted in terms not dissimilar to those of the Greek mysteries. As with Attis, Adonis, and Osiris, this Saviour-God had suffered, died, and risen again; and his worshipers were to repeat in their lives, in inward experience, this death and resurrection. The study of these contemporary cults shows the Pauline conception to have been one of several analogous

EARLY CHRISTIANITY

salvation-schemes.[1] With Paul it was an experience rather than a theory; that he had actually entered upon the New Life through the giving of his allegiance to Christ, he knew. Moreover, that Christ, having died, yet lived, and had revealed himself to Paul on that eventful day, was unquestionable to him. That his death had somehow been for men's sins was not only a deduction from certain verses of Scripture, but was the almost necessary explanation of such a strange and otherwise incomprehensible event. Death was the penalty of sin; but since Christ had been sinless, his suffering must have been vicarious, like that of the "Suffering Servant of Jehovah" prefigured in Isaiah 53 — a passage which Christ had no doubt applied to himself.[2] Somehow Christ had conquered sin and death, for himself and for all who clave to him. But in Paul the conception remained fluid, rhetorical, growing. The way stood open for bitter controversy over the question what the convert must do. Was it enough to believe, was salvation "by faith alone," did the mystical union with Christ suffice, in a magical sort of way? Or was continuance in "good works" essential to salvation?[3] And the way stood open for endless theorizing over the question *how* faith in Christ could redeem men. The

[1] Loisy calls them, including the Christian conception, *rêves apparentés* (*Hibbert Journal*, vol. 10, p. 45).

[2] Cf. Mark 10: 45: "For verily the Son of man came . . . to give his life a ransom for many." The Greek word ($\lambda \acute{\upsilon} \tau \rho o \nu$) may perhaps be translated 'liberation' — i.e., 'as a means of freeing many from sin and its penalty, death.' *How* his death could effect this liberation Christ does not tell us.

Cf. also, as typical of early Christian preaching, Titus 2: 14, "Jesus Christ gave himself for us, that he might redeem us from all iniquity." And Acts 3: 18, "But the things which God foreshewed by the mouth of all the prophets, that his Christ should suffer, he thus fulfilled." Cf. also Acts 17: 3; 26: 23. Luke 24: 26. 1 Cor. 6: 20. 1 Pet. 1: 18–21. Col. 2: 12–15. Heb. 2: 14–15.

[3] For the leading expressions of this controversy within the limits of the New Testament, see Gal. chaps. 3–5. Rom. 3: 19 to 8: 4. Jas. 2: 14–26. See below, pp. 180–86.

answers to this latter question constitute the various doctrines of the Atonement.[1]

II. *The Trinity?*

The prevalent Greek conception of God was that of an Absolute Reason, remote from men, ineffable, unknowable. Nor did the teaching concerning the war-god of the Old Testament, with his Jewish affiliations, and his rôle as Judge of men, in great degree break down that sense of aloofness. But Christ — that beloved personage, that Redeemer of men, who had suffered and died for them — appealed deeply to their hearts. Christ had been the great fact to Paul and the first Christians, union by faith with him their primary religious experience. The conception of him as Jewish Messiah was, indeed, unintelligible and uninteresting to the Greeks and Latins. But even to the believing Jews he had been a heaven-sent, more or less supernatural Being. A mass of legend and miracle had grown up around him; he had become a figure not unlike many with which the Greeks were familiar, gods who had walked the earth and shared human experiences. And so nothing could have been more natural and inevitable than the popular deification of Christ. Even Paul had spoken of the spirit of God, and the spirit of Christ, or again, simply the Spirit, indistinguishably. His mind was too practical to care for consistency or to spin out a satisfactory theory of it all. But the result of his preaching was that Christ assumed a far more exalted position to the Gentile world than he could have had to the Jews. Pliny's "carmen Christo quasi deo dicere" indicates the popular worship of Christ; and in the early creeds propositions about him far out-bulk those about God.

It would have been consonant with the polytheistic

[1] To be discussed below, pp. 174–78. See A. Sabatier, *Doctrine of the Atonement and its Historical Evolution.*

habits of thought of the Western peoples to have left Christ simply as another God by the side of Jehovah. But this was deeply repugnant to the ingrained monotheism of the Jews. And as the Jewish Scriptures had been taken over by the new religion, it became necessary to reconcile their emphatic monotheism with the deification of Christ. Fortunately there was a conception familiar to the contemporary Greek mind of just the sort to solve this paradox — namely, the Logos conception. Philo, a Jewish philosopher of Alexandria, contemporary with Christ, had already used it in expounding to the Greek world a Hellenized Judaism, which he had hoped to make the absolute religion of the future. He had taken up the term Logos, which meant to the Neo-Platonists the Word, or Emanation, or Creative Activity, of God — a sort of separate entity which bridged the chasm between God and man; he had applied this conception to Jehovah, and had been materially aided by the fact that the Greek translators of the Old Testament had made frequent use of this same term, Logos, in the phrases which we translate "word" of God. Even in the Old Testament this "word" or "wisdom" or "creative activity" of God had seemed at times half-personified, as if a separate Being.

From Philo or some other of the many writers who were using the term Logos the mystical author of the Fourth Gospel derived the word and most of its significance; his contribution was that he identified Christ with this Logos of God, and made it therefore clearly personal and incarnate.[1] This identification became generally accepted, although controversy long raged as to the exact relation between Christ and the Father. Thus the dominant tendency of Greek thought triumphed, and the popular worship of Christ was satisfied. From the conception of a man divinely anointed by God for the carrying out of his purpose for his chosen peo-

[1] See John 1: 1-14.

ple, to that of a supernatural Being sent by God to save men, thence to that of an Emanation of God himself, and finally to a flat identification with God as one of the "persons" of the One Godhead was a development that occupied several centuries. But in the end the instincts and concepts of the Western peoples triumphed over the Jewish monotheism — which must have seemed cold and bare to them at best; and Christ, like Buddha, and many another religious founder before him, became very God.[1]

The Neo-Platonic conception thus partially adopted was, in some of its forms, trinitarian;[2] and it may be a significant fact that it was by Greek-trained thinkers that the dogma of the Trinity was elaborated. The Spirit of God had been half-personified in the Old Testament; but it was now dispossessed of the right to be thought of as the Logos of God by Christians. This Holy Spirit, however, had been of striking importance in early Christianity — the "manifestations of the Spirit" being the undeniable proofs of redemption.[3] It was obviously detachable, so to speak, from God, could "descend upon men" and enter their hearts. According to the Fourth Gospel, Christ had promised his disciples to send this Spirit to live in their hearts when he should no longer be with them. Gradually this Holy Spirit became more and more a separate Being, until by the Christian thinkers of the second and third centuries it was made into the Third Person of a new and Christian Trinity. The deep and permanent truth enshrined in this dogma we shall speak of in chapter IX; but in the literal form which it assumed, e.g., in the Nicene creed, we must recognize an embodiment of contemporary Greek speculation of a sort very alien to our

[1] Cf. A. Réville, *History of the Doctrine of the Deity of Jesus Christ*.

[2] Cf. Plotinus' Trinity, $\tau\grave{o}$ $\H{\epsilon}\nu$, $\nu o\hat{v}s$, and $\psi v \chi \acute{\eta}$.

[3] See Scott, chap. III, and cf. 1 Cor. 12: 3, "No man can say, Jesus is Lord, but in the (or a) holy spirit." We read later ideas into these earliest sayings when we capitalize the words Holy and Spirit.

modern thought and irreconcilable with our maturer outlook.[1]

Christianity, indeed, went still further in its concessions to the polytheistic temper of the people. The saints, and especially the mother of Christ, were also worshiped. In 431 A.D. the Council of Ephesus decreed that the latter be received and honored — as a sort of supplement to the Trinity — under the title of the Mother of God.

III. Heaven, Hell, and Purgatory?

The beliefs of the Hebrews as to what lay beyond the grave were, like those of most ancient peoples, vague, fluctuating, and insecure.[2] The future life, if there was to be one at all, was to be rather dreaded than desired. It was not at all from these forebodings, but from the very different and far more eager anticipation of an earthly Messianic kingdom, that the Christian hope was developed. Jesus and Paul and the earliest Christians had expected the coming of the Messianic Kingdom within a few years.[3] As time went on, however, and Jesus did not appear, in his Messianic rôle, to establish it, skepticism naturally grew. Two tendencies then developed.[4] In the first place, the Judgment Day and inauguration of the Kingdom were put farther and

---

[1] God, Christ, and the Holy Spirit which had, according to promise, been poured out upon the Church and was the proof of its divine character, were the three important entities in early Christian belief; their conjunction in baptismal formulæ, and elsewhere, long antedated the conception of them as three Persons of a Triune God.

See J. Lebreton, *Origines du Dogme de la Trinité*; L. L. Paine, *Critical History of the Evolution of Trinitarianism*. Krüger, *Dogma von der Dreieinigkeit und Gottmenschheit* (Tübingen, 1905). A. Harnack, *Constitution and Law of the Church*, Appendix II.

[2] See below, pp. 383-85.

[3] Cf. above, pp. 60-62; 66-69; 75-79; 93-94. And Matt. 23: 39; 25: 13. Mark 8: 38; 9: 1; 13: 30-33; 14: 25, 62. Luke 22: 15-18. 1 Cor. 15: 51-52. Rom. 13: 11-12. 1 Thess. 4: 1. Heb. 9: 28. Jas. 5: 1.

[4] On all this, see S. Mathews, *The Messianic Hope in the New Testament*.

farther away;¹ and all those sayings that described this impending event as an obviously outward and earthly affair² were referred to that remoter future. On the other hand, the sayings that promised a speedy return had to be taken metaphorically, as meaning a coming in spirit in the hearts of the believers — an interpretation consonant, perhaps, with the early post-crucifixion experiences of the disciples.³ Further, the Kingdom of God — or Kingdom of Heaven, as it was sometimes called (owing to a reticence in speaking the Divine name) — which to the Jews had always meant a heavenly kingdom on earth, in Judæa, was interpreted by the Greeks, naturally out of sympathy with such local hopes, to mean a kingdom in the heavens. The vague "outer darkness" into which the wicked were to be cast crystallized gradually into a definite region of future torment, usually conceived, in harmony with widespread ancient notions of future existence, as a vast pit under the earth.⁴

Thus arose the Christian doctrine of Heaven and Hell. The Day of Judgment at the end of the existing order — that nightmare of the Middle Ages — was gradually put farther and farther into the future; though at several epochs a feverish anticipation of its imminent approach became widespread. At that great *dies iræ* the dead were to rise from the grave and assemble at the throne of God, where the sheep would be separated from the goats, the former to be rewarded with eternal happiness, the latter punished with eternal torment. The Devil, introduced into late Judaism, probably from Persia,⁵ apparently believed in but little emphasized

[1] Cf. 2 Thess. 2: 1–12. Rev., chap. 20; 21: 1–5.

[2] Such as Mark, chap. 13. Matt. 25: 31–45. Luke 17: 26–36. John 5: 28–29; 6: 40. 1 Pet. 4: 17–18.

[3] Cf. especially John 14: 16–29; 15: 26–27; 16: 7–14.

[4] Cf., in the Apostles' Creed: "He *descended* into Hell."

[5] See C. C. Everett, in *Essays Theological and Literary*. Also in *New World*, vol. 4, p. 1. *Harvard Theological Review*, vol. 5, p. 371. P. Carus, *History of the Devil*.

by Jesus, assumed importance in this scheme; though his relation to the God, who, although omnipotent, tolerated him, was a matter for much controversy. When the alternative between everlasting bliss or torment seemed too sharp, the doctrine of Purgatory, long familiar in the Orphic mysteries, crept in to soften it; but, not having a proper basis in Scripture, it was rejected by Protestantism.[1]

In such ways the various dogmas of the growing Church came into being. Council after council, in stormy debate, worked out what was to be for centuries the orthodox Christian belief. Much ingenuity and many acute disputations went to the forming of this body of doctrine, the mental energy and ability of the times finding in this way its outlet. In the subtle and elaborate work of Thomas Aquinas the system reached its completest form. The authority of the Church enforced its acceptance and thus fossilized it, ensuring it against healthy criticism or further development. In Dante's *Divine Comedy*, wherein deep religious feeling and the highest poetic genius vivified and illumined this gigantic framework of dogma, we have the greatest and most lasting product of Catholic theology. Opposing doctrines were vigorously stamped out; and this strange composite of popular faith and learned dialectic imposed itself with a grip of iron upon the mind of the Western world.

E. F. Scott, *Beginnings of the Church*. C. von Weizsäcker, *Apostolic Age*. A. C. McGiffert, *History of Christianity in the Apostolic Age; Rise of Modern Religious Ideas*. P. Wernle, *Beginnings of Christianity*. H. Harnack, *What is Christianity?* pt. II; *Mission and Expansion of Christianity; History of Christian Dogma*. G. Hodges, *The Early Church, from Ignatius to Augustine*. O. Pfleiderer, *Primitive Christianity*. H. Achelis, *Christentum in den ersten drei Jahrhunderten*. J. C. Ayer, *Source Book for Ancient Church History*. J. A. Faulkner, *Crises in the Early Church*. E. Du-

---

[1] The Scripture verses with which the doctrine supports itself are 2 Macc. 12: 43–46. Matt. 12: 32. Luke 12: 48. 1 Cor. 3: 15; 15: 29.

chesne, *Early History of the Christian Church.* S. J. Case, *Evolution of Early Christianity.* E. Hatch, *Influence of Greek Ideas and Usages upon the Christian Church.* C. Clemen, *Christianity and its Non-Jewish Sources.* T. R. Glover, *Conflict of Religions in the Early Roman Empire,* chaps. v–x. A. Sabatier, *Outlines of the Philosophy of Religion,* bk. ii, chap. iii. L. Abbott, *Evolution of Christianity,* chaps. v–vi. *Foundations,* chap. iv. G. Reinach, *Orpheus,* chaps. ix–x. F. Paulsen, *System of Ethics,* bk. i, chaps. ii–iv. H. B. Mitchell, *Talks on Religion,* chap. vi. G. Santayana, *Reason in Religion,* chaps. vi–ix. H. B. Workman, *Christian Thought to the Reformation. American Journal of Theology,* vol. 17, p. 63.

CHAPTER VIII

LATER CHRISTIANITY; MOHAMMEDANISM

By what process did the Roman Church become dominant?

JESUS founded no church and had no thought of one;[1] he merely called on his people to repent and be ready for the approaching world-change. And the earliest Palestinian Christians simply gathered informally to listen to the happy story, renew their faith in their Messiah, and strengthen one another in well-doing. It was rather with Paul's little groups of converts in Asia Minor and Greece, as time wore on, that church organization developed. At first they were very democratic, vesting whatever disciplinary and executive powers were necessary in their elders;[2] even into the second century, in Polycarp's time, their organization had proceeded scarcely farther. But for mutual helpfulness it became advisable to elect overseers — *episcopoi*, bishops; these were at first simply the most prominent elders. Gradually these bishops assumed greater and greater authority, until the government of the churches was rather monarchical than democratic. St. Jerome, indeed, warns the bishops [3] to "remember that if they are set over the presbyters, it is the result of tradition, and not a particular institution of the

---

[1] Matt. 16:18 and 18:17 employ the word ἐκκλησία. But the word must not be understood in our modern sense — if indeed the sayings are genuine at all. (See Holtzmann, *Life of Jesus*, pp. 319 n. 326–27). There was no *time* or motive for organizing a "church." On this whole matter see Scott, *Beginnings of the Church*, chap. II.

[2] The Greek word for elder, "presbyter," is the source of our word "priest." The Latin equivalent is "senior."

[3] *Ad Titum*, 1:7.

Lord." But by the fourth century they had taken over the functions — and even the titles, *sacerdos*, *pontifex*, etc. — of their predecessors, the pagan priests; and so, step by step, the pagan sacerdotal idea replaced the simpler conception of primitive Christianity.

Amid these bishops it was natural that the Bishop of Rome should have the greatest prestige. Rome was the capital of the Empire, and — especially now that Jerusalem had fallen — the natural center for the Church's life. Moreover, in the struggle against unbelievers and heretics it became necessary to have some central authority. Church councils were too clumsy a method of solving this problem; the leadership of the Roman bishops offered a promise of unity. Thus the Papacy was practically a *fait accompli* before it occurred to its apologists to justify it by the theory of divine right through Petrine succession.[1] That theory, as it was formulated toward the close of the second century, derived the powers of the Roman bishop, by an unbroken succession, from the apostle Peter, who was said to have ended his days in Rome, and upon whom Jesus was said to have conferred authority over the Church.[2] There was

[1] Just so the theory of the divine right of kings, which has lingered to our day, is a justification to the intellect, after the fact, of an antecedent status which it was desired to support.

[2] As a matter of fact, the earlier links in this chain are entirely untrustworthy. Peter may possibly have gone to Rome — though there is no evidence of it. But if he did, the fact has no significance. To any one who grasps the historic setting and real spirit of Jesus' anticipations, it is clear that nothing was farther from his mind than the transmitting of sacerdotal power to an institution. Peter was simply the man whom he trusted to keep his little band loyal until his Messianic coming. And then, there was in all probability no bishop at all in the little Roman church till long after Peter's death. The Catholic interpretation of Matt. 16: 18–19 does not appear until the third century. That text — which does not appear at all in the earliest narrative — may even be not from Jesus' lips at all. See Holtzmann, *Life of Jesus*, pp. 326–30. And cf. E. F. Scott, *Beginnings of the Church*, p. 51: "It is not too much to say that nowhere in the Gospels do we have stronger evidence of interpolation than in this memorable passage."

strenuous opposition from the other bishops and their churches to this assumption of authority by Rome. But the early Roman bishops were good politicians; and out of the general chaos they emerged triumphant. Thus, by an easily intelligible process, a powerful centralized Church, modeled in organization after the Roman Empire, and succeeding to its authority and prestige, grew up out of the democratic fraternities of primitive disciples.

During the same period a ritual and liturgy were evolved, and the Church more and more assumed control over the lives of men. The weaker the Empire grew, the stronger grew the power of priesthood and papacy. The division of the Empire led, indeed, to a like growth in authority of the Bishop of Constantinople; and a schism between East and West developed which was never healed. But though the Eastern Church remained, and remains to this day, separate from the Roman Church, the latter waxed steadily in authority in the West. In 386 Ambrose refused to obey the Emperor Valentinian; and a few years later another emperor, Theodosius, humbled himself and performed penance at the dictation of that bishop of the Church. In 800, Leo III placed the crown on the head of the Emperor of the Franks; and at the beginning of the thirteenth century Innocent III dominated Europe. Finally, in the nineteenth century, the dogma of the infallibility of the Pope was decreed — a desperate attempt to stem the rising tide of secularism which has shorn from the Papacy its political power and a large part of its hold on the minds of men.

What was the significance of the Reformation?

During the Middle Ages the decree of Pope and Council was accepted by all the Western peoples that had adopted Christianity. Not, indeed, without recurrent chafing and protest; there were many "reformers before the Reformation." But the masses were illiterate and ignorant, intercommunication of thought was not easy, and the various early attempts at rebellion proved abortive. So, although the way was prepared by Wyclif in England, Huss in Bohemia, and other independent and deeply religious spirits, the actual break with Rome did not occur until Luther's defiance of Papal authority in 1517. Luther, who was a priest, and a professor in the University of Wittenberg, did not foresee at first an actual secession from the Church; but circumstances drove him on. Excommunicated in 1520, he publicly burned the Papal decree. Others flocked to his standard; in 1529 a number of German princes and representatives of the cities signed the famous Protest which gave the name to the new movement. Political considerations entered in; especially the new sense of nationality among the Northern peoples welcomed the opportunity to get rid of the Roman yoke. In Switzerland, Denmark, Sweden, and the British Isles the challenge to Papal authority was particularly welcome. After protracted discussion and struggle, issuing in actual warfare in central Europe, the Northern nations became predominantly Protestant, while in the Mediterranean countries the old régime retained its hold.

The Reformation was really a revolution; and its name might better be applied to the so-called Counter-Reformation by which the Roman Church purged itself, under the stress of criticism and revolt, of its more flagrant abuses. The most palpable of these, and the immediate occasion of Luther's protest, was the shocking and cynical sale of indulgences, whereby those who had money were granted forgiveness of sins and eternal life. But this was only one embodiment of the corruption and wire-pulling in the Church of the times, corruption that was so snugly intrenched in high places as to need drastic measures. The protest of the reformers was directed, however, not only against the worldliness and politics in the Church, but against the paganized form of the Gospel which had become the official doctrine — the worship of the Madonna, of saints and relics, the dogma of transsubstantiation and the sacrifice of the Mass, the belief in Purgatory and the practice of prayers for the dead, the institution of Confession — such accretions of doctrine, which seemed to the reformers rather heathen than Christian. There was also an element of protest against the unwholesome asceticism favored by the Church and flourishing side by side with its worldliness — the monastic system, the celibate clergy, the fastings and penances whereby special merit with God was to be won.

Some of the practices thus criticized were presently reformed within the ancient Church. But the Protestant revolt was too fundamental to be checked by such concessions. With the revival of Greek culture and learning, the renaissance of the study of nature, and the awakening of the spirit of free inquiry, the control of a self-styled authoritative church over the minds of men was doomed. These humanizing and enlightening influences had been instinctively antagonized by the Church and long repressed. But the new ideas spread from the universities, and the authority of established beliefs could not remain unchallenged. The revolt from Rome did not imply an immediate and far-reaching change of beliefs; but it did mean a freedom from the choking ecclesiastical tyranny which was rendering freedom of thought and further growth impossible. It meant that henceforth the people were to have a hand in the government and creedal decisions of the Church. And it meant a setting aside of the sacerdotal system, with all its external machinery of salvation. Religion again, as in the hands of Christ and of Paul, became a first-hand and inward matter; salvation was not through sacraments and priestly absolution, but through the immediate relation of the individual to Christ and God.

Thus the independent and virile Northern races broke away from the domination of a stifling ecclesiastical system which had become, as time went on, in greater and greater degree alien to their temper.

The underlying and unexpressed ideal of the Reformation was that beliefs and practices must not be imposed upon men's minds by an external authority, but must grow out of experience and be tested by reason. But it is only gradually that Protestantism has come to full self-consciousness. The craving for outward and visible authority to lean upon long persisted; and a great deal of the Catholic absolutist spirit survived in the new churches. Moreover, in the struggle against Rome the need of some weapon was felt; the weapon at hand was the Bible. Thus the reformers escaped from slavery to a church only to fall into slavery to Scripture-texts. And many Protestants, advancing beyond their contemporaries in liberal thought, were persecuted not only by Catholics, but by their own more conservative brethren. The history of Protestantism is a record of intolerance and bigotry which goes far to dim its actual achievement in setting men on the path of progress.

Yet that it did set men on the path of progress is undeniable. Although when it broke with ecclesiastical authority it took refuge in the authority of Scripture, making that the basis and oracle of its faith, there was this momentous gain: instead of having to go to the priests to learn the truth, every one could henceforth find it for himself in God's written word. But the Bible, being a heterogeneous collection of writings expressing the points of view of many writers of widely separated times and beliefs, easily supplies a text for almost any doctrine — especially if its words are wrenched from their context and interpreted in the violent and arbitrary manner common to theologians. Thus Protestantism, while still, like its parent-faith, claiming the support of an infallible authority, lent itself to growth and change; a rapid divergence of belief resulted.[1]

What have been the subsequent tendencies of Christianity?

(1) At first, revolting from the loose and degenerate practices of contemporary Catholicism, Protestantism assumed a form of grim austerity; in Calvinism we have the severest form of Christianity. Calvin, with uncompromising logic, drew from the harshest verses of the Bible a clean-cut and relentless system, which bred a race of stern morality, but nearly banished all the natural joys of life. In England the new national church — established largely through political reasons — was, except for its independence of Rome, but a slightly expurgated Catholicism; and the Puritans — those who stood out for a *pure* church — looked upon it as a case of arrested development. They would have no images or candles or luxurious vestments, no mummery of ritual or liturgy, nothing luring to the senses or smacking of worldliness. Of priests and bishops they would have none; face to face with God and His word they lived, a stern, uncompromising and splendidly devoted band. New England was first settled, and made what it was to be, by them. Such men as Cotton Mather and Jonathan Edwards were fit to rank, in the power and purity of their lives and the depth of their religious feeling, with the great Hebrew prophets. And yet, Puritanism, with its firm belief in predestination and eternal punishment, was a religion to make one shudder. Such sermons as Edwards's *Sinners in the Hands of an Angry God* depict a deity beside whom the Devil himself pales into a

---

[1] For the Reformation, see, in addition to the books mentioned at the close of the chapter, T. M. Lindsay, *History of the Reformation*. C. Beard, *The Reformation in its Relation to Modern Thought and Knowledge*. R. M. Jones, *Spiritual Reformers in the Sixteenth and Seventeenth Century*.

mildly malevolent being. An arbitrary and cruel tyrant, damning the majority of his helpless creatures, and saving a remnant, not for their own merits, but to manifest his own power, or "glory," deserves at the least Channing's phrase — "a very injurious view of the Supreme Being." [1]

(2) And in fact this hideous doctrine became, as the times grew happier and more generally moral, too awful for men's increasingly humane instincts. The whole Calvinistic-Puritanic scheme, with its grim stress on the eternal gulf between sinners and saved, and its black picture of the natural state of man, however suited to the dark times of St. Augustine and Calvin, was not plausible in the easier and on the whole much purer conditions of modern life; and it has gradually come to seem nothing less than preposterous to all but the most tenaciously conservative of the descendants of those who, but a generation or two ago, firmly believed it. The conception of God prevalent at any time reflects the temper and ideals of the believers; and the modern mind, more sensitive to suffering than that of earlier ages, will tolerate no such tyrannical and brutal deity.[2]

Thus there has been in recent times, and particularly in

[1] He had already written (in 1809), "A man of plain sense, whose spirit has not been broken to this creed by education or terror, will think it is not necessary for us to travel to heathen countries to learn how mournfully the human mind may misrepresent the Deity."

[2] Cf. W. James, *Varieties of Religious Experience*, p. 329: "Few historic changes are more curious than these mutations of theological opinion. The monarchical type of sovereignty was, for example, so ineradicably planted in the mind of our own forefathers that a dose of cruelty and arbitrariness in their deity seems positively to have been required by their imagination. They called the cruelty 'retributive justice,' and a God without it would certainly have struck them as not 'sovereign' enough. But to-day we abhor the very notion of eternal suffering inflicted; and that arbitrary dealing-out of salvation and damnation to selected individuals, of which Jonathan Edwards could persuade himself that he had not only a conviction, but a 'delightful conviction' as of a doctrine 'exceedingly pleasant, bright and sweet,' appears to us, if sovereignly anything, sovereignly irrational and mean."

LATER CHRISTIANITY; MOHAMMEDANISM

America, a great revival of belief in the love of God, leading in many quarters to a conviction of universal salvation. Channing declared that the orthodox "have too often felt as if God were raised by his greatness and sovereignty above the principles of morality, above those eternal laws of equity and rectitude, to which all other beings are subjected.... We believe that God is infinitely good, kind, and benevolent, in the proper sense of these words; good not to a few, but to all; good to every individual." Theodore Parker wrote, God's "plan must be adapted to secure the ultimate welfare of each creature he has made." This gentler and happier view has permeated in greater or less degree all the Protestant churches, and bids fair to become the dominant Christian conception.[1]

(3) This great reversal of belief, together with many other changes of conception which we have not space to enumerate, involved the abandonment of tenets that seemed securely based upon the Bible, and naturally shook its authority. More and more, reason came to be upheld in its place as the ultimate criterion of truth. St. Augustine had said, "This is my faith because it is the Catholic faith." The early Protestants had said, "This is our faith because the Bible says so." But many were saying by the eighteenth century, with Toland, "We hold that reason is the only foundation of all certitude," and with Bishop Butler, "Reason is, indeed,

---

[1] C. C. Everett, late professor of theology at Harvard University, writing of this revolution of belief, said, "It was as if black and heavy clouds had rolled away, and the blue heavens stretched above them, and the clear sunshine gladdened their hearts. God was no longer the stern judge, demanding the death of the innocent before he could forgive the guilty — if that can be called forgiveness which has been purchased at such a price. Christ was no longer the substituted victim of the Father's wrath. Man was no longer under the curse of God. These men saw only the love of God reflected in the face of Jesus. Man was the child of God, still followed and ever to be followed by the Father's love."

Cf. Barrett Wendell, *Literary History of America*, bk. v, chap. iv.

the only faculty which we have to judge concerning anything, even revelation itself. . . . The faculty of reason is the candle of the Lord within us, against vilifying which we must be very cautious." In 1819 Channing, a Christian minister, could write, "If religion be the shipwreck of understanding, we cannot keep too far from it"; and a little later, "We must never forget that our rational nature is the greatest gift of God. . . . If I could not be a Christian without ceasing to be rational, I should not hesitate as to my choice . . . I am surer that my rational nature is from God than that any book is the expression of his will."

In pursuance of this spirit, modern Liberal Christianity studies the Bible more and more as it would study any other book, sees the Hebrew god Jehovah for what he really was to the minds of those early Semites, and recognizes him as being to them very much what the contemporary gods of Greece or Babylon were to their worshipers. Its God must be less barbarous, local, and anthropomorphic, revealed rather in the eternal moral law than in special miracles or Jewish codes. He is no longer thought of as favoring a special people or having the scope of his purposes limited by the history of Judaism and Christianity. The whole world-process is his plan; we are to read his will not so much in the sermons of Isaiah or the letters of Paul as in the conscience with which we are all endowed and the universal spiritual experience of man.

(4) The ultimate goal of Protestantism seems to be the complete rationalization of its beliefs, the acceptance by religion of science as the arbiter of truth, and the formulation of her insights and ideals in terms that science can accept. The promise of this eventual outcome lies in that individual liberty of belief whose germs were contained in the Reformation. There is even, in the movement known as Modernism, a push within the Catholic Church toward this goal. But

while such endeavors are strictly repressed by the Roman See, Protestantism, rejoicing in its comparative freedom, presents the spectacle of a chaos of experiments in reconciliation of the old and the new. On the one hand there are reactionary eddies toward traditional beliefs; on the other, all sorts of new and grotesquely irrational cults, tangential to the main line of development. Spiritualism, with its supposititious evidence of a future life, offers comfort to the credulous. Recently we have witnessed the extraordinary career of John Alexander Dowie, "Elijah II, The Restorer, General Overseer of the Christian Catholic Church in Zion," who made himself a multi-millionaire through the gullibility of his followers. Christian Science, so-called, has attracted many thousands by its radical optimism, its promise of physical health, and its frank abandonment of most of the older dogmas. All these phenomena are so many phases of that great doctrinal upheaval that is gradually changing the basis of authority in religion from ecclesiastical pronouncement and written word to reason and experience.

Meanwhile, as doctrines confront one another and crumble, more and more emphasis is laid upon the necessity and transcendent worth of the Christian Life. Churches of widely different beliefs are learning to coöperate for human uplift and to emphasize what they have in common rather than their creedal differences. In general, the thought of Christendom less and less concerns itself with another world, but sets itself the task of bettering this world. The Institutional Church, the Y.M.C.A., and kindred organizations, draw attention to the need of social regeneration. Some churches have arisen which discard the traditional beliefs *in toto*, and make their basis of fellowship solely the endeavor after the spiritual life, the life of purity and service. Thus, through all doctrinal changes, and although the intellectual formulation of the religion is profoundly changing, the Christian Ideal remains practically what it was to the earliest disciples, and a force of enormous potency in the world.

What are the essential features of Mohammedanism?

Six centuries after the birth of Christianity another Semitic religion emerged from the East, this time from Arabia, spread with extraordinary rapidity, and became, in point of numbers, one of the great religions of mankind. Mohammed, although unable to read or write, and of a rather morbid, neurotic temperament, had a gift of eloquent speech, with great personal magnetism, and aroused a fanatical devotion to his person and his teachings. By no means an impostor, he had a profound belief in himself, intense earnestness and sincerity in his mission, and accomplished reforms of importance for his people. From his childhood he was subject to trances and visions; and he undoubtedly believed himself, like the Old Testament prophets, — whom he in many respects resembled, — directly inspired and commissioned of God. It is true that in his later years he became an opportunist, manufactured visions to suit his needs, and blackened his record by some treacherous and cruel acts. But this was still in the service of an ambition that was truly national and religious. In the year 622 A.D. he made the famous journey — the Hegira — from Mecca to Medina, which has since become the starting-point of Moslem chronology. From that time on his success was meteoric; and before he died, a decade later, he stood at the head of a great politico-religious empire.

As is always the case with great religious or political successes, Mohammed appeared at just the right moment. The Arabian peoples were experiencing a great renaissance and a religious unrest; their sense of nationality was coming to consciousness, and a population grown too large for the sterile peninsula was on the point of one of those periodic overflows such as have so largely shaped the history of man. Mohammed's great work lay in unifying this people. It was their differing worship that most kept them apart; and by his war-cry, "There is One God, and Mohammed is his prophet!" he took the most effective means toward their consolidation. There was already a strong drift toward monotheism among the people; Jewish and Christian ideas had played considerable part therein. But it was reserved for Mohammed to complete the process. The unity and absolute sovereignty of Allah was his dominating idea; all the other gods were to be viewed as created and subordinate beings. The simplicity and universality of the conception won rapid allegiance; and the fierce Bedouin tribes united under the banner of Allah to spread their new gospel by the sword. By 700 A.D. the sway of the new religious state had become as wide as that of Christianity at the time of Constantine; and but for its defeat by Charles Martel, at the battle of Tours, it might have overrun western Europe as it did Asia, Africa, and the Balkan peninsular.

The chief religious value of Mohammedanism — besides its banishing of earlier superstitions — lies in its demand of absolute loyalty to Allah and acquiescence in his will. Allah is an absolute monarch, majestic, inscrutable, omnipotent; there is in him a complete lack of the intimate fatherliness and love of the Christian God. But the loyal allegiance to his commands and the loyal submission to his will have brought a large measure of selflessness and peace into the hearts of devout Moslems. And the fatalistic view of his purposes has endowed them with a reckless courage unsurpassed in the history of man. The Mohammedan creed is militant, prescribing a Holy War against infidels; it is lacking in the gentler and sweeter traits of Christianity; and it has not hitherto proved progressive. It legitimates slavery, polygamy, easy divorce on the part of the husband, and promises sexual delights in a very material Paradise. The humiliating position of women throughout the Mohammedan world of to-day is largely due to the insane jealousy of the Prophet. The injunction of almsgiving — emphasized by Mohammed because of his own needy and orphaned childhood — has been responsible for the maintenance of a perpetual horde of beggars wherever his doctrine is preached. The one great moral contribution of the religion is its prohibition of alcoholic drinks, which has kept the Mohammedan world reasonably free from that curse of Christendom. The Koran, with its bizarre visions and utter lack of charm of style or orderly arrangement, is among the most tedious and confusing of sacred books. A collection of fragments of remembered discourses of the Prophet, made some time after his death, and arranged in order of length, it has been rather barren mental food for the millions whose religion it contains. On the whole, and apart from its initial value in consolidating and arousing a hitherto disorganized and inarticulate people, Mohammedanism seems to have little in it of the highest worth for mankind.

S. Dill, *Roman Society from Nero to Marcus Aurelius*, bk. IV; *Roman Society in the last Century of the Roman Empire*, bk. I. C. Bigg, *The Church's Task under the Roman Empire*. A. Sabatier, *Religions of Authority and the Religion of the Spirit*, bk. I, chaps. II–V; bk. II, chaps. I–II. S. Reinach, *Orpheus*, chap. XI. A. V. G. Allen, *Christian Institutions*. J. B. Carter, *Religious Life of Ancient Rome*, chaps. IV–VIII. A. C. Flick, *Rise of the Mediæval Church*. H. B. Workman, *Church of the West in the Middle Ages;* and several other books. R. Sohm, *Outlines of Church History*. P. Schaff, *History of the Christian Church*. G. P. Fisher, *History of Christian Doctrine; History of the Reformation*. A. C. McGiffert, *Protestant Thought before Kant; Martin Luther*. E. C. Moore, *Outline of the History of Christian Thought since Kant*. S. Cheetham, *History of the Christian Church since the Reformation*. W. S. Crowe, *Phases of Religious Life in America*.

D. B. Macdonald, *Aspects of Islam; Religious Attitude and Life in Islam*. S. Reinach, *Orpheus*, chap. VI. A. Menzies, *History of Religion*, chap. XIII. T. W. Arnold, *Preaching of Islam*. W. St. C. Tisdall, *Religion of the Crescent*. E. Sill, *Faith of Islam*. F. A. Klein, *Religion of Islam*. Syed Ameer Ali, *Spirit of Islam*. Articles in *Hasting's* and *Schaff-Herzog Encyclopædia*, and *Encyclopædia Britannica*. *Harvard Theological Review*, vol. 5, p. 474.

SUMMARY OF PART I

What has been the trend of religious evolution?

FROM the welter of primitive superstitions to the pure and noble ideals of Buddhism, Judaism, and Christianity is a far journey. But the causes that have produced these profound changes in belief and practice are, in general, not difficult to discern. We are not to think of the mere unfolding of a universal and always latent "religious instinct"; nor is the road from the naïve animism of savage peoples to the concepts of modern liberal religion a highway along which mankind as a whole have advanced. Rather, there have been innumerable experiments and failures; beliefs have dawned, thrilled their converts, and disappeared; the religions that have survived have grown far from the visions of their founders, and show the marks of many a struggle and change. In this sphere, as everywhere, the evolutionary process has produced widely different results under differing conditions. And if a large proportion of living men to-day subscribe to rather closely analogous creeds, it is simply because the intercommunication of modern life, together with the many unifying forces at work, has made it possible for a few faiths to override and supersede their numerous rivals.

Religion is, at its beginning, not something new injected into human life; it emerges rather through that gradual differentiation of human interests which also marked out the spheres of art and science. Closely bound up with the social structure of primitive life, the development of religious ideas is to be explained largely in terms of contemporary social and intellectual change. Whatever activities and ideas and

SUMMARY OF PART I

interests are vital in the tribal life are sure to be reflected in religious practices. Thus religious evolution is not a self-contained process, carrying within itself its own explanation, as an acorn might be said to contain the germ of all that the oak is to be. On the contrary, a religion may veer in any direction, under the influence of current science and philosophy, the conscious or unconscious manipulation of priests, the political status and cultural development of the people. The mutual intercourse of tribes brought alien products into the various home-grown cults; and the eventual dominance of one or other was determined chiefly by the physical superiority of the conquering nations. Great personalities moulded the religion of their countrymen in the direction of their personal visions and ideals. The innumerable forces at work shaping tribal or national morals put their stamp equally upon religious practices and ideas, which are in early life a hardly distinguishable aspect thereof.[1]

Yet, as in the case of moral evolution, so in religious evolution, a few simple constant forces determine in the end the direction of development. Whatever variations of belief and practice may arise, there is in the long run a natural selection for survival of those that meet certain underlying human needs. These needs are threefold: for consolation, for inspiration, and for comprehension. In general, and in the long run, those conceptions tend to prevail which are happier and more hopeful; those which are more moral, or spiritual — i.e., which lead the believer into the better ways of life; and those which are more rational, more in harmony with men's observations of what is true or probable. Such beliefs have an inherent stability which is lacking to the gloomy or fearful beliefs, to the immoral practices, and to the more fantastic and obviously irrational conceptions. It is impos-

[1] For a detailed discussion of these forces see my *Problems of Conduct*, Part I.

sible for most of us to-day to believe, for example, in original sin and predestination to damnation; to worship the cruel and immoral gods of Babylon — or, for that matter, of the prophet Samuel [1] or of Calvin; to take seriously the predicted world-catastrophes of the book of Revelation or the Heaven and Hell of Dante. To judge from observable tendencies, the goal of religious evolution would seem to be a faith that shall be cheering, pure in its morality, and in harmony with the dicta of our scientific knowledge of the world.

The most striking example of the working of the first of these three forces is to be found in the growth and spread of monotheism. Polytheism, although a more natural and instinctive reaction to the complex and often opposed forces of nature, leaves the mind confused and hope uncertain. However favorably disposed a god may be, his power is limited by that of other and perhaps less beneficent beings. Athene, for example, was sure to work for the city that bore her name; but Hera's power was also to be reckoned with. Jehovah would fight for his tribes, but so would Baal and Chemosh for theirs. Only when the belief should grow up in a single god of all peoples, all-powerful and beneficent, could men feel wholly confident in his strength. Such a belief grew up in several places, under the influence of somewhat differing causes. But the monotheism of the Greeks was too speculative, too lacking in roots in the soil, to spread far beyond the circle of the educated or survive the overthrow of Hellenic culture. The monotheism of the Brahmanic priests was likewise too speculative, and lacking in warmth of human interests and idealism, so that it waned before the more spiritual atheism of Buddha — although the hunger for a God in whom to trust quickly found another object in the worship of Buddha himself.

But the monotheistic development of greatest ultimate

[1] Cf. 1 Sam. chap. 15.

significance was that which took place within the Hebrew religion. The enhancement of Jehovah's powers until he came to be thought of as the only god worthy of worship, and finally as the only existing god, was a process much closer to the practical life of men; it was linked with historical and local events, and brought into play the patriotism and moral fervor of an intense and ardent people. Instead of offering a vague hope, such as we find in Marcus Aurelius, that events are ultimately governed by reason and therefore to be patiently, even loyally, acquiesced in, it brought, in its eventual form, a pledge to the individual of the fulfillment of his personal hopes and longings. A belief so inspiring as this found ready and tenacious acceptance; no wonder that it swept over the western world. What made it prevail was, of course, not any evidence of its truth, but the immense consolation and hope it brought to the hearts of men.

The prevailing power of the higher moral conceptions in a religion is to be seen in the rise of many faiths, as, notably, Zoroastrianism and Buddhism. But its most striking example is the prophetic movement among the Hebrews, culminating in the tender and noble ideals of Christ and the early Christians. The dominance of Christianity is to be explained quite as much on the ground of the greater spirituality of its ideals as on the ground of its consolation and hope.

Finally, the survival value of rationality in a religion is best seen in the conflict of beliefs within Christianity, and the process, gradual but sure, by which those forms of the religion which are most sharply in conflict with reason and science are becoming discredited and yielding place to interpretations of the faith that are consonant with the intellectual outlook of the modern world.

PART II
PSYCHOLOGICAL

CHAPTER IX

THE GOD OF EXPERIENCE

WE have now glanced at the most significant landmarks in the history of religion, and are in a position to pick out its essential phenomena for closer scrutiny. Most prominent, perhaps, among these phenomena is the group of beliefs and attitudes and acts that cluster about the concept of God. And so we may appropriately begin our psychological analysis of religion by asking what the idea of God has meant to men. We are not yet to raise the philosophical — or theological — questions involved, to ask what the objective nature of God is, or to explain metaphysically his relation to the universe. We are to ask the prior question, How is God revealed in human experience? or — to put it in other terms — What in our human experience gives us the concept of God? For the place that the thought of God has in religion does not depend primarily upon any theory, and is not a mere matter of postulates or hopes or a blind act of credulity. It rests rather upon a solid foundation of experience. God-experiences (if we may use the phrase) are primary, God-theories are secondary. And even if our theorizing, our theistic arguments and theodicies, reach no conclusion satisfactory to the intellect, these significant experiences remain indisputable and precious; even were we to give up the name God, the Reality which we seek to express thereby would remain, of profound and momentous importance in the religious life of man.

How does God appear in human experience?

1. God in nature. The concept of God came into existence historically, as we saw in our opening chapter, in three principal ways; it was the crystallization of the awe and reverence and fear and hope felt in the contemplation of nature, in the thought of deceased heroes believed to be still alive, in the response to the inward pressure of conscience. Here already, in the convergence of these three great streams of mental tendency, we may detect the basic source of the Christian doctrine of the Trinity. God about us and beyond us, in the vastness of the cosmic life; God in Christ, the highest type of human hero, who sums up in himself, as it were, the spiritual power in other lives upon which we must lean; God in our own hearts, the Holy Spirit in us, to which we must give our whole allegiance if we would find lasting satisfaction and peace — our modern trinitarian conception, derived as it has been by a devious and blind process of intuition and reflection, has after all departed not so very far from primitive man's spontaneous reactions to the great and mysterious forces without and within him.

Man's earliest attitudes toward nature took a polytheistic bent, because the world seems at first an arena in which multitudinous diverse forces act and react upon one another. But in proportion as the world-life becomes understood, its underlying unity becomes manifest; and so, by whatever roads monotheism is reached, and from whatever causes it wins ascendency in men's hearts, it does certainly best fit in with our modern thought of the world as a universe. This universe we describe, as best we can, fragmentarily and imperfectly, in terms of natural law. But the mechanical aspect of the world-process is but one aspect. From the scientific point of view the universe may turn out to be throughout a vast machine. But, if so, that will still not be the whole story about it. For our worldly, industrial life this will be its most important aspect; but not for our emotional, contemplative, æsthetic, moral, religious life. The world will still be infinitely beautiful, ineffably wonderful,

THE GOD OF EXPERIENCE

endlessly inspiring; it will still be the source and matrix of all that is best in us, and the guaranty of the eventual dominance of that best. Regular and clock-like as may be the processes of its life-history, that life will nevertheless be moving on, irresistibly and surely, toward the ideal that it has itself engendered. Whatever else may be true of the cosmos, this also is true, and is the significant fact for our religious life; it is so constituted as to develop in us a spiritual life, and to push us, whether we will or no, into that spiritual life; it is a world-process that makes toward an ideal.

It were a sad incident in the intellectual and practical development of man if he should lose this primitive awe and humility before the beauty and wonder of the world. "You remember that fancy of Plato's, of a man who had grown to maturity in some dark distance, and was brought on a sudden into the upper air to see the sun rise. What would his wonder be, his rapt astonishment at the sight we daily witness with indifference! With the free open sense of a child, yet with the ripe faculty of a man, his whole heart would be kindled by that sight, he would discern it well to be Godlike, his soul would fall down in worship before it. . . . This green, flowery, rock-built earth, the trees, the mountains, rivers, many-sounding seas; — that great deep sea of azure that swims overhead; the winds sweeping through it; the black cloud fashioning itself together, now pouring out fire, now hail and rain; what *is* it? Aye, what? At bottom we do not yet know; we can never know at all. It is not by our superior insight that we escape the difficulty; it is by our superior levity, our inattention, our *want* of insight. It is by *not* thinking that we cease to wonder at it. . . . This world, after all our science and sciences, is still a miracle, wonderful, inscrutable, *magical* and more, to whosoever will *think* of it. . . . What is it? Ah, an unspeakable, Godlike thing; toward which the best attitude for us, after never so much science, is awe, devout prostration and humility of soul; worship, if not in words, then in silence. . . . To primeval men, all things and everything they saw exist beside them were an emblem of the Godlike, of some God. And look what perennial fibre of truth was in that. To us also, through every star, through every blade of grass, is not a God made visible, if we will open our minds and eyes? . . . Every object has a divine beauty in it . . . is a window through which we may look into Infinitude itself." [1]

The great seers and poets have been men who have felt more vividly than the average man the presence of this God "in whom we live and move and have our being." To the psalmist "the heavens declare the glory of God"; for Wordsworth there is in nature

> "A presence that disturbs me with the joy
> Of elevated thoughts; a sense sublime
> Of something far more deeply interfused,
> Whose dwelling is the light of setting suns,
> And the round ocean and the living air,
> And the blue sky, and in the mind of man;
> A motion and a spirit, that impels
> All thinking things, all objects of all thought,
> And rolls through all things." [2]

In similar vein Max Müller writes, "Look at the dawn, and forget for a moment your astronomy; and I ask you whether, when the dark veil of the night is slowly lifted, and the air becomes transparent and alive, and light streams forth, you know not whence, you would not feel that your eye were looking into the very eye of the Infinite?" And Emerson, "If the stars should appear one night in a thousand years, how would men believe and adore; and preserve for many

---

[1] Carlyle, *Heroes and Hero Worship: The Hero as Divinity.*

[2] Wordsworth's religion seems to have been based almost exclusively upon this nature-worship, this joyful recognition of the divineness of the natural world. And it seems to have been a stimulating and satisfactory religion. See Seeley, pp. 94–102.

generations the remembrance of the city of God which had been shown! But every night come out these envoys of beauty, and light the universe with their admonishing smile. . . . All natural objects make a kindred impression, when the mind is open to their influence. . . . In the woods, we return to reason and faith. Standing on the bare ground, — my head bathed by the blithe air, and uplifted into infinite space, — all mean egotism vanishes. I become a transparent eyeball; I am nothing; I see all; the currents of the Universal Being circulate through me; I am part or particle of God." [1]

In such moments of insight the religious man finds an added inspiration in the thought that he is himself a part of this divine order which overwhelms his imagination, caught by the same resistless currents of being, and sharing the universal destinies. No amount of scientific analysis and description can annul the truth of these hours of vision. And so, "when men say, 'As for God, we know nothing of him; science knows nothing of him; it is a name belonging to an extinct system of philosophy'; I think they are playing with words. By what name they call the object of their contemplation is in itself a matter of little importance. Whether they say God, or prefer to say Nature, the important thing is that their minds [be] filled with the sense of a Power to all appearance infinite and eternal, a Power to which their own being is inseparably connected, in the knowledge of whose ways alone is safety and wellbeing, in the contemplation of which they find a beatific vision. . . . I cannot believe any religion to be healthy that does not start from Nature-worship." [2]

II. God in our hearts — the Holy Spirit. The contemplative side of religion, the vision of God in nature, is important and abiding. But the directest avenue to God is through

[1] *Nature*, chap. I. [2] Seeley, pp. 22, 24.

obedience; he is not so much in the wind or the earthquake or the fire as in the still, small voice within us; and it is the pure in heart that see God. In the uprush of noble feeling and high resolve, in the power for good that wells up, sometimes so unexpectedly, within us, God is most surely revealed. It matters little whether this inflow of the Holy Spirit can be described or not in natural terms; the Spirit is holy not because of its miraculous way of working, but because its influence in our life is divine. The practically significant fact is that if we open our hearts, God will enter in and regenerate our lives; this power is ready for our use if we will cease to kick against the pricks, and lay hold of it. There, within us, is to be found not only our selfishness and our passion, but at least a seed of the Divine Will; and so all-important is this fact that religion has been defined as the life of God in the soul of man. Even when he sins and forgets God, this fountain of good is still invisibly within him, abiding even amid the riot and jungle of his inmost life, ever and again reminding him that there is a law above his own will which he may not, at his peril, disobey.[1]

By the "fear of God" truly religious men have meant, not their terror at a hostile environment, but their recognition of the authority of this higher law over their capricious wills. The direction conduct must take is not to be decided by our impulse or fancy; it is decreed from the beginning of the world. If we infringe these eternal laws, framed in the very constitution of the universe, we cannot escape the penalty. "The fear of the Lord — that is wisdom; to depart from evil

[1] Cf. Emerson, "It is a secret which every intelligent man quickly learns, that beyond the energy of his possessed and conscious intellect, he is capable of a new energy (as of an intellect doubled on itself) by abandonment to the nature of things; that besides his power as an individual man, there is a great public power upon which he can draw, by unlocking at all risks his human doors, and suffering the ethereal tides to roll and circulate through him."

THE GOD OF EXPERIENCE

is understanding."[1] "O Lord, I know that the way of man is not in himself; it is not in man that walketh to direct his steps."[2] That this unescapable authority of God has been supposed to imply a literal oral command by a "magnified, non-natural man," a tribal patron-god speaking from his home on his Sacred Mountain, need not disturb us; though no finger of Jehovah wrote the decalogue, it is no less binding upon us. No rationalization of religion can make duty less divine. Who is the fool who says there is no God? He is the moral nihilist, the cynic, or the worldly man, who laughs at duty and follows the passions of the moment. Nevertheless — "though there be many devices in a man's heart, the counsel of the Lord, that shall stand."[3]

But this fear of God, in the truly devout and aspiring soul, becomes the deepest joy; in loyalty to the God within him he finds the only road to lasting peace. He is now bound to his brother-men by the deepest bond; for the God-element in him is akin to that in them, a spark from the same eternal fire. Each separate reaching out for the good, each act of self-sacrifice, is felt not as standing alone, but as a part of the seeking and working of mankind toward God; or, to put it the other way, as a part of the gradual realization of God in human life.

---

[1] Job 28: 28. The peculiarity of Hebrew poetry by which the second line of a couplet repeats the meaning of the first line in other words shows clearly the practical equivalence in the poet's mind of the two phrases. Indeed, in Prov. 8: 13 we read, "The fear of the Lord is to hate evil."

[2] Jer. 10: 23.

[3] Prov. 19: 21. Cf. Arnold, *Literature and Dogma*, pp. 111, 38: "The idea of *God*, as it is given us in the Bible, rests not on a metaphysical conception . . . but on a moral perception of a rule of conduct not of our own making, into which we are born, and which exists whether we will or no; of awe at its grandeur and necessity, and of gratitude at its beneficence." "To please God, to serve God, to obey God's will, means to follow a law of things which is found in conscience, and which is an indication, irrespective of our arbitrary wish and fancy, of what we ought to do. There *is* a real power which makes for righteousness; and it is the greatest of realities for us."

III. God in Christ. But if in some degree in all of us the Holy Spirit lives, it is especially incarnate in the spiritual heroes of mankind; and above all — for us, at least, of Christendom — in Christ. "Somehow Jesus seems to sum up and focus the religious ideal for mankind"; [1] he is the supreme incarnation of the Divine in human nature; so that the words could fitly be put into his mouth, "He that hath seen me hath seen the Father." [2] We need not, therefore, however rationalistic our temper, balk at the phraseology that calls Christ divine; the truth that is to be conveyed by such language is not inconsistent with a truly historical view of his life and teachings, and does not necessarily imply anything miraculous or supernatural. To the popular mind, indeed, Jesus has often figured as very God; but the deity and the divinity of Christ are far from identical conceptions. The Church in its official dogma has steadily clung to the assertion that Jesus was thoroughly human; his divineness was only such as could be expressed in a human life. His will was wholly merged with the will of God, there was no selfishness left in him, no self-indulgence; it was his meat to do the will of the Father. The Christ-life is the divine life for men, the measure of the amount of godliness that our nature is capable of. To call his life divine is not in the least to assert that Jesus was born of a virgin, wrought miracles, or rose from the tomb; it is an entirely different sort of judgment, a value-judgment. The facts about his life must be decided by historical methods, as we would sift the records of the life of any other personage of the past; no ardent believer or intrenched ecclesiasticism ought to attempt to bias the impartial judgment of scholars upon them. But the question of the divine-

[1] R. J. Campbell, *The New Theology*, p. 70.
[2] Even those who most completely deify Jesus do not identify him with the *Father;* so that the sense of such sayings as these clearly is not that Jesus is God, but that he is a *revelation* of God; that if any one wishes to see what God is like, he must look at Jesus.

ness of this life is to be decided by men of spiritual vision. And the verdict of truly religious men is all but unanimous; the great warrior, the great statesman, the great inventor, the great poet, have a veritable spark of God in them; but the life that is most truly divine, that most fully reaches up to God, is the life of purity and charity and self-sacrifice. Preëminent among such lives, dazzling men of all races and degrees of culture for the two millenniums since he lived, is the life of the carpenter of Nazareth.

In view of the confusion in which the popular mind — and the mind, we may add, of many a theologian — has rested on this matter, it will be worth while to make more explicit what should have been clear enough from our study of the life of Christ, namely, his thoroughgoing humanity. Encrusted as the records are with miracles and marvels — which it is by no means possible or desirable categorically to deny — they do not fail to preserve hints and implications of his normal human limitations. He shared the physical weakness of men, being often weary and depressed, suffering all the anguish of other mortals as his cruel death drew near, and lacking strength to carry his cross. He shared the ignorance of men, not only in his boyhood,[1] but throughout his life; the hour when the Messianic Kingdom was to be inaugurated he said that no man knew, not even he himself, who expected to play the leading part.[2] He knew presumably no science, knew little of the life and history of the world, shared the local contemporary beliefs and hopes of his fellows, was possessed in the last months or years of his life by a passionate conviction which, in its literal form, can only be called a pathetic delusion. He was tempted, as all men are; and we have no means of knowing, really, that he was

[1] We are told that he "grew in wisdom" (Luke 2:52), which implies relative ignorance at least in his earlier years.
[2] Mark 24:36.

absolutely without sin. Human nature is not capable of omnipotence or omniscience; it is perhaps not capable of sinlessness. But Christ can be all the more surely our model of inspiration if we can think of him as facing life with only such resources and faculties as other men have, and yet making out of them so sublime a life.

Nor do we need to consider him as altogether unique in his divineness; if he said, "I and my father are one," he went on to pray that his disciples might be one with God even as he was. He summoned all men to the divine life, he thought of them all as sons of God; he was, as Paul said, but "the first born among many brethren," [1] the first to find the secret of life which was open to all. "As many as received him, to them gave he power to become the sons of God." [2] "The works that I do shall he do also, and greater works than these shall he do." [3] We all have a spark at least of the divine in us, and may aim to attain to the measure of the stature of the fullness of Christ.

> "Was Christ a man like us? Ah, let us try
> If we then too can be such men as he." [4]

We may not refuse to grant recognition to the divinity living in many a saint and prophet; there is no honor to Christ in setting him utterly apart from his brethren.

Nevertheless, as a matter of record, it was Christ who has done most to save men; his life remains in a sense unique in the realm of the spiritual. He not only lived his life divinely, but he has been ever since drawing men unto him. Many humble Christians have come close to the pattern; through their lives also God has been revealed. But after all, they are disciples; Christ was master. He blazed the

---

[1] Rom. 8: 29.   [2] John 1: 12.
[3] John 14: 12. Of course these sayings from the Fourth Gospel are not quoted as Christ's own words; but they may well echo genuine sayings.
[4] Matthew Arnold, *The Better Part*.

path; it is easier to follow. And such disciples are quickest to admit that they have fallen short of the pattern. "The difference between the Man of Galilee of the first century and the man of England and America in the nineteenth century, if I understand my gospels aright, is not in inherent capacity to draw near God, but in the relative degree of realization of a latent power common to humanity. It is this that has created the uniqueness of Jesus." [1]

Thus the doctrine of the Trinity, however foreign to our modern thought the terms in which the old creeds phrase it, has a very real basis in experience. If we try to regard it as the description of a quasi-human Being who is three persons and yet one, we may well balk at such an amazing example of the Greek genius for speculative subtleties. But if we take the conception in its inner and rational sense, we shall recognize that Christians attain to the vision of God in three leading ways — through the contemplation of the outer world, through obedience to the Holy Spirit in their hearts, and through faith in their Master Christ.

What is the nature of God as thus revealed?

God is usually conceived by the Christian as having consciousness, will, and emotions, as possessed of omniscience, omnipotence, and omnipresence, and as creator and ruler of the universe. Some of the arguments which are commonly offered in support of belief in these various attributes of God we shall discuss in due course. But it is only, at best, by some process of deduction that we can hope to arrive at such conceptions; as actually revealed in experience, God is — what we have just pointed out. God is the great Power that we see making for good in the world, that lives indestructibly in our own hearts, that burst into radiant flame in the soul

[1] Rev. Anson Phelps Stokes, in the *Outlook*, vol. 97, p. 505.

of Christ. The laws by which this Good works through the long evolutionary process we can dimly discern; its supreme importance we universally acknowledge; but what its ultimate nature, source, and goal may be is not writ upon the face of experience. We may then sympathize with Arnold's protest against the current "insane license of affirmation about God"; and, on the other hand, be tolerant and open-minded toward those conceptions of God — pantheistic, deistic, naturalistic, or what not — which are alien to that conception to which we have grown accustomed.[1]

But because we do not agree in our ideas of the objective nature of God, it by no means follows that there is any doubt of God's reality. On the contrary, when men call themselves atheists and speak of the belief in God as exploded, it is some specific and elaborated conception of God of which they are thinking, and which they mean to deny. And although belief or disbelief in the personality or the omnipotence of God, for example, is a matter for most serious thought, we must insist that to be unconvinced of these attributes is not at all to doubt the vital reality of God in the world and in our lives.[2] There are hypotheses about God,

[1] Cf. Arnold further (*Literature and Dogma*, pp. 10–11), "People use [the term "God"] as if it stood for a perfectly definite and ascertainable idea, from which we might, without more ado, extract propositions and draw inferences, just as we should from any other definite and ascertained idea. . . . But, in truth, the word 'God' is used in most cases as by no means a term of science or exact knowledge, but a term of poetry and eloquence, a term *thrown out*, so to speak, at a not fully grasped object of the speaker's consciousness, a *literary* term, in short; and mankind mean different things by it as their consciousness differs."

[2] Cf. Seeley, pp. 43–44, 104, 41, 50. "Controversies may be raised about the human as well as about the Divine Being. Some may consider the human body as the habitation of a soul distinct and separable from it; some may maintain that man is merely the collective name for a number of processes. . . . All these differences may be almost as important as they seem to the disputants who are occupied about them; but after all, they do not affect the fact that the human being is there, and they do not prevent us from regarding him with strong feelings. The same is true of the Divine

there may be a childlike trust in, say, Christ's conception of God, there may be a hundred reasons for pinning our faith to this or that theistic doctrine; but underneath these over-beliefs rests the basic fact that God exists — that there is an Ideal working itself out in the historic process, a great Power irresistibly drawing us on to some far off and unknown goal, and demanding our entire allegiance.

If we are tempted to become skeptical and discard the thought of God because we do not know what he is in himself, we must remember that we know nothing of what anything is in itself, except our own conscious stream as it passes. These material things that surround us we know only in terms of the qualities that our sense-organs give them. To a color-blind man the red flower is gray; to other eyes it might be blue; what is it for itself? We absolutely do not know. Or what is electricity? No one doubts its reality: we see it illuminating the arc-light, moving our trolley-cars, carrying our voices over the wires. But what *is* it? We talk of electrons, of the ether; but what are they? When we see the forked lightning, we say "electricity," we recognize the presence of a great power. When we see a sinner saved sud-

Being." "An age which is called atheistic, and in which atheism is loudly professed, shows in all its imaginative literature a religiousness — a sense of the Divine — which was wanting in the more orthodox ages. Before Church traditions had been freely tested, there was one rigid way of thinking about God. . . . Accordingly, when doubt was thrown upon the doctrines of the Church, there seemed an imminent danger of atheism, and we have still the habit of denoting by this name the denial of that conception of God which the Church has consecrated. But by the side of this gradual obscuring of the ecclesiastical view of God, there has gone on a gradual rediscovery of Him in another aspect. . . . The modern views of God, so far as they go, have a reality — a freshness that the others wanted. . . . His presence is felt really and not merely asserted in hollow professions." "Of atheism, that demoralizing palsy of human nature, which consists in the inability to discern in the Universe any law by which human life may be guided, there is in the present age less danger than ever." "Atheism in its full sense will become a thing impossible when no man shall be altogether without the sense, at once inspiring and sobering, of an eternal order."

denly from despair and filled with a humble consciousness of victory over sin, we say "God"; we recognize the presence of a power of vastly greater significance and far more worthy of our adoration. It is not a question of argument or proof, it is a question of sight; God is not a hypothesis but a fact.

Nor need we fret because our immediate knowledge of God is so limited; we know what it is necessary that we should know. We know that we are not alone in our endeavors, not futilely setting up mere subjective aspirations; the universe is on the side of our better selves. We know that at all costs we must follow the gleam.[1]

It would be foolish, then, and fraught with danger, to cease from thinking and speaking of God because much of unsophisticated man's thought of God is shown to be naïve and a projection of his own imagination. "To seek to discard, like some philosophers, the name of God and to substitute for it such a name as the Unknowable, will seem to a plain man, surely, ridiculous. For . . . no man could ever have cared anything about God in so far as he is simply unknowable. . . . Men cared about God for the sake of what they knew about him, not of what they did not. . . . It adds, indeed, to our awe of God that although we are able to know of him what so greatly concerns us, we know of him nothing more; but simply to be able to know nothing of him could beget in us no awe whatever. . . . Everything turns on its being at realities that this worship and its language are

[1] Cf. John Fiske, *Cosmic Philosophy*, vol. II, p. 470: "Deity is unknowable just in so far as it is not manifested to consciousness through the phenomenal world, — knowable just in so far as it is thus manifested . . . knowable, in a symbolic way, as the Power which is disclosed in every throb of the mighty rhythmic life of the universe; knowable as the eternal source of a Moral Law which is implicated with each action of our lives. . . . Thus, though we may not by searching find out God, though we may not compass infinitude or attain to absolute knowledge, we may at least know all that it concerns us to know, as intelligent and responsible beings."

aimed. Its anthropomorphic language about God is aimed at a vast, though ill-apprehended, reality." [1] God is a reality; and we must remember that though our actual experience of God be narrowly limited, he *may* none the less be all that the faith of the saints has deemed him to be — and how much more that we cannot now imagine, that it hath not entered into the mind of man to conceive! [2]

But however this may be, the important thing is, not to assent to the truth of God's existence, but to *feel* his reality and be dominated by it; to recognize a Law above our private wills, to cast aside all willfulness and cynicism and little-mindedness, to acknowledge the infinite worth of life and the infinite importance of duty. The true atheism is a want of belief in the meaning and value of life, a refusal to join forces with the great tides that are making for good in the world; a despair of human life and a deafness to its summons. There is no merit or value in a belief in God that makes no practical difference; the only important thing is to get into our lives the great experiences and the vital faith which that word connotes. For though our definitions of God be different, and our opinions about him vary from age to age, if we have the fear and love of God in our hearts, our theological opinions are of little moment.

[1] Arnold, *God and the Bible*, Preface. Cf. E. Renan, *Intolerance in Scepticism* (in *The Poetry of the Celtic Races and Other Studies*): "The word God being respected by humanity, having for it a long-acquired right, and having been employed in all beautiful poetry, to abandon it would be to overthrow all habits of language. Tell the simple to pass their lives in aspiration after truth, and beauty, and moral goodness; and your words will be meaningless to them. Tell them to love God, and not to offend God; and they will understand you perfectly. . . . Even supposing that for us philosophers another word were preferable, and without taking into account the fact that abstract words do not express real existence with sufficient clarity, there would be an immense inconvenience in thus cutting ourselves away from all the poetic sources of the past, and in separating ourselves by our language from the simple folk who worship so well in their own way."

[2] For our right to these further beliefs about God, see below, pp. 402–11.

God in human experience: T. H. Green, *Witness of God* (in *Two Sermons*). J. B. Pratt, *Psychology of Religious Belief*, chaps. IX–X. G. A. Coe, *Religion of a Mature Mind*, chap. XIII. M. Arnold, *Literature and Dogma*, chap. I. *God and the Bible*, Preface, and chaps. I–III. J. R. Seeley, *Natural Religion*, pt. I. W. E. Hocking, *Meaning of God in Human Experience*, pt. IV. O. Kuhns, *Sense of the Infinite*. H. A. Youtz, *Enlarging Conception of God. Hibbert Journal*, vol. 11, p. 394.

The Divinity of Christ: Traditionalistic: W. Sanday, *Christologies, Ancient and Modern.* W. N. Clarke, *Outline of Christian Theology*, pt. IV. O. A. Curtis, *The Christian Faith*, chaps. XVI–XVII. A. W. Moore, *Rational Basis of Orthodoxy*, chap. VII. J. Caird, *Fundamental Ideas of Christianity*, lectures XIII–XV. *Modern:* Foundations, chap. V. E. H. Rowland, *Right to Believe*, chap. IV. R. J. Campbell, *New Theology*, chaps. V, VII. J. V. Morgan, ed., *Theology at the Dawn of the Twentieth Century*, pp. 249–58. G. A. Gordon, *Christ of To-day.* Youtz, *op. cit.*, chap. VI. *New World*, vol. 1, p. 14. *Biblical World*, vol. 43, p. 295. *American Journal of Theology*, vol. 8, p. 9; vol. 11, p. 290; vol. 15, p. 584. *Outlook*, vol. 97, p. 503.

The Trinity: Traditionalistic: Clarke, *op. cit.*, pt. I, sec. IV; *The Christian Doctrine of God*, chap. II, sec. 7. Curtis, *op. cit.*, chap. XXXVI. *Modern:* Campbell, *op. cit.*, chap. VI. C. C. Everett, *Theism and the Christian Faith*, chap. XXVI. L. Abbott, *Letters to Unknown Friends*, p. 29 f. *American Journal of Theology*, vol. 12, p. 609; vol. 16, p. 528.

CHAPTER X

SACRIFICE AND SIN

INTIMATELY wrapped up with the concept of God are the allied concepts of sacrifice, sin, and salvation, which play a large rôle in the religious life. Born, like the idea of God, from the superstition and fear of primitive life, and having at the outset no spiritual value, these concepts have, like it, become gradually moralized until, in their highest expressions, they embody the noblest aspirations of the soul.

What is the history of the concepts of sacrifice and sin?

(1) Primitive sacrifice [1] was an outward and unspiritual act, performed in the hope of winning the favor of the gods or averting harm from them. Their disfavor is not at first attributed to men's sins, but is as capricious and irrational as the thunderbolts and storms and famines that are their weapons. Like the exacting and easily irritated tribal chiefs, they must be kept placated, must be propitiated if they become angry or for their own reasons threaten damage to the community or to the individual.[2] All important undertakings require their help, or at least their non-interference, and must therefore be initiated by some offering to them.[3] If the undertaking prospers, tribute must, in gratitude and with an eye to future favors, be awarded them.[4] If any act

---

[1] I do not mean to discuss the moot question, what the *earliest* form of sacrifice was. I am content to go back to the conceptions embodied in the earlier strata of the Old Testament.

[2] Cf. 1 Sam. 26:19. Gen. 8:20. Mal. 1:14.

[3] Gen. 46:1. Num. chap. 7.

[4] Gen. 4:3-4. Lev. 7:12; 21:29. Ps. 116:17.

unpleasing to them has been, however unwittingly, committed, it must be promptly expiated, by the sacrifice of something precious to the worshipers and therefore to them.[1] The commonest offering is that of food; the god enjoys the savory smell or in some invisible manner partakes of it.[2] This sharing of a meal with the god forms a bond between him and his worshipers; the notion of a blood-covenant thus ratified is found in many lands.[3]

So imminent loomed the potential wrath of the gods, and so anxiously was their assistance sought in the pressing struggles of early times, that among many peoples no animal food was eaten without the offering of a due share to them; and multitudes of priests lived at ease upon these offerings of their fellows' fear and credulity. In particular, any marked success might provoke the envy of the gods; or else it was due to their help; in either case it had to be followed by an apportionment to them of their share of the proceeds. The Jewish law required the sacrifice of the firstborn of every domestic animal, and the firstfruits of every harvest. Even the sacrifice of the firstborn child lingered into historic times in Israel; though as far back as the time of Abraham it had generally been commuted by the substitution of an animal.[4]

(2) Sacrifice as propitiation, tribute, or covenant has nothing religious, in the better sense of the word, about it; it is simply an act of worldly wisdom, involving no change of heart. Unhappily, such an unspiritual conception of sacrifice has not yet been entirely outgrown; the Jewish idea of the scapegoat[5] persists in the theological conception of

[1] Lev. 4:6; chap. 16.
[2] Gen. 8:21. Lev. 1:9, 13, 17. Ex. 29:18.
[3] Ex. 12:3 ff. Ps. 50:5.
[4] Cf. the reminiscence in Gen. 22:1–13. For lingering instances of human sacrifice, see 2 Kings 3:27; 17:31; 23:10. 2 Chron. 28:3. Ezek. 16:20–21. See *American Journal of Religious Psychology*, vol. 2, p. 24.
[5] See Lev. chap. 16.

SACRIFICE AND SIN

Christ as a propitiatory sacrifice to save men from the penalty justly attaching to their sins. But this merely exterior nature of sacrifice discredited it in the eyes of the great prophets of Israel, and they discarded it altogether. Jehovah, they said, desires mercy and not sacrifice. "Hath Jehovah as great delight in burnt offerings and sacrifices as in obeying the voice of Jehovah? Behold, to obey is better than sacrifice, and to hearken than the fat of rams." "Sacrifice and offering thou hast no delight in." "Thou delightest not in sacrifice, else would I give it; thou hast no pleasure in burnt-offering." "To do righteousness and justice is more acceptable to Jehovah than sacrifice." "What unto me is the multitude of your sacrifices, saith Jehovah; wash you, make you clean, cease to do evil, learn to do well." "For I desire goodness and not sacrifice."[1] This point of view was taken by Christ; and the early Christians understood that the whole Jewish sacrificial system was definitely abrogated.[2]

(3) But while this tendency to let the ancient custom of sacrifice lapse prevailed ultimately among most peoples, among the Jews and Christians another idea won its way, namely, the transformation of sacrifice from an outward to an inward matter. Some of the keenest Hebrew moralists made effective use of the old phraseology and ingrained habits of the people by demanding, not the abolition of sacrifice, but the substitution of a new and higher form of sacrifice. "Offer sacrifices of righteousness." "The sacrifices of God are a broken spirit; a broken and a contrite heart, O God, thou wilt not despise."[3] And this new conception, blending admirably with the Christian gospel, found notable expression in apostolic teaching. What was demanded by

---

[1] 1 Sam. 15:22. Ps. 40:6; 51:16. Prov. 21:3. Isa. 1:11. Hos. 6:6. Cf. also Amos 5:21 ff. Mic. 6:6 ff. Jer. 6:20.

[2] Cf., e.g., Matt. 9:13. Mark 12:33. Heb. 10:4.

[3] Deut. 33:19. Ps. 4:5; 51:17.

God was no longer a material gift, the renunciation of some worldly possession, but the gift of a pure and loving heart, the renunciation of selfish and sensual desires. "I beseech you, therefore, brethren, to present your bodies a living sacrifice, holy, acceptable to God — which is your rational worship." "To do good and to share forget not; for with such sacrifices God is well pleased."[1] To-day in the venerable Greek and Roman Catholic churches the primitive conception of penance and propitiation still to some extent persists; but wherever liberal conceptions of Christianity prevail it has been quite supplanted by the more rational and spiritual idea. God does not need to be appeased; we need to be cleansed. The eternal laws of life demand sacrifice — not for those laws' sake, but because, ultimately, human welfare itself requires it. And however pathetic and futile have been most of the renunciations demanded throughout the course of history in the name of religion, man has been through them stumbling and groping toward the great truth that the best way of life is the way of sacrifice of desire — that he must lose his life who would truly find it.

Parallel with this evolution of the idea of sacrifice has gone an evolution of the idea of sin. Early religion everywhere includes a sense of frequent transgression, with an accompanying fear of disaster, attempts at purification, and anguish of heart.[2] There was little thought of why an act

[1] Rom. 12:1. Heb. 13:16.

[2] Cf. E. L. Schaub, in *Harvard Theological Review*, vol. 5, p. 123: "While the extent and nature of the particular acts that are considered sinful naturally vary with differences in intellectual and spiritual development, the consciousness of sin itself, in some form or other and to some degree, is, anthropology seems to teach, universal to all peoples of whom we have definite knowledge. There is always a more or less explicit consciousness of a discrepancy between our actual life and conduct and those ideals and postulates which urge themselves upon us as objectively valid."

SACRIFICE AND SIN

was wrong; it was simply taboo, it must not be done. Even acts that were necessary, such as the killing of enemies, the handling of sick people and corpses, midwifery, and the like, produced a feeling of aversion and pollution and a sense of the need of purification; the old Jewish laws are very exacting in their demands in all such cases. Mishaps were usually attributed to some, perhaps unconscious, impropriety; especially tribal catastrophes were a sign that something had been done amiss. As the gods came to be more and more clearly personified, these transgressions became distinctly offenses against them; to learn to obey their will became an elaborate art, bringing into being oracles, soothsayers, augurs, and the like. But still sin was an outward matter, denoting no more than ignorant blunder, heedless folly, forgetfulness or indifference; unwitting, even well-intentioned or unavoidable transgression brought on its penalty as well as perverse or passionate disobedience.[1] The sense of sin was simply the uneasy feeling of having incurred punishment; and the rituals of purification had for their object to wipe off a stain as material as blood upon the hands.

Here, too, however, the vision of the Hebrew prophets saw clearly; to them the important matter was not the outward act, but the inward loyalty or disobedience. Purity became a matter, not of proper observance, but of intent, of the direction of desire and the meditations of the heart. Jesus put it in classic form in his saying, "There is nothing from without the man that going into him can defile him; but the things which proceed out of the man are those that defile him. . . . For from within, out of the heart of men, evil thoughts proceed . . . and defile the man."[2]

A similar moralization of the concept of sin and purity is

[1] Cf. the case of Uzzah, who was struck dead by Jehovah for his apparently well-meant, and surely very natural and instinctive, movement to prevent the sacred Ark from toppling over. 2 Sam. 6: 6–7. 1 Chron. 13: 9–10.
[2] Mark 7: 14–23.

to be traced in other religions. In the Buddhist scriptures we read, "Neither abstinence from fish or flesh, nor going naked, nor shaving the head ... nor sacrifices to Agni, will cleanse a man. Reading the Vedas, making offerings to priests ... these do not cleanse a man. Anger, drunkenness, obstinacy, bigotry ... these constitute uncleanness."[1] In the *Zend Avesta*, "Purity is for man, next to life, the highest good; that purity, O Zarathustra, that is in the religion of Mazda for him who cleanses himself with good thoughts, words, and deeds." And in the later Hellenic religion we have sentiments like this from the Golden Song of Hierocles, "Purity of soul is the only divine service." Thus from a superstitious uneasiness at vague and ill-understood dangers, and a frantic search for deliverance from impinging pollution, there was evolved here and there in the clearing consciousness of men a loathing of those acts and desires that led them from their own ideals and blurred their vision of God.

What are their dangers?

The Emperor Julian, cleaving, in a world rapidly growing Christian, to the sturdy pagan ideals, scorning the sentimentalism and self-distrust which was becoming the fashion, is reported to have said on his deathbed, "I die without remorse, as I have lived without sin." And many a modern thinker — Sir Oliver Lodge is one of the latest — has said that men ought to concern themselves little with sin and sacrifice, but rather with positive effort and achievement. Certainly the sense of sin and the pursuit of purity have had their distortions and dangers for men; what these are we may now pause to note.

(1) Too dominant a sense of sin adds a burden to life that may overbalance the gain won through the resulting power

[1] *Amagandha Sutta*, 7:11.

over temptation, and indeed may even paralyze effort. Religious chronicles are full of the distress and overconscientiousness and despair of reasonably good men. St. Paul could call himself the chief of sinners;[1] and a hundred parallels could be found in the utterances of the saints to his outburst, "I know that in me, that is, in my flesh, dwelleth no good thing; for to will is present with me, but to do that which is good, is not. For the good that I would I do not, but the evil that I would not, that I do. . . . For I delight in the law of God in the inward man, but I see a different law in my members, warring against the law of my mind, and bringing me into captivity under the law of sin which is in my members. O wretched man that I am! who shall deliver me out of this mortal body?"[2] Modern church liturgies are full of such sentiments as, "We have all sinned and there is no health in us." "Lord have mercy upon us, miserable sinners!" There is in this groveling and self-distrusting attitude a lack of grit or nerve which revolts the manly soul; and religion, countenancing such flabby self-abasement, has seemed to many a morbid and sickly affair.

(2) The longing for purity has led some men to a futile asceticism, wherein a cruel self-repression has been practiced, apart from its excuse in the real needs of life. St. Simeon Stylites on his pillar, the whirling dervishes of India, the self-torturing Mohammedan fanatics, the hermits, with their ceaseless scourgings and fastings and mortifications of the flesh, — these have distorted the true spirit of religion, which should bring men life, and life more abundantly. "An overemphasis upon self-denial sacrifices unnecessarily the sweetness and richness of life, stunts it, distorts it, robs it of its natural fruition. The denial of any satisfaction is cruel except as it is necessary. Purity carried to a needless ex-

[1] If, indeed, the saying is actually Paul's; 1 Tim. 1: 15.
[2] Rom. 7 : 18–24.

treme became celibacy; the virtue of frugality became the vice of a starvation diet, producing the emaciated and weakened saints. The attempt radically to alter and repress human nature is nearly always disastrous. Most of the ascetics had to pass their days in constant struggles against their temptations; and many of them recurrently lapsed into wild orgies of sin, the result of pent-up impulses denied their natural channels."[1] A pure religion rejects these deformations of its spirit. In so far as renunciation is necessary it brings to it a gladness of endurance; beyond that stern necessity it bids us not repress but develop our natures; it comes not to destroy but to fulfill.

(3) Another distortion to which the striving for purity is subject lies in the extreme of unworldliness. Worldliness consists in forgetting the ends of life in absorption in the means. The business man who gives his whole thought to making money without learning to use it well, the ambitious politician who spends his life in seeking office without thinking how through the office he may serve the people, the woman who devotes her days to dressmakers and milliners, all those whose minds are occupied with the mere instruments and mechanism of life, are choked with the tares of worldliness. They may live on a higher plane than the idler or *débauché;* they may escape the worst pitfalls of life; but they do not attain to its highest rewards. The unworldly man sees deeper into life, lays hold of the eternal things; if he seeks wealth or fame, or cultivates society, it is for the ideal ends he can attain therethrough, for the better service of his fellows or of God.

So far unworldliness is good. But it may easily go too far, becoming a dread of contamination by the ordinary machinery of life. When the longing to keep himself unspotted from the world leads a man to become a hermit or an idle monk,

[1] Durant Drake, *Problems of Conduct,* p. 121.

to spend his days in useless vigils and prayers instead of using his strength for active service, it may bring him an inner peace; it may, by removing him from temptation, keep him from positive sin; but it leaves him a useless encumbrance upon the earth. The truly religious man, though not of the world is yet in it, sharing its burdens, meeting its temptations, willingly letting himself be tainted, if need be, by its dirt and squalor, so his arm can be of use and his determination avail in some degree for his fellows. The anchoritic and monastic ideals of the Middle Ages did enormous harm in absorbing the spiritual enthusiasm of the men who might otherwise have put their energies and idealism into regenerating in some measure the life of the age.[1]

What is their permanent value?

Morbid and perverted in such ways the sense of sin and the longing for purity may become. We should by all means seek to avoid these excesses and to cultivate something of the healthy common sense of the Greeks, while following the deeper insight and finer ideals of Christianity. But if not carried too far, the sense of sin and the sting of remorse are valuable auxiliaries to the positive religious impulse, never without need of every form of help. For after all is said, the power of temptation still remains strong for poor stumbling human nature; and the religious life must be for most men a militant life. If we agree with Arnold that "All thinking about [sin] beyond what is indispensable for the firm effort to get rid of it is waste of energy and waste of time," we must also realize the truth of his further words, "This sense of sin, however, it is also possible to have not strongly enough to beget the firm effort to get rid of it."[2] The danger of our

[1] For an estimate of the good and evil in monasticism, see H. B. Workman, *The Evolution of the Monastic Ideal*; J. O. Hannay, *Spirit and Origin of Christian Monasticism*.

[2] Matthew Arnold, *St. Paul and Protestantism*, chap. i.

times lies rather in this latter direction, in ceasing to think enough of the awfulness of sin. This at least can be confidently said: if our theory of life includes no sacrifice, no stern self-repression, if it makes life out to be an easy task and offers impulse and passion right of way, it is a mistaken theory. Success in life is not to be so cheaply bought. The prohibition is not external but internal, inherent in the very structure of human nature; sin is the wreck of life, and purity its natural ideal.[1]

Religion has, therefore, been right, not only in demanding instant and unquestioning obedience to the right, but in bidding a man hate the wrong and label it by an odious name. His inner conflicts are thereafter no longer between two opposing impulses that differ only in relative worth, they are between Right and Wrong, between Duty and Sin. The first stage of the religious life begins at the point when a man accepts what were else merely an expedient manner of life as unconditionally binding upon him, as the will of God. The highest stage is reached when all his random and mistaken impulses are eradicated, when he no longer desires to follow anything but the right, and out of the snare of temptation has emerged into the blessedness that belongs to the pure in heart. But because absolute purity is beyond the attainment of mortal men, religion lies chiefly along the road, in the yearning and aspiring life, that is not content with any compromise with evil, but struggles ever on and on

[1] Cf. W. James, *Varieties of Religious Experience*, p. 51: "When all is said and done, we are in the end absolutely dependent on the universe; and into sacrifices and surrenders of some sort, deliberately looked at and accepted, we are drawn and pressed as into our only permanent positions of repose. Now in those states of mind which fall short of religion, the surrender is submitted to as an imposition of necessity, and the sacrifice is undergone at the very best without complaint. In the religious life, on the contrary, surrender and sacrifice are positively espoused; even unnecessary givings up are added in order that happiness may increase. Religion thus makes easy and felicitous what in any case is necessary."

toward perfection. From the first conception of an objective duty that has authority over his subjective caprices and personal desires, a duty grudgingly and heavily obeyed, religion develops into an ardent pursuit of righteousness, a happy and whole-hearted dedication to an ideal of life.

The saints and the great religious teachers have been those who have loved purity and seen the beauty of holiness. In the Psalms, in the teachings of Jesus, in the letters of Paul, we have the classic expressions of delight in the law of righteousness. Renunciation, instead of being a grim necessity, is welcomed with open arms; self-denial is no longer a yoke and a burden, to be borne because there is no way of escape, it has become the deepest desire of the heart. Such is the temper of the deeply religious man: he loves Duty not only because it is the only path to sustained happiness, but for its own glorious sake. He says, —

> "I give nothing as duties,
> What others give as duties I give as living impulses."

The ultimate goal of the religious life — of any worthy life — is indeed service, achievement; but achievement unspotted and unhampered by selfishness, by sensuality, by worldliness and sin. All indolence and frivolity, all coarseness and dissipation, all gluttony and immoderation and drunkenness and lust, are its eternal enemies. From the clutch of these passions man climbs toward the heights where he shall no longer hear the seductive voice of temptation, where his will shall be in harmony with the will of God, the will which the ideal of his life prescribes. Between these two poles of the animal life and the ideal life lies his pilgrim's progress; from the world of unchecked inclination he journeys over a long and toilsome road, with much effort and travail of spirit, to the spiritual world, which is the world of perfected human nature.

The doctrine of Original Sin

To the great idealists sin has often appeared not merely as an individual matter but as a universal inheritance and burden; the Hebrew prophets, for example, were sweeping in their denunciation of the general wickedness of men. That this omnipresent wickedness dated back to the first man and was due to his original fall from innocence, came to be a popularly accepted belief. We find it in some of the Apocryphal writings that preceded the Christian era; and Paul fitted it into his conglomerate theological structure. "As through one man sin entered into the world, and death through sin, and so death passed unto all men, for that all sinned — as through the one man's disobedience the many were made sinners, even so through the obedience of the One shall the many be made righteous." Such an assertion of universal depravity was plausible in that age, when the old virtues were tottering and the new had only begun to appear. To Paul it was a matter of plain observation: "Jews and Greeks — they are all under sin; as it is written, there is none righteous, no, not one." On himself the curse equally rested — "I delight, in my heart, in the law of God; but I see a different law in my body, warring against the law of my mind, and bringing me into captivity under the law of sin which is in my body." Under this curse "the whole creation groaneth and travailleth till now."[1]

To Paul the important matter was the fact of universal sinfulness and the need of salvation; Adam was useful rhetorically, to contrast with Christ — the first sinner with the first sinless man. But the Christian fathers, with their hunger for theoretical precision, crystallized his hints into a hard-and-fast doctrine of Original Sin. Adam's sin has demoralized the race; his guilt is transmitted to us all, and

[1] Rom. 5: 12–19; 3: 9–23; 7: 14–25; 8: 22.

we are hopelessly entangled unless the supernatural grace of Christ is accepted. St. Augustine, in particular, converted in middle life after a youth whose wildness he afterward, by a natural psychological tendency, exaggerated into unrelieved blackness, saddled upon the Church the conviction of man's natural depravity.[1]

But as times grew gentler and men more humane, this gloomy view of human nature was bound to give way. Particularly in America, with its unbounded hopes and its freedom from old-world problems, the sense of the natural goodness of man, already vigorously preached by the eighteenth century romanticists, became dominant; and the official pessimistic doctrine of the Church appeared a sad and chilling untruth. "The progress of society," said Channing, "is retarded by nothing more than by the low views which its leaders are accustomed to take of human nature." "It is a duty to estimate highly the nature which God has given. It should be regarded with reverence, rather than contempt."[2] And Emerson cried out impatiently to his Divinity School listeners, "None believeth in the soul of man, but only in some man or person old and departed."

To the modern man there is evidently truth on both sides of the controversy. Man is neither inherently bad nor inherently good. No impulse or instinct is in itself evil; but any may lead to evil if undisciplined and unrestrained. We do inherit tendencies that bring pain and wrong and premature death; from the burden of these passions men have universally longed to be delivered. We do start handicapped

[1] See G. F. Wiggers, *Historical Presentation of Augustinism from the Original Sources;* F. R. Tennant, *Sources of the Doctrine of the Fall and Original Sin;* Jonathan Edwards, *The Doctrine of Original Sin Defended;* Jeremy Taylor, *Scripture Doctrine of Original Sin.* For a modern interpretation of the doctrine see J. Royce, *Problem of Christianity,* vol. I, chap. III. For a modern criticism, see Edmond Holmes, *In Defence of What Might Be,* chap. II; J. J. Hall, *Evolution and the Fall;* and the literature of Eugenics.
[2] *Mem.* I, 288.

and hampered by this common human inheritance; we are all potentially sinful before our first sinful act, there is in us a predisposition to evil. The doctrine of the Fall puts into the form of a single historical incident what is really a general truth about human nature — the fact that its present state does not correspond to its real estate. Not only the Hebrews, with their unusually acute consciousness of shortcoming or imperfection, but many other races, have postulated a golden age in the past wherein this discordance did not exist. Anthropology discredits such an idea; there has not been any general degeneration. But universally, practice does not correspond to ideal. A truer formulation of the fact which the doctrine of the Fall has sought to explain would be to say that man has not *fallen*, he has never *risen* to his potentialities, or found the life of happiness and power that might be his.

But if there is weakness and imperfection in us all, there is also much good in us all; any normal child, if rightly trained, and subjected to just the right influences, could become a saint. If some seem so hopelessly fallen as to need supernatural grace, it is for lack of the proper influences at the right time. Environment is more responsible than heredity. Nor need we trouble ourselves about predestination and election. Some undoubtedly start better off than others; modern science is showing why, and pointing the way toward an ultimate improvement. In this matter we have more to learn from eugenics than from theology. We shall always have to fight against the evil tendencies inseparable from human nature; but proper breeding and training of the human species can remove from the situation most of its hopeless aspects. The doctrine of the inevitable sinfulness of man has had its day.

Historical: L. R. Farnell, *Evolution of Religion*, chap. III. F. B. Jevons, *Sacrifice* (in *Introduction to the Study of Comparative Reli-*

SACRIFICE AND SIN

gion). W. R. Smith, *Religion of the Semites*, lectures VI–XI. P. V. N. Myers, *History as Past Ethics*, chap. XIII. C. H. Toy, *Judaism and Christianity*, chap. IV. A. Lang, *Custom and Myth*, pp. 105–20. *American Journal of Theology*, vol. 4, p. 257.

Traditionalistic: O. A. Curtis, *The Christian Faith*, chaps. XIV–XV. W. N. Clarke, *Outline of Christian Theology*, pt. III. C. A. Beckwith, *Realities of Christian Theology*, chap. V.

Modern: W. E. Orchard, *Modern Theories of Sin*. E. S. Ames, *Psychology of Religious Experience*, chap. VII. G. B. Cutten, *Psychological Phenomena of Christianity*, chap. XI. F. J. Peabody, *Jesus Christ and the Christian Character*, chaps. III–IV. G. A. Coe, *Religion of a Mature Mind*, chap. XII. G. Santayana, *Reason in Religion*, chaps. X–XI. J. Royce, *Problem of Christianity*, vol. I, chaps. III, V. J. Martineau, *Studies in Christianity*, pp. 466–77. W. de W. Hyde, *Sin and its Forgiveness*. C. C. Everett, *Theism and the Christian Faith*, chaps. XXI–XXII. F. R. Tennant, *Concept of Sin*. R. Mackintosh, *Christianity and Sin*. *Schaff-Herzog Encyclopedia*, arts. *Sin*, *Sacrifice*. *Harvard Theological Review*, vol. 5, p. 121.

CHAPTER XI

SALVATION, CONVERSION, AND ATONEMENT

What is the meaning of salvation?

IDEALLY, there ought to be no need of salvation for men; education and eugenics should breed a race of men adapted to their environment and able to live in harmony and inner peace. This, however, is but a remote ideal; actually, most men have consciously failed in adjustment somewhere, and felt the need of salvation. Most men at one time or other have cried out as Paul did, "To will is present with me, but to do that which is good is not.... Wretched man that I am, who shall deliver me from this body of death!" To the felt need of deliverance from sin there has generally been added the dread of the punishment of sin, the fear of future retribution. To be saved meant to the early Christian propagandists the promise of admittance to the Messianic Kingdom shortly to be set up by Christ; to the modern evangelist it means escape from the torments of hell and the hope of sharing the delights of heaven. But this aspect of salvation need not concern us here;[1] it has varied with the differing conceptions of God and the future life, and has necessarily been a matter of speculation or faith rather than of actual experience. What we have to consider is rather the means of escape from sin here and now; a matter as to which practically the whole human race are in the same case, and which can be discussed independently of theological or eschatological dogmas.

There is a modern tendency to discard the terms "salva-

[1] The question of the future life will be discussed in chap. XXIV.

tion," "conversion," "regeneration," and the like, because they have become colored for most of us by theological presuppositions and often applied to acts and forms which have no real spiritual value. Baptism, partaking of the wine and bread, confession, joining the church, profession of belief, — such outward acts are symbolical and suggestive, but have no direct intrinsic efficacy. All assumption by any church of power to save men or to pronounce them saved, except as they actually experience an inward change, is sheer insolence. Nor can we in these days hold that only Christians have been saved — a mere handful out of the myriads of men and women who have peopled the earth. Salvation, deliverance from sin, is open to all. Jew and Christian, Brahman and Buddhist, have felt alike the need of it; and by all the great faiths the way of salvation has in some measure been found: in some measure — for there are degrees of salvation. We can no longer separate men into sheep and goats, the saved and the lost; moral differences are infinitely numerous, and no man is wholly good or bad. There are indeed cases of abrupt transition from great sinfulness to purity; but more often salvation has to be worked out gradually through years of effort and failure.[1]

Yet, if it is true that salvation has come in greater or lesser degree to multitudes of men of all faiths, it is also true that it has come in most striking measure through Christ. No other power ever let loose in the world has accomplished nearly so much in freeing men from the bondage of sin as the power of his life and death. The great highroad of deliver-

---

[1] Cf. James, *Varieties*, pp. 238–39: "The real witness of the spirit to the 'second birth' is to be found only in the disposition of the genuine child of God, the permanently patient heart, the love of self eradicated. And this, it has to be admitted, is also found in those who pass no crisis, and may even be found outside of Christianity altogether.... No chasm exists between the orders of human excellence, but here as elsewhere nature shows continuous differences, and generation and regeneration are matters of degree."

ance for sin-ridden men is that of overcoming evil with good; a great love, a great loyalty, can banish temptations against which a direct struggle is futile. So a spiritual union with Christ has for millions wrought that transformation of character which we call regeneration; and the surest way to save men who have sunk far into sin has proved to be, after winning their will to repent, to bring them to Christ.

What is the meaning and value of conversion?

When a man, after a life of indifference to spiritual values, is suddenly saved from such religious apathy, roused to a new set of interests, delivered from the power of sin — and therefore from its consequences, natural or supernatural — we call him converted. "Conversion" means, literally, a "turning round"; the term is usually restricted to cases of a turning from a lower to a higher level of life.[1] Conversion is not by any means always accompanied by extremes of nervous excitement; on the contrary, the process is usually quiet enough in outward manifestation. It is by no means always abrupt; rather, it may be so gradual as to have no special significant moments to mark the change of heart. There are all sorts of types, from that of the convert who is thrown into unconsciousness by the stress of battling emotions to that of the man who, though truly religious, is conscious of no conversion at all, but seems to have always cared for the best

---

[1] Starbuck defines it as follows (p. 156): "Conversion is suddenly forsaking the lower for the higher self. In terms of the neural basis of consciousness, it is the inhibition of lower channels of nervous discharge through the establishment of higher connections and the identification of the ego with the new activities." James defines it (p. 189) as, "The process, gradual or sudden, by which a self hitherto divided, and consciously wrong, inferior, and unhappy, becomes unified, and consciously right, superior, and happy, in consequence of its firmer hold upon religious realities." And (p. 196), "To say that a man is 'converted' means that religious ideas, previously peripheral in his consciousness, now take a central place, and that religious aims form the habitual centre of his energy."

SALVATION, CONVERSION, AND ATONEMENT

things. There is not necessarily any sharp line between the converted and the unconverted; if a child is rightly trained, and grows up into the Christian life, he will need no turning-round. Only those who have become addicted to wrong habits, who have gone so far astray that they have, for the time, lost the power or inclination to follow virtue, need such a right-about-face, such a forcible shaking out of their old ruts and turning to a new direction.

Yet conversion has played a large part in Christianity, and rightly so. For to most of us, however outwardly blameless our lives have been, there comes at some time or other the vision of a higher spiritual level on which we might live; and even with the best of training the average child is naturally self-centered and but slightly, if at all, religious. There comes commonly a moment when the youth or maiden realizes as never before the meaning of life and its duties, and turns from a hitherto half-unconscious selfishness to a conscious devotion to the duties which love and religion demand. Professor Starbuck, who, in his valuable *Psychology of Religion*, has collected many statistics of the various types of conversion, is decided in his affirmation that it is a normal accompaniment of adolescence. The period of the teens is naturally a time of profound mental upheaval, the most critical period of life, when the youth, yet plastic, is forming his character and choosing his ideals. Many primitive religions took advantage of this transition period to awaken the dormant instincts of the young and enlist their loyalty; the Christian Church should certainly aim to reach and influence them at that susceptible age.[1] It is by no means true that children are radically and inevitably sinful until a super-

[1] "The Church," says Starbuck, "takes the adolescent tendencies and builds upon them; it sees that the essential thing in adolescent growth is bringing the person out of childhood into the new life. . . . It accordingly brings those means to bear which will intensify the normal tendencies. It shortens up the period of storm and stress."

natural grace has transformed them; in normal cases they should grow imperceptibly into a spontaneous religious life. But that religious life can usually, at the right moments, be greatly stimulated by appropriate suggestion, in forms varying with the individual need.

To those who have passed through such a quickening and illuminating experience, it naturally seems important that others should feel it also. And so some Christian churches — notably the Methodist — have proclaimed a process of this sort necessary and have refused their fellowship to those who cannot profess to have undergone it. Their methods of fostering the experience have become stereotyped; its particular form in a given church is largely determined by imitation or suggestion. This specific type of experience is then expected of all who are to belong to that church; and every one in that circle who yearns at all toward religion feels in duty bound to go through this experience, or to persuade himself that he has gone through it. It is an interesting side-light on human suggestibility, this readiness with which a certain measure of conformity is attained, in experiences which appear so individual and spontaneous. But it is generally to be noted that an elaborate and skillful technique has been employed to produce precisely such manifestations; and they usually occur under the influence of contagion. The danger is, of course, that it degenerate into a perfunctory and mechanical ceremony with the great numbers who are not mentally ready for just that type of experience. But we must never forget that the form without the spirit is worthless; conversion is not actual unless there is a real change of attitude, a new dedication of the heart, once wavering or indifferent, to the religious life.

We are accustomed, perhaps, to associate conversion with revivalistic orgies, with visions and voices, tears and exhortations, and intense emotional stress. In fact, there has been much of the abnormal, much of the irrational and disgusting, connected with Christian evangelism. But we should not despise methods, however repellent to our sensibilities, that have been efficacious in turning men from sensuality or selfishness to a godly life. The emotional outflows — shoutings and gesticulations, jerkings, hallelujahs, jumpings up and down, and the like — are natural enough. To overcome deeprooted habits of wrongdoing and direct a life into new channels may well involve much stress of spirit, be accompanied by deep emotions, and, in those of the proper temperament, by "automatisms" of various sorts — blinding flashes, luminous figures, voices, and kindred phenomena. Yet it is unfortunate that such abnormal experiences, experiences not accessible to all men, and not always of actual spiritual benefit, should ever have been deemed an essential mark of the Christian life. Christ certainly never required them; all that he demanded was, "Take up your cross and follow me." Many of the Christian churches have never encouraged cataclysmic conversion, but have instead elaborated a gradual process of religious education. But the apostle Paul and St. Augustine, perhaps the two men who had the greatest influence in controlling the direction of development of Christianity, were both men of psychopathic temperament, subject to these violent experiences; it is largely due to that fact that catastrophic conversion has seemed to some churches a necessary prelude to the Christian life.

From another point of view Christian evangelism has been often disparaged, namely, because its fruits are held to be but transitory, a mere ephemeral burst of emotion that when it ebbs leaves a man no better than before. But very many cases fall within the observation of any student of these phenomena in which the spiritual level has been permanently and strikingly raised as a result of the conversion experience. Backsliders there will be; and few can hope to retain through a long succession of common days the vision of their supreme moments. It is impossible to keep the glamour and the glow that go with "falling in love" through the humdrum years of married life; yet the radiance of that glorious period may bind the two into an eternal union. So the great moments when the soul passionately espouses the religious life should, and often do, effect a permanent raising of the level of the whole subsequent life. And any one who has once known the joy and peace of the Christian spirit, even if for a few days or hours only, can never wholly forget that blessed time, and is forever after more receptive to religious pleading than one who has never, even for a moment, caught the vision of that better Way.

Space is lacking for a description of the very various types of the conversion experience. But one great distinction we must note. William James has familiarized us with this distinction, between Volitional Conversion, as he termed it, and Conversion by Self-Surrender. The former type is that of those who attain the new level of life by an agony of struggle and sweat and constantly renewed consecration, who need to retain the militant attitude toward sin. The latter type includes those who best attain the higher life by surrendering themselves at the critical moment to its power. A profound sense of impotence and despair is followed abruptly, in these cases, by a wave of joy and a sense of victory. The prior discouragement is often intensified by the lurid preaching of the evangelist, the doctrinal obsession of the natural sinfulness and helplessness of human nature, and the fear of impending punishment; when the final release comes, the relaxation of pressure and conviction of salvation produces by contrast a keen joy; the self is no longer divided, the struggle is over.[1] This type of mental process produces

[1] This second type of conversion will be further discussed, in the following chapter, in connection with the inquiry into the nature of faith. See pp. 180–86.

SALVATION, CONVERSION, AND ATONEMENT

obviously the most striking cases; and some Christian bodies have held it to be the only genuine form of conversion. But, after all, what the particular type of conversion is, matters little; it is only a question of the most efficacious means to an end. The ultimately important thing is not how a man is converted, but what he is converted to.[1]

There are dangers in the practice of evangelism. There is the danger of encouraging a mere emotionalism, divorced from sane and accurate thinking; and of fostering erroneous doctrines through their alliance with such stimulating emotions. There is the danger of making the conversion experience an end in itself, producing little fruit in an altered life. There is the danger of making religion appear something apart from normal life, something violent and absurd and repugnant to people of refinement and common sense. There is the danger of stereotyping the conversion experience till the converts go through it perfunctorily, like so many sheep, as a necessary doorway to the church, without its having a vital meaning to them or being a genuine and organic part of their own life. There is the danger of stimulating an abnormal craving for excitement, which may satisfy itself upon a later occasion in some disastrous way. There is the danger of neglecting, through reliance upon conversion, the normal processes of religious education. Nevertheless, properly

[1] Cf. Coe, p. 144: "The ultimate test of religious values is nothing psychological, nothing definable in terms of *how it happens*, but something ethical, definable only in terms of *what is attained*." And Bishop McConnell (in *Constructive Quarterly*, vol. 1, pp. 135–36): "We no longer lay stress upon incidental and accidental features in religious experience.... The essential is the new life itself, and the emphasis should be on the features which seem to make for larger life in the most natural and normal fashion. ... All these experiences are subject to psychological law. The problem in Christian life is to bring the psychological movement under *moral* law, to make the emotional reaction come out of moral purpose and lead to the moral control of the will." Both of these writers, it may be noted, are prominent living Methodist ministers, one a professor in a leading theological school, the other a bishop of the church.

controlled and directed, the practice of abrupt conversion may be of enormous value; because it has been misunderstood and abused, we need by no means utterly discard it.[1]

The doctrine of the Atonement

Through Christ men were saved; that was the great fact that illuminated the early Christian preaching. The old sacrificial systems were done away with; priests and burnt offerings were finally and forever displaced by the One Saviour. The good news consisted largely in the relief from former burdens. But there was also the positive gospel: somehow by Christ's life or sacrificial death the power of sin had been broken, and the New Life had been opened up to men. Redemption was an actual experience — which merged into a greater hope. But what was the objective side to this subjective fact? *How* were men saved through Christ? Paul and the earliest Christian teachers, being almost exclusively practical in their interests, left the matter open; there is no definite theory of redemption or atonement in the Bible. But the later theologians found in the rhetoric of these earliest preachers many a suggestion and metaphor that served as scriptural basis for their various theories.

(1) The earliest theory to obtain wide currency was that of a price paid to the Devil. That the power of the Evil One had been broken was clear; and the words "redeem," "ransom," etc., appear frequently in the primitive teaching.[2] Irenæus and Origen developed, with the relentless logic of the theologian, the apparent implications of these terms. Satan had won, by the successful temptation of Adam, a right to the souls of men; he held them as his captives. Over Christ, however, because of his sinlessness, he had no power;

---

[1] Some of the theological inferences drawn from the conversion experience will be discussed below, on pp. 322–25.

[2] Cf. Matt. 20:28. Mark 10:45. Titus, 2:14. 1 Pet. 1:18. Col. 2:15. Heb. 2:14–15.

and by causing him to be put to death he made himself in turn liable to a penalty, and had to forfeit his claim over his former prisoners. Christ's death was, then, a price paid for the souls of men; the transaction was variously thought of as a bargain, or as a stratagem; at any rate, the Devil was outwitted and spoiled of his prey. Variant forms of this ransom-theory were formulated by St. Jerome, St. Augustine, St. Bernard, and other pillars of the church; it has not yet wholly faded from Christian thought.

(2) This dualism, however, this struggle between God and Devil for the souls of men, was repugnant to many Christians; and the learned doctor Anselm, in answer to his famous question, *Cur Deus homo?* propounded the legal theory. According to this, the Devil had no rights which God was bound to respect. But the guilt of sin had to be somehow atoned for to maintain God's honor and satisfy his sense of justice. Christ offered himself, to bear man's punishment in his stead; God accepted the substitution; man can therefore go free. The theory was worked out by Thomas Aquinas, and became the dominant Christian conception. It is embodied by Milton in the lines, —

> "Man, . . . losing all,
> To expiate his treason hath naught left,
> But, to destruction sacred and devote,
> He with his whole posterity must die; —
> Die he or Justice must; unless for him
> Some other, able, and as willing, pay
> The rigid satisfaction, death for death."

This theory, however, with its picture of God as the stern and relentless judge, was also opposed from the beginning; Socinus once for all showed the weakness of its judicial fictions, and it has been pretty widely abandoned by the Church as immoral. That God should insist upon "justice," i.e., upon a full measure of punishment for every sin, and be unable or unwilling simply to forgive and forget wrongdoing, — which is the result of the instincts and impulses with which men are endowed, and is usually wretched enough in itself, without added punishment, — has to the sympathetic and sensitive seemed incredible. That prior to Christ's suffering he should have damned poor ignorant men to torments in hell, and should still exact that frightful penalty of them except as they realize their situation and consciously accept Christ's vicarious sacrifice, is a doctrine too awful for the modern taste. The revenge-conception of punishment has been abandoned in inter-human relations; and the humaner spirit of the times demands an equally humane God. We see too clearly the causes of sin; we pity the sinner and seek to reform him; if we imprison him it is only to restrain him from further wrongdoing, to bring better influences to bear upon him, and to deter others from similar folly. Any punishment beyond what is necessary for these ends is sheer cruelty. Moreover, if God's relations to men are to be conceived in terms of criminal law, if we must at all costs have justice, *is* it justice to punish myriads of men for Adam's sin — even granting that sin to be far more heinous than it would naturally appear? And what sort of justice is it that could be satisfied with the punishing of one innocent man and the free pardon of myriads of guilty men? The theory seems a remnant of the ancient idea that the gods need to be placated; but by the side of the pagan gods, who were content with humble offerings of flesh and fruit, the Christian God, demanding the suffering and death of his own Son, appears a monster of cruelty.

(3) As far back as Abelard, in the twelfth century, the "moral influence theory" had its exponents; and it has been gradually, if slowly, winning its way in the Church.[1]

---

[1] Cf. for a modern expression of it, Sabatier, pp. 94–95: "The redemptive element is to be found, not in the death of Christ, but in the power and brilliancy of his religious consciousness, to the benefits of which we are

According to it, the power of the death of Christ lay in its awakening in men an answering love powerful enough to conquer their sinfulness. That sacrifice was necessary, not to pay the Devil or to placate God; it was psychologically necessary, to stir men's hearts and arouse their latent powers. Christ's life was saving; if his death was necessary, it was as a capstone and climax to his life of sacrifice. Historically, his teaching failed to win many adherents; the uttermost sacrifice was needed. And that death on the cross actually proved the saving fact. By it, not by his sinless life, was Paul impressed; it was the preaching of the cross that converted, that saved, the world.

Without pausing to note any of the other, less-known theories, we may assert that in this "moral" theory lies whatever truth there is in the doctrine of the Atonement. Good men do have to atone for the sins of bad men; if it had not been for the wickedness of men, Christ, our type of spiritual hero, would not have had to suffer and die. That widespread human wickedness cost him dear; he paid the full price; and he is the fitting type of the vicariousness of so much of human suffering. Moreover, that suffering, that supreme example of self-sacrificing love, has had a great redeeming power, breaking down men's resistance and winning them to God. The individual is often unable to cure his own perverted will; it is the devoted love of others, such love as is typified in Christ, that softens the hard heart and rescues men from the power of sin. "It is only suffering love that avails to bring back the prodigal sons; and only as parents

admitted through faith, and in which we find peace, joy, and salvation. Christ suffered for us only . . . as a result of human solidarity, from the painful consequences of sins in which he had no personal part. . . . His death is not the cause of an objective atonement made before God for sin, but the historical means of a subjective atonement which is effected in the human consciousness through faith, by the death of the old man and the birth of the new."

have it for their children, pastors for their people, friends for their friends, can they be real soul-winners." [1] It is the spirit of Christ, the ministry of love and self-sacrifice, that is slowly lifting men upward; that event on Calvary, nineteen hundred years ago, symbolizes this age-long process; the doctrine that has crystallized round it expresses in concrete and tangible form a profound and pathetic truth.

But there is always the danger of so preaching this doctrine as to relax rather than quicken men's efforts; contented reliance upon Christ's sacrifice has led many a Christian to forget that it is only by following Christ, by repeating in his own experience Christ's sacrifice and victory, that he can share the great reward. Yet this was what Paul meant; redemption was to him not an outward transaction but an inward transformation. To Paul's experience Christianity must cling fast. We must let Christ's sacrifice touch us, include us, destroy our desire for sin; we must catch the spirit of atoning love and reënact the great Atonement, in our humble way, in our own lives.

Salvation: H. Höffding, *Philosophy of Religion*, pp. 41–57. J. V. Morgan, ed., *Theology at the Dawn of the Twentieth Century*, pp. 159–222. R. J. Campbell, *New Theology*, chap. XII. M. Arnold, *St. Paul and Protestantism*.

Conversion: W. James, *Varieties of Religious Experience*, chaps. IX, X. E. D. Starbuck, *Psychology of Religion*. G. A. Coe, *Spiritual Life*, chaps. I–III. G. B. Cutten, *Psychological Phenomena of Christianity*, chap. XVIII. E. S. Ames, *Psychology of Religious Experience*, pt. III. A. W. Moore, *Rational Basis of Orthodoxy*, chaps. XI–XII. H. Begbie, *Twice-Born Men*. *American Journal of Psychology*, vol. 7, p. 309.

The Atonement: Morgan, ed., *op. cit.*, pp. 261–99. Various authors, *The Atonement in Modern Religious Thought* (Whitaker, 1901). *Foundations*, chap. VI. C. A. Dinsmore, *Atonement in Literature and Life*. A. Sabatier, *Doctrine of the Atonement and its*

---

[1] H. W. Pinkham, in *Theology at the Dawn of the Twentieth Century*, p. 298.

Historical Evolution. R. C. Moberly, *Atonement and Personality.* J. Royce, *Problem of Christianity*, vol. i, lects. vi–vii. B. P. Bowne, *Studies in Christianity*, chap. ii. R. J. Campbell, *New Theology*, chaps. viii, ix, x, xii. Moore, *op. cit.*, chap. x. J. Caird, *Fundamental Ideas of Christianity*, chaps. xvi–xviii. *Biblical World*, vol. 42, p. 67.

CHAPTER XII

FAITH AND PRAYER

IF the outward source of salvation, for Paul and the many Christians who have followed in his steps, was Christ, the inward and coöperating factor, equally necessary, was Faith. "By faith are ye saved," the great apostle taught his converts; and there is no directer way to grasp the meaning of this term than through a study of the experience that we call "Salvation by Faith." Just as the doctrine of the Atonement resulted from an attempt to explain the ultimate causes and conditions of this experience, so the Pauline-Lutheran dogma of Justification and Sanctification by Faith was an interpretation of the event itself in terms of the then current theological and psychological conceptions. Our aim should be, not to accept as inerrant and unalterable these speculations of a former day, but to revert to the personal religious experiences which gave birth to them and to interpret those indubitable and significant facts in terms of our modern scientific knowledge.

What is the nature and value of faith?

Paul is the type of earnest, aspiring man for whom a sensitive conscience and a keen sense of sin are not enough to overcome temptation; they need to be reinforced by a great loyalty and a new assurance. The long struggle to live up to outward standards left him discouraged and lacking in inward power; what he needed, and found, was an influx of new life, to lift him to a higher plane. It was the getting of a "new man"; it was "the spirit of life in Christ Jesus" that

FAITH AND PRAYER

"freed" him "from the law of sin and death."[1] His redemption from inner discord had come, with an intense emotional crisis, when he yielded his heart to the Christ whose followers he had been persecuting. So for him always, to be saved — made safe from falling — required the giving of the heart to Christ. If a man was willing to die, as it were, with Christ, to his former lusts and passions, and to lay hold of the Christ-life, or, in Paul's language, let Christ live in him, Christ's victory over sin might be his also.

What Paul thereafter opposed (and what should always be contrasted with salvation by faith) was not salvation by good conduct, but salvation by mere external compliances. The surrender of heart and will to Christ, which he demanded, involved purity of life, involved a flat abandonment of all the old lusts; good conduct was its outcome and test — "faith without works is dead." The secret of success was the substitution of the positive forces of loyalty and optimism for the paralyzing sense of impotence and struggle; the mind was henceforth to be centered on Christ and the old life forgotten. In the old endeavor to fulfil a casuistic list of rules there had been no inspiration, but a perpetual realization of failure; the attainment of spirituality seemed hopelessly far off. But with the new hope attainment became possible at a bound. So to many another it has happened that godliness has been best won, at a certain critical point, by grasping the higher life through the imagination, and claiming it, though yet unrealized, as an actual possession; the joyous expectancy of success turning the scales in favor of the new habits.[2]

---

[1] Rom. 8: 2.

[2] The value of the method, as preached, in varying theological terms, by so many followers of Paul, in bringing a new force of hope into a life, is well illustrated by this extract from one of John Wesley's sermons: "You think, I must first be or do thus or thus [to be saved]. Then you are seeking it by works unto this day. If you seek it by faith, you may expect it as you

The psychology of the situation would be explained to-day somewhat as follows: The unhappy sinner, in many cases, has the power to live aright locked up in his heart, but unable to get control of him because it is blocked by the realization of his sinfulness; the formation of new habits is interfered with by his very concentration of thought upon his previous failures. Suddenly he is told that he need not think of his temptations any longer, that he has but to let go, yield himself to some one who is his Saviour, or to the Holy Spirit in himself, and the power of right living will be his, he will be saved. The suggestion of the possession of power is potent enough to make the power actually sufficient. The mind is fixed upon the goal instead of upon the obstacles, is freed from the demoralization that comes from a remembrance of past weakness, and lives in the atmosphere of attainment.[1]

That this experience was not understood, that it was deemed miraculous and materialized into an outward transaction, wherein God, that his justice and mercy might both be satisfied, imputed the sinlessness of Christ to whosoever should accept his offer of forgiveness, has not wholly undermined its efficacy as a vital means of deliverance from sin. The interpretation put upon it is of small importance compared with the fact of its existence. While men are prone to sensuality and selfishness, to inner discord and unhappiness,

are; then expect it now. It is of importance to observe that there is an inseparable connection between these three points: expect it *by faith*, expect it *as you are*, and expect it *now*."

[1] Cf. J. H. Leuba, in *American Journal of Religious Psychology*, vol. 1, p. 74: Faith "means greater suggestibility to the circle of ideas the subject is intent upon realizing, and deliverance, if not from the presence, at least from the power, of those other tendential ideas against which he has been struggling."

William James's memorable description of the salvation-by-faith experience may be found in his *Varieties of Religious Experience*, p. 205 *ff.* His particular contribution lay in pointing out the important rôle played by the subconscious life in producing these experiences of abrupt and passive salvation.

they will need the help of outward influences to turn them to the right life; and theology, though naturally, before the very recent development of the science of psychology, far astray in its comprehension of the phenomenon, has in its blind fashion clung hold of this valuable method of Salvation by Faith, and through it brought to many purity and peace.

The true importance of this method, however, has been greatly obscured by its veil of prescientific conceptions; and we are only to-day, with our better understanding of its essential nature, beginning to appreciate what can be accomplished by it for health of mind, even for health of body. More or less gropingly various sects of recent growth are making use of it — "Mind-Cure," "Faith-Cure," "New Thought," "Christian Science." In varying phraseology, and with widely different theoretical explanations, by all of these cults the same fundamental psychological truth is exemplified and made of practical service.

But what should already be clear is, that this faith, which is so efficacious in spiritual, and even in physical hygiene, is something very different from, and much more important than, an assent to doctrines, i.e., to statements concerning supposed historical or cosmological facts. Faith, in its good sense, is not credulity; it is not rightly opposed to free inquiry, to the historical spirit, or to intellectual conscientiousness. An acceptance of beliefs of any sort has never saved any one's soul; "it is not on any estimate of evidence, correct or incorrect, that our true holiness can depend." We cannot too earnestly oppose all demands for acceptance of doctrines which would not of their own obvious reasonableness command assent. Such a "virtue" would really be a vice; and if Faith could only be taken to mean that, it would be our duty to refuse it.[1]

[1] Cf. T. H. Green, sermon on *Faith*: "If faith were really belief in the occurrence of certain miraculous events upon transmitted evidence of the

There are, indeed, other legitimate uses of the term besides that which we are considering. It may be used in the sense of trust in a person and what that person says. There are those whose vision is deeper than ours; it is often necessary and sweet to rest our judgment upon theirs. Multitudes of Christians thus pin their faith to the beliefs that Christ held and taught. But such a leaning upon another must be only provisional; we cannot ultimately surrender our judgment, or follow blindly a leader, however dear and worthy of our reverence.

In a slightly different sense, faith may mean the adoption of a belief as a working hypothesis, in lack of sufficient evidence to convince the intellect one way or the other. Such a faith is, again, often necessary, and of great value; but it must remain open to challenge and criticism, be freely discarded if evidence against it appears, and never assume a certainty that it does not actually possess.[1]

In the best sense, however, in the sense in which faith actually saves, it is not a belief in alleged facts (which would ultimately require evidence of the truth of those facts to justify it), but a moral state, a disposition of the heart and will, which is quite independent of the existence or nonexistence of any outward facts. It is not the acceptance of doctrines on scanty evidence, it is the laying-hold, through the imagination, on a higher life; the keeping of the mind set on it when lower passions obtrude themselves and mar the vision; a steadfast refusal to let the concrete failures and

senses of other people, its certainty would after all be merely a weaker form of the certainty of sense. Such a faith is neither intrinsically worth maintaining, nor in the long run can it maintain itself, against the demands of reason. Reason will not be kept at bay by being told that certain truths are above it, when these 'truths,' if they are anything at all, are propositions concerning matters of fact to which from their nature the principles regulating all knowledge must be fully applicable."

[1] The ethics of faith, in these two senses, will be discussed below, in chap. xxv.

discouragements of the day turn our eyes away from that ideal of our life whose presence is our inspiration and power. It is the "assurance of things hoped for" — that is, an optimistic attitude, a believing attitude toward the future; it is "the conviction of things not seen";[1] that is, a keeping firm hold of the intangible realities of the spiritual life, even when their worth cannot be felt and their glow is gone.[2]

Faith is then not rightly opposed to reason — nor is it so opposed in the Bible — but to sight; it is not a way of ascertaining truth, but a way of holding on to truth that there is ample justification for believing. Faith cannot tell us that water will buoy us up; but when experience has taught us that it will, it requires faith to let ourselves plunge in. So in religion: we recognize the truth of the laws of the spiritual life, but it requires faith to use them; we admit the superiority of Christ's way of life, but it takes faith to cleave to it when passion possesses us and desire points another way. Faith, thus, in its highest and moral sense, is the believing in and holding on to an ideal of life against all the temptations and foreshortening illusions of the senses. The difficulty in the way of it is not an intellectual but a moral, not

[1] Heb. 11: 1.

[2] Cf., for current definitions of faith, Rev. Elwood Worcester: "Faith makes the invisible world real to us, convinces us that the things of the spirit are not fancies but ultimate realities." W. R. Inge: "Faith is the faculty that makes real to us the future and the unseen . . . frees us from the trammels of time, enabling us to assume a heroic attitude in face of temporal sufferings by regarding events *sub specie eternitatis*." Dewey and Tufts: Faith is "the staking of one's self upon the truth and worth of one's ideal." So Matthew Arnold (*St. Paul and Protestantism*, chap. II): Faith is "a power, preëminently, of holding fast to an unseen power of goodness."

In Hastings's *Dictionary of the Bible*, Faith is defined as "a trustful appropriation of Christ and a surrender of self to his salvation." "Intellectual acceptance is not at all the Biblical meaning."

Leuba defines it as "the formation of a vital partnership with the representative of an ideal (or with the abstract ideal itself) by which life rises to greater intensity, more complete inner harmony and fuller self-realization." (*American Journal of Religious Psychology*, vol. 1, p. 80.)

an objective but a subjective difficulty. There come times to the best of us when ideals seem visionary and warm throbbing human passions alone of worth. We have learned that the way of self-restraint is the best way and our duty, but for the moment we cannot see that it is so. We have to "walk by faith, not by sight."[1] But however the temptation presses, however it bids us call purity an illusion and yield to the demands of the senses, if we keep the faith, if we are faithful to our ideal, we shall be saved.

There is nothing mysterious about this, nothing irrational. It is the same attitude in religion that has made men successful in other matters. Faith is not to be found exclusively in religion. Columbus, refusing to let fear daunt or warnings dissuade him, keeping steadily his faith in the possibilities that lay before him, found a new continent for man. Alexander setting out to conquer the world, Grant before Vicksburg, Lincoln facing the chaos of a severed country — all great men have needed a strong faith in their ideals to nerve them to carry them successfully through. Men are proud to have faith in the women they love, mothers in their sons, patriots in their country and its destiny. How much more do we need it in the religious life, in that intangible realm where the greatest truths so easily elude us or become obscured by the mists of pettiness and passion! The Christian personifies his ideal in Christ, and through faith in him rises above his weaknesses. But whether it come through Christ or some other inspiring leader, or through our own experience and courage, matters little, so we sternly lay aside all discouragement and cynicism, and have faith in our spiritual possibilities, faith in a better life for man, a faith vivid and real enough to bring our whole souls to the realizing of those possibilities and the bringing about of that better order.

[1] 2 Cor. 5: 7.

What has been the evolution of prayer?

The religious life, instinctive as under certain conditions and in certain moods it is, maintains itself with difficulty in the average human soul, and has need of every possible support and stay. It needs that dogged devotion through all doubts and temptations that we call faith; it needs also that daily communion with God and rededication of spirit that we call prayer. Prayer, however, like so many other of the concepts and practices of developed religion, has sprung historically from a non-religious and superstitious source. Its beginnings lay in the frantic and haphazard attempts of primitive man to avert disaster when no practical methods suggested themselves — in the cries and gesticulations and prostrations that were the instinctive reaction of his uneasy and bewildered body. Thence it developed in three main directions, of which we may in turn speak.

(1) *Spell-prayer.* Certain experiences of the power of a dominant personality over other men, combined with chance successes which seemed to prove a power over nature, gave rise to practices of incantation, conjuration, and elaborate strategy, which are commonly summed up by the term "magic." In magical practices the supernatural powers are summoned, domineered over, utilized, without need of winning their favor. By the proper spells the savage believes he can bend their wills to his and command their services. The Arabian Nights' tales amply illustrate this widespread primitive conception; the genie whom Aladdin summons, for example, is his bounden slave; only, just the right act must be performed, just the right words spoken. In other cases the effect of the magic may be directly upon one's enemy or friend. But in all these cases there is no appeal, no petition, but rather coercion, through some mysterious and occult means. There is something exciting and alluring about such

operations; and in spite of the skepticism of modern science magic dies hard. The belief in witchcraft flourished in the cultured New England of a few generations ago; the "evil eye" is an undoubted fact in some parts of Italy to-day. Multitudes of Catholics attribute a magical efficacy to the making of the sign of the cross or the telling of beads. Exorcisms are still practiced, relics and bones of saints are believed to have healing power; one may even suggest that the phrase "for Christ's sake" is felt by many petitioners to exercise a sort of compelling influence upon God.

(2) *Petition-prayer.* Magic perhaps antedated animism. But with the development of animistic conceptions of nature, supplication was naturally made for favors needed and for the averting of calamities feared. So widespread did this habit become that the word "prayer" means to most men to-day "petition." But with the discovery of the seeming omnipresence of natural law, and the widespread modern doubts as to the existence of personality behind nature, the habit has, among educated people, become severely shaken. Is God a Being who hears and answers petitions? If he can be assumed to be such a conscious Ruler of the universe, with the interests of men at heart, does he deflect his great purposes at the wish of individuals, or even of groups? Is it not rather a worthier conception of God that he should know and plan what is best for men, and hold to that plan in spite of their blind and foolish requests? Or do we know, after all, that God is omnipotent, that he can break the chain of natural law if he would, that he can give to men all the blessings he might long for them to have?

All such questions must wait upon our particular conception of God and the universe; they cannot be answered, even as a matter of probability, at this stage in our inquiry. And, to anticipate the outcome of our later discussion,[1] we may

[1] See, especially, chaps. XVIII and XXIII.

FAITH AND PRAYER

frankly confess here that, in the present state of our knowledge, they cannot be answered at all with assurance. Modern conceptions of the nature of God, of the relation of God to the world, and of the possibility of supernatural intervention in the natural order, are as yet fluctuating and fluid; no safe deductions can be drawn, *a priori*, as to the answering of petitions. And when we come to *a posteriori* evidence, we must admit, if we are as scrupulous here as in other matters, that there is none that approaches conclusiveness. Innumerable cases of apparently answered prayer are, of course, available; but if cases of apparently unanswered prayer were as zealously collected they would probably far outbulk the others. No scientifically conducted statistical study has ever been made, to the knowledge of the writer of this volume, to ascertain whether the number of "answers" exceeds the probabilities of coincidence, coupled with the human efforts that are usually also made.[1] The fact that so many saints, that Jesus himself, our spiritual leader, believed implicitly in the power and desire of God to grant human petitions, can no longer be felt as proof. In so many ways these peerless souls were mistaken in their conceptions; if they were above their age in spiritual insight, they shared its errors as to matters of fact. Saintliness and moral power are no guaranty of the truth of the theological conceptions that in any given environment go with them; on the contrary, practical religious genius rarely goes hand in hand with power of analysis or a scientific sense.[2]

[1] Cf. the proposal for such an inquiry made by Tyndall in 1872. Quite a discussion ensued. See *Contemporary Review*, vol. 20, pp. 205, 430, 763, 777; vol. 21, pp. 183, 464. *Fortnightly Review*, new series, vol. 12, p. 125.

[2] In a questionnaire conducted by the author of this volume among college graduates in this country, the question was asked, "Does prayer avail to change the sequence of natural events in addition to its effect upon him who prays?" Nearly all the respondents were professed Christians. Of these twenty-five per cent were convinced, and eleven per cent more clung to faith, or hope, that it does so avail. Thirty-eight per cent positively dis-

But not to be able to prove is by no means to disprove. So, however unsatisfying the results of candid investigation may be, millions of petitions will continue to arise from yearning hearts the world over; and the desired blessings, if they come, will be deemed answers thereto. And even if these happy believers are cherishing an illusion, no harm can possibly come therefrom, but rather much good, unless human effort is relaxed, in reliance upon superhuman help, or unless the judgment of men as to evidence and logic is blurred by their practical reliance upon an unproved postulate.

(3) *Communion- and consecration-prayer*. But the controversy over the outward efficacy of prayer must not too exclusively engage us. For the usefulness and rationality of prayer do not stand or fall with our verdict upon that point. In any case, prayer is *chiefly* useful for the production of inward and spiritual changes. If we finally learn that the universe is so made that prayer cannot produce rain, or prevent a shipwreck, if that is not the *kind* of thing that prayer accomplishes, religion need not hesitate to acknowledge the fact. If obtruding our personal petitions upon the Universal Life is futile, communion with God, and repeated dedication of our hearts to God, is a practice of unquestionable reasonableness and worth. There are sources of spiritual energy which we can tap; they were very early found by praying men, and prayer tends to become, in ever-increasing degree, communion and consecration.[1]

believed it, twenty-six per cent had no opinion. See *Independent*, vol. 75, p. 755.

[1] Cf. James, *Varieties of Religious Experience*, p. 464: "Every one now knows that droughts and storms follow from physical antecedents, and that moral appeals cannot avert them. But petitional prayer is only one department of prayer; and if we take the word in the wider sense as meaning every kind of inward communion or conversation with the power recognized as divine, we can easily see that scientific criticism leaves it untouched. Prayer in this wide sense is the very soul and essence of religion."

So M. W. Calkins, in *Harvard Theological Review*, vol. 4, p. 496: "Histor-

What is the function and value of prayer?

Leaving open, then, the question as to the outward efficacy of prayer, we can at least say that its chief efficacy is inward. Prayer is vital for the soul's life; and no man, whatever his theological position, can afford to do without it. Jesus gave the reason when he said, "This kind goeth not out but by prayer." He prayed constantly himself, and doubtless drew from that source much of his inward strength. The apostle likewise bids us "pray without ceasing" — because men are "sanctified by the word of God and prayer." [1] So down the centuries the strong men have been the praying men. More things, truly, are wrought by prayer than the heedless, happy-go-lucky world dreams of; the experience of the saints testifies abundantly to its almost limitless power over temptation, fear, and even physical weakness.[2] Whether or not prayer can alter the face of nature, it certainly can alter us — and far more radically than a superficial thought might suggest. Beneath our shallow and fleeting conscious life lie the unplumbed depths of the subconscious; thoughts and moods that make no immediate outward mark upon a man's conduct have their slowly accumulating effect therein, which, some day revealing itself, may surprise every one, perhaps no one more than the man himself. Prayer reaches down to these hidden strata of our

ical investigation and psychological analysis unite in the demonstration that prayer is more than petition."

And Rev. J. H. Crooker, *The Church of To-morrow:* "The simple fact is that God has not given human desire a mechanical efficiency in the physical world, any more than He has given the force of gravity a psychological efficiency in the world of human thought. . . . And yet true prayer is not ruled out of even those realms by this interpretation. Whatever helps the bridge-builder, the engineer, and the farmer to a divine life makes possible a stronger bridge, a safer train, a better harvest."

[1] Mark 14: 38. Matt. 17: 21. 1 Thess. 5: 17. 1 Tim. 4: 5.

[2] For one testimony to the marvelous efficacy of prayer inwardly, see the *Outlook*, vol. 83, p. 857.

lives, and may profoundly influence them. Through it many a man has overcome faults of temper or of sense that sorely beset him, and has emerged from his closet master of himself and easily virtuous in the eyes of a world that knew nothing of his secret struggles.

To take then some regular time of the day for meditation upon our duties and our needs, for turning our minds back from the practical affairs or the pleasures that choke our higher aspirations, to the fundamental and serious aspects of life — this practice, steadily and undeviatingly followed, is the only safe method by which most men can keep even approximately true to their own ideals. At such moments the irritation, the petulance, the passions that may have overswept the heart are hushed and brought sharply into contrast with the purity and unselfishness and self-restraint to which it is pledged; if the prayer is sincere, their gathering momentum cannot but be stopped and the heart purged and reinvigorated. Even if no violent passions have invaded its sanctuary, the dust of petty thoughts and paltry feelings inevitably gathers and calls for a periodic house-cleaning that should be not too infrequent. Out of the whirl and distractions of the day, out of the mistakes and the failures, back to the pure atmosphere of the ideal let a man turn, where strength is to be gathered to meet the perplexities and temptations that await him.

By the thoughts that are in a man's heart will his actions be guided. Wisely spake the lawgiver when he wrote, "Thou shalt talk of these things when thou sittest in thine house, and when thou walkest by the way, and when thou liest down, and when thou risest up." [1] Wise are the apostle's words, "Whatsoever things are just, whatsoever things are pure . . . think on these things." [2] A hundred times a day is none too often to think on them; if the pause is only for a

[1] Deut. 6: 7.   [2] Phil. 4: 8.

moment it may lighten an hour, like a sudden burst of sunshine in cloudy weather. But at least once in a day, and at a regular hour, lest it be forgotten, there should be a lull in the active life and a consecration prolonged enough to bring the heart well under the spell of its ideals.[1]

Surely the time and effort thus spent, even if taken from a busy and useful life, are richly rewarded. That is, if the prayer is directed to the actual needs of a man's heart and is not a vague emotional debauch or mechanical repetition of words. Prayer may be a sort of æsthetic ecstasy; it may be an anæsthetic that blinds us to our pressing duties; it may be a vain agonizing over our own troubles or those of our loved ones; it may be nothing but "vain repetitions," such as Jesus denounced. There are many possible distortions of prayer, — the complacent praise of the well-fed congregation, that ignores the hopeless misery of its poorer neighbors, the parrot-like mumbling of the churchman whose

---

[1] Cf. Matthew Arnold (*Literature and Dogma*, chap. 1): "All good and beneficial prayer is in truth, however men may describe it, at bottom nothing else than an energy of aspiration towards the eternal not ourselves that makes for righteousness, — of aspiration towards it, and of coöperation with it. Nothing therefore can be more efficacious, more right and more real."

Cf. also Tolstoy (in a private letter): "But because petitionary prayer has no meaning, it does not follow that one cannot or should not pray. On the contrary, I believe it is impossible to live without prayer, and that prayer is the necessary condition of a good, peaceful and happy life. . . . In every man there is a divine spark, the Spirit of God. Prayer consists in calling forth in one's self the divine element while renouncing all that is of this world, all which can distract one's feelings. . . . Free solitary prayer consists of all which in the words of other wise and righteous men, or in one's own, brings the soul back to the consciousness of its divine source, to a more vivid and clear expression of the demands of one's conscience, i.e., of one's divine nature. Prayer is a test of one's present and past actions according to the highest demands of the soul. . . . I also endeavor to pray during the daily round of my life, while I am with men and passions are getting hold of me. It is in these cases I try to recall to mind all that took place in my soul during my solitary prayer, and the more sincere that prayer was, the easier it is to refrain from evil."

mind in its blankness is vaguely soothed by the rising and falling cadences, the sanctimonious orisons of the monk whose hands are unsoiled by practical service, the wail for alleviation of their lot from the discontented. Only that prayer is right that is manly and brave, that accepts without cringing whatever lot befalls; only that prayer is useful that is relevant to the practical duties of a life; only that prayer is worthy that is spontaneous and earnest and into which a man's whole heart is poured; only that prayer is to be urged which is necessary to keep a man living up to the best of his capabilities and at the height of his powers.

Familiar phrases have their value, especially if they come from the pen of some loved teacher or revered sage. Few men have pondered and read enough to be able to clothe their own aspirations adequately in words; except for this borrowing of others' prayers, their aspirations would remain largely inarticulate and lacking in that powerful reinforcement that they might receive from embodiment in fitting terms and moving periods. Then, to repeat the expression of another's resolves, and to find that they coincide with one's own, is to draw close in spirit to him and to feel one's own aspirations as a part of the whole uplooking heart of humanity. In the repetition of such prayers a breath of the other's aspiration, a strengthening influence from the other's resolve, a new insight and higher vision may come, that one groping alone with his problems would never have found.

The danger in such repetitions is that they become mere words and fail to reach the heart; that they miss the real needs of the struggling soul and represent duties and longings alien to its problems. Better than such empty forms is the freshly worded prayer, the personal cry of the individual heart, however confused and incoherent, that expresses its own longings and its genuine resolves. And in the task of putting into words the ideals one wishes to attain, or stigmatizing in its proper light the particular sin one wishes to overcome, a good deal is accomplished. No one whose battle with his lower nature is a real and pressing matter will rest content with a mere use of another's phrases; his own extremity or the particular beauty that lies to him in some noble manner of life will formulate for him better than any other could do the words he shall say.

No half-hearted prayer will do, no perfunctory murmuring of words, as if the very exercise itself were commendable and a duty. If it is worth doing at all it is worth doing effectively. It may be well for the child to grow into the habit of prayer before he is old enough to make it a vital thing to him; it may be that phrases repeated with little thought or earnestness will linger in his mind and come to his rescue in some later trouble. But what counts ultimately is the consecration of heart, the spirit of willingness and resolve; and the constant bringing of that spirit into the foreground of consciousness until it becomes the dominant mood, so wholly the dominant mood that not even in some careless or tired moment can the unkind word or impulse of passion slip out and pass into irrevocable fact.

Faith: G. B. Cutten, *Psychological Phenomena of Christianity*, chaps. xv–xvi. H. Höffding, *Philosophy of Religion*, pp. 116–35. P. Strutt, *Nature of Faith*. J. H. Skrine, *What is Faith?* C. C. Everett, *Theism and the Christian Faith*, chap. xxxii. T. H. Green, *Faith* (in *Two Sermons*). C. Gore, ed., *Lux Mundi*, chap. i. G. L. Dickinson, *Religion, a Criticism and a Forecast*, chap. iv. W. R. Inge, *Faith and its Psychology*. *American Journal of Religious Psychology*, vol. 1, p. 65.

Prayer: L. R. Farnell, *Evolution of Religion*, chap. iv. F. B. Jevons, *Prayer* (in *Introduction to the Study of Comparative Religion*). A. Sabatier, *Outlines of a Philosophy of Religion*, bk. i, chap. iv, sec. 4. R. R. Marett, *Threshold of Religion*, chap. ii. A. L. Strong, *Psychology of Prayer*. D. W. Faunce, *Prayer as a Theory and as a Fact*. G. S. Merriam, *Prayers and their Answers* (in *The Man of To-day*). W. James, *Varieties of Religious Experience*, chap.

19. G. B. Cutten, *Psychological Phenomena of Christianity*, chap. XXVIII. E. S. Ames, *Psychology of Religious Experience*, chap. VIII. E. H. Rowland, *Right to Believe*, chap. VI. W. E. Hocking, *Meaning of God in Human Experience*, chap. XXIX. G. A. Coe, *Religion of a Mature Mind*, chap. XI. W. N. Rice, *Prayer* (in *Christian Faith in an Age of Science*). J. Wendland, *Miracles and Christianity*, chap. VII. G. Santayana, *Reason in Religion*, pp. 38–48. R. C. Cabot, *What Men Live By*, pt. IV. *Hibbert Journal*, vol. 9, p. 385. *Harvard Theological Review*, vol. 4, p. 489. *American Journal of Religious Psychology*, vol. 1, p. 129; vol. 2, pp. 108, 160.

CHAPTER XIII

RELIGIOUS LOVE AND PEACE

The spirit of love and service in religion

SACRIFICE, faith, and prayer are necessary as means of saving the individual life from its pitfalls. But if the adjustment of a man's impulses to his own needs forces itself perhaps most unavoidably upon his attention, the disciplining of his attitude toward others is in the long run even more essential. That he sink into the mire of unrestrained vice himself is less of a harm than that he hurt those about him; and though he save his own soul, if he help not his neighbor his religion is a narrow and petty affair. Human life, being necessarily social, demands, not only that we harmonize with one another our chaotic impulses, but that we adapt them, at whatever cost, to the wills and needs of others. Pure religion and undefiled has these two leading aspects: ministering love — "to visit the fatherless and widows in their affliction"; and personal purity — "to keep one's self unspotted from the world." [1]

These two aspects of the religious life naturally go together, self-restraint for one's own sake merging with self-restraint for the sake of others. But there is also a certain tendency of purity, when unbalanced by charity, to be unsympathetic, hard, and narrow; and the purest are sometimes the most unlovable of people. As we grow higher in our ideals and stricter with ourselves we loathe sin more and more, and very easily fall into loathing the sinner. Faults that are readily overlooked by the average easy-going man

[1] Jas. 1:27.

incite the vigorous condemnation of the purist; with weakness which he has himself conquered he has scant patience, and for ideals foreign to his own he has no sympathy. The Psalms, for instance, with their hunger and thirst after righteousness, are full of maledictions against evildoers, and show a temper often far from charitable. By the noblest religion, however, not only self-indulgence and avarice and lust are branded as sins, but haughtiness and self-conceit, the spirit that says, "Lord, I thank thee that I am not as these!" For even these are our brothers too, whom we are to save from sin if we can, but in any case to love. If they offend against us we are not to give way to "righteous indignation," — that phrase by which Christians have justified anger and enmity, — but are to forgive seven times — nay, seventy times seven times. "For love suffereth long and is kind, love seeketh not her own, is not provoked, taketh not account of evil — endureth all things."

But even when religion has not led men to a positively hard-hearted attitude toward their fellows, it has often concentrated their thoughts unworthily upon personal salvation, to the neglect of their proper office of helpfulness. They have built cathedrals that soothed their spirits and drew them individually nearer to God, they have with prayer and mortification of the flesh striven to conquer some trivial fault that weighed on their conscience; but at the end the world has been little better or happier for their lives. Against this spirit many a religious reformer has striven. The real saint is he who asks, not "What shall I do to be saved?" but, "What shall I do to be of service?" Not the hermit in his solitary fastings, not the monk with his endless concern that his sins be forgiven, but St. Francis, binding with his own hands the leper's wounds, Darwin, devoting the toil of a lifetime for the benefit of human knowledge, those private soldiers who risked their lives in the fight against yellow fever in Cuba, a million hard-working, self-sacrificing men and women the world over — these are the true Christians, the true saints and heroes of humanity.[1]

Worse than scorn or indifference, however, have been the persecutions, inquisitions, and crusades into which religious zeal has led men. Families have been divided, man has gone to war with brother man, and religion has at times seemed the greatest enemy of human concord. In the mediæval ideal of chivalry — that curious and romantic blend of Christianity and paganism — the combative instinct received a religious consecration. It might have been supposed that Christianity, with its initial proclamation of peace and good-will toward men, would put an end to war; the early Christians, indeed, condemned it, even to the point of refusing military service. But Constantine fought under the cross, Augustine and Ambrose defended war, the aggression of Islam had to be met; and so "the cross became the handle of a sword." This martial religion, this militant church, had its noble and glorious side, to which we cannot but respond, as we read, for example, in Shakespeare's glowing words, of Norfolk's death: —

> "Many a time hath banished Norfolk fought
> For Jesu Christ in glorious Christian field,
> Streaming the ensign of the Christian cross
> Against black Pagans, Turks, and Saracens;
> And, toiled with works of war, retired himself
> To Italy; and there, at Venice, gave
> His body to that pleasant country's earth,
> And his pure soul unto his captain Christ,
> Under whose colours he had fought so long."

Nevertheless, in its best days religion has known how to unite personal zeal with sympathy, a passionate devotion to its ideal, and a stern self-denial with tenderness toward the weak and erring and those of alien faith. It has taught, on

[1] Cf. Mazzini, "When I see any man called good, I ask, 'Whom, then, has he saved?'"

the one hand, "Be ye perfect," and, on the other hand, "Judge not, that ye be not judged." The *pietas* of the Romans — their truly religious loyalty to family and state — and the intense national consciousness of the Jews were widened by Christianity into a recognition of universal brotherhood. The parable of the Good Samaritan taught the lesson. "We who are many are one body," wrote the Apostle; and again, to Jews and Greeks and Romans, "All ye are brethren." [1]

It was not enough to refrain from judging one's neighbors and pointing at them the finger of scorn; Christianity insisted upon positive sympathy and service. The precepts of Isaiah were followed — to "seek justice, relieve the oppressed, secure justice for the orphaned and plead for the widow." [2] The great Hebrew prophets had been spokesmen of the common people; the Jewish lawgivers had shown a marked humaneness toward the poor of the land, and even the resident alien. Jesus had mingled with all classes, rebuked the pride and self-seeking of his disciples, and set an incomparable example of tenderness and practical charity. To the rich young man of stainless reputation he said, "One thing thou lackest; go, sell whatsoever thou hast, and give to the poor"; on another occasion he bade his hearers, when they asked guests to dine, invite not the rich who could repay the kindness, but the poor who could not repay.[3] In similar vein Paul and the author of the Book of James had rebuked their churches for their caste spirit and lack of brotherliness.[4] In accordance with this teaching, the collections in the primitive church were spent almost wholly for the service of the poor; indeed, the very organization of the church was designed primarily for this fraternal helpfulness. The sick, infirm, and disabled were cared for, the richer

---

[1] Rom. 12:5.   [2] Isa. 1:17.   [3] Mark 10:21. Luke 14:12–14.
[4] 1 Cor. 11:17–34, etc. Jas. 2:1–4.

members gave their property freely, work was found for the unemployed, and the paradox of Jesus was followed seriously and with joy — "Whosoever will be great among you, let him be your minister; and whosoever will be chief among you, let him be your servant." [1]

So important for early Christianity was this spirit of love and service that it seemed to many — as it has seemed to many since — the quintessence of religion. Jesus had said that the two greatest commandments were the love of God and of man; Paul went so far as to say, "The whole law is fulfilled in one word, even in this: Thou shalt love thy neighbor as thyself"; and again, of faith, hope, and love he said, "The greatest of these is love." [2]

Nor is this *caritas* of Paul's matchless eulogy a product exclusively of Christianity. Buddhism is full of it. Marcus Aurelius, the Stoic, has many passages in such vein as these: "Be always doing something serviceable to mankind; and let this constant generosity be your only pleasure." "It is man's peculiar power to love even those who do wrong. And this is possible if, when they do wrong, it occurs to thee that they are kinsmen, and that they do wrong through ignorance and blindly, and that soon both of you will die; and that the wrong-doer has done thee no real harm." "Gently admonish him and calmly correct his errors, when he tries to do thee harm, saying, 'Not so, my child; we are constituted by nature for something else. I shall not be injured, but thou art injuring thyself.'" [3] And in a prayer of a certain Eusebius, an early Platonist, we read, "May I be no man's enemy, but may I be the friend of whatever is eternal and abiding. May I never quarrel with those nearest me; but if I do, may I be quickly reconciled. May I never devise evil against any man; if any devise evil against me, may I escape uninjured

---

[1] Matt. 20: 26-29.   [2] Mark 12: 28-31. Gal. 5: 14. 1 Cor. 13: 13.
[3] *Meditations*, bks. VI, VII, IX.

and without the need of hurting him. May I wish for all men's happiness and envy none. May I never rejoice in the ill-fortune of one who has wronged me...."[1]

Certainly no aspect of religion is more beautiful or more important than this. As in the personal sphere religion lifts the necessity of self-repression into a passionate love of purity, so in these wider relationships its task is to exalt the conception of duties to others into a longing to love and forgive and serve. Religion shifts the focus of a man's interests from his own welfare to that of his family, his neighbors, his fellow men; it so depersonalizes him that he finds his aims and his joys, not so much in his private fortunes as in the fortunes of that larger whole of which his life is but a part. Religion is a change in the center of gravity of life, a widening of the boundaries of self. What it exists, above all else, to teach us, is that the way of love is the perfect way of life.

And then, through this love of men, whom we see, we pass to the love of God, whom in his fullness we have not seen. This is love passing beyond its individual objects to the Universal Spirit of Good that shines through them all and makes them for us hints and glimpses of the Ideal, of that Perfect Good which eludes us in earthly things, but which we must ever love and follow. Tired of the transient and the changing, torn between the fleeting and fading objects of its love, the mind longs for something stable and eternal. Disillusioned in his idealization of particular creatures, to what may a man safely pay his adoration? To nothing but to God, the Absolute Good, dwelling in all loveworthy persons and beautiful things, but nowhere on earth perfectly realized. Only, indeed, in individual men and things can we find God in tangible, visible form; and to these particular persons and objects, with their flaws and their ephemeral existence,

[1] Quoted by G. Murray, *Four Stages of Greek Religion*, p. 182.

our loyalty should rightly cling. Yet it is not their imperfections that call out our love, but the revelation of God that we find in them. In this thought the heart may find a new comfort and peace. For though this or that particular object vanish and die, God persists, and will still rejoice the heart that has learned to love him wherever he may be found.

Religious peace

The natural result of the life of purity and love is peace. When the inner discord of an undisciplined life and the conflict of selfish desires with the needs of others are done away with, the greatest enemies of our happiness are overcome. Yet the pure and loving heart is not always for that at rest. For the longing for purity and the ability to love bring in their train new occasions for suffering; and there are in any case many natural ills, not remediable, which come even to the most loyal and sinless souls. These agonies and losses and catastrophes that torture the innocent as well as the guilty are irretrievably in the world; religion cannot remove them. What it can do is to help a man to bear them, to lift him into a state of mind which shall be above their assaults, so that he can say, "O grave, where is thy victory; O death, where is thy sting!"

If religion is to be at all profound, it must thus stoop to meet the pain and the misery of life, it must abide with them and somehow soften their sting. The noblest religions — as, notably, Buddhism and Christianity — have had much to say of sorrow, and have, for this reason, sometimes been called pessimistic. But neither of these religions is really pessimistic, neither ends in repining, or adds to the burden of life; instead, they inexpressibly lighten that burden and rob it of its worst aspects. "Come unto me," said Buddha; "I teach a doctrine which leads to deliverance from all the miseries of life." "Come unto me," said Christ. "Come unto me, all ye that labor and are heavy laden, and I will give you rest."

The secret of this peace has been, primarily, the freeing of the heart from worldly desires. The added vistas of hope beyond the grave, and the Christian conception of a Father God who watches and loves his children, have given great comfort and consolation. But a large share of the peace that they have brought is due to the new valuations they have induced; they have taught men to set their hearts, not upon what is transient and uncertain, but upon what is sure and abiding. "Lay not up for yourselves treasures upon earth, where moth and rust doth corrupt and where thieves break through and steal; but lay up for yourselves treasures in heaven, where neither moth nor rust doth corrupt and where thieves do not break through or steal."

At times the attempt has been made by distracted men to take these precepts with a thoroughgoing literalness. The deliberate cult of poverty, which has characterized some phases of Christianity as well as of other religions, has the secret of its fascination in the freedom it gives the soul. He who makes it his own will to have nothing is secure from all those disappointments and worries and temptations that hover near the man who has possessions and does not know how to get along without them. Poverty — when relieved of anxiety for the means of subsistence — is, as a Catholic writer says, "A great repose." The pursuit of poverty is impracticable in our modern organization of society; and it has its great drawbacks at best, rendering impossible much that makes life most desirable. But it is possible for us in some measure to attain the end those mendicant monks attained; we can, while owning things to a reasonable extent, and enjoying fully whatever pleasures come our way, remain inwardly above their power, not counting upon them, not basing our happiness upon them, and so not becoming miserable if they are taken away.

This unworldliness may easily lead, however, to a dampening of human energies and a paralysis of practical activity. The power to rise above ordinary troubles may lead to a neglect of available means for averting or curing them; the ability to endure our own ills may become a disinclination to bestir ourselves to lessen the ills of others. This has been, in fact, one of the insidious dangers of the religious life.

> "On the terraced walk aloof
> Leans a monk with folded hands,
> Placid, satisfied, serene,
> Looking down upon the scene,
> Over wall and red-tiled roof;
> Wondering unto what good end
> All this toil and traffic tend,
> And why all men cannot be
> Free from care and free from pain,
> And the sordid love of gain,
> And as indolent as he." [1]

For such a man religion has become a mere personal luxury, not a stimulus and driving power; it has degenerated into a cowardly escape from the problems of humanity instead of being a force for their solution — a retreat from life instead of its transformation.

There is a better way to peace than this: namely, not by ceasing to care for worldly matters, but by caring more for spiritual matters; the way of self-forgetfulness by self-surrender to something greater than our private fortune and worthy of our entire devotion. Indifference to our personal welfare is an impoverishment of life unless we put in place of that primary interest some deeper purpose, something noble to live for, to give meaning and worth to life. To become concerned, not with what we are to get out of life, but with what we can put in, to let ourselves become mere instru-

[1] Longfellow, *Amalfi*.

ments, to merge our wills with the will of God, is to learn the secret that Dante teaches in his great line, —

"*In la sua voluntade è nostra pace.*"

Nothing can take from us the joy of doing our part well, however humble a part it be, of belonging to the great army of those who are battling for the welfare of man against his ancient enemies, pain and ignorance and sin. For no matter how little we may be able personally to do, our cause is advancing, its triumphs are ours; every stroke made for the right, every act of love or of heroism the world over adds to our rejoicing. Slowly but steadily our cause is advancing; if we can learn to care supremely for its triumphs and to consecrate to its service what strength we have of heart and hand, we too may find the peace that passeth understanding. "Let it make no difference to thee," says Marcus Aurelius, "whether thou art cold or warm, if thou art doing thy duty; and whether thou art drowsy or satisfied with sleep; and whether ill-spoken of or praised; and whether dying or doing something else." "Let our lives be kindness and our conduct righteousness," says Buddha; "then in the fullness of gladness shall we make an end of grief." But it must not be a mere modicum of kindness and righteousness, it must be an utter self-forgetfulness in them; it must be that veritable losing of our lives through which, as Jesus taught, we shall most truly find them.

Mysticism and Christian Science.

In conclusion, we may mention two phases of the religious life which have in a peculiar degree brought peace to the human heart. The one consists in cultivating an emotional sense of the wonder and joy of life, ranging from a passing mood to a prolonged trance-like state or an almost continuous exaltation of spirit. This cultivation of the beatific vision is best known as "mysticism." The other phase consists in an obstinate refusal to admit the existence of evil or to respond to it with the usual reactions — fear, grief, disappointment, regret. Practiced in many forms, as a part of many faiths, it is best known to us under its contemporary name of "Christian Science." We shall not now concern ourselves with the implications of these experiences for our knowledge of the world; whatever inferential value they possess must await discussion at a later point in our study.[1] But just as experiences, worth repeating in our own lives as a means of heightening their intrinsic value, we may here briefly consider them.

Mysticism is many centuries old. A careful training in the attainment of its illumination was practiced in Brahmanic India, under the name of "Yoga"; attention was paid to such physical details as diet, posture, breathing, concentration of mind, as well as to an antecedent moral discipline.[2] Catholic manuals teach the art; it is known in Mohammedan Persia; no religion or creed has a monopoly of it. Its extreme forms, which are a sort of self-hypnotization and actual trance, are open, no doubt, only to certain temperaments; but in some degree all, of whatever faith, can attain, at least at moments, to its blessed assurance and bliss.[3]

---

[1] See pp. 326–30.

[2] Cf. "The bliss of Brahman! Speech and mind fall back baffled and ashamed; all fear vanishes in the knowing of that bliss." See S. Abhedananda, *How to be a Yogi*.

[3] No two writers agree in their definitions of mysticism. Inge speaks of it as "an attempt to realize the presence of the living God in the soul and in nature. . . . Complete union with God" (p. 5). Cutten says: "Mysticism is subjective religion. It is religion seeking to emancipate itself from the tyranny of external media. It is religion bringing the soul into the immediate presence of God" (p. 24). William James (whose discussion in lectures XVI–XVII of his *Varieties of Religious Experience* remains the most illuminating presentation of the subject) declares that mystical experiences are "states of consciousness of an entirely specific quality"; "a deepened sense of the significance" of things; "incommunicable transports"; "the over-

Space is lacking here for a discussion of the best means of attaining to these moments of insight into the wonder and beauty of life.[1] Our lives are, in any case, too rushed, too full of practical duties, to allow us to undergo the elaborate training of the adepts in mysticism; the best most of us can hope is, in moments now and then, under the spell of some glorious sunset, some peculiarly lovely landscape, or a strain of exquisite music, when in love, or when deeply moved by a book, a sermon, a play, or some great experience, to draw this deeper breath, get this deeper vision. We may catch it from some poet — from Wordsworth, when he speaks of

> "That serene and blessed mood
> In which . . .
> . . . with an eye made quiet by the power
> Of harmony, and the deep power of joy,
> We see into the life of things."

Or from Amiel, when he writes of those "moments divine, ecstatic hours, in which our thought flies from world to world, pierces the great enigma, breathes with a respiration broad, tranquil, and deep as the respiration of the ocean, serene and limitless as the blue firmament, . . . instants of irresistible intuition, in which one feels one's self great as the Universe, and calm as a god." Or from Emerson, when he says, "Crossing a bare common, in snow-puddles, at twilight, under a clouded sky, without having in my thoughts

coming of all the usual barriers between the individual and the Absolute"; a "feeling of enlargement, union, and emancipation"; a "sense of ineffable importance in the smallest events"; "excitements like the emotions of love or ambition, gifts to our spirit by means of which facts already objectively before us fall into a new expressiveness and make a new connection with our active life." A recent definition is this of G. P. Adams (in *Harvard Theological Review*, vol. 4, p. 236): "A profound discontent with the obvious, a search for those more remote meanings which overflow the barriers of the common presuppositions and discourse of men."

[1] For a chatty discussion of some of the avenues thereto, see O. Kuhns, *The Sense of the Infinite*. See also *Atlantic Monthly*, vol. 117, p. 590.

any occurrence of special good fortune, I have enjoyed a perfect exhilaration. I am glad to the brink of fear." Or from Richard Jefferies, when he writes, "With all the intensity of feeling which exalted me, all the intense communion I held with the earth, the sun and sky, the stars hidden by the light, with the ocean — in no manner can the thrilling depth of these feelings be written — with these I prayed, as if they were the keys of an instrument, of an organ, with which I swelled forth the notes of my soul, redoubling my own voice by their power. The great sun burning with light; the strong earth, dear earth; the warm sky; the pure air; the thought of ocean; the inexpressible beauty of all filled me with a rapture, an ecstasy, an inflatus." [1]

But besides cultivating these ecstasies, this ravishing sense of the worth and glory of life, we may set to work to blind ourselves to its defects. The Stoics developed this possibility in antiquity, sometimes half-unconsciously, and again with a sophisticated comprehension of the psychology involved. Marcus Aurelius, for example, realizes that the process is subjective. "Take away thy opinion," he says, "and there is taken away the complaint. Take away the complaint, and the harm is taken away. If thou art pained by any external thing, it is not this thing that disturbs thee, but thine own judgment about it; and it is in thy power to wipe out this judgment now." [2] Just such a persistent optimism, that refuses to label anything trouble and smiles at whatever befalls, has been taught, far more blindly, but with great practical effectiveness, in our contemporary world by Christian Science.

[1] His *Story of My Heart* is full of such rhapsodical expressions of his mystical moods.
[2] Most of his utterances, however, are less sophisticated. Cf., e.g., "But life or death, honor or dishonor, pain or pleasure . . . are neither good nor evil. . . . Nothing is evil which is according to nature."

There is much in Mrs. Eddy's book and in the contemporary teaching of the sect that does not commend itself to the enlightened. As in the case of most religions, what is untrue and what is barren is reverenced and retained through its association with a great and needed truth. But if we are to reject a faith because its founders mingled with it much that is irrational, which religion can retain our allegiance! There are, indeed, practical dangers connected with Christian Science — the danger of neglecting the resources of modern medicine and surgery, together with the proved advantages of disinfection, quarantine, and hygiene in general; the danger, potential in every highly centralized organization, of dominating the minds of multitudes and using its power and money for harmful ends; the danger of opposing scientific education and keeping the minds of its followers on an irrational level. That Christian Science is not scientific needs no argument; and in what material or mental ways that Church may harm the life of the community is yet to be seen. But surely the physical and spiritual good that it has done far outweighs any present evil.

We must recognize that when Mrs. Eddy's disciples say that pain and evil are "unreal," they are using the word in the Platonic sense; "real" is to them a eulogistic word — as it has been, and is, for so many philosophers — meaning what belongs to the spiritual or ideal order. Whatever does not belong to this order has a less worthy kind of existence, and is to be counted out. Plato called it Μὴ ὄν — "nonexistent" — or, perhaps we should translate it, "not to exist"; Mrs. Eddy calls it "error." The words matter little; the practical point is, these evils *must* not exist for us, must not find a place in *our* world. Just as when we adopt any ideal we cease to compute and calculate, but throw ourselves whole-heartedly upon that side, so in our emotional reaction upon life we are to have eyes only for the good and refuse to see anything else. It is treating the world that is our home as we ought to treat our wives and mothers and dearest friends; it is our world, we love it and are loyal to it, for us it shall have no faults.

No doubt for the Christian Scientist himself our appreciation of his faith would seem inadequate; for him it is not an attitude, it is a recognition of what is objectively *so*. But, leaving this point for the present,[1] we may at least agree that Stoic and Christian Scientist and the other thoroughgoing eulogists of the world attain to an inward peace that marks out their faith as having in it something of great human worth. It is possible in far greater degree than most of us realize to banish fear and grief from our lives and attain to an invulnerable peace. The early Christians attained to it — cf. Justin Martyr's, "You can kill us, but you cannot hurt us!"[2] The early Buddhists attained to it — "Enter on this path and make an end of sorrow; verily the path has been preached by me, who have found out how to quench the darts of grief.... He who overcomes this contemptible thirst [the desire for the good things of life and rebelliousness at ill fortune], ... sufferings fall off from him like water-drops from a lotus leaf."[3] In recent years it has been attained in marked degree by Bahaists,[4] by some of the followers of the "New Thought,"[5] as well as by many humble Christians of all sects, and by one here and there who has

[1] For further discussion of Christian Science, see pp. 182-83 and 325-26. And cf. S. L. Clemens, *Christian Science;* L. P. Powell, *Christian Science;* J. H. Leuba, *Psychological Study of Religion*, pp. 301-07; J. V. Morgan, ed., *Theology at the Dawn of the Twentieth Century*, pp. 369-401; G. B. Cutten, *Psychological Phenomena of Christianity*, chap. XVI; W. Riley, *American Thought*, pp. 43-53.

[2] For illustrations of the inward peace of the early Christians, see Edgehill, *The Spirit of Power*, chap. VI.

[3] *Dhammapada*, vss. 275, 336.

[4] See, e.g., *Harvard Theological Review*, vol. 7, p. 339.

[5] See, e.g., Horace Fletcher's *Forethought minus Fearthought*, or R. W. Trine's *What all the World's A-Seeking; In Tune with the Infinite*.

found the way for himself.[1] But Christian Science deserves praise for doing more than any other contemporary force to turn human lives to the sunlight and banish the shadows from their hearts. The therapeutic value of this sunnier attitude is great. But Christian Science is more than a method of bodily healing, it is a way of bringing inward unity and peace into distracted and restless human nature. Its insight must be incorporated into the catholic and inclusive Christianity of the future.

Charity, Piety, Service: A. Harnack, *Mission and Expansion of Christianity*, bk. II, chap. III. F. J. Peabody, *Jesus Christ and the Christian Character*, chaps. IV–VI; *Jesus Christ and the Social Question*. H. Drummond, *Greatest Thing in the World* (in *Essays*). Harnack and Herrmann, *The Social Gospel*. J. H. Newman, *Love, The One Thing Needful* (in *Parochial and Plain Sermons*). J. Royce, *Problem of Christianity*, vol. I, pp. 74–105. E. A. Edghill, *The Spirit of Power*, chap. VII.

Religious Joy and Peace: J. H. Newman, *Religious Joy, Religion Pleasant to the Religious* (in *Parochial and Plain Sermons*). G. M. Stratton, *Psychology of the Religious Life*, pt. I. G. B. Cutten, *Psychological Phenomena of Christianity*, chaps III–IV. G. K. Chesterton, *Heretics*, chap. XVI; *Orthodoxy*, chap. V. W. James, *Varieties of Religious Experience*, chaps. XVI–XVII. E. Underhill, *The Mystic Way; Mysticism*. W. R. Inge, *Christian Mysticism*. W. M. Scott, *Aspects of Christian Mysticism*. O. Kuhns, *Sense of the Infinite*.

---

[1] Cf. Emerson, *History*, in *Essays*, vol. I, "To the poet, to the philosopher, to the saint, all things are friendly and sacred, all events profitable, all days holy, all men divine."

CHAPTER XIV

THE ESSENCE OF RELIGION

How shall we determine the essence of religion?

WITH this hasty outline of the salient phenomena of religion, historical and psychological, before us, we may approach the question, What is the essence of religion, and how shall we define it?

We must at the outset realize the impossibility of framing a definition of religion that shall cover all of its historic aspects. There lie here before our eyes a confused and ever-changing mass of emotions, beliefs, rites, and acts; there is no common factor that runs through them all, no one thing that all phases of religion have had in common that is not also to be found in other spheres of human activity. The religions are bound together by a historic development; but our contemporary civilized religion is as different from the religion of some barbarous tribe as it is from our own æsthetic life or our patriotism. For the matter of that, religion is apt to be so bound up with morality, with superstition, art, politics, all the other phases of man's life, that it is exceedingly difficult to sift out the elements to which its name should be given. This is particularly true, of course, of primitive life, where the differentiation of activities has not progressed far;[1] but even in our modern life other emotions and activities so interpenetrate and blend here and there with religion that it is a perplexing problem to draw boundaries and mark out its distinctive field. To attempt, then, to make our defi-

---

[1] Cf. F. de Coulanges, *The Ancient City:* "Law, government, and religion in Rome were three confused aspects of one thing." See, for an elaboration of this thought, Shotwell, chap. I.

nition inclusive would be, not only to make it so long and cumbersome as to be practically useless, but to include elements which are not present in all religions, and elements which religion shares with other human interests.

It is easy enough to point out, in the case of any of the familiar definitions of religion, that the formula, on the one hand, omits much that is conspicuous in historic faiths, or, on the other hand, covers acts or attitudes not usually thought of as religious. If, for example, we define religion, with Mr. Fielding Hall, as "the recognition and cultivation of all our highest emotions,"[1] we seem to include in it love, patriotism, appreciation of beauty, and the rest. If we define it, with Reinach, as " a sum of scruples,"[2] we seem to include all of our morality, customary and individual. If we define it, with Menzies, as "the worship of higher powers,"[3] we seem to include a mass of barbarous superstitions and empty observances which had no value that we should usually call religious. And no one of these, or of the thousands of other definitions that have been proposed, connotes all of the aspects that have in this religion or that been most strikingly prominent.

The search for a common factor tends, moreover, to emphasize what is trivial rather than what is vital. Not by its early and crude forms, not by its sodden and uninspired devotees, is religion to be judged, but by what it becomes in the lives of the prophets and saints. No one who has known the loyalty and peace of a deeply religious life can be content to think of religion as an emotional debauch, or as a set of scruples, or, with Herbert Spencer, as a sense of the ultimate inscrutableness of the universe. Mystery and emotion may be, as Professor Shotwell says, "constant elements"; they may be the connecting links between the primitive welter of

---

[1] *The Hearts of Men*, p. 298.   [2] *Orpheus*, p. 2.
[3] *History of Religions*, p. 7.

superstition and a religion worthy of the name. But a sense of mystery, or emotional thrills, are not, of themselves, *important* enough; they give no hint of the vital nature of mature religion and its value for life. Religion is a growing and changing thing; as we think of an oak not in terms of what it has in common with the acorn, and man not in terms of what he has in common with his ape-like ancestor, so we may think of religion not in terms of what it was at this or that stage, but in terms of what it has become and bids fair to become in its ripest development.

In fine, the only purpose of offering a definition of religion is to pick out from this ever-changing and infinitely various segment of human experience what seems most important and destined to be permanent. Our definition will be a value-judgment, representing what we deem fit to honor with the eulogistic term " religion," what we consider essential, amid all these many-colored experiences, for the best human life, a norm by which to measure a religion's worth. Such a matter is not to be decided by *a priori* desire or personal prejudice; our decision must be based upon a deep knowledge of the world we live in and the needs and conditions of man's success therein; upon a sympathetic acquaintance with the manifold activities to which the name has been applied, an insight into human nature, and a trained ability to distinguish truth from error. What we shall call the heart of religion, and what its accretions and unessential concomitants, must depend upon what a wide experience teaches us to be needful and what a mature criticism shows us to be true.

What is the relation of religion to theology?

One of the commonest misconceptions is that which thinks of religion as consisting primarily of beliefs — beliefs, in particular, about gods, saviors, a future life, or some sort of supernatural world enveloping our human experience. Such beliefs may have immense power to comfort and inspire; and it is in the midst of them, as its matrix and background, that the religious life has, historically, come into being. But shall we deny the name "religion" to a life that is, in spirit and fruits, the same, when such beliefs are not present? And at what point among these infinitely varying beliefs shall we draw the line between religion and superstition, or between religion and philosophy? Primitive men, and uncultivated men still, are full of supernatural beliefs that have no religious value whatsoever. Philosophers of every stripe have elaborated their convictions upon such matters with no appreciable influence upon their lives. Many a man to-day believes unquestioningly in God, attends church regularly, or fulfills whatever observances he supposes to be required of him, who is no more religious than a courtier who pampers his sovereign's desires. On the other hand, we have one of the greatest of the world's religions, Buddhism, with (in its original purity) no God and no immortal hope. And many an agnostic among us, with no belief in God or a supernatural Christ, and no expectation of heaven, has a truly religious temper and lives a truly religious life.[1]

[1] Cf. Dickinson, *op. cit.*, p. 57, 52: "Religion is an attitude of the imagination and the will, not of the intellect; . . . It is possible, it is common, to believe in God without having religion; it is less common, but it is not less possible, to have religion without believing in God. . . . It is not, in a word, the doctrine that makes religion, it is the spirit; and the spirit may inspire the most diverse and contradictory doctrines."

And Cf. James Martineau, *The Godly Man* (in *Hours of Thought*): "If I see a man living out of an inner spring of inflexible right and pliant piety; if he refuses the colour of the low world around him; if his eye flashes with scorn at mean and impure things which are a jest to others; if high examples of honour and self-sacrifice bring the flush of sympathy upon his cheek; if in his sphere of rule he plainly obeys a trust instead of enforcing an arbitrary will, and in his sphere of service takes his yoke without a groan, and does his work with thought only that it be good; I shall not pry into his closet nor ask about his creed, but own him at once as the godly man. Godliness is the persistent living out an ideal preconception of the Right, the Beautiful, the Good."

It may, indeed, be said of such religions as ignore or reject the concept of God that they have a God under another name. Buddhism has practically made a God of Buddha, as popular Christianity has of Christ. Richard Jefferies, who (in his passionately religious *Story of My Heart*) indignantly scorns the belief in God, speaks constantly of a "something higher than Deity." It is obviously a matter of nomenclature — most men in his case would speak simply of a "higher conception of God." Emerson with his Oversoul, Comte with his idealized Humanity, and many an avowed atheist who serves an abstract Ideal, have a God as truly as the naïve Christian who pictures an anthropomorphic Being in the skies. Something supreme there must be in a religion, something to love, reverence, and worship, something that awakens man's loyalty and wins his allegiance away from his petty affairs. But the intensity of the religious spirit, and its worth in a life, have little relation to the particular concept of God about which it is entwined.

May we not agree, then, to give the name "superstition" to these supernatural beliefs when they remain the crude reflection of blind hopes and fears; to call them philosophical or theological beliefs when they have been worked upon by the intellect, lifted above the level of folklore, and formulated into legitimate theories; and to call them religious only when they have come to have a moral meaning, giving outward and cosmic sanction to an inward and natural ideal? Religion has too long been defined as a set of beliefs, with its spiritual, its ideal aspects treated as a mere corollary or addendum. The study of comparative religion has been too largely a tabulation of the various gods and their characteristics, just as secular history has until lately been little more than a list of kings and their doings. The religion itself, that swayed the hearts of men and glorified their lives, lies buried under all these strange names and grotesque legends. But really it would matter little whether men called their god Isis or Bel or Brahma or Zeus or Jupiter or Jehovah; these differing names have all meant their acknowledgment of a higher supremacy over their animal instincts and selfish passions; and what is important is not their beliefs but their behavior. Back of all the superstitions and dogmatisms, beneath the artificial creeds and the rites that are so often strange to our thought, the seeing eye can discern passionate aspirations, loyalties, and ideals that roused men from their spiritual torpor, steadied their flickering impulses, and made their passions flexible to their will.

> "Which has not taught weak wills how much they can?
> Which has not fall'n on the dry heart like rain?
> Which has not cried to sunk, self-weary man,
>   Thou must be born again!" [1]

Every religion, even the humblest, has had something of this noble and uplifting power. From the outside each seems a pathetic medley of superstition; but within men's hearts each has been in some measure a bulwark against sin, an appeal to the finer instincts, a call to a better life. All the great religious founders and reformers — Zoroaster, Buddha, Confucius, the Hebrew Prophets, Christ, St. Francis, Luther, and the rest — were, above all, teachers and exponents of a higher and purer way of life. Religion is — the spirit that flamed in these men; their cosmological views were but the crust that enveloped it, the concepts through which they gave it expression. Beliefs change and vanish, theologies wax and wane, but the life of charity, consecration, and peace remains. Not opinions and not observances are important in the end, but purity and honor, tenderness, and sympathy, and love. The devotion to these ideals has gone hand in hand with every sort of theological belief, has crystallized into a personal devotion to this or that saint or

[1] Matthew Arnold, *Progress*.

seer, has lifted many a crude and fantastic world-conception into the dignity of a religion.[1]

Theology is man's stumbling and blundering attempt to express and explain this religious life. Each people, in its own language and its own way, has made the attempt; the resulting theories have naturally been full of naïveté and error; and even when they have satisfied men's minds for an epoch, they have proved sadly out of accord with the mental dialect of a later day. "Theology takes the facts of the religious experience and codifies and relates them, puts them in logical order, gives labels to them, explains their inferences, and fits this portion of our experience into the whole of our lives, sets these facts in their right perspective and place in any given view of the world. Theology has the same relation to religion that botany has to flowers or that physics and chemistry have to the material universe.... Theology is a philosophy, religion the life which furnishes the material for that philosophy.... Down through two thousand years men have been working at the indubitable and transforming facts of the Christian experience. They have tried to state those facts in the language of their own generation. They have spoken of them, from the point of view of their own day. They have related them to the view of the world of their time.... And meanwhile, men's views of the world have been changing.... And so you will find it true of

[1] Cf. James, *op. cit.*, p. 505: "When we survey the whole field of religion, we find a great variety in the thoughts that have prevailed there; but the feelings on the one hand and the conduct on the other are almost always the same; for Stoic, Christian, and Buddhist saints are practically indistinguishable in their lives. The theories which religion generates, being thus variable, are secondary; and if you wish to grasp her essence, you must look to the feelings and the conduct as being the more constant elements."

And cf. Emerson, *Sovereignty of Ethics* (in *Lectures and Biographies*), "If theology shows that opinions are fast changing, it is not so with the convictions of men with regard to conduct; these remain."

much of your inherited science of religion, that it will need large modifications and restatements. . . . But do not let this readjustment of your intellectual apprehension of religious truth dim the sense of the reality of that experience to which all this science is but the witness and of which it is but the expression."[1]

Defining religion in terms of life rather than in terms of belief makes it not only a much more vital matter and a far more universal possession, but puts the attainment of a true religion within the reach of humanity. What the actual facts were concerning the creation of the world, or the life and resurrection of Christ, what the truth is concerning the nature of our personalities and their future fate, the nature of God and the destiny of the universe, it is not within our present resources really to know. We may construct more or less probable theories, and stake our lives upon this or that hope. But if religion consisted essentially of dogmas of this sort, the intellectually scrupulous would be obliged to admit it to be merely a set of conjectures or hypotheses. And a realization of the infinitely varied beliefs which men have actually held on these matters would lead the cultivated and sympathetic spectator more and more to an attitude of bewilderment or agnostic neutrality.[2] But it *is* possible for

[1] Albert Parker Fitch, *The College Course and the Preparation for Life*, pp. 134–40. This statement, from the pen of the president of one of our leading theological schools, is a typical expression of the point of view now rapidly gaining ground, that religion is essentially a life rather than a belief or set of beliefs. The modern terms "philosophy of religion," and "science of religion," which are largely displacing the older term "theology," make the relation clearer. Theology is a philosophizing *about* religion.

[2] This step has actually been taken by many who regard religion as a set of beliefs. Cf. J. M. E. McTaggart, *Some Dogmas of Christianity*, pp. 292–93: "It follows that no man is justified in a religious attitude except as a result of metaphysical study. . . . Since [men] are confronted on all sides with religions different from their own, it is inevitable that they should ask themselves why they believe their religions to be true. And when the question is once asked, what can avert a widespread recognition that the truth

men to contrast different ideals and estimate their relative worth; to try different ways of life and know which is best. The truth of religion, in our sense of the word, is experimentally verifiable; it is *practical* truth. And if we give Christianity our allegiance it is because nineteen centuries of repeated experience have conclusively shown its insight into human needs to be most profound and its Way to be the solution for the eternal problem of human life.

The important thing, then, about a religion is not the rationality or irrationality of its intellectual conceptions, but the spirituality and vision of its ideals. The lack of rationality may limit its influence and detract from its power; but without the glowing fire of moral idealism it is dead. What though creeds and rites are foolish and fanciful, so the spiritual vision is high and ennobling! Seeing this precious treasure, which no faith has been utterly without, we may be gently tolerant of all theoretical blunders, and of the "old clothes" — to use Carlyle's picturesque metaphor — in which religion is so commonly wrapped.

Our generation needs the warning that enlightenment cannot take the place of religion. We have learned to understand the facts of life better than our forefathers; but that intellectual gain is but dust and ashes in our mouths if we lose the secret of their religious experience. Grim old Puritans that they were, narrow-minded and bigoted and ignorant of all our science, their picture of history the sheerest melodrama, at least their religion had a deep practical meaning to them, saved them from much sin, and threw a halo about their lives. Again, no normal man can read such a book as James's *Varieties of Religious Experience* without

of religion can only rest on foundations too controversial to be taken on trust, and too obscure for many people to investigate?"

The opening chapter of this book is a good defense of the conception of religion as a set of theological conceptions.

perceiving, on the one hand, the grotesqueness and unreality of the beliefs of many whose experiences are there related, and yet realizing that they had hold of a great secret. The unquestionable fact is that religious people have found something precious that other folk have missed. And among these religious folk are to be counted, not by any means all those who have belonged to this church or that, or believed this, that, or any creed, but all those who have risen above the ordinary, humdrum level of human existence into the realm of deeper breathing and brighter vision, all those who have felt the power and peace of an altered life.

What is the relation of religion to morality?

If religion is to be conceived as a way to live rather than as a set of cosmological or historical beliefs, wherein is it different from morality?

Historically speaking, the religions have been something more than the moral codes which they incorporated. They have framed those codes with some sort of cosmic significance, have invested them with emotional values, and made them dynamic. "Merely moral" men are those who have been correct in their behavior, but who have failed to see the super-personal setting of the restraints which they obeyed, have missed the far vistas, the calling forth of loyalty, the unction and the joy that religious men have known. The moralist approaches the problems of life through intellectual comprehension, and the result is the life of reason; the prophet approaches them through his heart and intuition, and the result is religion. Mere morality is prosaic, cool, exact; religion is imaginative, emotional, exaggerated. Benjamin Franklin's maxims are moral, the Sermon on the Mount is religious. In religion a cold necessity has become a glorious privilege, the latent enthusiasms in a man's heart have been awakened; the religious man is he who feels the infinite importance of moral choice, the boundlessness and depth of duty, and yearns for a noble and sinless life. Morality may be a matter of policy or of habit; religion is an inward thing, a dedication of heart and will, a positive espousal of ideals.[1]

The Greek philosophers supposed that wisdom alone would be enough to steer men aright in their problems of conduct. But the rational view of morality developed by Plato and Aristotle failed to regenerate the world. Men's instincts and passions are too strong; they need to conquer emotion by emotion, to be caught up by a great conception that can arouse their dormant idealism, awaken their loyalty, and make them care for the Way that reason approves but leaves so uninviting. Most of our temptations owe their appeal to our craving for happiness, for excitement, for something great, the quickened heartbeats and deeper breathing of a passion given rein. Morality is dull, repressive, cold; and while we acknowledge its utility, we often lack the power to care for and follow its behests. Religion satisfies this need, meeting excitement with excitement, joy with a purer joy, giving us something bigger and better than the temptation from which it turns us. It not only tells a man what to do, it pushes him into doing it; it not only sets up a code, it gets into a man's heart and saves him. Historically, this is what the religions, as contrasted with the mere philosophies and moral codes, have done; and any man

[1] Cf. Matthew Arnold, *Literature and Dogma*, chap. 1, pp. 13, 17: "The object of religion is *conduct*. . . . Religion means simply either a binding to righteousness or else a serious attending to righteousness and dwelling upon it. Which of these two it most nearly means, depends upon the view we take of the word's derivation; but it means one of them, and they are very much the same. . . . Is there, therefore, no difference between what is ethical, or morality, and religion? There is a difference, a difference of degree. Religion, if we follow the intention of human thought and human language in the use of the word, is ethics heightened, enkindled, lit up by feeling; the passage from morality to religion is made when to morality is applied emotion. And the true meaning of religion is thus, not simply *morality*, but *morality touched by emotion*."

deserves to be called religious by whom an ideal of life has been so heartily and loyally espoused that it lifts him, in some measure, above the power of temptation to seduce or of ill fortune to depress.¹

A rational study of ethics presents us only with relative values; this way, it says, will lead to such and such results, this duty is on the whole and in most cases the higher. It speaks in terms of probability and approximation; the ideal remains for it always problematic and open to doubt. But men cannot live by probabilities; success demands definite choice. Religion is such a choice; it *commits* a man, for better or worse, to a clear-cut, concrete ideal. It is, as has been said, a "great bias." The religious man pledges his allegiance, he no longer weighs and considers, no longer deals with advantages and utilities; he obeys the command, "Thou shalt not!" he labels the one act Duty and the other Sin. The classic Greek ideal was one of moderation; "nothing in excess" was its motto. And the worldly man of all times has sought this *via media;* as much altruism and honesty and purity as pays, no more. Not such is the temper of the religious man; he is an extremist, quixotic, weighing no

¹ Cf. James, *op. cit.*, pp. 41–51: "Morality pure and simple accepts the law of the whole which it finds reigning, so far as to acknowledge and obey it, but it may obey it with the heaviest and coldest heart, and never cease to feel it as a yoke. But for religion, in its strong and fully developed manifestations, the service of the highest never is felt as a yoke. Dull submission is left far behind, and a mood of welcome, which may fill any place on the scale between cheerful serenity and enthusiastic gladness, has taken its place. . . . Whereas the merely moralistic spurning takes an effort of volition, the Christian spurning is the result of the excitement of a higher kind of emotion, in the presence of which no exertion of volition is required. . . . If religion is to mean anything definite for us, it seems to me that we ought to take it as meaning this added dimension of emotion, this enthusiastic temper of espousal, in regions where morality strictly so called can at best but bow its head and acquiesce. It ought to mean nothing short of this new reach of freedom for us, with the struggle over, the keynote of the universe sounding in our ears, and everlasting possession spread before our eyes. . . . Religion thus makes easy and felicitous what in any case is necessary."

loss against his gain. Christianity demands not a modicum of love and purity, but boundless love and absolute purity. No man, it says, but is our brother and must be loved to the end; no ideal is too high to put up as our goal. By demanding all, it touches the deepest springs in our nature, opens up infinite horizons, gives us a sense of quickened living.

Another characteristic of religion is its simplicity. Morality consists in following a heterogeneous set of precepts; religion unifies, gives a single direction and aim.[1] Amid the tangle of possibilities and the conflicting calls of impulse it points the finger and says, "Do thus and so!" Confused by the manifold instincts that his life engenders, beset by insidious temptations that he knows not how to resist, the religious man gives his allegiance to a definite ideal; though it be not ultimately the best, he takes it for his, he devotes his heart to it, he makes it a part of himself; and through this single-heartedness he solves the problem of his life.[2]

What is the essential nature of religion?

Religion, in the best sense of the word, is the devotion of the heart and will to some great ideal of life. It is the universal war against sin and wrong, greatly and imaginatively conceived. It is the divine urge in the human breast — "the life of God in the soul of man." It summons men from their haphazard, animal life, rescues them from their passions, is

---

[1] Cf. F. Adler, *The Essentials of Spirituality:* "The spiritually minded person [= the religious person] is one who regards whatever he undertakes from the point of view of hindering or furthering the attainment of a supreme end."

[2] Discussions of the relation between religion and morality, besides those of Matthew Arnold and William James from which excerpts have been quoted, will be found in G. H. Palmer's *Field of Ethics,* chap. IV; G. Galloway's *Philosophy of Religion,* pp. 195–204; G. T. Ladd's *Philosophy of Religion,* vol. I, chap. XIX; *New World,* vol. 2, p. 453; *American Journal of Theology,* vol. 7, p. 259; *Harvard Theological Review,* vol. 4, p. 229; *Hibbert Journal,* vol. 12, p. 529.

never without the sense that they need correction, adjustment, salvation. Its presence means emancipation from the cares and fears of worldliness, release from anxious, burdened moods, a new tranquillization, poise of spirit, power; a widening of horizons, an easing of strain, an inner resourcefulness and stability. The individual loses himself in a larger life, and thereby finds that life has more dignity and worth than the natural man knows.

Religion, if it is worthy the name, always brings this sense of revelation, of profounder insight into the meaning of things, a new evaluation and perspective. Its task is "the salvation of men through the transformation of a natural life into a life whose dwelling-place lies beyond human woe and sin." There is a way to live — it has been found over and over again by this saint and that — that ennobles life and gives it a heavenly radiance; it is of the pathos of human existence that so few have caught the vision, so few have learned the precious secret that might be the heritage of all. But some dim measure of the truth has been grasped and passed on from age to age, some glimmers of spiritual insight, shining through the superstitions and dogmas that have enveloped them, giving a certain unity to the variegated religious practices of men. This core of spiritual life at the heart of so many diverse systems — marred as it is by many excrescences, mingled with all sorts of blunders and illusions, and overlaid by the laborious interpretations of the groping intellect — is the essence of religion.

There are many possible attitudes toward life. A man may be cowed and despairing, he may be unemotional, indifferent, sodden; he may be rebellious, or cynical, or frivolous, or melancholy. There is the rake, who makes of life a debauch; there is the Epicurean, who makes of it a dainty pursuit of enjoyment; there is the humorist, who makes of it a joke. To all these attitudes religion is sharply opposed. The religious attitude, through all its variations, is an earnest, aspiring attitude. It seeks to wean men from their haphazard, hand-to-mouth existence, to save them from the satiety and restlessness and heart-hunger that are inevitably engendered by selfish and sensual, and even by trivial and flabby, living. Sad it may sometimes be, when confronted by the ineffaceable pain and disillusions of life, ecstatic and light-hearted it may be in brighter moments; but it is always serious, demanding restraint of conduct and discipline of will. Goethe, with all his genius, and whatever the strength of his theological convictions, was not a religious man, because he lived for the exploitation of his passions and the gratification of his personal ambitions. Rousseau, with all his pious sentiments, was palpably irreligious, because he had in his heart no principle of loyalty or consecration that even struggled to overcome his animal instincts and worldly desires. In sharp contrast with such "carnal" men, the great religious seers, from Buddha and Zoroaster to Wesley or Phillips Brooks, have been men whose lives have been dedicated to a great ideal, and who in its service have found daily inspiration and joy.

It may be thought that this is too simple a matter to constitute religion. But religion does not exist to persuade men to believe something unnatural and a mystery; it exists to express and keep before them those natural ideals which they do in their better moments believe in, but tend forever to forget; to make them, in despite of temptation and inertia and willfulness, steadily remember and care for and obey them. To reinforce the weak voice of these ideals men need to make a religion of them, to devote themselves to their commands with ardor, and become possessed by them. Not only must the mind be convinced, the heart must be won from sin, the imagination must be stirred, the ideal which the needs and conditions of our life prescribe must be thought of not as a yoke, to be heavily and grudgingly obeyed, but as a vision to be passionately loved and followed. And religion, because it does that for man, is the greatest and most beautiful thing in his life.

H. B. Mitchell, *Talks on Religion*, chap. I. E. S. Ames, *Psychology of Religious Experience*, pt. IV. W. James, *Varieties of Religious Experience*, chaps. I–II. L. Tolstoy, *What is Religion?* H. Höffding, *Philosophy of Religion*, pp. 105–16. G. Galloway, *Philosophy of Religion*, chap. IV. G. B. Foster, *Function of Religion in the Life of Man*. G. L. Dickinson, *Religion, a Criticism and a Forecast*, chap. III. M. Arnold, *Literature and Dogma: Preface, Introduction*, chap. I. J. H. Leuba, *Psychological Study of Religion*, pt. I, and *Appendix*. H. F. Hall, *Hearts of Men*. W. Bender, *Wesen der Religion*. B. P. Bowne, *Essence of Religion*. J. R. Seeley, *Natural Religion, Preface*, and pt. I. J. Royce, *Philosophy of Loyalty*, chap. VIII. J. M. E. McTaggart, *Some Dogmas of Religion*, chap. I. Emerson, *Character, The Preacher, Sovereignty of Ethics* (in *Lectures and Biographies*). G. T. Ladd, *Philosophy of Religion*, vol. I, chap. XXII. B. Russell, *Philosophical Essays*, II. *Hibbert Journal*, vol. 11, p. 46. *Harvard Theological Review*, vol. 4, p. 229. *Monist*, vol. 11, p. 536.

CHAPTER XV
THE CHRISTIAN RELIGION

Is Christianity the true religion?

THE traditional conception of Christendom has been that it is the only true faith and all others are false; on the one hand, a God-given and ultimate religion, on the other, nothing but man-made and erroneous superstitions. Such a judgment, we have now come to see, was a presumptuous and narrow conceit. Christianity is one of several widespread and inspiring religions, by which men have been helped to live and for which they have been ready to die. Only Christians are to be "saved"? And Christianity has existed less than two thousand years, out of the hundreds of thousands since man emerged from the brute! There were flourishing civilizations, men and women honorable, pure, religious, centuries before Christ, or Jehovah, was ever heard of. The old Christian conception of history covers but six thousand years in all — and leaves out during that time the matchless Greek civilization, spurns the splendid Roman order, includes everything but its own local and brief phase of history in one sweeping condemnation. Because, forsooth, all these did not worship the Jewish Jehovah!

If to believe this were Christianity, then Christianity would be doomed to speedy extinction. It were too parochial an affair, with too small a range of vision, inapplicable to the wider stage of human history. This arrogant and perverted perspective is out of line with all else that we learn of man and his progress, this singularly partial God unworthy of our worship; and a dogmatic structure based on this conception, however buttressed by argument, and however full of precious consolation to its believers, cannot but fall as men grow more enlightened and more humane. Not merely in the two thousand years of Christianity, but in some degree in all religions and among all races, man's groping spiritual life has found expression.

Yet if all the great religions have truth in them, Christianity, we may justly claim, has the fullest measure of truth. The Christian life, at its best, is the highest type of life proposed to man; and Christ is humanity's profoundest teacher and most fitting guide. The particular concepts and phraseology of the religion that centers about him, though open to narrow misinterpretations and leading often to an unhappy dogmatism, are of the deepest and most vital significance. The Fatherhood of God, the Holy Spirit in our hearts, the Divinity of Christ, the Cross that we must bear, the Kingdom of Heaven toward which we strive — such language represents so adequately the highest yearnings and insights of the spiritual life that mankind may well come more and more to employ it to express, in appropriate symbols, its perennial aspirations and its eternal joys.[1]

[1] Cf. S. Reinach, *Orpheus* (Eng. tr.), p. 232: "Christianity ... is the mightiest spiritual force which has ever transformed souls, a force which continues to evolve in them. ... It is the morality of the school without a school, purified and distilled in ardent souls, with all the charm and all the persuasive force of popular conceptions."

So Loisy, *The Gospel and the Church*, "The spirit of the Gospel is the highest manifestation of the human conscience seeking happiness in justice."

And J. Royce, *The Problem of Christianity*, vol. 1, p. 10–11: "The Christian religion is, thus far at least, man's most impressive vision of salvation, and his principal glimpse of the home-land of the spirit ... the most effective expression of religious longing which the human race, travailing in pain until now, has, in its corporate capacity, as yet been able to bring before its imagination as a vision, or has endeavored to translate, by the labor of love, into the terms of its own real life."

For none of these authors is Christianity marked off by supernatural revelation from the other religions, or radically different in kind. It is sim-

The Gospel of Christ

To find the essence of Christianity, we must go first, of course, to the teachings of Christ, as recorded in the Synoptic Gospels. We need not here repeat the summary of that teaching which we made in an earlier chapter.[1] But we may pause to point out that subsequent Christianity, though it moved far from its founder's spirit in its creeds and ceremonies and institutions, yet retained, and retains to this day, a bright glow from that original fire.

Christ's first word was "Repent!"— which meant, not "Do penitence!" but "Turn about, live a new kind of life!" Men were to care for heavenly, spiritual treasures rather than for worldly treasures, to lose their lives in order really to find them, to seek to minister rather than to be ministered unto. The radicalism of this demand is obscured for us by its familiarity; but it was hardly straining the metaphor to say, "Except a man be born again he cannot enter the Kingdom of Heaven." For Paul this need of regeneration was symbolized by the Cross — "they that are Christ's have crucified the flesh with its passions and lusts"; they must die with Christ to the old life and rise with him to the new. Paul told also of miraculous occurrences — of the earthly life, the resurrection, and the future coming of the Christ. But the heart of his gospel was the possibility of a new Life for his hearers, the putting off of the old man and putting on of the new. "In Christ Jesus neither circumcision availeth anything nor uncircumcision, but a new nature." The Church has clung throughout all its changing theologies to this fun-

ply the best of many good religions. For criticisms of Christianity, see H. Sturt, *The Idea of a Free Church*; H. Holley, *The Modern Social Religion* (Bahaism), pt. IV; G. L. Dickinson, *Religion and Immortality*, chap. I; W. Rauschenbusch, *Christianity and the Social Crisis*, chap. IV; *New World*, vol. 1, p. 618.

[1] See above, pp. 75-81.

damental sense of the need of a radical turnabout from the desires and passions of the natural man to the new passions and loyalties of the spiritual life.[1] This teaching was foolishness to the Greeks whom Paul addressed; it is foolishness to the worldly-minded to-day. But the accumulating experience of nineteen centuries proves, for those who have eyes to see, that it is the deepest wisdom.

But the teaching of Christ was not, as has so often been supposed, an other-worldliness, a snatching away of a few saved souls from a world left to its fate into a heaven in the skies. On the contrary, he prayed that God's will be done on earth as in heaven; he foretold, and bade men prepare for, the coming divine age when righteousness and peace should reign in men's hearts, and injustice, cruelty, and sin should be done away. His faith in and ardor for this new era of a bettered human life on earth dominated all his teaching; his plea was that there and then his listeners should begin for themselves the New Life and form the nucleus of the new community. And though we may have to restate them in modern language, the same great Hope and the same great Duty that flamed in Jesus' gospel can still fire our hearts. For the Kingdom is coming now "with observation"; though it is not so much a "Lo, here!" or "Lo, there!" that reveals it as the long vista of history. Pessimism as to human progress is shallow observation; great as is the evil in

---

[1] Cf. T. H. Green, *Two Sermons*, pp. 16, 70: "The primary Christian idea is that of a moral death into life." "The great concern of the best Christian teachers has been . . . to bring their people to enact in their own hearts and lives the work which the creeds rehearse; not to convince them that Christ was miraculously born and died and rose again, but so to affect them as that they shall die and rise again with him. . . . " And C. Bigg, *The Church's Task under the Roman Empire*, Introduction: "Christianity *per genus* is a religion; *per differentiam* it is the religion of the Cross. The Fatherhood of God, the immortality of the soul, revelation, sacrifice, prophecy, and law are common to many religions. . . . But the Cross is the peculiar property of the Gospel. This is the emblem the first Christians adopted."

human life, and many as are its setbacks, amelioration is, on the whole, a fact beyond dispute. And every Christian should work with those who are battling with the forces of evil and helping to bring in the new time.[1]

If Christian evangelism and zeal for regenerative work derive thus from the Gospel of the Master, so nearly all the ideals which the Church has stood for can be found adumbrated in his teaching. The summons "Back to Christ!" has been the cry of most of the great reformers since his time. Humanity is forever losing the vision, thinking to be saved by sacraments and outward conformities, drifting away from the spiritual insights that the Church exists to perpetuate. Men are reading the Gospels less to-day than formerly, and in the rush and prosperity of modern life forgetting or even despising the simple precepts of the Galilean. But outward prosperity is a fickle goddess to worship; and even when her favors are constant she leaves the heart parched and empty. If we would learn the deepest secrets of life we must turn not to the captains of industry, the statesmen, or even the poets, but to those who have lived in passionate loyalty to a religious ideal; and of them all the peerless leader is Christ.

"We are weak, dragged down by animal instincts and impulses; helpless often, before the sins which do so easily beset

[1] Cf. J. S. Mill, *Theism* (end): "A battle is constantly going on, in which the humblest human creature is not incapable of taking some part, between the powers of good and those of evil, and in which every even the smallest help to the right side has its value in promoting the very slow and often almost insensible progress by which good is gradually gaining ground from evil, yet gaining so visibly at considerable intervals as to promise the very distant but not uncertain final victory of Good. To do something during life, on even the humblest scale if nothing more is within reach, towards bringing this consummation ever so little nearer, is the most animating and invigorating thought which can inspire a human creature; and that it is destined, with or without supernatural sanctions, to be the religion of the future I cannot entertain a doubt."

us: the religious consciousness of Jesus kept him, not only pure in deed, but pure in heart. . . . We are selfish, lovers of ease, concerned for personal comfort: the religious consciousness of Jesus held him tranquil when he knew not where to lay his head. . . . We are troubled about many things, eager for possessions: the religious consciousness of Jesus kept him free from the clutch of material things, held him peacefully assured that even food and raiment are but things to be added unto the true life. . . . We are despondent, morose, afraid to be glad: the religious consciousness of Jesus led him to rejoice in the beauty of the world, made him no less welcome at the feast than in the house of mourning. We are hampered at every turn by conventions, concerned for the outside of the platter: the religious consciousness of Jesus held ever clearly before him the true values of life. . . . We are dull of sight, given to miserable misunderstandings: the religious consciousness of Jesus gave him a quick and sure insight into the hearts of men and women, so that the common people heard him gladly and all the city was gathered together at his door. We are bitter, unforgiving, ungenerous: the religious consciousness of Jesus enabled him to forgive all things, because 'they know not what they do.' We are cowardly, afraid of suffering, physical and mental, afraid, continually, of what may happen: the religious consciousness of Jesus rendered him absolutely fearless, capable of defying without hesitation a religious conservatism bitterly intolerant and vindictive, carried him from one danger to another with a courage quiet, steady, magnificent. We are cold, indifferent, unsympathetic: the religious consciousness of Jesus filled him with a compassion so profound, so tender, so mighty, that the very sound of his voice, and touch of his hand, brought healing to the sick in body and in mind. . . . In brief, the religious consciousness of Jesus made his life, so full of privation, discouragement, and suffering, the life that, whatever may be our creed, we all know in our hearts was the life preëminently worth living." [1]

The Christian religion, whatever of new insight it may add to its gospel from age to age, as it develops and adjusts itself to the changing conditions of man's existence, must ever go back to its source, the life and teachings of Jesus, and make the spirit that was there so gloriously manifested the heart of its message.

The Gospel about Christ

Not a few have maintained that the real Christianity is simply — the teachings of Christ. Whatever is not there found is an extraneous addition to the religion which should be stripped off, that it may shine in its original purity. To such a plea we may all, with considerable sympathy, respond; whatever, certainly, is alien to the spirit of the Master should find no place in a church that calls itself by his name. That admission would shear from the Church its reliance upon sacraments and forms, its insistence upon orthodoxy, and many another corruption abhorrent to his spirit. But, on the other hand, we must recognize that man's problems change from age to age, his knowledge widens, and his needs develop. If any religion is to be permanent and universal in its appeal and in its help, it must keep pace with

[1] *The Religion of Christ in the Twentieth Century*, pp. 176–80, abridged. Cf. also R. E. Spear, in *Constructive Quarterly*, vol. 1, pp. 544–45: " My thesis is that in our search for the essential and constructive principles of Christianity, we can get more help from foreign missions than from any other source. . . . Foreign missions embody the elements of Christianity which are essential to its life. . . . They are the present expression of the primitive Christian spirit fresh from its first contact with God in Christ. To go straight to the heart of the matter, they are the purest embodiment of the spirit of absolute loyalty to duty and of utterly unselfish love. And these are the two highest characteristics of the life of our Lord, and therefore of the Christian mind. They were the two commandments of the Law when the Law had passed through the alembic of his soul who fulfilled it. They were the emphatic notes of his own doctrine."

this evolution and develop *pari passu* with these needs. An evolution of this sort there has, in fact, been. The Christianity of the Greek fathers was very different, in many ways, from the gospel of Christ, mediæval Christianity still more different; and our modern Christianity, although in its "liberal" phases harking back to considerable extent to the earliest form of the faith, yet includes elements foreign to Christ's own mind and preaching. And this is as proper as it is inevitable; it is the churches that have changed and grown that have been most alive and imparted most life to their members. We must not confuse the question, What is Christianity? with the question, What was primitive Christianity? The Christian religion is a living reality now, and entitled to definition in terms not merely of what it was at the outset, but of what it has since become.[1]

The most conspicuous element that has been added by the Church to the teaching of Jesus is, of course, the Christological element, its recognition of him as the great Revealer of God and spiritual truth, and its reverent devotion to him. Jesus himself — in spite of the picture of him drawn, in a later day, in the Fourth Gospel — did not go about preaching his own importance or teaching a doctrine of his own nature. He talked not of himself but of his ideals for men, and of the blessed time to come when those ideals should be realized on earth. Nevertheless, to the Way of Life taught by him there was bound to be added an interpretation of his life and mission; to the gospel *of* Christ a gospel *about* Christ. And this has been an indispensable part of the religion ever since.

The importance of the emphasis upon Christ himself — rather than upon the abstract truth of his teaching — lies in the fact that abstract truths lack power to move the average

[1] Cf. S. J. Case, *Evolution of Early Christianity*, chap. I: "The Developmental Nature of Christianity."

man; he needs something concrete and visible, he finds God chiefly in men, the best men he knows. Such hero-worship is one of the most potent of upbuilding forces; through the contemplation of their ideal as actually wrought into earthly life in Christ many a man has been saved from sin who would have remained indifferent to the bare teaching itself. Christ was what we long to be; the goodness, the purity and power and peace, that was in him is the ideal of Christianity. In him the word became flesh, the ideal became incarnate. And so the central point in the religion is not a set of abstract ideals but a living, glowing, appealing personality. Christianity is, and will always be, for most men, primarily a personal loyalty to Christ.[1]

It is true that — judged *a priori*, and apart from the actual course of history — some other spiritual leader might have been idealized by his followers and subsequent generations, and become our banner-bearer and inspiration. There is something arbitrary about this exclusive devotion to one man, however pure and however great. But by a conjunction of historical events he has become the one about whom the ideals of humanity have clustered; he has become a summation and apotheosis of all human virtues. And it is he who

[1] Cf. Professor D. C. Macintosh, of Yale School of Religion: "Christianity is the religion of discipleship to Jesus." And Professor G. W. Knox, of Union Theological Seminary, "Christianity in its broadest definition is the religion of all those who call Jesus Lord." And E. Lewis, in *The Atlantic*, vol. 114, p. 735: "That which distinguishes the Christian religion from every other is the supreme position it gives to a personality and a personal ideal once actually incarnated in terms of human life and character, and the central emphasis it places upon identification with the spirit of the Master as the determinant of conduct in the professed disciple."

And cf. Carlyle, *Heroes and Hero-Worship: The Hero as Divinity:* "No nobler feeling than this of admiration for one higher than himself dwells in the breast of man. It is to this hour, and at all hours, the vivifying influence in man's life. Religions I find stand upon it; not Paganism only, but far higher and truer religions, — all religion hitherto known. Hero-worship, heartfelt prostrate admiration, submission, burning, boundless, for a noblest godlike Form of Man, — is not that the germ of Christianity itself?"

was actually the spring and source of the movement that spread a spiritual religion over the weary and wicked world of the West, lighted a flame of aspiration and joy and hope, amid dark and troubled times, that has changed the face of civilization and bids fair to change it far more in the future. And if we consider not only what his life and death effected, but what he himself was, if we catch the vision of his inward purity and outward sweetness, his freedom from bondage to the orthodoxy of his time, his fearless obedience to his dominating purpose in a hostile environment, the steadfastness with which he kept true to it even at the cost of his life, we shall confess him a fitting model for our contemplation and founder for our Church.[1]

But we must insist that to believe in Christ is, essentially, to believe that he is our fitting master, that we should live as he lived.[2] Our Christological theories matter little; what matters is that we should take up our cross and follow him. That, at least, and not any particular belief about him, was what he asked of men. Those that were to enter the Kingdom were not those that called him "Lord, Lord!" but whoever obeyed the Divine will.[3] Blasphemy against him was to be forgiven; it was only blasphemy against the holy spirit itself that was the hopeless sin.[4] So long as men are turned to the right life it matters little whether they recognize or not the sources of their healing and inspiration; a "Christless Christianity," if men would actually live it, would be infi-

[1] Cf. C. F. Dole, in *Theology at the Dawn of the Twentieth Century*, p. 250: "Reserving all matters of dissent and criticism, it remains that Jesus stands as the historical type, as well as the teacher, of a new order of human life. . . . Grant that these teachings were not original with Jesus. Nevertheless, he is the conspicuous figure of the man who adopted them, trusted them, and went to his death for their sake. The teachings took his name, because somehow he contrived to give them reality and working power."

[2] Cf. E. Lewis, *loc. cit.*, "Faith in Jesus is self-identification with him in the spirit and practice of life."

[3] Matt. 7:21.   [4] Matt. 12:32. Luke 12:10.

nitely better than a devout belief in Christ which bore little fruit in conduct. But actually it has been the personal figure of Christ, blessing the little children, healing the sick, firing the hearts of his disciples, facing the bigoted priests, and dying on the Cross, that has brought poignantly home to men the ideals for which he lived and died. And the Church has done well to cling, through all its permutations of doctrine and practice, to its allegiance to the person of its Founder.

The Christian life and Christian creeds

The early Christians called their religion not a belief but a *Way*.[1] According to the Fourth Gospel, Christ came that men might have *life, and life more abundantly*. So Origen speaks of "the life that Jesus taught." The help that he gave — and that we most imperiously need — was a practical help, an insight into the true values of life and a method of attaining them. This gospel came to be clothed in the concepts of current Greek thought and enshrined in an organization of Roman lineage. But "creedless Christianity is older than any creeds." And that the gospel requires no particular world-view for its acceptance is proved by the fact that it has persisted and leavened human life through the profoundest changes in outlook and belief. The simplicity of Jesus and his early followers was the high-water-mark of Christianity; for them the Life was more and the doctrine less than in the subsequent history of the Church. Afterward dogmas grew up, varying from century to century,. but always standing more or less in the way of free acceptance of the Life. Yet through all these changes Christianity has preserved some measure of its initial insight and evaluations. The *Weltanschauung* of Christ, of Paul, of Tertullian, of Athanasius, of St. Augustine, of Thomas Aquinas, of Calvin, of Phillips Brooks, of Martineau, were as widely different as

[1] Cf. Acts 9:2; 19:23.

can well be imagined; but for them all the Life was essentially the same. This ideal of life, together with a personal allegiance to him who taught it, is what all Christians have in common.

From time to time reformers have arisen who have sought to remove some of the crust of speculation from the preaching of the Christian Life. In our generation, after an era of keen theological disputation, the current is again setting toward the spiritual conception of religion; and the Church is putting its emphasis upon charity and purity and service. But always beneath its forbidding formularies and elaborate theologies it has kept alive a spark of the spirit of brotherliness and earnest consecration that inspired its Master, Christ, that glowed in the bosom of Paul and the apostles, that led St. Francis out to nurse the sick and dying, that has lifted many a humble and uncultivated man to a level above that of Cæsar or Napoleon. Read the Nicene or the Athanasian Creed, and Christianity will appear to be a sort of intellectual jugglery; look at the lives of the faithful, and you will see Christianity in its true essence and ultimate significance, as the life of the spirit, illuminating men's troubled hearts, bringing them inward power and peace.

"The first Christian associations were formed on a basis which was less intellectual than moral and spiritual. . . . It was a fellowship of a common ideal and a common enthusiasm of goodness, of neighborliness, and of mutual service, of abstinence from all that would arouse the evil passions of human nature, of the effort to crush the lower part of us in the endeavor to reach after God. . . . It is even possible that the baptismal formula may have consisted, not in an assertion of belief, but in a promise of amendment." But "the flocking into the Christian fold of the educated Greeks and Romans, who brought with them the intellectual habits of mind which dominated in the age, gave to the intellectual element an importance which it had not previously possessed. Agreement in opinion, which had been the basis of union in the Greek philosophical schools, and later in the Gnostic societies, now came to form a new element in the bond of union within and between churches. ... The insistence on that intellectual basis ... checked the progress of Christianity. Christianity has won no great victories since its basis was changed." [1]

Who is the true Christian?

A Christian is — any one who is consciously a follower of Christ, who looks to Christ as his pattern and guide, and sincerely tries to live the Christ-life — the life of self-surrender and purity and love, the life that aims not to be ministered unto but to minister — in the midst of a selfish and sensual world.

The Christian will naturally wish to know what can now be known of God, and Christ, the human soul and its destiny; and he will gladly profess publicly his belief in what appears to him to be the truth. But Christ imposed no creedal test; rather, he had scant consideration for the orthodoxy of his times, and flung to men the question, "Why judge ye not of yourselves what is right?" So the Christian need know nothing of theology, hold no particular conception of the person of Christ, and bind himself to no creed.

The Christian will probably find inspiration for himself and be able best to help others by allying himself with one of the churches that have grown up about the name of Christ; and he will glory in open confession of his discipleship to the Master. But Christ founded no organization, and offered salvation to men not through sacraments or church-going but through repentance and espousal of the New Life. So

[1] E. Hatch, *The Influence of Greek Ideas and Usages on the Christian Church*, pp. 335–49, abridged.

the Christian need belong to no church; and if he does join one of the churches he will look upon his membership therein not as in itself constituting him a Christian but only as a means to quicken his spiritual life and enable him the better to serve his fellows.

The one essential requirement of the Christian is that he heed the admonition of the Apostle, "Let him that nameth the name of Christ depart from iniquity!" And yet, if he is conscious that he has sinned, if he despairs of his strength to keep pure and loyal, he will remember that Christ came to save that which was lost, called his followers from among just such sinful men, and bade his disciples forgive seventy times seven times. Whoever is sincerely repentant for past faults, is ready to take up his cross again and follow Christ, is willing to fight on against the sensual nature within him and to think most not of himself but of others, may, humbly but proudly, take to himself the name of Christian.

W. A. Brown, *Essence of Christianity*. C. C. Everett, *The Distinctive Mark of Christianity* (in *Essays, Theological and Literary*). A. Sabatier, *Outlines of the Philosophy of Religion*, bk. II, chap. II. Anon., *Religion of Christ in the Twentieth Century* (Putnam's, 1906). A. Harnack, *What is Christianity? Christianity and History*. J. Royce, *Problem of Christianity*, vol. I. B. W. Bacon, *Christianity Old and New*. L. Feuerbach, *Essence of Christianity*. A. Loisy, *Gospel and the Church*. G. Tyrrell, *Christianity at the Crossroads*. W. Rauschenbusch, *Christianity and the Social Crisis*. W. Bousset, *What is Religion*, chap. VII. B. H. Streeter, *Restatement and Reunion*, chap. I. W. H. P. Faunce, *What Does Christianity Mean*, chap. I. *Hibbert Journal*, vol. 11, p. 717. *New World*, vol. 1, p. 401; vol. 9, p. 246. *American Journal of Theology*, vol. 16, p. 256. *Harvard Theological Review*, vol. 7, p. 16. *Biblical World*, vol. 44, p. 398.

SUMMARY OF PART II

What function does religion have in the life of man?

LIFE may be said to consist broadly of two activities, the adjustment of things to ourselves and the adjustment of ourselves to things; the former is the object of all practical work, the latter is the object of religion. If men are to live in any safety and comfort much labor must be performed upon the outer world; nature must be subdued and refashioned to become adapted to man's needs. But this is not all. When the highest degree of physical security and material luxury is wrested from mother earth, when knowledge is won and art developed, there remain sources of dissatisfaction and distress. That residuum in the nature of things which man cannot change confronts him and warns him that his human nature too must be tamed and reshaped if he is to attain to a sure and abiding happiness.

Thus, religion is not a merely adventitious source of satisfaction, an extra solace tacked on to life; it is a psychological necessity. In the broad and natural sense in which we are now using the word, every man must be religious if his life is to be a complete success. Beset as he is by warring and unwise impulses, surrounded by other human beings with wants and wills of their own, confronted by the obdurate facts of pain and separation and death, he must learn to weed out and harmonize his desires, to adjust his will to the welfare of those about him, and to set his heart upon such things that the uncertainties of life cannot take away his joy in living and plunge him into despair. To these fundamental and irremovable aspects of life he must adapt himself; he must struggle till he attain to the life of purity, the life of love, the life of peace.

The necessary adjustment of life to its conditions is made when we have attained a harmony of our impulses with one another, with the wills of other people, and with the fortune that befalls us. By enlisting men's devotion to such ideals, by teaching a way of life that can save them from sensuality and sin, unite them in brotherhood and mutual service, and lift them above sorrow, religion has, for those who have really grasped its secret, proved a solution of the great problem of life. From the cold necessity of obedience to moral laws and of self-repression religion leads men to a love of righteousness and purity; from an enforced tribal loyalty and a legally prescribed justice religion lifts them to a love of their fellows, to a genuine unselfishness and charity; from a mere stunned submission to fortune or defiance of its injuries, religion lifts them to the peace that comes from complete self-surrender in the service of the Ideal. This disposition of the heart and will, through which a man comes to care for the highest things and to live in gentleness and inward calm above the surface aspects and accidents of life, we call, in its inner nature, Spirituality; when it is embodied in outward forms and institutions, and spreads among whole communities, we call it a religion.

This spiritual significance is to be found in some degree in all the religions, but in the fullest and highest expression only in Christianity. Christianity seeks to turn men from the life of impulse and selfishness to the larger and holier life; and the turning it calls Conversion. Often the change of heart is brought about only by long struggle and repeated endeavor. But not infrequently it is effected better, at a certain critical point, by grasping the higher life through the imagination, and claiming it, though yet unrealized, as an actual possession. This process orthodox Christianity calls

Salvation by Faith; or rather, this is the vital experience underlying the dogma which has grown up under that name. Faith, thus, in its highest and moral sense, is the believing in and holding on to an ideal of life against all the temptations and foreshortening illusions of the senses. Conversion is the soul's initial acceptance of that life, and Faith is its retention of grasp upon it when the push of lower interests makes it seem far away and unreal.

The function of religion is then, in a word, to create in men a clean heart and renew a right spirit within them. Christianity is the greatest of the religions because it has held up the highest ideal of life and furnished the greatest dynamic for its realization.

PART III
PHILOSOPHICAL

CHAPTER XVI

THEOLOGICAL METHOD AND THE SCIENTIFIC SPIRIT

So far in our study we have been content for the most part to describe the facts of religious experience without seeking to draw inferences therefrom. We have now to consider the more important of the great mass of theological beliefs, whose existence is due, primarily, to the attempt to relate and explain those experiences. And first we must glance, in turn, at the three sharply contrasting methods by which men have constructed and justified their theologies: the interpretation and elaboration of pronouncements taken as unquestionably authoritative, the manipulation of concepts and derivation from them of *a priori* truths supposed to hold good of the outer world, and the observation of facts and formulation of inductive generalizations that offer shorthand descriptions of them.

The three methods of theology

I. Authority. Truth may be hit upon in many ways — by intuition or clever guessing, by accepting the statements of others, by short cuts of all kinds. But these are also ways of acquiring error, and are not of guaranteed trustworthiness. So man has long sought some certain warrant of truth, some reliable method upon which he can stake his belief and conduct. The earliest method, and one that still retains the allegiance of a large proportion of religious people, is that of setting up some book or human voice as the agent of a divine revelation and therefore of indubitable authority; whatever can be deduced from these supernaturally warranted pronouncements may be held with an assurance to which men can in no other way attain. We have already spoken of the process by which during the lapse of centuries an anthology of Hebrew writings, and later of early Christian writings, came to be invested with a peculiar sanctity and authority; and then of the steps by which the Roman Catholic hierarchy came to arrogate to itself the right to interpret those sacred books and formulate for universal acceptance the truths which they contained. The Church assumed to guard the deposit of faith and to define it more and more clearly as questions arose, dubbing all new ideas, not therein contained, as heretical and false. But actually it read into its oracles much that could not by an impartial exegesis be found therein, and developed new dogmas according to the exigencies of its situation. So successfully did the Church maintain its position, in the West, that the pious declared, with St. Augustine, "I should not believe the Gospel if the authority of the Church did not so decide me."

We cannot do better, in seeking to grasp this dogma of an infallible Church, than to quote from an official pronouncement. In the "Dogmatic Constitution of the Catholic Faith," adopted by the Council of 1870, "The Holy Mother Church holds that God can be known with certainty by the natural light of human reason, but that it has also pleased Him to reveal Himself and the eternal decrees of His will in a supernatural way. This supernatural revelation, as declared by the Holy Council of Trent, is contained in the books of the Old and New Testament. . . . These have God for their author, and as such have been delivered to the Church. And, in order to restrain restless spirits, who may give erroneous explanations, it is decreed — renewing the decision of the Council of Trent — that no one may interpret the sacred Scriptures contrary to the sense in which they are interpreted by Holy Mother Church, to whom such interpretation belongs. All those things are to be believed which are written in the word of God, or handed down by Tradition, which the Church by her teaching has proposed for belief. No one can be justified without this faith; nor shall any one, unless he persevere therein to the end, attain everlasting life. Hence God, through His only-begotten Son, has established the Church as the guardian and teacher of His revealed word. . . . We therefore pronounce false every assertion which is contrary to the enlightened truth of faith. . . . For the doctrine of faith revealed by God has not been proposed, like some philosophical discovery, to be made perfect by human ingenuity, but it has been delivered to the spouse of Christ as a divine deposit, to be faithfully guarded and unerringly set forth. Hence, all tenets of holy faith are to be explained always according to the sense and meaning of the Church; nor is it ever lawful to depart therefrom under pretense or color of a more enlightened explanation." [1]

Pleasant and soothing as this doctrine is, the "restless spirits" that the Church has tried to drug into acquiescence would not be so restrained; and the vast majority of educated men the world over have become convinced that the pretensions of the Church to a special revelation of truth are unwarranted. One has but to look at the beliefs which the Church has declared true! One has but to see the palpable errors of fact in the Book which she holds up as infallible! For example, for the writers of the Bible, and so for the Catholic Church, the earth was a flat disk about which the sun revolved, the sky a dome, with openings through which the rain descended, and above which was heaven, where God dwelt and whither the saved arose after death. The naïve account in Genesis holds to this primitive view; and the story of the Ascension of Christ, in the opening chapter of

[1] For an eloquent defense of this position, see J. H. Newman's *Apologia pro Vita Mea.*

Acts, presupposes it. Every one knows how bitterly the Church antagonized the rival Copernican system, how Galileo was tried and Bruno burned. This is one of the most familiar instances of the naïveté and falsity of the supposedly supernatural revelation which the Church has proffered. But there is scarcely a scientific truth of importance which has not contradicted some part of her teaching and been opposed in the name of her "deposit of Divine truth." The facts of evolution have had to be rejected because they conflict with her doctrine of the Creation; the discoveries of anthropology and archæology and geology concerning the antiquity of the earth and of man flatly contradict her chronology; and a recognition of the validity of historical criticism is incompatible with her dogmas as to the authorship and dates of the Bible documents — dogmas which, in many instances, unprejudiced historians have with one voice declared absurd. In view of this obviously and grossly false nature of so much of her declared "revelation," we cannot base our theological structure upon any such supposed certainties; we must find some other avenue to truth.

II. A priori reasoning. From the beginning of the Church's life, even when the possession of a supernatural source of revelation was unquestioned, Christian apologists sought to justify their beliefs by the use of the unaided intellect; system after system was constructed based on pure reason. One such system became standardized during the Middle Ages; we call it the "Scholastic Theology," and find its most elaborate expression in the *Summa Theologiæ* of Thomas Aquinas. But this is simply the system which the Catholic Church accepted. Multitudes of equally ingenious and convincing — or unconvincing — systems have been spun out of the brains of closet philosophers; the attempt to reach theological truth through the use of the mind's inner resources, its logical powers and innate intuitions, has resulted in such diverse world-views as those of Anselm, Spinoza, Leibnitz, Kant, Hegel, Bradley, and Royce. There is no need of refuting any of these systems — they refute one another. Since the publication of Bacon's *Novum Organum*, this whole method of seeking truth by *a priori* reasoning has become more and more discredited. No system has received widespread recognition — except that which was favored by the official support of the Church. No results from this method have passed into our common knowledge.

Particularly from British and American thinkers has come the refutation of the claims of *a priori* reasoning to objective validity. Locke, in his famous *Essay concerning Human Understanding*,[1] pointed out that "universal propositions of whose truth or falsehood we can have certain knowledge concern not existence. . . . These universal and self-evident principles, being only our constant, clear, and distinct knowledge of our own ideas . . . can assure us of nothing that passes without the mind. . . . That any or what bodies do exist, *that* we are left to our senses to discover to us as far as they can." Mill wrote, in his *Logic*,[2] "A large proportion of the erroneous thinking which exists in the world proceeds on a tacit assumption that the same order must obtain among the objects in nature which obtains among our ideas of them." More recently we have Pearson speaking with scorn of the method "which does not start with the classification of facts, but reaches its judgments by some obscure process of internal cogitation . . . and results, as experience shows us, in an endless number of competing and contradictory systems."[3] And William James tells us,[4] "By the ancients, *a priori* propositions were considered, without further ques-

[1] Bk. IV, chap. VII, sec. 14.
[2] Bk. V, chap. III. See also bk. II, chap. V, sec. 6; and chap. VII, secs. 1–4; *Examination of Sir William Hamilton's Philosophy*, chaps. VI and XXVIII.
[3] K. Pearson, *Grammar of Science*, chap. I, sec. 6.
[4] *Principles of Psychology*, vol. II, p. 664.

tion, to reveal the constitution of Reality. Archetypal things existed, it was assumed, in the relations in which we had to think them. The mind's necessities were a warrant for those of Being. . . . But . . . the eternal verities which the structure of our mind lays hold of do not necessarily lay hold on extra-mental being; nor have they, as Kant pretended later, a legislating character even for all possible experience. They are primarily interesting only as subjective facts."

The truth is, these systems are far more a result of unconscious assumption and mental bias than of logic. One after another has been enthusiastically worked out, only to have its fallacies exposed and be rejected by other thinkers. But ever new systems arise to replace the old. Thus to argue against dogmatic theology is a guerrilla warfare; every position in turn is taken, but the enemy forever eludes capture. It would require a library to hold all the dogmatic systems and their refutations; and were all to have their inadequacies painstakingly exposed, new systems would spring up tomorrow. Nor can any counter-argument, without endlessly tedious expansion, be made so complete that the theologian cannot find some gap or pick some verbal flaw, and so, by discrediting the refutation, seem to reëstablish the presumption in favor of his argument. It is not worth while, then, except for practice in analysis and exact thinking, to bother with picking these *a priori* systems to pieces. Of far more importance is it to point out the proved validity of another method of truth-seeking, and by stimulating a loyalty to that scientific method, to overcome evil with good.

III. The scientific method. The spirit of all true science can be epitomized by the Biblical summons, "Come and see!" It never seeks to impose antecedent conceptions; it lets things "tell their tale in their own way." Absolutely faithful to observed facts, letting them suggest their own laws, describing them impartially, as they are, and never picking out or emphasizing those particular facts which bolster a desired conclusion, distrusting all authority which observable facts do not corroborate, not seeking first to construct a system and then looking for evidence to support it, but following with a delicate responsiveness the leading of the evidence, and abiding by its dictates — such is the temper by which science is slowly conquering human ignorance. There is but one way to learn what are the facts in any department of human life. *A priori* assumptions cannot ascertain them, pious aspiration cannot mould them according to its desire, postulates imperiously demanding that the universe conform to our needs or cravings cannot produce them. Only by studying experience concretely, observing it with painstaking exactness, freeing ourselves from bias, from preconceived opinions and wishes in the matter, and making with due caution generalizations that shall include all the observed facts and contradict none, can we be sure that we have what is really knowledge and not mere speculation. This is the scientific method; and the keeping to it is the scientific spirit.[1]

[1] Cf. Boutroux (Eng. tr.), p. 352: "The special mark of the scientific spirit is shown in unwillingness to admit any starting-point for research, any source of knowledge, other than experience." Pearson, chap. I.: "The classification of facts and the formation of absolute judgments upon the basis of this classification — judgments independent of the idiosyncrasies of the individual mind — essentially sum up the aim and method of modern science. . . . The classification of facts, the recognition of their sequence and relative significance, is the function of science; and the habit of forming a judgment upon these facts unbiassed by personal feeling is characteristic of what may be termed the scientific frame of mind." Wenley, p. 59: "Free, with complete freedom to inquire into anything, man is as completely bound — bound to abide by discernible testimony. Of such is the spirit of science." G. B. Foster, *Finality of the Christian Religion*, p. 190: "The new method may be expressed in one word: observation. Formerly science was a captive of dogma; now it is a captive of nature. . . . Formerly one subjected reality to the categories of the understanding; now one subjects the understanding in sovereign obedience to facts. Formerly one said things

Not all students of science actually follow this ideal of open-mindedness and impartial recording of the evidence. But such is the recognized ideal of science, such is the way in which it has won its successes; where it is not earnestly espoused there is no possibility, except by mere chance, of arriving at truth. Scientists make mistakes, observe inaccurately, generalize incautiously; scientific books are not always free from prejudice and passion. But the essence of science lies in this, that its calculations are always open to correction, its inferences are open and above board; if the evidence does not warrant them, that fact will soon become clear. Science is not a fixed doctrine, it is a spirit; and in this spirit lies man's hope for knowledge. In those fields where the emotions and loyalties least enter in, science has won general allegiance; only the hopelessly ignorant set up their superstitions against the authority of the latest textbooks of astronomy or physics. But it is as yet sadly different with philosophy, politics, and religion. Books widely read and applauded do little more than "confuse problems and caricature investigation." With much brilliant and eloquent writing on these matters, there is still little that is scrupulously cautious, clings to observable facts, and is actuated by a truly scientific spirit. Yet to a scientific study of these most vital of matters we must come, even if it mean the relinquishment of former assurances and the recognition of the narrow limits of our knowledge. We must be willing to give up "sweet comforts false, worse than true wrongs," throw overboard our most obstinate convictions, subject the

must be so, therefore they are so; now one says things are what they are, and one looks at them and into them to see what they are." And Seeley, p. 9: "The scientific spirit is simply a jealous watchfulness against that tendency of human nature to read itself into the Universe, which is both natural to each individual and may mislead the greatest investigators, and which can only be controlled by rigorously adhering to a fixed process, and rigidly verifying the work of others by the same."

facts of the religious life to the same critical scrutiny that we should give to astronomical phenomena, and build our theology upon a strictly empirical basis. Only so shall we find it built upon a rock, and able to survive the doubts and questionings of an increasingly scientific age. We shall have less truth for a while than we thought we had; but in the end we shall have more, and what we have will be as universally acknowledged and believed as the conclusions of the physical sciences. The use of unscientific methods only discredits theology and postpones, by putting us on the wrong track, the attainment of actual knowledge.

Fortunately the last few decades have witnessed a noteworthy change of attitude on the part of the younger theologians; and the time seems not far distant when a scientific theology — or philosophy of religion, to use the newer term — may actually take its accredited place among the sciences. Huxley wrote, a generation or more ago, "The greatest intellectual revolution man has yet seen is slowly taking place by the aid of science. She is teaching the world that the ultimate court of appeal is observation and experience, and not authority; she is teaching it to estimate the value of evidence." [1] And in the opening years of the Twentieth Century we find books on religion laying down such principles as these: "I have urged that there is only one method of knowledge, that of experience and legitimate inference from experience. And while freely admitting, and even insisting upon, the importance of every kind of experience as material for analysis and discussion, I have argued that any truth that is to be elicited from such experience must be elicited by the method of science, in the broad and proper sense of the term." [2]

[1] *Lay Sermons:* "On the Study of Zoölogy."
[2] G. L. Dickinson, *Religion, A Criticism and a Forecast*, opening paragraph. First published in 1903–04. As long ago as 1875, Seeley wrote

It is a sign of our growing mental maturity that we are at last learning to ask for the evidence of whatever we are bade believe — for verification of religious truth as clear as that which we should be given for the laws of astronomy or biology. There is in certain quarters a profound distrust of this spirit; it is felt to be subversive of the faith, the sign of an unbelieving and materialistic generation. But if there is no proper evidence for our beliefs, we wish to know it; while if our theology is true and well-founded, it can stand the test of doubt. The intrusion of the scientific spirit into the study of religion is a matter for congratulation; it has been the goal of much patient labor and earnest pleading on the part of the intellectual leaders of the race, as the absence of that spirit has been one of the greatest obstacles in the way of the attainment of truth. With the general acceptance by the Church of scientific methods and the scientific spirit we may expect a new era in religious thought.[1]

The opposition of the Church to the scientific spirit

Religion and art and material progress long antedate science; it was not until the classic period of Greek history — at least so far as extant records show — that any portion of the human race emerged from the superstitious and magical view of Nature into a truly empirical study of her processes.

(*Natural Religion*, p. 7): "In theology, metaphysics, moral and political philosophy, history, the principle of authority has reigned hitherto with more or less exclusiveness, and the repudiation of it makes a revolution in those departments of knowledge. . . . The important change is in the extension of the methods of physical science to the whole domain of knowledge. While one part of the 'wisdom of the world' has been discredited as resting solely on authority, another large division of it is now rejected as resting on insufficient induction, and another as resting on groundless assumptions, disguised under the name of necessary truths, truths of the reason, truths given in consciousness, etc." Scientists, of course, have been urging this for a century or two.

[1] The possibility of *super*-scientific methods of attaining truth will be discussed on pp. 337–41, 361–64, and 406–09.

A natural science and philosophy was rapidly developed; and for a brief brilliant period there might have been a hope that human enlightenment would anticipate its actual development by twenty centuries. But the Greek thinkers were a small band, soon overwhelmed by political cataclysms; their science disappeared under a flood of supernatural explanations and superstitions. In Rome, though she absorbed much of the Greek culture, natural science never became firmly established upon a solid footing; and the torrent of Christianity that swept over the decaying empire carried away what rudiments existed. So was lost man's first great opportunity of understanding and mastering the world in which he lives; such was the price he paid for that renewal of moral earnestness and deepening of his spiritual life that the new religion brought.

Christianity, though it was "foolishness to the Greeks," and a silly fable to the wise,[1]—a $\beta\acute{a}\rho\beta\alpha\rho\text{o}\nu$ $\delta\acute{o}\gamma\mu\alpha$,— spread among the masses of ignorant and downtrodden, because of the glorious message of hope and of brotherhood which it brought; spread not, of course, through any evidence of the truth of its doctrines — for who stopped to examine the historic testimony by which it was supported? — but through its instant and powerful appeal to the heart. When, during the later Roman times, this religion of the masses became politically dominant, there was no natural science and no scientific spirit even among the upper classes to dispute its rapidly crystallizing dogmas. Men of acumen, lacking a solid foundation of knowledge, or any criterion of evidence, devoted their intellects to elaborating the new dogmas and interpreting in philosophical terms the supernatural faith they had received. All independent thinking was dubbed heresy by the Church, violently denounced and

---

[1] "Not many men wise after the flesh [i.e., according to the usual standards of rating] are called." 1 Cor. 1: 18–26.

ruthlessly stamped out; no thought was allowed but that which defended the Church doctrines. The pagan systems were regarded as impious; Hypatia, distinguished lecturer on philosophy, was murdered by a mob of monks in 441; the great schools of Athens were closed by order of the Christian Emperor Justinian, in 529.[1] There followed the long slumber of the Dark Ages, wherein the intellect, having no free play, was the bounden slave of dogma.

But the restless spirit of man could not forever be bound by these chains. We have noted how in the sixteenth century a widespread revolt occurred against ecclesiastical tyranny and corruption, and the Northern nations especially began to seek an altered basis for their religion. Abandoning ecclesiastical authority, they retained the authority of the Scriptures, which offered as safe a haven to the spirit as the authority of Church and Council, but allowed far greater opportunity for individual interpretation and construction. The classic Greek texts had already been reintroduced into Europe, where they had been almost forgotten, through the Mohammedan Arabs; and men again began to think for themselves. Slowly they ventured on the study of Nature, on invention, on exploration. The newly invented printing press spread the news of discoveries and theories, and once more enlightenment began to go forward.

Bitterly did the Church oppose every step of this progress. The newly won knowledge conflicted with some of her doctrines, the spirit of free inquiry menaced her whole system. Even the Reformers could not shake off the shackles of the old idea of authority. Luther wrote: "People give ear to an

[1] "The public manifested such indifference toward these ruins of the past, that the edict was scarcely noticed. Christianity had taken possession of the Empire two centuries ago; the concrete and thrilling questions of religion, and the troubles caused by the invasions of the barbarians, superseded the serene and peaceful θεωρία." A. Weber, *History of Philosophy* (Eng. tr.), p. 184.

upstart astrologer who strives to show that the earth revolves, not the heavens or the firmament, the sun and the moon. Whoever wishes to appear clever must devise some new system, which of all systems is, of course, the best way! This fool wishes to reverse the entire science of astronomy. But sacred Scripture tells us that Joshua commanded the *sun* to stand still, and not the earth." And similarly the scholarly Melancthon: "Certain men, either from the love of novelty or to make a display of ingenuity, have concluded that the earth moves. Now it is want of honesty and decency to assert such notions publicly, and the example is pernicious. It is thé part of a good mind to accept the truth as revealed by God and to acquiesce in it. The earth can be nowhere except in the center of the universe." [1] Bruno was burned at the stake by Catholics, Servetus by Protestant Calvin; Galileo, under pain of death, was forced to retraction. "But the world does move!" he is said to have muttered as he left the trial chamber. Aye, verily, the world does move, and no power of authority or tradition or of persecution could stop it!

It would take too long even to summarize here the process by which, step by step, the new knowledge won its way against the Church. The story has been excellently told in Andrew D. White's *History of the Warfare between Science and Theology in Christendom*. One by one the conceptions of traditional Christian theology which deal with the history and nature of this world have yielded to the scientific ideas; many of the Protestant churches have revised or dropped their creeds, and kept pace in considerable measure with the new conceptions; all of them, and the Catholic Church as well, have been compelled in some degree to rephrase and reinterpret them. But every inch of the way has been fought; a huge mass of literature has been evolved in the ever-

[1] Both quoted by Foster, *op. cit.*, pp. 162-63.

repeated attempts to square the creeds with the advance of knowledge, and the greater part of modern philosophy has concerned itself with the reëxpressing of inherited beliefs in forms less and less obviously inconsonant therewith. Stamped and creased with these traditional forms of thought, philosophy has not been able, to any great extent, to become purely scientific, or to show the free spontaneity of the Greeks; and some of the sciences have been seriously hampered by the theological prepossessions of so many of their devotees. But science has grown, through the sheer force of truth, and through the practical usefulness of her discoveries. Scientific knowledge has become widely diffused; and the Church, in contending against it, has lost the allegiance of large numbers of her sons.

The battle has been a losing one for the Church, a gradual retreat from vantage-point to vantage-point, a steady recession of once assured dogma and concession to scientific knowledge. Stumbling and slipping, grasping at this crevice and that ledge, but sliding surely down, once it left the secure rock of an unquestioned authority, theology is coming to earth, abandoning its pretensions to a special avenue to truth, and becoming absorbed in such scientific studies as the psychology of religion and the history of religions. Meanwhile everything is confusion. Scientific knowledge has become widely diffused; but the scientific spirit, which won that knowledge and which has much yet to win out of the unknown for man, finds common comprehension and acceptance much more slowly. Facts that scholars everywhere proclaim become before long the public possession; but the spirit of impartial observation and generalization through which those facts were patiently wrested from the chaos of experience is as yet but the possession of the few. Protestant churches pretty generally accept the results of science, but not so generally her method. But not till Christianity openly welcomes this spirit of free criticism and inquiry, and seeks to base her beliefs on as solid grounds of experience as anything else that we call knowledge, can she put an end to the long, unhappy, shameful conflict between religion and science. It is not enough to make timid expurgations and leave unremedied the fundamental mistake. Once the secure basis of revealed authority is abandoned, there is no intermediate resting place for thought until it rests on the authority of scientific knowledge.

A. D. White, *History of the Warfare between Science and Theology.* J. W. Draper, *History of the Conflict between Religion and Science.* J. B. Bury, *History of Freedom of Thought.* W. N. Rice, *Christian Faith in an Age of Science*, pt. I. A. Sabatier, *Religions of Authority and the Religion of the Spirit.* R. M. Wenley, *Modern Thought and the Crisis in Belief*, II. W. F. Adeney, *A Century's Progress*, chap. IV. G. B. Foster, *Finality of the Christian Religion*, chap. V. J. T. Shotwell, *Religious Revolution of Today.* G. L. Dickinson, *Religion, A Criticism and Forecast*, chap. II. J. R. Seeley, *Natural Religion*, pt. I, chap. I. K. Pearson, *Grammar of Science*, chap. I. T. H. Huxley, *Science and Hebrew Tradition*, chap. I. G. Forester, *Faith of an Agnostic*, chaps. II–III. E. Boutroux, *Science and Religion in Contemporary Philosophy*, "Conclusion." *Harvard Theological Review*, vol. 7, p. 1. *New World*, vol. 9, p. 285. *Biblical World*, vol. 43, p. 178.

CHAPTER XVII

THE INTERPRETATION OF THE BIBLE

THE Christian Bible consists of the sacred books of the Jews, together with certain narratives and letters and a fragment of apocalyptic literature dating from the early Christian era. All these documents were slowly sifted out of a much larger mass of similar literature, the collection reaching that definite limit which it has since maintained in the fifth century A.D. A heterogeneous corpus as it is of divers sorts of writings, by men of many different beliefs and convictions, accumulated during ten centuries of marked religious transition,[1] an unbiased mind would certainly never suspect it of being a book of supernatural origin or authority. It is true that the Hebrew prophets, like the prophets of other religions, believed themselves inspired of God in their utterances, and used, fearlessly and freely, the formula, "Thus saith Jehovah," when they expressed their burning convictions of right and wrong. But even those of their contemporaries who believed them to be inspired of God were free to criticize their specific pronouncements. The Old Testament historians, in compiling their chronicles, referred now and then to earlier and well-known books as authority for their statements,[2] as they would hardly have done if they had expected their accounts to be taken on Divine authority. The author of Luke, in prefacing his work, claims attention only as a painstaking historian, not

[1] The J document of the Hexateuch was written about 850 B.C., and the latest books of the New Testament about 130 A.D.

[2] See, e.g., Joshua 10: 12 *ff*; Num. 21:14. Sixteen books, now lost, are thus alluded to in the Old Testament.

as a vehicle of supernatural inspiration. And certainly Paul would have been bewildered to find his hasty and occasional letters taken by pious Christians as the very Word of God!

How did the conception develop of the inerrancy of the Bible?

It is not difficult to trace the historic process by which these particular Jewish and Christian writings came to be set apart as having special authority, and finally as essentially different from all other books. The first document to be thus regarded was the Book of Deuteronomy, which, in its original and briefer form, was published under peculiar circumstances during the reign of Josiah, about 621 B.C.[1] Written actually not long before, it purported to come from the ancient lawgiver Moses, and as such was accepted by the king and the pious among the people, and declared the religious law of the land. In 444 B.C., after the return of a remnant of the faithful from the exile, Ezra promulgated the so-called Priestly code, which was also accepted as Mosaic. About this nucleus other books gradually gathered: the words of the great prophets of an earlier time, chronicles of the former golden age of Hebrew history, religious hymns, tales, and proverbs. Slowly the idea of a canon, or authoritative collection, was evolved. What books should be included therein was for long uncertain; the pious hesitated, for example, over the Song of Songs and Ecclesiastes, ultimately admitting them because of their reputed Solomonic authorship. Collections varying from a score or so to over four score books were made. But formal and second-hand as the Jewish religion had largely become, the need was strongly felt of an authoritative code to which to cling; and by the time of Christ the Hebrew Scriptures had attained practically the limits which have since been retained, though cer-

[1] See 2 Kings 22 and 23.

tain books were still hotly disputed, and the canon was not definitely fixed for another century.

The early Christians, convinced that a New Dispensation [1] was at hand, and eager to share and deepen their new convictions, began to read at their meetings the accounts of Jesus' life and some of the letters of his apostles which best conveyed the new gospel. At first many books were read and cherished which have since been discarded — such writings as the *Epistle of Barnabas*, the *Epistle of Clement*, and the *Shepard of Hermas* being ranked with the letters of Paul. Luke tells us that many Gospels were in existence in his day; fragments of a number of these have been found. On the other hand, a number of the books which were eventually included in the Christian collection were for long regarded with little favor by many of the churches; Hebrews, James, Jude, 2 Peter, 2 and 3 John, and Revelation were especially the subject of debate. Finally, however, by chance or circumstance, the canon came to include those books which now form our New Testament, and to reject all others; an ecclesiastical decree of 495 A.D. settled the last open questions, and the intellectual torpor of the Middle Ages put an end to controversy and change.

Contemporaneously with the gradual determination of the canon there developed a greater and greater reverence for these new sacred books. At first the Gospels were quoted simply as memoirs, and their statements justified by quotations from the Old Testament. But as the age of Jesus and the apostles faded farther and farther into the past, the surviving literature that contained their teaching grew more and more precious; and these writings, far more important to the Church than the old Jewish Scriptures, came to be ranked as equally inspired. The name Bible — $\beta i \beta \lambda \iota a$, the

[1] Hence the title New Testament — *testamentum*, $\delta\iota a\theta\eta\kappa\eta$, meaning "dispensation" or "covenant."

Books — dates from the fourth century, and marks the definite fusion of these two sacred anthologies. For a long time the Bible books were freely criticized. St. Jerome exercised his individual judgment in accepting or rejecting. Luther called the Book of James "a veritable epistle of straw," and said of the Old Testament that we sometimes find in it "wood, hay, and stubble, and not always gold, silver, or diamonds." But free criticism means divergence in belief. And the Church, in its struggle to maintain a standard of orthodoxy, gradually came to that insistence on the absolute truth of every word of her sacred books which for so long dominated the minds of men — a conception vehemently preached even to-day, and holding its own here and there even in the face of the general diffusion of historical and scientific knowledge.[1]

What facts have altered our conception of the Bible?

The word "criticism" (from $\kappa\rho\iota\nu\epsilon\hat{\iota}\nu$, to judge) does not properly imply caviling or fault-finding; it means judgment, discernment, comprehension. Biblical criticism, which had its beginning, perhaps, in Spinoza's *Tractatus Theologico-Politicus*, and has had a marvelous development in the past century, is simply an open-minded attempt to understand the various documents that make up the Bible, their dates, authorship, purpose, and meaning. Our increasing knowledge of nature, of history, of psychology, and of comparative religion, the reconstruction of more accurate texts through the discovery of new manuscripts and the patiently minute

[1] Cf. this passage from a sermon preached as late as 1861 at Oxford University, by Dean Burgon: "The Bible is none other than the voice of Him that sitteth upon the throne. Every book of it, every chapter of it, every verse of it, every syllable of it (where are we to stop?), every letter of it, is the direct utterance of the Most High. The Bible is none other than the Word of God — not some part of it more, some part of it less, but all alike the utterance of Him who sitteth upon the throne, faultless, unerring, supreme."

comparison of the thousands now available, the study of contemporary inscriptions and remains, of the development of the Hebrew and Greek languages and the precise meanings of their words, and the growth of a maturer historical method, that knows how to read between the lines of a narrative and discriminate trustworthy from unreliable materials — these manifold new resources have brought us to a far more intelligent appreciation of this mass of Jewish and Christian writings. Differences of opinion on many points still exist; and there are many things which we should like to know that must forever remain beyond reach of our investigation. But the general conclusions of modern scholarship with regard to the Bible "cannot be denied without denying the ordinary principles by which history is judged and evidence estimated. Nor can it be doubted that the same conclusions, upon any neutral field of investigation, would have been accepted without hesitation by all conversant with the subject." [1]

(1) It has, for one thing, been definitely proved that the traditional ascriptions of authorship of many of the Bible books are mistaken. The Pentateuch, for example, was not written till centuries after the time of Moses — as on the surface would seem probable from the fact that kings of Israel are mentioned therein, not to speak of the description of Moses' own death! These books have been proved to be compilations dating from the period of the exile, incorporating two parallel narratives of the eighth and ninth century, together with considerable later material; the parallel strands run side by side through a large part of them, and the compiler has not always well reconciled the divergent accounts. Again, few, if any, of the Psalms were written by David; most of them are post-exilic. Neither Ecclesiastes

[1] Canon Driver, *Introduction to the Old Testament*, Preface. A good book to study in this connection is H. B. George's *Historical Evidence*.

THE INTERPRETATION OF THE BIBLE 269

nor the Song of Solomon was written by Solomon. The greater part of the Book of Isaiah comes from a much later time. The probabilities are strongly against the authorship of the Gospels — with the exception of the Second Gospel — by the men whose names they bear. Some of the supposed epistles of Paul are certainly not from his hand,[1] James is not by its reputed author, and 2 Peter is a barefaced forgery. The Book of Revelation is a medley of apocalyptic literature, some of it pre-Christian, none of it by the author of the Fourth Gospel. These commonplaces of Biblical scholarship can be substantiated by a study of any of the good recent introductions to Old and New Testament.[2]

(2) But other facts have been brought to light much more significantly at variance with the old conceptions of the Bible. For one thing, many inconsistencies exist between different traditions that have both been incorporated. When one verse flatly contradicts another, it is only by a difficult evasion that the believer can preserve his devout belief in the truth of both. For instance — to mention but a few — in Acts 9:7, speaking of Paul's vision, we read, "And the men who journeyed with him stood speechless, *hearing a voice*, but seeing no man," while in Acts 22:9, which narrates the same experience, we read, "And they that were with me saw indeed the light, and were not afraid; but they *heard not the voice* of him that spake to me." Again, the first three Gospels make Christ eat the Last Supper on the eve of the Passover, and die on that day, while the Fourth Gospel relates that he died on the day of preparation for the Passover. Of the same census we read in 2 Sam. 24:1, that the Lord commanded David to take it, and in 1 Chron. 21:1, that it was Satan

---

[1] Hebrews is certainly not his, and the Pastoral Epistles (1 and 2 Timothy and Titus), at least in their present form. Very many scholars are confident that 2 Thessalonians and Ephesians are not from Paul.

[2] See the references on pp. 49–50 and 66.

that put it into his mind. The two genealogies of Christ — both purporting to trace his ancestry back to David through Joseph — are flatly contradictory of each other, as indeed both conflict with the tradition, also accepted in the same two Gospels, of the virgin birth, whereby Joseph was held to be not his father at all. The infancy and resurrection stories at the beginning and end of Matthew and Luke are in many respects mutually incompatible.

(3) Not merely inconsistent with one another, however, but obviously untrue, are many of the Biblical statements. For example, the world was not made in six days (which were real days, "morning and evening," to the narrator) nor in six geological epochs, except by a very arbitrary straining of facts. The order of creation given in Genesis differs from the order in which things really came into being. The sky is not a "firmament" (or partition) which divides the "waters which are under the firmament" from the "waters which are above the firmament." This whole account of creation, which is closely parallel to earlier Babylonian accounts, reflects a very primitive conception of nature. Again, not a few statements in the historical books have been proved untrue by extant monuments and the records of surrounding nations; it is plain to the historical student that the Jewish chronicles are biased and to considerable extent untrustworthy. It is clear that the evangelists were in many points mistaken in their views of the events of Jesus' life. And the author of Acts, by his irreconcilable differences from the statements of Paul, shows a radical misconception of the nature of some of the events in the early history of the Church.

(4) But still more strikingly incompatible with the supernatural view of the Bible are the gross and immoral ideas that are mingled with its noble and elevating inspirations. No worse than contemporary cults, the Jahweh-worship of

the Jews was at first no better; and even down to and beyond the times of Jesus certain ideas persisted that are repugnant to our humaner instincts. God's anger and desire for vengeance are repeatedly mentioned; and the picture the unprejudiced reader would form of this Jewish deity from many Old Testament passages is that of a cruel and bloodthirsty tyrant. He "hardens Pharaoh's heart" [1] that he may punish the Egyptians in a spectacular manner; he throws stones down from heaven on Israel's foes; [2] he commands the sun to stand still that more of them may be slain before dark; [3] he bids his chosen people invade the land of a neighboring tribe, burn all their cities, slay all the males, adults and children, and all the married women, and keep the virgins for their own enjoyment; [4] he slays seventy thousand innocent Israelites for David's sin in taking a census of the people.[5] Jael and Rahab are praised, though guilty of the blackest crimes, because they were on Israel's side. To the usurper Jehu, who entraps and murders numbers of innocent people, including children, to establish his power, the Lord declares, "Thou hast done well in executing that which is right in mine eyes." [6] Even the Psalms, with all their intense religious feeling, have much in them that is low and unworthy — whining complaints over troubles, anathemas upon other peoples whom the Jews hated, vindictive appeals to Jehovah to persecute them.[7] "O daughter of Babylon," the psalmist says, "Happy shall he be that rewardeth thee as thou hast served us. Happy shall he be that taketh and dasheth thy little children against the stones!" [8]

Even worse than the revengeful longings of the psalmist is the bitter threat of everlasting punishment for unbelievers

[1] Exod. 14:4–8. [2] Joshua 10:11. [3] *Ibid.*: 12–13.
[4] Num. 31. [5] 2 Sam. 24:15.
[6] 2 Kings 10:1–30. For other cruel Old Testament teachings see Deut. 2:34; 7:2–16; 20:10–17; Lev. 25:44–46; 1 Sam. 15:3.
[7] Cf., e.g., Ps. 69:22–29; 109:6–21. [8] Ps. 137:8–9.

in the Book of Revelation. He that worships falsely "shall drink of the wine of the wrath of God, which is poured out without mixture into the cup of his indignation; and he shall be tormented with fire and brimstone in the presence of the holy angels, and in the presence of the Lamb. And the smoke of their torment ascendeth up for ever and ever; and they have no rest day nor night." [1] Paul too had a grim and revolting side to his faith: "[God] saith to Moses, I will have mercy on whom I will have mercy, and I will have compassion on whom I will have compassion . . . he hath mercy on whom he will have mercy and whom he will he hardeneth. . . . Hath not the potter power over the clay, of the same lump to make one vessel unto honor and another unto dishonor?" [2] And in one of the epistles we read, "God shall send them strong delusion, that they should believe a lie; that they all might be damned who believed not the truth." [3]

Surely such sentiments need no comment! In the light of them, to teach that the teachings of the Bible are throughout divine and authoritative is to barbarize our moral ideas; to claim that such words as these are inspired of God is to worship a god who is at times a very devil. Wicked dogmas have been based on some of these texts, cruelties have been justified by them. Our forefathers put poor old women to death because of the verse "A witch shall not live." [4] Religious persecutors have pointed to the texts," Constrain them to come in," and "Gather up the tares in bundles and burn them." [5] The subjection of women has justified itself from the saying, " I suffer not a woman to teach . . . but to be in silence." [6]

These bits of dross amid the gold do not destroy the worth of the Bible, but they do make sharply against the

[1] Rev. 14: 10–11. [2] Rom. 9: 15–24. [3] 2 Thess. 2: 11–12.
[4] Exod. 22: 18. [5] Luke 14: 23. Matt. 13: 30. [6] 1 Tim. 2: 12.

conception of it as everywhere inspired and authoritative. It is important, to get a right appreciation of it, that we face these facts. Indiscriminate praise hurts rather than helps in the long run. The Bible is a very human book; it pictures the progress of a very primitive people toward a love of the highest things; its writers are often mistaken, often biased, often possessed with illusions, sometimes possessed with human weakness and passion. We must read it as we would read any other book, passing lightly over the unhelpful parts, dwelling on what is true and elevating, and thus making it a stimulus, never a hindrance to our inward growth.

Is the Bible inspired, the Word of God, authoritative?

(1) The Bible is by no means of even value; to use it wisely we must recognize that fact. It is not inspired in all its teachings. And even where we may call it inspired, we must not take that inspiration as a warrant of infallibility. The Church has never agreed upon a definition of the term "inspired"; but in the Bible, inspiration is ascribed to very imperfect men — as, Balaam, Gideon, Saul, David. It means the entrance into the heart of a holier spirit, a loftier spiritual vision. But the most inspired teachers have had their illusions and sometimes judged amiss. The only way to know what is inspired is to find what has the power to inspire others — what illumines life, reveals its deeper meanings, quickens men's spiritual loyalty. And surely so much inspiration could not have come out of the Bible for all these generations of men if a very real inspiration had not gone into it. The best passages in it are inspired as are few other passages in the whole range of the world's religious literature.

Spiritual insight in the degree here found is rare. But there is no need, in our loyalty to the Bible, of disparaging the holy books of the other religions or such other Jewish and Christian writings as did not get included within the Bible canon. Ecclesiasticus, for example, has at least as much inspiration in it as Ecclesiastes, and Tobit surely more than Esther; in the Buddhist Scriptures are many passages more truly inspired than the less inspired parts of our Bible, and surely Dante at his best was inspired, and Tennyson, and Emerson, and Phillips Brooks. We must cease to think of the Bible as different in kind from other books, or of its teachings as unique. The religion of Israel was not an isolated phenomenon, requiring a supernatural explanation and recorded in a miraculous manner; it was rather a stage in the natural evolution of Semitic religion, quite intelligible in view of the influences under which it developed, and finding documentary expression through the natural zeal of its priests and prophets. Biblical religion is an outgrowth of earlier phases of religious development; its legends and rites and codes are variants of earlier ones which may, to some slight extent, still be deciphered in Babylonian, Assyrian, and Hittite inscriptions. In short, God is revealed, as the apostle said, "by divers portions and in divers manners"; he is God "not of the Jews only, but of the Gentiles also." The Bible, if it is an invaluable record of man's consciousness of God, is, after all, but one of many such records. He who finds inspiration and sustenance therein should learn to find inspiration also in the other precious monuments of the religious life of humanity.

(2) Can we say, then, that the Bible is the Word of God? It is noteworthy that that phrase, although used over four hundred times in the Bible, is in none of those instances applied *to* the Bible. The formula of the Reformation was, that the Scriptures *contain* the Word of God; that is to say, the truth is in the Bible, but the Bible as a whole is not to be identified with it. It is the vehicle of it, and a

vehicle that is by no means perfect. The devout reader can find there much precious religious insight; God is revealed therein. But that revelation of God is mingled with much else that the children of Israel, in their long quest for divine truth, could not disentangle therefrom. The familiar assertion, attributed to the evangelist Moody among others, that the Bible is "the Word of God from cover to cover," is one calculated to blur our perception of religious values and do incalculable mischief.

(3) Finally, how, or in what sense, has the Bible authority? In a word, its authority is that of the truth which it contains, no more. We cannot call a statement true simply because the Bible says so; but whatever of truth the mature experience of Christendom finds in the Bible demands our allegiance — not because it is in the Bible, but because it is true. We may thus be spared all that far-fetched exegesis, those strained interpretations of Biblical statements that aim to commend them to us against conscience or common sense, and freely admit that the Biblical writers, however inspired in their best moments, were at other times, or even in the midst of their most inspired utterances, often deluded in their hopes and mistaken in their facts. We never dream of accepting the sweeping claims of the other holy books of the world to an absolute authority; we read the Vedas, the Zend-Avesta, the Koran for whatever of truth we can find in them, and discard the rest. Were it not that Christianity grew up out of Judaism, and in its infancy rested upon it for support, we should no more think of accepting the authority of the Jewish Scriptures than that of any of these other sacred writings. In the last analysis, we must follow Christ's precept — "Why even of yourselves judge ye not what is right?" We must judge every Book and Church and Teacher by the light of our own reason and conscience; and we shall know that the Bible contains

a great revelation of truth because we are able to judge for ourselves of what is true and what is false. Calvin saw clearly when he wrote, "As to this inquiry, 'Whence shall we be persuaded that Scripture hath flowed from God unless we have recourse to the decrees of the Church?' This is as if one should inquire, 'Whence do we learn to distinguish light from darkness, white from black, sweet from bitter?' For Scripture lets us have a no more obscure perception of its truth than black and white things of their color, sweet and bitter of their taste."

Wherein consists the greatness of the Bible?

(1) The primary value of the Bible will doubtless always lie in its power to inspire, to awaken a devotional spirit, and deepen men's insight into spiritual truth. No book was ever so surcharged with religious feeling or makes it so concrete and living. Heterogeneous as its various documents are, we find throughout an endless faith in the laws of righteousness, a never-fading consciousness of God. The great seers and prophets and saints of the last two millennia, together with countless humble souls, have to an extraordinary degree been moulded by it and drawn from it their inspiration and their power. National ideals have been formed under its influence; it has been one of the two or three greatest influences in modern life. "This collection of books has taken such a hold on the world as no other. . . . It is read of a Sabbath in all the ten thousand pulpits of our land. . . . It goes equally to the cottage of the plain man and the palace of the king. It is woven into the literature of the scholar, and colors the talk of the street. . . . Some thousand famous writers come up in this century, to be forgotten in the next. But the silver cord of the Bible is not loosed, nor its golden bowl broken, as tens of centuries go by." [1]

---
[1] Theodore Parker, *Discourse of Religion*, pp. 302-04.

In view of the proved inspirational power of these writings, we must take care that they be read still by the generations to come. The collapse of the old pretensions concerning the Bible has turned many a man away from it in impatience or contempt. Others, who have not heard the call to the higher life, are bored with its solemnity and prefer to do their reading in the lighter and gayer literature of the hour. But if the people ever cease to read the Bible for its spiritual dynamic, our young men will, we may fear, cease to see visions, and lose their belief in the things of the spirit.

(2) Even from a purely cultural point of view the loss would be great. The splendid Elizabethan English of the King James Version has done more than any other force to preserve the beauty and rhythm of our speech; conversance with it has been the source of the literary power of many a master. And an acquaintance with this winnowed literature of a great people is an education in itself. All the great human emotions find expression between the covers of this book with the deepest sincerity and in inimitable language. Here are chronicles unsurpassed in vivid terseness and dramatic power; here are ancient legal codes, folk-tales, sermons, letters, biographies, love-poems, hymns, an epic, charming tales of rustic life, of Oriental courts, of war and passion; conjugal fidelity is dwelt upon, ambition, filial devotion, patriotism, and mother-love; fascinating stories, exquisite lyrics, earnest exhortations, memorable aphorisms, aptest of parables, combine to form an anthology of the deepest interest to all lovers of what is abiding and excellent in human life. "Wholly apart from its religious or from its ethical value, the Bible is the one book that no intelligent person who wishes to come into contact with the world of thought and to share the ideas of the great minds of the Christian era can afford to be ignorant of. All modern literature and all art are permeated with it. There is scarcely a

great work in the language that can be fully understood and enjoyed without this knowledge, so full is it of allusions and illustrations from the Bible. It is not at all a question of religion, or theology, or dogma; it is a question of general intelligence." [1]

(3) From the historian's point of view, also, we must acknowledge the importance of these records of the development of the greatest of religions. They are not always accurate or trustworthy in their conception of the facts; but they are priceless sources, landmarks of religious history, monuments of some of the most important events that have happened on earth. From them we can understand the movement that culminated in the great sermons of the prophets, and later led to the supreme event in religious history, perhaps in all history, the Christian conquest of the Western world. The memorabilia of Jesus picture the purest of men teaching the highest way of life that man has conceived. The Bible is the greatest source-book of the religious life, its supreme and classic expression. As the Greek statues are in the realm of sculpture, as Homer and Dante are in the realm of poetry, as Shakespeare is in the realm of drama, so is the Bible in the realm of religion.

(4) And finally, however antiquated or unintelligible to us its ancient conceptions may sometimes appear, and however we may be drawn to other, more recent and more sophisticated books, we must never forget what the Bible has meant in the life of our Church and of our race. Tattered and worn as it is, only the fragments of a great literature, its text often corrupted through the errors of a thousand loving but humanly fallible copyings by hand, discredited in many of its statements by the onward march of historical and cosmological knowledge, obsolete in many of its ideas and obsolescent even in some of its most cherished ideals, it

[1] Charles Dudley Warner, quoted by Selleck, p. 5.

is yet our Book of books, the banner about which Christendom has so long rallied, and the ultimate source of very much that is best in our lives. Like a flag that is battle-scarred and torn, it has inspired so many men to heroic endeavor and sacrifice, consecrated for them the long effort of so many dragging days, soothed the sting of sorrow of so many breaking hearts, that the man who is capable of any deep and natural sentiment can hardly see or handle it without emotion. As the flag is the symbol of our nation and a summons to her service, so the Bible is a perpetual summons to the spiritual life and the immortal symbol of man's unquenchable faith in God.

J. Warschauer, *What is the Bible?* J. T. Sunderland, *Origin and Character of the Bible.* W. C. Selleck, *New Appreciation of the Bible.* Driver and Kirkpatrick, *Higher Criticism.* F. W. Farrar, *History of Interpretation; The Bible, its Meaning and Supremacy.* J. E. Carpenter, *The Bible in the Nineteenth Century. Foundations*, chap. II. W. Gladden, *Who Wrote the Bible?* B. P. Bowne, *Studies in Christianity*, chap. I. G. T. Ladd, *What is the Bible?* L. Wallis, *Sociological Study of the Bible.* J. P. Peters, *The Old Testament and the New Scholarship.* E. von Dobschütz, *Influence of the Bible upon Civilization.* A. Sabatier, *Religions of Authority*, bk. II; *Outlines of a Philosophy of Religion*, bk. I, chap. II. R. M. Wenley, *Modern Thought and the Crisis in Belief*, III–V. G. H. Gilbert, *Interpretation of the Bible.* W. G. Jordan, *Biblical Criticism and Modern Thought. New World*, vol. 3, pp. 23, 250. *Methodist Review*, vol. 93, p. 899. *Biblical World*, vol. 44, p. 3.

CHAPTER XVIII

MIRACLES

WITH the passing of the credulous acceptance of Bible legends and the blind trust in Bible texts, the miraculous element in Christian belief has tended steadily to diminish. Many of the leaders of Christian thought now reject miracles *in toto*; and others who are not ready to abandon them altogether have ceased to use them as supports for their faith. We will first note the reasons for this waning of belief in miracles, and then consider how far, if at all, they can serve as foundations or aids for our theology.

What considerations have weakened the belief in miracles?

Judging by its etymology, the word "miracle" means simply a marvelous event, one which excites our wonder.[1] In this broadest sense we speak of the sunrise or the coming of spring as a miracle, and may, indeed, find the whole pageant of nature miraculous. "This green, flowery, rock-built earth . . . that great deep sea of azure that swims overhead. . . . What *is* it? Ay what? At bottom we do not yet know; we can never know at all. . . . It is by *not* thinking that we cease to wonder at it. . . . This world after all our science and sciences, is still a miracle; wonderful, inscrutable, *magical* and more, to whosoever will think of it."[2] More particularly, a miracle is a wonderful event in which God is revealed, or which works for man's salvation; the

---

[1] So the Latin *miraculum*, the Greek θαυμάσιον, and the German *Wunder*.
[2] Carlyle, *Heroes and Hero-Worship*, chap. I.

greatest of miracles is the conversion that takes place in a sinner's heart, the power of the indwelling God to regenerate a life. In this sense there can be no objection to the use of the term; it in so far implies no violation of natural law, no break in the regular sequence of cause and effect. And since the very idea of natural law is a recent one, the conception of miracles can hardly be said to have generally implied such a break in a fixed natural order. But the conception has usually implied something abnormal, an intrusion into the ordinary and expected course of events; and the modern technical sense of the word, as a break in the natural chain of cause and effect due to supernatural intervention, scarcely more than makes explicit and precise what was vaguely meant. Taking the term in this sense, then, what grounds have we for mistrusting the existence of miracles?

(1) In the first place, there has been in the past century or two a rapid accumulation of evidence pointing to the invariable regularity of natural processes — what is called the reign of natural law. The more closely we analyze events in any field of study, the more clearly we see that their apparent confusion is the result of an extremely complex tissue of underlying uniformities. Things do happen in exactly the same way if exactly the same circumstances are repeated; the enormous development of science has been possible only because of that fact. Whenever an experiment has been properly made, it holds good for all time; for the way things behaved yesterday is the way they will behave to-morrow. There are indeed many groups of phenomena too intricate for us as yet to unravel; particularly is this true of mental phenomena. But the field of observed uniformity is constantly being extended. Even mental and social facts are suggesting underlying laws to investigators; and if concrete mental and social events are too complex and include too many disturbing factors for these underlying laws to be any-

thing but tendencies, the results of statistical study, where these disturbing factors counterbalance one another, exhibit a regularity often very striking. Altogether, it looks more and more as if the whole world were, from the analytic point of view, an enormously elaborate mechanism; and this increasingly insistent look of things constitutes a very great presumption against the existence of those alleged irregular events that we call miracles.

We must, indeed, beware of falling into a scientific dogmatism upon the matter. After all, the universality of natural law is no more than a very big generalization resting upon a long series of observations; if any facts to the contrary can be surely established, the generalization is thereby disproved. We have no *a priori* certainty of this "reign of law." It rests upon just such an unbroken induction as the generalization that "all swans are white," which was utterly smashed by the discovery of one black swan. Let but one miracle be proved, and we must revise this conception of the universal life as an unbroken web of uniformities. Our science will be rendered in so far more precarious; we shall have to recognize the possibility of exceptions to the laws which we have come most confidently to rely upon. But whether this be the case or not we cannot determine *a priori;* we must simply sharpen our observation, keep our eyes open for evidence. Hume, in a famous argument, declared the evidence for the universality of natural law to be so vast that the falsity of any amount of evidence for a miracle was more supposable than a break in law. But the universality of natural law is by no means so firmly established; in some fields we have as yet hardly a few glimpses of law; and, on the other hand, we have a great deal of human testimony offered in support of alleged breaches of law. The most that we can say is, that in view of the very remarkable recent extensions of the realm of ascertained law into regions that once seemed hopelessly lawless, it should require much more certain evidence to convince us of a miracle than we should ask in support of any fact against which there is no such antecedent presumption.[1]

In recent years the deterministic conception of the universe — the conception that whatever happens is absolutely determined by antecedent causes, and, therefore, theoretically predictable — has been sharply questioned. We have, for example, Driesch's Vitalism, and Bergson's Creative Evolution — theories that postulate certain variable and indeterminate factors at definite points in the universal life; uncaused causes, that veer events this way or that to an extent and in a direction unforeseeable even by omniscience. As yet none of these anti-deterministic theories is anywhere near being proved; and the arguments offered in support of them have been pretty severely handled. In spite of the lure of these conceptions of a more fluid and plastic world-life, the weight of scientific opinion seems to incline toward the belief in the universality of law. But, after all, the slight veerings from mechanically determined effects in the human brain, or in the conduct of a bit of protoplasm, cannot be conceived to produce such effects as the turning of water into wine or the restoration of a corpse to life. That is to say, the concrete instances where we are asked to believe in a miracle are such as to come within the field of law in any

---

[1] Huxley has a good illustration of this principle in his book *David Hume* (p. 132): "If a man tells me he saw a piebald horse in Piccadilly, I believe him without hesitation. The thing itself is likely enough, and there is no imaginable motive for his deceiving me. But if the same person tells me he observed a zebra there, I might hesitate a little about accepting his testimony, unless I were well satisfied, not only as to his previous acquaintance with zebras, but as to his powers and opportunities of observation in the present case. If, however, my informant assured me that he beheld a centaur trotting down that famous thoroughfare, I should emphatically decline to credit his statement; and this even if he were the saintliest of men and ready to suffer martyrdom in support of his belief."

case; and the difference between the differing world views we have mentioned is not such as to affect the question of miracles in any appreciable degree.

Nor need this other suggestion detain us, that the alleged miraculous events may be true and yet not contrary to law, since the law may really be more complex than we had supposed, and, in its adequate formulation, such as to cover the given case.[1] Certain supposed miracles, such as the healing-acts of Jesus, and of present-day Christian Scientists, or the abrupt conversions made by evangelists, may thus be ultimately explicable in terms of law, and so not miracles at all. But that the laws of chemistry are in need of such drastic amendment as to include the case of water turning into wine at a word, that the laws of astronomy are so far from adequate as to need inclusion of the possibility of the sun's standing still upon occasion, is too grotesque a supposition to entertain. Most of the miracles that men argue for are of this type; they so flatly contradict well-ascertained uniformities as to present a clear alternative. Either our most certain natural laws are really broken now and then, or else the supposed evidence for these breaks is untrustworthy, and the alleged events never happened.

(2) What, then, is the strength of the evidence for miracles? It must be confessed that while the evidence for natural laws has been growing steadily greater, the evidence for miracles has been growing as steadily less. Remote and credulous times are full of miracles; we hear of them but rarely, if at all, to-day. They flourish in the dark and vanish with the light of day, with the growth of the habit of accurate observation and recording of observations. They seem to have an affinity for uncultivated minds and superstitious habits of thought; we do not find them entering into the

[1] For a clear exposition of this suggested possibility, see Rice, pp. 329-36.

experience of the educated. No single case of what would clearly be a miracle has ever been vouched for by such careful scientific observation as to leave no room for doubt of the facts.[1] Even if we had apparently unimpeachable evidence, in some isolated instance, of a fact which, if it existed, would be a miracle, we should have to bear in mind the great fallibility of human testimony,[2] and reserve our acquiescence

[1] Some "spiritualistic" phenomena are vouched for by men of high scientific repute; so are some of the "miracles" wrought by the holy relics at Trèves, etc. But these phenomena, even if we can feel sure of their existence, do not contradict clearly ascertained laws, and are, in most cases, not regarded as miracles by the scientific men who are persuaded of their existence. The case would be very different if we could get scientific guaranty of such facts as the turning of water into wine, a man's walking upon the sea, being born of a virgin, etc., etc.

[2] Any reader of Münsterberg's *On the Witness Stand* will realize the extraordinary unreliability of the witness even of well-trained men, speaking in the best of faith. The testimony of ignorant and untrained men is almost worthless, except as probed by expert examiners. Especially is this the case where the emotions and imagination are implicated. I hardly know of a more telling argument against miracles than this little book — which, of course, was written without any such reference.

Even Catholic writers, in their treatment of the miracles ascribed to the saints, have been free to point out the unreliability of such testimony. Cf. H. Delahaye, *Legends of the Saints*, p. 15: "Even the most veracious and upright of men unconsciously create legends by introducing into their narratives their own impressions, deductions, and passions, and thus present the truth either embellished or disfigured, according to circumstances. These sources of error, it need scarcely be said, become multiplied with the number of intermediaries. Every one in turn understands the story in a different fashion and repeats it in his own way. Through inattention or through defective memory some one forgets to mention an important circumstance, necessary to the continuity of the history. A narrator, more observant than the rest, notes the deficiency, and by means of his imagination does his best to repair it. He invents some new detail, and suppresses another, until probability and logic appear to him sufficiently safeguarded. The result is usually only obtained at the expense of truth; for the narrator does not observe that he has substituted a very different story for the primitive version. These things happen every day; and whether we are eye-witnesses or mere intermediaries, our limited intelligence, our carelessness, our passions, and above all perhaps our prejudices, all conspire against historical accuracy when we take it upon ourselves to become narrators."

until it had been corroborated by testimony from other observers or in other similar cases. The fact seems to be, however, that the belief in miracles flourishes in primitive life, and among naïve peoples far into civilized times; miracles cluster, in particular, about men of unusual power and personality, above all, about great religious teachers. But they belong to the thought of uncritical peoples and disappear with enlightenment.

(3) This fact, at any rate, is to be borne in mind: Christianity has by no means an exclusive lien upon miracles. All the religions are full of them; and, as a recent theologian has said, it is not only the weakness of the evidence for the Christian miracles but the strength of the evidence for the non-Christian miracles that gives us pause. It is only by our bias and partisanship that we accept ours and reject theirs. Many miracles are better authenticated than those which Christian faith has clung to; yet no Christian dreams of accepting them. Herodotus, for example, tells us of miraculous events that happened in his own times; he was a writer of a more critical temper than most of the historians of early Christianity, and of unblemished character. Yet we dismiss his tales with a smile. We read that Buddha was born of a virgin, that Zoroaster was miraculously conceived, that Mohammed was visited by the angel Gabriel; nearly all of the Biblical miracles can be paralleled by equally well- (or ill-) substantiated similar miracles in other religions. The study of comparative religion shows how the same legends and miracles tend constantly to recur. But the believers of each religion stoutly affirm their own miracles and deny those of the other faiths. "The time has come when the minds of men no longer put as a matter of course the Bible miracles in a class by themselves. Now, from the moment this time commences, from the moment that the comparative history of all miracles is a conception entertained and

a study admitted, the conclusion is certain, the reign of the Bible miracles is doomed." [1]

If, then, we accept some miracles — as, the raising of Lazarus, or the emergence of the reanimated body of Jesus from the tomb and its ascension into the sky — there seems to be no place to stop. Shall we go on to believe in Elijah's raising of the dead, or his bodily translation to the skies? in the talking of Balaam's ass, in the collapse of the walls of Jericho at the blowing of horns? Shall we go on to believe in similar stories in the Buddhist or Mohammedan or other Scriptures? The Biblical accounts are not contemporary records; the resurrection stories, in the form which we now possess, date from at least fifty years after the time of which they speak, the Lazarus story from at least sixty, and more likely eighty years after. Then why not accept the marvels in Bonaventura's life of St. Francis, written but forty years after that saint's death, and in a more enlightened age? The fact is, if we allow ourselves to believe in the one case and refuse to believe in the other case, it is not because we have any better evidence for the miracles we accept, but because we have an antecedent bias toward belief therein. We believe primarily because we wish to believe.

(4) Another interesting fact is that we can often catch miracles in process of growth. A harmony of the Gospels, for example, reveals, here and there, a development from a simple event as recorded by Mark into a much more marvelous happening in Matthew or Luke. We can see how the antecedent expectation of miracle-working on the part of the Messiah, and the need of pointing to miracles in proof of their assertion of Jesus' Messiahship, led the early Christian believers to an unconscious embroidering upon the primitive tradition. There was a nucleus of marvelous healing-acts

[1] Arnold, *God and the Bible*, p. 40. An interesting comparative study of miracles follows.

about which further accretions could easily gather; and any tale, once started, in whatever way, would gain uncritical acceptance. In some cases we can conjecture with considerable confidence that an apparent miracle resulted from the misunderstanding of a parable, as in the matter of the blasted fig tree and the raising of Lazarus,[1] or of what was originally poetic hyperbole, as in the case of the sun standing still.[2] In the later, noncanonical gospels, we have all sorts of legends which had not yet been accepted when our Gospels were written. The stories of the birth of Jesus in Bethlehem, the virgin birth, and the reanimation of Jesus' body, had almost certainly not gained currency in the time of Paul and the apostles; neither in Paul's Epistles nor in the account of the primitive Christian preaching in Acts do we find allusion to them, though they would have been precisely the most telling arguments if known.[3] Again, if all the miracles imputed by the evangelists to Jesus were really performed, in the presence of so many witnesses, it is incredible that he should have made so little impression upon people's minds. The priests assumed without question that he was a blasphemer; even his disciples were slow to accept him as the Messiah; and at his death he had, in spite of his extraordinary personality and spiritual power, but a small following.

[1] Cf. Mark 11: 12-14, with Luke 13: 6-9; and John 11: 1-46, with Luke 16: 19-31.

[2] The historian takes literally (Joshua 10: 13b-14) the lines of poetry, from the book of Jashar, which he has just quoted (vss. 12b-13a). The verse-division here conceals the situation badly.

[3] It may be necessary to say again that the rejection of the stories at the end of the Gospels, concerning the emergence of Jesus from the tomb and the appearance of his reanimated body here and there, by no means implies a rejection of the belief in the continued life of Jesus after death. *That* belief was held by the disciples from the very beginning, was corroborated by their experiences (whatever those experiences may have been) and was accepted by Paul on the testimony of *his* experience on the road to Damascus.

Such considerations, brief as our summary has been, should sufficiently explain the growing skepticism in regard to miracles. We may now ask of what value the belief in miracles may be if we can still, in spite of these considerations, retain it.

Of what value is the belief in miracles?

According to the traditional view, the power to work miracles must come from God, and is therefore a witness, not only to the presence of God in his world, but to the truth of the teaching by which they are accompanied. They are God's endorsement of his chosen prophets, their credentials before an unbelieving world. Let us examine this conception more closely, taking as our concrete example the case of Christ, which is the crucial case for Christian thought.

(1) Do Christ's miracles, if proved, guarantee the truth of his spiritual teachings? How can they? What connection is there between extraordinary physical powers and spiritual truth? "Suppose I should say to you that hate is better than love, and then should work a miracle, — for instance, the turning of this pencil into a serpent, — would that prove it true that hate *is* better than love? Or suppose I should turn a thousand pencils into serpents, or work a thousand other miracles, would they all combined have anything whatever to do with proving that hate is better than love?"[1] The validity of Christ's principles of living is witnessed, not by any marvels that may have accompanied their proclamation, but by the inward power and peace they bring. If they do not *work*, if they do not prove the best solution of the prob-

[1] J. T. Sunderland, *Miracles in the Light of Modern Knowledge*, p. 6. Cf. Carlyle, *Sartor Resartus*, bk. III, chap. VIII: "Here too may some inquire, not without astonishment: On what ground shall one, that can make iron swim, come and declare that therefore he can teach religion? To us, truly, of the Nineteenth Century, such declaration were inept enough."

lem of life, then we shall do well to discard them for a better solution, though all the thunders of Sinai proclaimed their supernatural source. The authoritative religious teacher is not he who has power to calm the sea or turn water into wine, but he who has an insight into human hearts, their needs and temptations and inherent ideals; whoever has such insight is our spiritual master, even if he be physically the most impotent of mortals. It is a *hysteron proteron* to say that Christ's teachings must be true because they are *his* teachings; we should rather say that he is proved a great teacher because he taught what we see to be so *true*.

(2) But if spiritual truth must be tested by other criteria than its source, is it so with knowledge of facts? Do not Christ's miracles prove his supernatural nature and therefore afford a presumption that he knew more than we do about God, the human soul and its destiny, and other matters beyond our ken? Unfortunately, such a presumption is overthrown (quite apart from our doubts as to the actuality of the miracles) by the fact that so many other people are reported to have performed equally striking miracles; and their teachings do not agree. How can the orthodox regard miracles as a guaranty of the correct knowledge of a teacher, when the Bible itself imputes them to all sorts of magicians and miracle-mongers? Should we credit the teachings of the Egyptian wise men because they were able to turn their rods into serpents, transform the waters of the Nile into blood, and bring a plague of frogs upon the land?[1] The New Testament refers in several places to miracles wrought by "false prophets"; the "sons of the Pharisees" were working them, as Jesus says. How then do they give any particular authentication to Jesus' teaching rather than to that of these others?[2]

[1] See Exod. 7: 11-12, 22; 8: 7.
[2] See Matt. 12: 27; 7: 22; 24: 24. Mark. 9: 38-41. Luke 9: 49-50. Acts 19: 113-15. Rev. 13: 13-14; 16: 13-14; 19: 20.

(3) But do not miracles at least manifest God's goodness, since they were usually wrought for the benefit of some sick or suffering person? On the contrary, it is difficult to reconcile the belief in miracles with the belief in God's goodness. For if he can and does at rare intervals allow them, to save this man or that, why does he not allow them oftener, to save so many other equally innocent victims of undeserved suffering? So few saving miracles would be gross favoritism. If a miraculous draught of fishes was granted to one discouraged band of fishermen, why not to thousands of others who have toiled as hard and gone to bed hungry? If one leper was healed, and sent on his way rejoicing, why not all the wretched sufferers from that loathsome disease? Such a little intervention might so often have averted so many unspeakable horrors! If the divine order permits of miracles at all, it would seem as if God, in not exercising this power oftener, must be singularly callous and hardhearted. Again, some of the recorded miracles, while of benefit to the favored person, were quite unfairly cruel to others who had to suffer therefrom. For example, if God intervened with a miracle to enable Joshua and his host to capture the city of Jericho, it was hard on the innocent women and children in the city who were put to the sword. If he intervened to save Peter from prison, it was hard on the guards, who, though really not at fault, were thereupon, we are told, put to death by Herod for dereliction of duty.[1]

(4) About the only miracle that would seem of much worth to us is that of the resurrection. If we could know beyond possibility of doubt that Jesus rose superior to death, and is still alive, in some heavenly sphere, that knowledge would go far to strengthen our faith in our own immortality. Of course, most of those who believe the resurrection

[1] See Joshua 6: 20-21. Acts 12: 19.

stories hold Jesus to have been a supernatural Being, whose continued life would not therefore guarantee ours; while if we doubt the previous miracles stories, which prove his supernatural powers, we shall be likely to doubt the resurrection stories also. Yet to have evidence of life after death, even in a unique case, gives a vast stimulus to hope. To be sure, we may well continue to believe Jesus to be immortally living, even if we reject these stories; but we shall no longer have tangible evidence of it. The genuine experiences of Paul and the other Apostles, of which we know so little, may conceivably have been purely subjective, and their conviction that Christ had revealed himself to them, or "in them," an illusion. So that a loss of confidence in the resurrection stories must be acknowledged to be a loss of no small moment.

What should be our attitude toward miracles?

Certainly our attitude toward miracles should be that of the open mind; to refuse to listen receptively to the great mass of proffered evidence would be a stupid dogmatism. But as certainly we must, in the present state of the evidence, render a verdict of "Not proven"; many would be inclined to go further and say, "Not even very plausible." The main current of contemporary thought is setting strongly against belief in the miraculous. Once men believed in Christ because they accepted the fact of the miracles; now they believe in miracles, if at all, because they have accepted Christ, and suppose the belief in miracles to be a necessary corollary. But from being a prop of faith, they have become a stumbling-block in the way of faith. That being the case, it is at the least a tactical error on the part of Christian apologists to thrust them upon their would-be converts. The great truths of Christianity are verifiable now, in repeatable human experience; they should not be said to rest upon marvels that are alleged to have happened centuries ago and cannot at best be proved. The great theologians have seldom leaned hard upon miracles; Christ himself is reported to have shown impatience with those who came to him seeking for a miracle as a sign, and to have told them that they should have for a sign only a summons to repentance.[1] To-day we have many leaders in the Church who are seeking to free Christian truth from the embarrassment of the miraculous element.[2]

Finally, we may insist that to lose belief in miracles is by no means to lose faith in God. Surely God may be revealed as clearly in the normal as in the abnormal, in the sweep of the cosmic laws as in interventions that break them. Some critics have even ventured to suggest that miracles would be a sort of patching up of a cosmos that needed mending, and find them incompatible with their theology. But at any rate, supernaturalism is by no means essential to Christianity. Matthew Arnold was absolutely right when he wrote, in a well-known passage,[3] "Some people, when they have got rid of the preternatural in religion, seem to think that they are bound to get rid of the notion of there being anything grand and wonderful in religion at all; at any rate, to reduce this element of what is grand and wonderful to the very smallest dimensions. They err."

Traditionalistic: G. P. Fisher, *Grounds of Theistic and Christian Belief*, chaps. VIII–IX. T. J. Dodd, *Miracles*. G. P. Mains, *Modern Thought and Traditional Faith*, chap. XIV. W. N. Rice, *Christian Faith in an Age of Science*, pt. II. J. Wendland, *Miracles and Chris-*

---

[1] Mark 8: 11–12. Matt. 16: 1–4. Luke 11: 29: 32. In the duplicate passage in Matt. 12: 38–42, some editor has completely mistaken the allusion and inserted a ridiculous interpretation (vs. 40).

[2] Cf., for example, Gordon, p. 7: "My plea is not against miracles, but against the identification of the fortune of religion with the fortune of miracle."

[3] *God and the Bible*, chap. III.

tianity. J. H. Newman, *Two Essays on Miracles; Apologia pro vita sua*, note B. A. M. Fairbairn, *Philosophy of the Christian Religion*, pp. 23–27.

Modern: M. Arnold, *Literature and Dogma*, chap. v; *God and the Bible*, chap. I. T. H. Huxley, *Hume*, chap. VII; *Science and Christian Tradition*, chaps. v–vi. H. Höffding, *Philosophy of Religion*, p. 27 f. A. Sabatier, *Outlines of a Philosophy of Religion*, bk. I, chap. III, secs. 1–2. G. A. Gordon, *Religion and Miracle*. G. B. Foster, *Finality of the Christian Religion*, pp. 115–147. J. M. E. McTaggart, *Some Dogmas of Religion*, secs. 41–43. *American Journal of Theology*, vol. 8, p. 240; vol. 15, p. 569. *Harvard Theological Review*, vol. 3, p. 143. *Hibbert Journal*, vol. 12, p. 162. *New World*, vol. 5, p. 9. See also references in footnotes on pp. 66 and 84.

CHAPTER XIX

CREATION AND DESIGN

IF we can deduce no safe theological conclusions from alleged irregularities in nature, can we do so from the regularity of the natural order, from any peculiar phenomena which it includes, or from the sheer fact of its existence? We shall examine some current inferences of this sort.

Can we draw theological inferences from

I. The sheer existence of the universe? Many have held that the very existence of the universe, with its causal order, requires us to postulate God as its creator; here, then, would be a big step beyond that empirical knowledge of God of which we spoke in chapter ix. The form of the argument varies with its various exponents, but one quotation must suffice: "No movable body moves itself. A does not move unless acted upon by B; nor can B move A unless preceded by C. Somewhere there must be an X which is unmoved, and yet which is in itself sufficient to explain the motion in D, C, B, and A. If X is not given, none of the series will move.... At last, somewhere or other in this series, we are forced to admit the existence of an uncaused cause.... This first efficient cause we call God."[1] Generalized, the argument is that every event must have had a cause; we are involved then in an endless regress unless we can get back to some First Cause which needs no prior cause to explain it. Our causal chain must have some peg to

[1] Aveling, *op. cit.*, pp. 63–76.

hang from; only in the creative fiat of God can we find such a satisfactory end to our search.

(1) But, if every event must have its cause, what caused that creative fiat of God? Must we not, in consistency, postulate a prior cause for that — and find ourselves still involved in the endless regress? How is it easier to account for God than for the universe? If one may be conceived as eternal, why may not the other? If God can exist uncaused, why may not the other realities? The universe is, at bottom, an inexplicable fact; but to postulate another and equally inexplicable fact to explain it leaves us with as many questions to ask as before. Putting God at the point where we cannot read history any farther back, because we crave some explanation, is like the ancient acceptance of the belief in a gigantic turtle that supported the earth. Surely the earth must have some support, and what else could the skeptic point to? But how did they know it was a turtle? And what supported the turtle? So we may ask our theologian: How do you know that the earth was created by *God*? And what created God? The modern inference is as precarious, as much a leap in the dark, as the ancient one.

(2) Well, then, we shall be asked, how else *did* the universe come into being? The answer is simply — we have no means of knowing. Perhaps the law of cause and effect did not always hold — as, indeed, it may not hold everywhere today; perhaps the world just began to be, without any antecedent cause. Or perhaps it is eternal. Eternal existence baffles our realization; but the limitations of our power of clear conception should not bias our acceptance of conceptual possibilities. Or the world may be the product of many gods; this is, indeed, man's earliest idea, and in spite of our predilection for unity, there is no proof that there was but one first cause. The idea of the creation of the world by God is the idea which comes most readily to most of us, with our

theistic education; it is the most consoling and emotionally satisfying answer to the question how the world came into being. But it has no more *evidence* in its favor than any other answer, and may not, for all its pleasing associations, be the *true* answer.

(3) Granted that there must be a first cause, what right have we to capitalize it into a First Cause, and call it God? God we know in experience, as the great Power making for good. What right have we to identify that Power with the original creative-power? The first cause may have been a Devil, or a non-rational cause. As a matter of fact, the farther back we can read the causal process, the nearer we get — not to God, but to a nebula, scattered atoms, or ether — all purely material states. There is no hint that we should reach any other *kind* of a cause. And so a First Cause, even if we can logically assume it, and even if we choose to give it the name God, is not proved to be what we mean by God in experience; it is only a force at the beginning of things, not necessarily a living, present, helpful, or good God, and so of no interest to religion.

In a word, how the universe came into existence, or whether it has always existed, we do not know; and wherever we are ignorant, imagination readily leaps in to fill the void. Creation by an intelligent Being is a conceivable explanation; but there are many other explanations equally conceivable, and for neither the one nor the others does the mere existence of the cosmos afford the least evidence.

II. The existence of certain classes of facts. But do not the particular characteristics of this universe of ours imply creation by an intelligent Being? Theologians have thought to find such an implication in the existence of natural law, of organic life, of mental life, and of morality.

(1) Curiously enough, some of the same theologians who

point to irregularities in the natural course of events — i.e., miracles — as a witness of God, point also to the regularity of the course of events as a witness of God. This marvelous mechanism, they say, must have been created by an Intelligence. One way of putting it is to say that "natural law implies a lawgiver." That is, however, a palpable play on words. For the term "natural law" is merely a metaphor for the uniformities which we find in the sequence of events; and uniformities of behavior do not imply a lawgiver, but may be quite spontaneous or produced by non-intelligent causes. Another play on words has it that the "objective reason" or "rationality" of the world presupposes a "subjective reason" or "intelligence" as its source. This so-called "rationality" of the world turns out to mean, again, only its orderliness, its mechanistic character, which may not be imposed upon it from without at all. The fact that the universe is a marvelously intricate structure, which we can to some degree map in our minds, comprehend, and master, cannot logically afford the inference that that intricate and intelligible structure was planned and moulded by an antecedent Mind. Perhaps this complex world-life has evolved, unplanned and unforeseen, through the simple but uniform habits of its innumerable component parts, which have become gradually more and more intricately intermingled.[1]

[1] This argument merges into a consideration of the problem of knowledge; and all sorts of theories have been constructed around the assumption that the intelligibility of the world must be the work of Intelligence. Into these deep philosophical waters we cannot here go. But let me quote a typical writer of this sort, B. P. Bowne. He speaks of the "numerical exactness of mathematical processes," and asserts that "the truly mathematical is the work of the spirit." The atheist has to "assume a power which produces the intelligible and rational, without being itself intelligent and rational. . . . There is no proper explanation except in theism." (*Theism*, pp. 67–70.) "Things which are to be known must exist in intelligible, that is, rational, order and relations. The world as we grasp it is a world of thought relations; for thought can grasp nothing else. Now if the real world were an expression of thought, this would be quite intelligible.

CREATION AND DESIGN

(2) But do we not, then, need to assume the hand of God to account for the existence of organic life on earth? or of psychic life? or of moral life? "Organic life had a beginning in the material universe. But life could not have its origin in mere material forces. Therefore that origin is to be assigned to the action of a living being altogether different and extraneous to that matter which it endowed with the various substantial principles of life." [1] Again, "this rare and lonely endowment [human intelligence] must have its roots in the universe. . . . The problem then arises how to deduce the conscious from the unconscious, the intelligent from the non-intelligent. . . . The more clearly we conceive physical elements or processes, the more clearly we perceive the impossibility of such a transition." [2] Again, "He that implanted in man an unalterable reverence for righteousness, shall not he himself be righteous? This inference is so spontaneous and immediate that it is seldom questioned when the moral interest is strong and thought is clear. . . . As there is no known way of deducing intelligence from non-intelligence, so there is no known way of deducing the moral from the non-moral." [3]

These three arguments are alike in alleging the necessity

The world without exists through a mind analogous to the mind within. . . . But on the atheistic scheme the thing-world has no thought whatever in it. It just exists in its own mechanical way. . . . But in that case there is no way to thought at all, and still less is there any provision for knowledge." (*Ibid*, pp. 132–33.) An introductory survey like the present volume cannot afford the space to discuss the epistemological problem, about which many bulky volumes have been written. It must suffice to refer the reader to such books as Perry's *Present Philosophical Tendencies*, or the coöperative volume, *The New Realism*, or Fullerton's *The World We Live In*, or Strong's *Why the Mind has a Body*, as illustrations of the contemporary tendency to abandon all of this older epistemological theory. According to the reigning modes of philosophic thought there is no logical inference to theism to be found in the fact of knowledge.

[1] Aveling, *op. cit.*, p. 134.   [2] Bowne, *op. cit.*, p. 120.
[3] *Ibid.*, pp. 251–52.

of an interposition by God in the natural course of evolution in order to account for the origin of these particular developments. They are based upon our supposed inability to explain the higher stages from the action of the forces present at the earlier stages. They are purely negative arguments, then, offering no positive sign of an interposed divine fiat, and no explanation of how or where such an intervention took place. They are based purely upon our present ignorance, and have the weakness of all such arguments — no one can say how soon we may find a clue which shall suggest a purely natural transition from lower to higher stages. In view of the absence of any assured sign of intervention in the natural order in our own times, and the absence of positive evidence for such intervention at these remote points in the process, the arguments can hardly be said to be more than plausible conjectures.

But more than that, we are finding continuity in so many places where men formerly assumed breaks in the natural course of development, that a pretty strong presumption arises that we shall ultimately be able to explain the whole cosmic process in terms of natural law — or, at least, that the natural law is there, whether or not we shall ever be able to formulate it. As a matter of fact there are already in the field "mechanical" theories of organic life, i.e., theories which account for it in terms of known physical and chemical laws; such theories have won widespread acceptance among biologists. And organic life of a low order, or something of the sort, seems to have actually been brought into existence out of non-living matter in the laboratory. The line between organic life and the activities of "non-living matter" is so exceedingly fine, that biologists differ, in borderland cases, as to what shall be considered "life" and what not; and no student can come away from a survey of these phenomena without at least suspecting that they

CREATION AND DESIGN

are all purely natural, that "living" organisms are simply a more complex form of the universal restless activity of the cosmic substance. And finally, if "law" does not prevail through all this process of increasing complexification, the intervening factor may be "entelechy," "chance," "free will," or what not. The "vitalists" who oppose the conception of a completely mechanistic universe by no means all draw theistic inferences; it is the theologians who, while knowing little themselves of the phenomena in question, seize upon their anti-mechanical arguments to draw therefrom a rather far-fetched conclusion.

The question of the origin of mind takes us over into the realm of metaphysics, where all is as yet confusion. But here again it must be said that few of the current philosophical theories lead over into theistic inferences. The writer of this volume has elsewhere hinted at a way in which the origin of consciousness may be conceived in terms of natural law,[1] and hopes to return to the subject in a future volume. The whole problem of the nature of consciousness and its relation to the material world is as yet so unsettled that no safe inferences can be drawn one way or the other.[2]

As to the origin of morality out of a non-moral background, any scientific treatise on ethics will show conclusively that there is no need of assuming any supernatural intervention.[3] So that we must admit that our knowledge of God is not to be furthered through any inferences that we can at present draw from the apparent jumps in the evolutionary process.

(3) There is, however, an assumption behind these cur-

[1] In a dissertation, *The Problem of Things in Themselves* (Ellis, Boston, 1911).

[2] This problem would require, again, too much space to take up here. See the books mentioned in the footnote on p. 299.

[3] Cf. the present writer's *Problems of Conduct*, pt. I; or Dewey and Tufts, *Ethics*, pt. I; or Herbert Spencer, *Data of Ethics*, chaps. I–VIII.

rent arguments that may still linger in the mind of the reader. It is, that results cannot be "higher" than their causes — "shall a man be more pure than his maker?" Aveling makes this assumption explicit in the words," "An effect requires a proportionate cause. . . . The essential perfection of the effect preëxists in the cause."[1] But have we not daily examples of effects more precious than their causes? A beautiful flower grows from an uninteresting seed, a lovely child from an ugly fœtus. If you point out that, tracing the process a little further back, the flower and the child come from a similar flower and human being, we can reply that, tracing the process still further back, the flower comes from some flowerless form of vegetation, and the human child from an ape-like brute. Everything of most worth in our life has sprung, visibly, from dissimilar and humbler beginnings. Why may not this be the case with the evolutionary process as a whole; why may not our earthly life, with its intricate diversity and richness of interest, be a flowering-out of the world-process into something never attained before? At any rate, it is pure assumption to say that effects can be no *better* than their causes; we might as well say that they can be no *worse* — in which case we should be led to postulate a Devil as creator, to account for what is evil, instead of a God to account for what is good and beautiful.

III. Marks of design or purpose? A far more plausible argument than any of the foregoing is that which draws from the apparent marks of design in the universe an inference that it was created by Intelligence. In so many cases, it is said, rational, desirable ends are attained by the intricate combination of causes not themselves intelligent or capable of consciously coöperating, that we have no choice but to assume a Master-hand behind the process. We are

[1] *Op. cit.*, p. 78.

CREATION AND DESIGN

equipped, for example, with eyes for seeing, with ears for hearing, and with the most delicate machinery for procuring our survival and happiness; water is provided for us to drink, air for us to breathe, beautiful scenes to delight our hearts. Surely it is absurd to say that such a carefully adjusted world came into being by the coöperation of blind forces. May we not then assume with confidence that God is Creator of the universe?

This forcible argument, in its current forms, is analyzable into three strands, which we may examine in turn: —

(1) The first, and weakest, strand is an argument from analogy. In Paley's famous parable,[1] a watch is discovered upon a desert island; though there be no other trace of human life, the finder knows that a complex mechanism of that sort, adapted to a rational use, must have been made by an intelligent being. How much more surely, then, can we infer that the universe, so much more complex and wonderful, and attaining so much more glorious ends, was created by a greater Intelligence!

But an argument from analogy is always precarious. It may be, for all the analogy can prove, that *some* kinds of complex mechanisms, like the watch, are created by intelligence, while *other* kinds, like flowers and animals, and the universe as a whole, have come into existence in other ways. As a matter of fact, we should not judge the watch to be a product of intelligence on any such inferential grounds; we *know* empirically that watches are made by men, and do not grow, like flowers and animals. But we have no such empirical knowledge of intelligence as concerned with the creation of these other complex mechanisms. Hence we must pass over this analogical form of the argument and consider, more at length, the causal argument.

(2) It is not conceivable that this coöperation between

[1] *Natural Theology*, vol. I, chaps. I-III.

thousands of unintelligent factors to produce a valuable adjustment should be a mere matter of chance. Democritus, lacking a Darwinian conception, and unwilling to assume a Providence, felt obliged to assert that eyes and ears, and all the other delicately adjusted organs, were the fortuitous result of the blind whirl of atoms. But this is as grotesque a supposition as to hold that a bag of printer's types, flung down ever so many million times, would eventually happen to fall into just the right order to form the text of this volume. If our canons of cause and effect hold in these matters at all, there must be some cause adequate to account for the assembling and adjustment of the thousands of parts of these intricate organs. The logical Method of Agreement, discovering that the only point in which all of these diverse elements agree is in their function of conducing to the usefulness of the organ, suggests that the cause of the formation of these organs has something to do with their use. But the usefulness of the eye (for example) is subsequent to its formation and so cannot itself be the cause sought. What then can that cause be but a design-to-cause-the-ability-to-see? We may not be able to see how or where this conscious intention got in its work; but unless some other equally plausible cause is suggested, must we not assume it as the only alternative to the inconceivable hypothesis of mere chance aggregation?

No. Because another cause has been pointed out, which is not merely plausible, but is actually known to exist. This is the-fact-that-better-and-better-eyes (or, approximations-to-eyes)-conduce-better-to-survival. In the reproductive process, wherethrough all organisms come into existence, innumerable obscure physical forces are at work producing innumerable slight variations; offspring are not quite exactly like their parents. In the struggle for existence between the members of a given generation, those will tend to outlive

CREATION AND DESIGN

the others, and so reproduce their particular type, whose variation has given them any sort of advantage over their rivals. A slight sensitiveness to light would be such an advantage; any physiological change that chanced to produce a greater responsiveness to differences in light would give its possessor a superiority. Thus, as thousands of generations kept providing varying types, that type would (other things being equal) tend to survive which had in each case the best developed organ that responded to light-waves. And so by hundreds of thousands of slight steps, each a lucky variation out of thousands of useless or harmful ones, the delicately adjusted eyes of existing animals would be formed. This blind process, called Natural Selection, working through intelligible physical laws, automatically discards the myriad useless experiments which organisms in their exuberant fertility are producing, and preserves for future development those few variations that chance to be steps in the right direction. Or, in other words, useful variations tend, in a purely mechanical way, to ensure their own survival; and an accumulation of useful variations leads ultimately to any degree of intricate development.

It is true that biologists cannot yet explain in detail every case of adaptation in terms of this process. But every year clears up some hitherto obscure steps; and there are few biologists but are led by their observations to the conviction that all the manifold adjustments of organic forms will ultimately be explained in these terms. Moreover, the apparent adjustments of inorganic nature to the needs of organic forms can be explained in terms of the adjustment of the organisms to inorganic nature. That is, instead of marveling, for example, that the earth's atmosphere should have just the right proportions of oxygen, carbonic acid gas, etc., to maintain the organic life which exists upon its surface, we can point out that organic life has come to be of such a nature as to utilize precisely such proportions of gases because it has crept into existence under those conditions. On another planet, where much more CO_2 exists, living forms, if any have there come into existence, will be of such a nature as to thrive on a greater proportion of that gas.

The causal argument, therefore, loses all its cogency. Where a known cause is sufficient, or probably sufficient, to account for given phenomena, it is illogical to infer another and unseen cause. Moreover, Natural Selection accounts for all the failures, all the maladjustments, all the hit-or-miss character of the process, as the theological hypothesis does not. It is still possible to believe that God stands back of the whole evolutionary process; but the supposed *evidence* of his causal activity vanished, once Natural Selection was proved to be a *vera causa*. It is sometimes said that the Argument from Design can be restated in terms of Evolution. That is not true of this causal argument. The *belief* in God's creative activity may indeed be retained, but it becomes pure assumption; the *argument* is gone.

(3) The third form of the argument rests upon the presence of values in the world. We may not need to assume a supernatural agency to account for the mutual adaptations of organisms and environment considered merely as physical facts; but when we see what precious values emerge here at the end of this apparently blind process, are we not irresistibly led to suppose that God, in his infinite goodness and wisdom, planned and initiated the whole process?

But consider, first, the clumsiness and cruelty of the method employed. Does it look like the work of infinite goodness and wisdom to make a thousand useless forms for every one that is of use, to kill off a thousand young creatures, equally endowed with the craving for life, for every one that can survive? The process is infinitely more wasteful than the Chinese method of getting roast pig, in Charles Lamb's famous tale. It is as if a man, ignorant of what constituted the target, were to fire in all directions at random until eventually, by mere chance, he hit it. The more closely one studies the evolutionary process, the more it seems a blind struggle, and the less it suggests an intelligent creator. Millions of ill-adapted creatures have prematurely perished for one that was lucky enough to live long enough to reproduce its type. We, the handful of fortunate survivors of this age-long struggle, assume that it was all intended for our benefit. So might some microbes, borne about by the air currents till they fell into a glass of milk, assume with complacent thankfulness that that congenial home was designed by a benevolent Creator for their needs. But how about the millions of similar microbes that the winds blew elsewhere to perish?[1] Cicero tells us of a temple of Poseidon where were hung many votive tablets offered in gratitude by those who had been saved from shipwreck. "But where," said a visitor, "are the offerings of those who were *not* saved?" In short, our complacency is like that of the prize-winners in a lottery; the process seems to us benevolent because we are the favored survivors. If we could look through the eyes of the myriads that have fallen by the way, we should not see any evidences of creative wisdom or love; we should see nothing but a merciless doom.

Consider further the very partial nature of the success attained even with us who have survived. Even to-day, after millenniums of elimination of the unfit, the bodies of the best of us carry round a hundred marks of our hit-or-miss origin, vestiges of organs which, useful to our remote ancestors, serve no present use and are often of great danger to us in our present conditions of life. The vermiform appendix, the cause of appendicitis, is perhaps the best-known instance;

[1] This illustration is Paulsen's.

but even our most useful and most admired organs are burdened with useless inheritances and imperfectly adapted to their work. Man is too limited in his powers to reproduce these extraordinarily complex and highly unstable forms which nature, working with her vast forces through the ages, has brought into existence; but given the power, he could much improve upon her handiwork. Of all organs the eye is the most admired; but Nature, as the great physiologist Helmholz said, "seems to have packed this organ with mistakes, as if with the avowed purpose of destroying any possible foundation for the theory that organs are [intentionally] adapted to their environment." And how many organs, or developments of existing organs, do we lack which would be of the greatest value to us! Look at the great majority of men, heirs of all the ages: dull of vision they are, cloudy in mind, torn by passion, uncomely to look at, hardly capable of reason or of virtue, stumbling blindly forward, but unequally matched against a baffling and tormenting environment. Look at the idiots, the deformed, the repulsively ugly, the underwitted. How many successes have there been, and how many failures; or what degree of success has been attained in the best of us?

Again, consider what seems to be the end designed. Is it human happiness, or virtue? Or the happiness of the whole sentient creation? Frankly, the marks of design, if such they are, do not point in that direction. If pleasure has been attained, so has pain; it looks as if both were but incidental, chance means to the end of mere survival. Nothing seems more clearly designed than rattlesnakes' fangs, tigers' claws, the suctorial organs of bedbugs and mosquitoes and fleas. Many adaptations ensure a living being's welfare; but many others, that show as clear marks of design, ensure his suffering and death.[1] Creatures are made to prey upon and devour

[1] Cf. Mill, *Nature:* "If a tenth part of the pains which have been ex-

one another, parasites are ingeniously adapted to live upon our entrails, insects to sting us, the germs of smallpox and cholera and tuberculosis, and a thousand other diseases, are admirably fitted to feed and thrive at our expense within our bodies. The Designer, then, would seem to be interested only in adjustments for their own sake, and callous to the suffering they often produce. Do we *wish* to believe in a Designer of such a character as we can legitimately infer from a study of the things designed? [1]

To discover the character of a Creator we must judge by the ends attained and the means employed. To find marks of design, infer a creator, and then assume that that Creator is to be identified with the God whom we worship, is a *non sequitur*. Plato was much more cautious, in postulating a Demiurge, or Creator, quite distinct from his God; the latter existed not as a first and efficient cause of things, but as a goal or magnet toward which the creation was being irresistibly drawn. But indeed, to speak of existing phenom-

pended in finding benevolent adaptations in nature had been employed in collecting evidence to blacken the character of the Creator, what scope for comment would not have been found."

[1] Cf. James, *Varieties of Religious Experience*, p. 438: "Conceived as we now conceive them, as so many fortunate escapes from almost limitless processes of destruction, the benevolent adaptations which we find in Nature suggest a deity very different from the one who figured in the earlier versions of the argument."

And Mill, *Theism*, pt. II: "The greater part of the design of which there is indication in nature, however wonderful its mechanism, is no evidence of any moral attributes, because the end to which it is directed, and its adaptation to which end is the evidence of its being directed to an end at all, is not a moral end; it is not the good of any sentient creature, it is but the qualified permanence, for a limited period, of the work itself."

And Paulsen, *op. cit.*, bk. I, chap. II: "Pleasure and pain are . . . means to the preservation of life. The animal is impelled by pain to escape injury and destruction, enticed by pleasure to seek what is useful and tends to preservation. And as far as I can see, the biologist would add, nature employs both means without preference. If, however, one of them is preferred, it is most likely pain rather than pleasure. . . . How can the [mere] existence of all these forms of life be the end of a mind similar to our own?"

ena as "ends attained" is to beg the whole question. A teleological interpretation of desirable or interesting facts is always alluring, but it cannot be more than a conjecture. And logically, the evil events are equally susceptible of teleological interpretation. The eruption of Mont Pelée and the earthquake at Messina can be considered as ends very nicely attained by the evolutionary process; the conjecture that such catastrophes were designed stands on the same level with the conjecture that our blessings were designed. And so, until a satisfactory solution can be found for the problem of evil, it is a very dubious inference that one would draw from the ends actually attained in this world, and the method by which they are attained, to an Intelligence planning and producing them.

Nevertheless, in spite of the logical weakness of the argument and the dubious conclusion to which, if consistently carried out, it would apparently lead, most men will continue to have, in their happier moments, an instinctive sense that so wonderful a world must have its origin in intelligence, and so beautiful a world in love. "When we call before us the full sweep of the world's advance from the time when it was a mere whirling and fiery mist, and see how marvellously out of its seeming chaos there grows order and intricate regularity, how the wonders of plant and brute life come into being, how finally man appears, the paragon of animals, with eyes to see the beauty of the world and reason to bring its forces into subjection, and, most of all, with the power to create the ideal world of truth and honor, righteousness and love; when we see these supersensible ideals more and more ruling his life, till we have the promise of a society wherein the poet's dream and the prophet's forecasting shall be an actual thing, — when all this, I say, comes before us, it is not easy to resign ourselves to say that all has merely happened so."[1] The dysteleologies in the world do not disprove a benevolent Designer, they simply counteract the evidence that we gather elsewhere for his existence. It is possible to conceive of other facts which, if they exist, render the existing universe compatible with the idea of design by Benevolence.[2] These facts, being merely conjectural, cannot be used as evidence; but their possibility leaves a loophole for faith.

First-cause argument: Pro: W. N. Clarke, *Outline of Christian Theology,* 9th ed., pp. 109–13. H. Schultz, *Outline of Christian Apologetics,* p. 103 f. F. Aveling, *God of Philosophy,* chaps. v–vii. *Con:* J. M. E. McTaggart, *Some Dogmas of Christianity,* secs. 156–60. H. Höffding, *Philosophy of Religion,* pp. 35–41. G. Galloway, *Philosophy of Religion,* pp. 387–89. J. G. Schurman, *Belief in God,* lecture iv. J. S. Mill, *Theism,* pt. i. W. H. Mallock, *Religion as a Credible Doctrine,* chap. viii.

Special Phenomena: Pro: Clarke, *op. cit.,* pp. 105–09. Schultz, p. 108 f., 114 ff. Aveling, *op. cit.,* chap. viii, xi, and p. 133 ff. B. P. Bowne, *Theism,* pp. 67–75, 119–22, 127–34, 251–54. A. M. Fairbairn, *Philosophy of the Christian Religion,* pp. 48–55. *Con:* Mallock, *op. cit.,* chaps. ii–iii.

Design: Pro: Aveling, *op. cit.,* chap. ix. Clarke, pp. 113–17. Schultz, p. 105 ff. Bowne, *op. cit.,* pp. 75–119. G. P. Fisher, *Grounds of Theistic and Christian Belief,* p. 30 ff. J. G. Schurman, *Belief in God,* lecture v. A. R. Wallace, *The World of Life; A Manifestation of Creative Purpose, Directive Mind, and Ultimate Purpose.* H. K. Rogers, *Religious Conception of the World,* pp. 93–120. *Con:* Mill, *op. cit.,* last part of pt. i, pt. ii. Mallock, *op. cit.,* chap. ix. McTaggart, *op. cit.,* secs. 161–65, 196–207. F. Paulsen, *Introduction to Philosophy,* bk. i., chap. ii. F. C. S. Schiller, *Humanism,* viii.

---

[1] Rogers, *op. cit.,* pp. 97–98.   [2] See, e.g., pp. 380–82.

CHAPTER XX

THE INTERPRETATION OF RELIGIOUS EXPERIENCE

MODERN theology shows a widespread tendency to abandon the older lines of inference, that drew conclusions from the existence or characteristics of the outer world, and to base its theory now upon the spiritual experience of mankind. Such a procedure has been adopted in this volume as the only method that promises to be fruitful; the psychological phenomena surveyed in Part II are the data which theology has to work with. But the correct description of these data and drawing of safe inferences therefrom is a much more difficult task than most pious people imagine. Introspection is notoriously liable to deception; and just because the reality and significance of an experience is unquestionable, we are not warranted in accepting any belief that the experiencer himself supposes to be implied by it, or attributing it to whatever he assigns as its cause. There is altogether too much confusion and looseness of thought in these matters; and if our religious philosophy is to stand the test of criticism we must be on the lookout for these pitfalls.

What cautions should be observed in interpreting religious experience?

(1) Observation errs most naturally through defect. Our faculties are capable of attending to but few aspects of a situation at once; and no one observes half of what goes on before his eyes or passes through his mind. Especially in meeting experience that is new to us are we bewildered and helpless; if we do not know what to look or listen for,

we usually fail to catch the essential points. So a believer testifying to a supposed answer to prayer may entirely overlook some natural train of causes which would have brought about the desired result quite apart from his prayer. Or a neurasthenic healed, as he believes, by Christian Science may never consider the fact that his "treatments" coincided with a cessation of worry, an adoption of a more hygienic way of life, or some other change that may really be the important factor in his cure.

(2) If we wish to prove a certain theory we are apt to overlook facts that impugn it. Our minds pounce upon every instance that makes for our pet beliefs, and ignore equally obvious instances that make against them. Cases of apparent answer to prayer accumulate in the believer's memory; the cases of apparently unanswered prayer pass out of his mind. He dwells lovingly upon the instances of fulfillment of Old Testament prophecy; the cases of non-fulfillment do not exist for him. Facts turn up daily that confirm his creed and bely his neighbor's; and all the time his neighbor sees a thousand signs that warrant his own belief and none or few that discredit it. The Christian Scientist sees people all about him who have been cured; the many who, though treated, have not been cured go unnoticed. In short, men see what they are looking for and are blind to facts that point the other way; observation and introspection are usually onesided.

(3) On the other hand, observation often errs through excess; that is, we think we have perceived more than our actual data. The mind is extraordinarily influenced by suggestion; a preconceived idea of what one is going to see or feel easily affects one's belief as to what one does see or feel. A child who believes in ghosts sees them in every bush, a nervous woman hears a burglar in every creak or rustle. So when New England divines testified to having

seen victims "bewitched" by some poor accused old woman, when Jesus spoke of casting devils out of some "possessed" person, when Paul thought of himself as having "seen the Lord," when the early Christians, in their moments of emotional ecstasy, felt themselves possessed by the Holy Spirit, or when a Hindu mystic speaks of himself as having attained to oneness with Brahma, it is conceivable that these unquestionably sincere witnesses, under the influence of preconceived ideas, read more into their experiences than was actually there. Where conversion is practised on a large scale, a certain sequence of experiences tends to become stereotyped. To a certain extent the emotions and ideas thus suggested are actually experienced by succeeding groups of converts; their experiences are different from what they would be under the influence of some other form of evangelism. But where the actual experiences fall short of the expected program they tend almost irresistibly to be filled out by the imagination with the expected and orthodox details. Thus while religious experience is often really formed or colored by antecedent belief, the description of that experience still oftener mingles elements of the belief with the observation, so that the resulting conceptions of the believer are an inextricable blend of fact and faith.[1]

[1] Cf. G. Galloway, *Philosophy of Religion*, p. 255: "The fact that you have an experience does not guarantee the truth of the meaning you read into the experience." A typical instance may be quoted from the pen of one of our eminent contemporary theologians (Albert Parker Fitch, *The College Course and the Preparation for Life*, pp. 133–34): "Religion is an experience of the inner life. It is our own personal awareness of God and self and sin; our own actual finding out, that when through Jesus we know God and come to Him, *sin is forgiven* and we are set free. That is n't a theory or a philosophy or a science. It is a fact in human life, which generation after generation of men have known for themselves. It does n't admit of argument, it just is." I have italicized a statement here which, though expressly and vigorously asserted to be a fact of our experience, cannot possibly be so. God's forgiveness of our sins does not take place in *our*

(4) Much false recording of facts is due to errors of memory, which is a tricky faculty at best. People vary greatly in the kind of psychic stuff of which their recollections are chiefly composed; those who remember in auditory or motor images are particularly unreliable in their visual memories, and vice versa. Especially in matters in which we have an interest is our memory liable to corruption by that interest. Autobiographies, chronicles of wars, and religious histories are especially to be accepted with caution. It is so easy, in looking back, to remember things a little more in accord with the way they ought to have been than with the way they were.[1] The natural tendency to embellish an incident and make a good story out of it, the subconscious desire to impress the listener, to extol a hero, to prove a point, to make converts, must continually be discounted by the historian. Where strong feelings or prejudices enter in, few men are to be trusted, however honest they may mean to be, in the statement of their own past experiences. Where a story has passed from mouth to mouth and reaches us only at second or third or tenth hand, as in the case of the Gospel narratives, it is only with the utmost pains, by a continual process of reading between the lines and watching for the subtlest signs, that the historian can become reasonably sure of an event.[2]

conscious experience; at the most, we have a feeling of relief from remorse, renewed inner peace, and a new outflow of love, which we may take as signs of forgiveness — if we believe in the existence of a God who forgives. Those inner experiences themselves do not contain the fact of forgiveness, and may conceivably exist without any such fact being true.

[1] Cf. H. Münsterberg, *On the Witness Stand*, p. 58: "We find an abundance of cases reported which seem to prove that either prophetic fortune tellers or inspired dreams have anticipated the real future of a man's life with the subtlest details and with the most uncanny foresight. But as soon as we examine these wonderful stories, we find that the coincidences are surprising only in those cases in which the dreams and the prophecies have been written down after the realization."

[2] Cf. what was said above, on p. 63 and pp. 269–73.

(5) Many unintentional misstatements of observation or misunderstandings on the part of others result from a lack of realization of the exact meaning of words. Even with words that have a precise and generally accepted value, extraordinary divergences of description occur among men of quite similar training and habits.[1] In the use of words which have no such fixed and ascertainable meanings still greater divergences obtain. Did Paul mean by his doctrine of salvation by "faith" what the framers of the Athanasian creed took him to mean? Did Jesus, when (or if) he spoke of himself as Son of God, mean to imply what later orthodoxy read into those words? When the early Christians spoke of the presence of the Holy Spirit (or should we read "a holy spirit," uncapitalized?) did they refer to the Third Person of a trinitarian God? The word "God" is notoriously ambiguous; the devout theist who has his faith mightily cheered by a First Cause argument, or some work of idealistic metaphysics, or some account of mystical experience, utterly fails to realize that the "God" reached in those ways may have little or nothing in common with the God of his religious life. The use of an identical word hides the most radical differences in conception; and many a man's beliefs rest largely upon the testimony or faith of other men whose beliefs are really fundamentally alien to his own. Religious experience is peculiarly apt to be vague, confused, inarticulate; there is an utter lack of a precise and generally accepted vocabulary for its various phases. Consequently, in no realm is there more verbal confusion or more fallacious reasoning.

[1] Cf. Professor Münsterberg's account of his experiments with his Harvard students in the book just referred to. In answer, e.g., to a question how long a certain event that took place before their eyes lasted, some called the time two or three times as long as others. Equally divergent answers were given to such questions as, How far? How often? How many? How fast?

(6) Experiences themselves do not inform us of their causes; to discover them requires a process of further observation, comparison, and inference, which must be subject to the ordinary laws of logic. But the man who is in the glow of a great emotional experience is in no mood for cool analysis, for the proper application of logical tests, the isolation of factors, the elimination of assumptions. He inevitably explains his experience in terms of whatever conceptions he has at hand, and considers that explanation to be as assured as the experience itself. For example, many or all of the striking experiences that have reinforced for their subjects the belief in supernatural Beings may conceivably be attributable merely to invasions into the ordinary consciousness from what we now call the "subliminal" region of our minds. Certain temperaments are liable to visions, automatisms, possessions, inexplicable to the subject and inspiring a sense of awe and wonder, of terror or rapture, according to their nature. These phenomena are psychologically similar whether they have any religious significance to the subject or not. The vision of the apostle Paul, the "speaking with tongues" of the early Christians, the trances of the saints, are only in the happiness they gave and the belief they fostered, not in their psychological nature, different from a million other visions and possessions and trances which have only brought to their subjects uneasiness or alarm. They no doubt accelerated the spread of Christianity, as of other religions — Mohammed was particularly subject to such experiences. They have produced spiritualism in our day. The Society for Psychical Research has investigated many thousands of cases, and the books on pathological psychology are full of them. Some of them are as yet but dimly understood. We are certainly not yet in a position to be dogmatic about these experiences, one way or the other. But the point is that if, for example, the

sound of the Saviour's voice or the vision of his face that comes to the saint is a proof of the outer reality of this voice or face, then the number of objective realities equally well authenticated by psychologically similar sounds and sights is appalling.

At any rate, whether a given visual experience is really a veridical vision of Christ, whether a given auditory experience is really the voice of Christ, or of God, or of the angel Gabriel (as in the case of Mohammed), cannot be decided by the believer's conviction; the experiences may be just as they are and yet be merely subjective, due to the previous excited condition of his mind and nerves. Only some external test can determine their cause. Sometimes the inference is so unconscious that the inferred cause figures in the subject's thoughts as an actual part of the experience itself (as in paragraph (3) above); at other times the inference is conscious but irresistible, as in St. Theresa's statement, "I felt my soul inflamed by ardent love to God; this love was evidently supernatural, for I knew not what had set it alight in me and I myself had done nothing in the matter." [1] But in any case, what we report as a certainty of experience is very likely to be colored by inference; the statement intended to describe the experience really includes a theory of the cause of the experience.[2]

(7) A very different sort of error is made by those rationalists who assume that if they can explain a religious

[1] Quoted by H. Höffding, *Philosophy of Religion*, p. 102.

[2] Cf. Mill, *Logic*, bk. IV, chap. I, sec. 2: "In almost every act of our perceiving faculties, observation and inference are intimately blended. What we are said to observe is usually a compound result, of which one-tenth may be observation, and the remaining nine-tenths inference." And Galloway, *op. cit.*, p. 255: "The so-called data of religious experience are not pure data. They imply a system of beliefs, and involve, in a greater or less degree, a process of interpretation . . . We shall hardly understand the diversified character of religious experience in different races and civilizations, if we do not keep this in mind."

man's experience in natural terms they have explained away the significance of the experience. Modern psychology is making the attempt, at least, to find natural causes for the phenomena of conversion, faith-healing, visions, photisms, glossolalia, and all the other peculiarly religious experiences. But if this attempt is successful, will God be ruled out of the world? On the contrary, this will simply turn out to be the way in which God works in the world. Paul has been disparaged as an epileptic, and it is commonly pointed out that the saints as a class are "abnormal," "morbid," "eccentric," or "psychopathic"; their experiences then, being due to pathological conditions, are to be rejected as no longer illuminating. It is said that the insane asylums are full of people whose experiences are, from the psychological point of view, rather strikingly similar. But what of it? It may be that religious insight is most penetrating in those whose minds are close to the verge of, or actually in, a condition that unfits them for the ordinary business of life. The same phenomenon is noted often in the case of poets and musicians. The abnormal is, after all, merely the unusual; and the man best fitted for "practical" affairs may have least of value to tell us in these higher realms. So we may let the students of abnormal psychology study the experiences of the saints and trace what natural laws they can. There may be something gruesome about this analysis and comparative study, as there is about embryology and all dissection. But the value or truth of an experience has nothing to do with its origins or the physical laws that condition it; and we must not let these physiologists of revelation disturb our appraisal of the worth and truth of what religious experience has to reveal.[1]

[1] I wish it were possible to quote here the entire first chapter of James's *Varieties of Religious Experience*, which so forcibly and delightfully discusses this error — which he labels "medical materialism."

(8) Finally, the student must beware of ignoring or doing too scanty justice to forms of experience which he has not himself had, or which do not form a part of the orthodox tradition of his community. An investigator who has no capacity for mystical experiences is apt to dismiss them all as mere moonshine. And the Christian theologian is apt, in interpreting such experiences, to fix his attention upon Christian mysticism entirely and ignore the great field of non-Christian mystical experiences. What is not intelligible in terms of one's own experience generally seems unreal, or else unimportant. It is easy to assume that an experience that seems to you fantastic, or is out of line with your world-view, has been exaggerated or wrongly described; and if rationalists have not reached the conclusions which the theologians have reached, it may well be in part because they have not had the same data to go on.[1] So, if we must be critical of alleged experiences, we must also be open-minded toward them. There probably are, as Hamlet said, more things in heaven and earth than are dreamt of in our philosophy; and we are not yet in a position to dismiss any alleged experiences as inherently impossible. They may be misnamed, and may mingle interpretation with their record of fact; but where there is much smoke there is apt to be some fire. And even if an experience has its elements of illusion or delusion, it may yet contain elements of precious truth, and be of importance for our theory of religion.

We may now consider briefly the warrant for some inferences commonly drawn from certain concrete types of religious experience.

I. The voice of conscience. The undeniable authority of conscience has seemed to many to imply the existence of a

[1] For an able presentation of this point, see *Journal of Philosophy, Psychology, and Scientific Methods*, vol. 10, p. 296.

THE INTERPRETATION OF RELIGIOUS EXPERIENCE

personal law-giving God. Whence this command that contradicts our personal desires and imposes itself upon our wills, if it be not the voice of such a Being in our hearts? "From the existence within us of this strong feeling of responsibility, this rooted sense of duty, this consciousness of obligation, pervading all our being and colouring all our thoughts and actions, the existence of a being to whom we are each personally responsible is to be directly inferred."[1]

But a study of any modern scientific treatise on ethics will make plain the reasons for the authority of conscience, an authority which could not be enhanced by any supernatural behest. No voice from without, even of a Creator and Ruler of the universe, could alter the duties that inhere in the very nature and conditions of human life now that it exists; such a command could not make right other than right, or wrong other than wrong. If God is a conscious Being, aware of and interested in our fortunes, he does no doubt wish us to do right; but the rightness or wrongness of an act is independent of his desire, and just as real if there be no such Being interested in it. Right and wrong are terms applicable to human actions according to their normal results; actions that conduce to the welfare of mankind we call right, those that tend to lessen it, wrong. The individual has to submit his personal will to the universal good, his momentary will to his own ultimate good and that of his fellows. This is, in a word, the basis of duty and responsibility.

Moreover, a man cannot stop to weigh and consider in each separate case of conduct, or trust his will to keep free from selfish impulses and irrational desires. So conscience has been developed. It is the voice of the experience and needs of the race speaking in a man's heart. It is, indeed, forever readjusting itself to fit changing needs and impulses;

[1] F. Aveling, *The God of Philosophy*, p. 115.

but at any given time and to any individual it comes with the authority of his own accumulated experience and the wider experience of the society whose traditions he unconsciously accepts. Thus neither the *fact* of duty and responsibility, on the one hand, nor the *sense* of duty and responsibility, on the other, need any supernatural postulates for their explanation. We *are* responsible to our own future selves and to all those whom our conduct affects; that we should *feel* this responsibility as a vague and half-understood pressure within our own minds is a natural result of the social influences under which we have grown up.

This should not be taken to mean that God is not revealed in the moral life and in conscience. In Goethe's drama, Thoas deprecates Iphigenia's conscientious purpose with the skeptical remark, "It is no God, but thine own heart that speaks"; but she replies, "'T is only through our hearts they speak to us." The discovery of the natural function of morality and the natural genesis of conscience do not lead to atheism; the Power which is working through natural channels to produce these good results, and, in a sense, speaking in our hearts, we may still call God. But that this Power is conscious, personal, purposive, or all-powerful, these facts cannot honestly be said to imply.

II. Conversion. The experiences of abrupt conversion, of which we spoke in an earlier chapter, have seemed, to many, a witness of supernatural agency; this inrush of a new spirit, often to the astonishment of the subject, this new joy and power for right living — how else can it be explained than as the working of Divine Grace in the heart? Bishop McConnell writes, for example, "What conclusion can we reach save that the experiences point to the reality of the forces which the seekers assume to be at work?" [1]

The workings of a Divine Power we may indeed call such

[1] *Constructive Quarterly*, vol. 1, p. 129.

THE INTERPRETATION OF RELIGIOUS EXPERIENCE 323

beneficent experiences. But modern psychology is venturing to explain those workings in purely natural terms; and indeed, since closely similar phenomena occur in connection with many incompatible religions, they can hardly substantiate any particular one of the numerous supernatural causes assigned. There have, for that matter, been conversions as striking as those the theologians point to quite apart from any belief in the supernatural, deeply emotional conversions from selfishness to self-surrender, from vice to self-mastery, from credulity to atheism.[1]

For the comprehension of these experiences, especially, much illumination has come from the study of "the subconscious." Many a change of mood and character, we are learning, ripens in the dark, as it were, before being consciously recognized; and often a new mood or impulse suddenly invades our consciousness, coming from this hidden region into the broad daylight of our minds. There are crises and upheavals in our mental life as well as in the life of nature. Some of these crises bring about a change for the worse, some for the better; the latter sort of abrupt change has been cultivated by the Church under the name of conversion. At such times the mind of the believer is filled with the belief in a supernatural power which may work upon him, and is ready to attribute his change of heart to that

[1] Cf. James, *Varieties of Religious Experience*, p. 111: "A form of regeneration by relaxing, by letting go, psychologically indistinguishable from the Lutheran justification by faith and the Wesleyan acceptance of free grace, is within the reach of persons who have no conception of sin and care nothing for the Lutheran theology." J. H. Leuba (in *American Journal of Psychology*, vol. 7, p. 343) records the remarkable and permanent conversion of the great temperance lecturer, John B. Gough, saying, "It is practically the conversion of an atheist; neither God nor Christ is mentioned." He goes on to say: "Names, persons, and representations — a sympathetic fellow-man, Jesus Christ, or God — are practically one, in so far as they are able to determine the same life of love. . . . What imports is that the regenerating psychic process takes place; through what instrument, matters little."

agency. But there is not necessarily to the psychologist anything more miraculous in these religious conversions than in any other changes of heart. When a young man who has lived for himself falls in love; when, his latent patriotism suddenly aroused, he answers the call of his country and offers his life in her service, his center of interest has shifted as completely as that of a religious convert. Unsuspected susceptibilities in his heart, dormant loves and passions, are awakened and become the dominant interest.[1]

Conversion is usually preceded by a period of restlessness and conflicting impulses. Two natures struggle in the breast: the lower self kicks against the pricks, still holding sway and seeming to be the real self, while all the time the higher passions are smouldering underneath, ready to burst forth at the proper stimulus and become a consuming flame. Similar abrupt changes of equilibrium often occur in the outer world; in the spring, after weeks of gradual thawing, suddenly the ice in a river breaks up. So may the cold selfishness of a heart be slowly but invisibly melted, till finally it gives way and the stream of love flows out in a torrent all the stronger for having been so long dammed up. The forces playing upon the heart may be storing up their effects invisibly; the youth may not realize that he is changing; but gradually his unselfish impulses, his longings for purity and loyalty and deliverance from sin, are ripening, maturing,

[2] Cf. Leuba again (*American Journal of Psychology*, vol. 1, p. 75): "The wonderful vitalizing effect of Faith is not, as many suppose, its exclusive property. Are not these characteristics also those of every form of sthenic emotion — of anger, of jealousy, of love? May not love come upon us with the suddenness of a clap of thunder; may it not transport us to the seventh heaven; may it not, as it were, push our energies into specific channels and thus enormously reinforce our reactions to the side of life upon which love shines and at the same time make us irresponsive to the other calls of life? May it not inspire us with a non-rational, boundless confidence in the object of our love and in whatever notion may, in our mind, be attached to it? Observe, also, that love, like Faith, needs in order to break out but the slightest outward incentive or possibly none at all."

till some stimulus, just enough to change the equilibrium, discharges them into the full sunlight of consciousness, and he feels himself suddenly a new man.[1] That this experience is supernatural cannot be proved from its apparent abruptness.

III. Faith-healing. A closely similar class of experiences which seem to attest definite theological beliefs are the physical cures that so frequently follow on faith. The healing miracles of Christ and the apostles, the cures wrought by Catholic relics, by Christian Scientists, by faith-curers, or by prayer, very naturally inspire in the man who is cured a belief in the truth of the doctrine by or upon belief in which he is cured. This was one of the important factors in the growth of the primitive Christian church; and the lapse in the practice of healing has given rise in recent times to several extra-orthodox bodies, which rest the truth of their doctrine upon the practical success of their method.[2]

[1] C. James again, *op. cit.*, pp. 228–37: "It is natural that those who have personally traversed such an experience should carry away a feeling of its being a miracle rather than a natural process. . . . [But] so many peculiarities in them remind us of what we find outside of conversion that we are tempted to class them along with other automatisms, and to suspect that what makes the difference between a sudden and a gradual convert is not necessarily the presence of divine miracle in the case of one and of something less divine in that of the other, but rather a simple psychological peculiarity, the fact, namely, that in the recipient of the more instantaneous Grace we have one of those Subjects who are in possession of a large region in which mental work can go on subliminally, and from which invasive experiences, abruptly upsetting the equilibrium of the primary consciousness, may come."

[2] There can be no doubt of the actuality of vast numbers of these alleged cures, many of them very striking. Cf., for one instance out of thousands, O. Holtzmann, *Life of Jesus* (Eng. tr.), p. 193: "When the Holy Coat was displayed at Treves in the year 1891, the sight of the relic, seen with the eye of faith, did, as an actual fact, according to the perfectly trustworthy evidence of German physicians of unimpeachable reputation, effect in eleven cases cures for which no other medical reasons whatever could be offered. . . . [A description of the cases follows.] . . . Facts like these, which are not really open to question, will make Jesus' works of healing also seem not impossible." Not, of course, that we need accept uncritically every story of his healing!

But modern physiology may not need the hypothesis of supernatural causation. It recognizes that the bodily activities which are controlled or influenced by the sympathetic nervous system can be disorganized or paralyzed by fear or anxiety or mental depression, or a multitude of other causes, and greatly stimulated by confidence and hope and joy. It is not the particular theological belief, much less the object of the belief, that works the cure; it is the tonic effect of the patient's faith that gives the powers of the body the needed stimulus to assert themselves and overcome the malady.[1] Whether the belief is in something real or in something imaginary seems not to matter, so long as the believer has the necessary faith. This power of the mind over the body is receiving at last the recognition it deserves from scientific students; and the art of psychotherapy is becoming an increasingly important part of medical study. As striking cures, perhaps, as ever saint or relic or Christian Scientist performed are being wrought to-day, without the aid of any theological belief, by the ordinary physician who has learned to practise skillfully the art of "suggestion." Certainly, if all the beliefs which have cured men were true, truth would be a very variable or self-contradictory thing! But it "is, indeed, one of the central dangers of all non-medical suggestive cures, that while any belief may cure, through the mere emotional power of the act of believing, the content of the belief gains an undeserved appearance of truth."[2]

IV. Mysticism and intuition. The general nature of the mystical experiences we have briefly described in an earlier chapter.[3] Persons of a certain temperament are liable to

---

[1] It is noteworthy that even Jesus could perform few healing acts at Nazareth, his own home — "because of their unbelief." See Mark 6: 5–6. Matt. 13: 58.

[2] H. Münsterberg, *Psychotherapy*, p. 381.

[3] See above, pp. 137–39, 203–09.

invasion by such moments of ecstasy without any conscious endeavor after them, others can cultivate them; in either case, if they are believers in some form of theism, the exaltation of spirit inevitably seems an inpouring of the Divine Life. And there can be no objection to recognizing such an experience as a communion with God; indeed, it is through just such experiences, among others, that our conception of God is formed. But, as with the experiences we have been considering, there is a danger that the particular antecedent conceptions of the believer, being imported into and coloring the experience, should receive in his mind unwarrantable corroboration from it. The mystic may say, for example, that he has "felt the boundless love of God," that "the mystery of the Trinity has been revealed to him," that "Christ came into his heart with assurance of forgiveness." That is, the experiences are taken to be not merely subjective but objective, not merely emotional, but perceptional; they are felt to have supernatural implications, to be inexplicable in terms of preceding conscious states plus the natural influences of the environment, and therefore to afford proof of the objective existence of the God or Saviour upon whom the subject's mind has been fixed. To many a mystic the reality of this Being with whom he has felt himself to be communing is as unquestionable as that of the human beings with whom he talks, and his personality and love equally assured.

But our belief in other human minds is not only instinctive, it is *corroborated* by a vast amount of evidence. It is the only plausible hypothesis to account for multitudes of our experiences which are inexplicable in terms of antecedent subjective states. Is it so with the mystical states? Or are they merely subjective, explicable without the hypothesis of a divine mind affecting them, and affording us therefore no avenue to extra-psychological truth? Whatever our answer may be — and the matter is hotly disputed — we must be willing to subject mystical experiences, like all others, to the criticism of the intellect. Any single type of supposed "perception" is always to be doubted until confirmed by other senses. "The fact that experiences such as those called mystical are different in kind from ordinary experiences does not exempt their deliverances from the authority of the test of truth. And unless we abandon all rational standards of thinking, we are bound to conclude that mystical experiences may testify to error." [1]

Again, the exact psychological inferences to be drawn from these mental states, their transcendent implications, if they have any, will be a difficult matter to determine. For there have been mystics in all the religions; and the truth so immediately "known" has been one thing for one and quite the opposite for another. "The fact is that the mystical feeling of enlargement, unison, and emancipation has no specific intellectual content whatever of its own. It is capable of forming matrimonial alliances with material furnished by the most diverse philosophies and theologies, provided only they can find a place in their framework for its peculiar emotional mood. We have no right, therefore, to invoke its prestige as distinctly in favor of any special belief. . . . [Indeed] religious mysticism is only one half of mysticism. . . . It is evident that from the point of view of their psychological mechanism, the classic mysticism and these lower mysticisms spring from the same mental level, from that great subliminal or transmarginal region of which science is beginning to admit the existence, but of which so little is really known. That region contains every kind of matter: 'seraph and snake' abide there side by side. To come from thence is no infallible credential. What comes must be sifted and tested, and run the gauntlet of confron-

[1] Bode, *Logic*, p. 249.

tation with the total context of experience, just like what comes from the outer world of sense."[1]

The same two criticisms are applicable to the arguments of those who assert that the direct knowledge of God is not a matter of occasional and extraordinary experience, but is open to all — that man has a "religious sense," if he will but use it. Just what this supposed sense is, what its organ and physical mechanism, we are never told; its very existence remains hypothetical, with nothing to vouch for it but the word of those who claim to possess it. But even if clear evidence of the existence of such a "sense" were offered, its dicta would have to submit to sifting at the hands of the intellect and the other senses. We know that a seen object is an objective reality because we can also touch or hear or smell it, or in some way check up our optical sensations; otherwise we suspect them to be mere hallucinations or malobservations. So with the data offered by a "religious sense"; they must be corroborated by the rest of our experience. And since we find, as a matter of fact, that the "religious sense" of one man perceives one kind of a God, and that of another a radically different God, we not unnaturally suspect that this "sense" is a merely supposed

[1] James, *op. cit.*, pp. 425–27. Cf. G. L. Dickinson, *Religion, A Criticism and a Forecast*, pp. 40–41: "All of these revelations cannot be true. One may be true and the others false. But in that case we must find our criterion of truth and falsehood somewhere else than in the subjective certainty of the converted person. . . . It is indisputable that the test of validity must be sought somewhere else than in the sense of certainty felt by the person who claims to have had the revelation. In other words, the truth of a doctrine supposed to be thus conveyed, or the goodness of a moral intuition, must be sifted, before they can be accepted, by the ordinary critical processes; and, except as the result of such a sifting, performed deliberately again and again, in calm and normal moments, no man who is at once religious, honest, and intelligent, will or ought to accept the deliverances of any so-called revelation of this type."

As Galloway puts it (*Philosophy of Religion*, p. 238): "The psychological feeling of certainty does not in itself give the assurance of epistemological validity."

source and explanation of those deep-rooted beliefs that in most men's minds antedate and outlive argument and evidence.

Such sub-rational beliefs form a large part of the mental equipment of most of us. But it is better to label them as prejudices, preconceptions, suspicions, conjectures, or hopes. At best we may call them intuitions, implying by that word our belief that in spite of the lack of supporting evidence they point us toward the truth. So, of course, they may. But we must be honest enough to confess that intuition can give us only possibilities, not assured knowledge. We may think of them as coming from "deeper levels" of our nature, or as being "super-rational," and so a sort of extra eye; and we may personally pin our trust to them. But until we can show solid reasons for believing in these "intuitions," they can become no more than private sources of comfort, and suggestions for our mind to work upon. Until we have tangible evidence to go on we can never be sure that they are anything but prejudices or delusions.

Examples of arguments: G. P. Fisher, *Grounds of Theistic and Christian Belief*, chaps. IV–VI. D. A. Curtis, *The Christian Faith*, chap. XXVI. W. N. Clarke, *Outline of Christian Theology*, pp. 123–26; *Christian Doctrine of God*, chap. IV, sec. 3.

Criticisms: J. S. Mill, *Logic*, bk. IV, chap. I, *Theism*, pt. I, toward end. J. H. Leuba, *Psychological Study of Religion*, chap. XI. G. B. Cutten, *Psychological Phenomena of Christianity*, chaps. I, II, XXI. J. M. E. McTaggart, *Some Dogmas of Christianity*, chap. II. W. James, *Varieties of Religious Experience*, chap. I. *Hibbert Journal*, vol. 4, p. 485.

The Interpretation of Mysticism: H. Delacroix, *Études d'Histoire et de Psychologie du Mysticisme*. W. E. Hocking, *Meaning of God in Human Experience*, pt. V. James, *op. cit.*, chap. III, XVI, XVII. B. W. Bode, *Outline of Logic*, pp. 247–52. G. Santayana, *Poetry and Religion*, chap. I. *Mind*, (N.S.), vol. 14, p. 15.

The Interpretation of Faith-healing: G. A. Coe, *Spiritual Life*, chap. IV. E. Worcester, *Religion and Medicine*, *Christian Religion as a Healing Power*. H. Münsterberg, *Psychotherapy*. L. P. Powell, *Christian Science*, chap. VII. Cutten, *op. cit.*, chap. XV. P. Dubois, *The Influence of the Mind upon the Body*. C. Lavaud, *Guérison par la Foi. American Journal of Theology*, vol. 14, p. 533.

CHAPTER XXI

PRAGMATIC ARGUMENTS

THE discouraging lack of evidence as yet found by a strictly scientific method to support traditional theological beliefs has given rise in recent years to a number of closely related arguments which aim to base the proof of dogma upon practical needs in place of evidence. These arguments we may group under the rather loose and fluctuating term "pragmatism"; and to the consideration of some of their commoner variations we may now turn.

Can we trust a belief:

I. Because its untruth would be intolerable? The apostle Paul, in a familiar passage, wrote: "If there be no resurrection of the dead, then is Christ not risen; and if Christ be not risen, then is our preaching vain, and your faith is also vain. . . . If in this life only we have hope in Christ, we are of all men most miserable. . . . If the dead rise not, let us eat and drink, for to-morrow we die." [1] To him the possibility of his being deceived was so abhorrent that his mind refused to entertain it; the implications of such a situation were so unpleasant that it could not be the true situation. In similar vein we are told by many modern apologists that atheism must be mistaken because it is so dreadful and dangerous: it drives men to despair, it paralyzes their energies, it leads naturally to a reckless disregard of morality. Schiller tells us that the belief in God and immortality will alone save us, and must therefore be accepted; our phi-

[1] 1 Cor. 15: 13, 14, 19, 32.

losophy must "support, or at least not paralyze, moral effort." [1] Mallock tells us that although "scientific observation and analysis can discover no place in the universe" for God, and though "the mind is incapable of representing consistently to itself" the theistic idea, yet "our whole system of practical life involves the assertion" of it. "Some system of doctrine equivalent in its effects to the doctrines of theistic religion is an element absolutely essential to the higher civilization of man." [2] In fine, these beliefs are essential to an optimistic view of the universe, and optimism is our duty; they are essential to keep man moral, so they *must* be true. Their untruth would be intolerable.

This argument, which has properly been called the "*reductio ad horrendum*," may be answered in several ways: —

(1) Perhaps the universe *is* "intolerably" bad; how can we know until we investigate? What right have we to assume that it is constructed so as to comfort and inspire us? If it is n't, we must make the best of it. We may hide our heads, like the ostrich, from so unpleasant a thought; but wincing and averting our eyes will not alter the facts, whatever they are. Our lives are continually offering instances of catastrophes that would have been intolerable to contemplate that have nevertheless come to pass; we have daily evidence of Nature's indifference to our hopes and desires. It is notorious that many of our purest longings remain unfulfilled. If optimism means being cheery under all circumstances, then optimism is clearly our duty; if it means assuming, in despite or in advance of the evidence, that the world is as we should like it, then it may still be our duty, and is certainly our privilege, to cultivate such a faith; but such an attitude of ours can in no wise inform us of what the cosmic facts really are.

[1] *Humanism*, pp. 347, 5.
[2] *Religion as a Credible Doctrine*, pp. 249, 259.

(2) The loss of beliefs that once seemed essential to men's happiness may after all prove not intolerable. Often they are replaced by other equally stimulating beliefs. It may be that only a part of a complex belief is really essential to a man's happiness, and that part may be preserved in a new view. Thus, some of those who believe in "creative evolution" — a tendency inherent in the universe to develop of itself toward ideals — maintain that for them it quite satisfactorily takes the place of the theistic conception. Some who find it impossible to believe in personal immortality declare that "ideal immortality" is a worthy and inspiring substitute. Comte felt that his natural religion could supply all the consolation and inspiration of the current supernatural doctrines. "Tastes differ and tastes change. A Viking or a Maori warrior might well find that the prospect of an immortality without fighting made the universe intolerable."[1] Indeed, men can stand even a complete loss of theological beliefs without a paralysis of their practical life. It is a matter for plain observation that atheists are about as often energetic and good and happy as theists; men who are agnostic with regard to a future life nevertheless act with enthusiasm and joy while they live. It is, after all, a gratuitous apprehension to fear that men are going to sit still and fold their hands and die of despair, or plunge into depths of depravity, if they cease to credit what seems to the believer so essential. There is very little actual relation between cosmic beliefs and morality or energy or happiness. What is agonizing and paralyzing is the transition-period, during which a belief is being renounced, and while the sweetness which it once had for the heart refuses to be forgotten. The man bred to a certain cosmic conception may indeed never get over the loss of it. But his children, who grow up without those beliefs, will very likely never feel

[1] McTaggart, *op. cit.*, p. 52.

their lack. It is a matter of adjustment; we can adapt ourselves to altered conditions, mental as well as physical, far more easily than we suppose.[1]

(3) If it be said that men can get along without the theistic beliefs — or what not — merely in their unreflective hours, and because they are short-sighted and illogical, it may be replied that the lack of logic is rather with those who suppose their particular beliefs to be a necessary implication of morality or of a hopeful view of the universe. The reasons for morality, at least, are purely natural and have nothing to fear from theological skepticism; morality being simply the best way to live, that way remains the best way even if there be no personal God or no heaven. If any men are restrained from vice and sin simply by their fear of God's anger, or by the hope of reward, they are in sad need of moral education. To "eat, drink, and be merry" — if that means to indulge in immoral dissipation — is a short-sighted and foolish philosophy of life, even if this life be all. Teach men the rationale of morality and it will no more be disturbed by theological perturbations than agriculture or transportation. A sensible man would not cease to want to live in the best way simply because life was brief and there

[1] Professor Pitkin (in *Journal of Philosophy, Psychology, and Scientific Methods*, vol. 8, p. 302) calls attention to "the normal man's invincible indifference in practical life to the intellectualist's demand that we allow metaphysics to sour our breakfast porridge and paralyze the nerves which give us a good time. What may be truth of the cosmos through all the reaches of time is not, as a matter of fact, true of little spots in it at some brief moments; and men, who live and move only in little spots and only at brief moments, always have reacted and always will react only to these intimate near tracts of time and space." It is not true "that a theory about the cosmic drift *must* regulate our practical attitudes, feeling, and conduct from moment to moment," or that "if the world isn't engineered so as to guarantee unlimited bliss for all hands, your knowledge of this must *logically* pervade your dinner, the evening at the theatre, and to-morrow's boat-ride; must, in short, throw its lights or its shadows across each hour. ... As a matter of psychological *fact*, these lights and shadows do not fall upon men's paths as the logic of the case demands."

was no God watching him. And if a man is not sensible, and chooses the worse way? Well, so do men now. Motives and encouragements and driving forces exist on all hands; if they do not keep men up to their best, it is because of our failure properly to utilize them. Certain incentives might be lost, but plenty would remain.

And how could the mere fact of God's existence guarantee us immortality or a desirable outcome of the universe? For if he is omnipotent, he still evidently does not remove what are to us evils; seeing that he has permitted so much that crosses our desires, how can we be sure that he will not cross our other desires? If he is not omnipotent, how can we be sure that he can secure immortality for us? or the ultimate victory of good? In short, theism alone does not imply the fulfillment of our desires, nor does atheism necessarily imply their non-fulfillment. So the theological beliefs which are defended on the ground that they alone imply the satisfaction of our needs often do not really guarantee any such satisfaction.

(4) Finally, this argument, that if a state of things would be bad it cannot be true, is immoral; for it logically implies that if a fact is true it cannot be bad. If we are to refuse to believe in an atheistic world because it would be an evil, we may logically refuse to hold any of our acts evil, since they are actual facts. But "it is our duty to be humble in judging of reality, and imperious in judging of goodness. What is real is real, however we may condemn it. On the other hand, what we condemn — if we condemn rightly — is bad, even if it were the essence of all reality. The moral evil of the argument from consequences seems to me to be that it makes us imperious in the wrong place, where our humility is wrong and servile. When the reality of a thing is uncertain, the argument encourages us to suppose that our approval of a thing can determine its reality. And

when this unhallowed link has once been established, retribution overtakes us. For when the reality is independently certain, we have to admit that the reality of a thing should determine our approval of that thing. I find it difficult to imagine a more degraded position."[1]

II. Because our hearts vouch for it? The thoroughgoing pragmatist is not daunted, however, by such considerations. Our intellect, he admits, warns us from letting our hopes and desires bias our judgment. But why should we let our intellects tyrannize over us? Why should we be slaves to what Emerson calls "this arid, departmental, post-mortem science." We are, after all, more than intellect; and every part of our nature has its rights in court also. Kant asserted for his "postulates of practical reason" a validity equal to that of the conclusions of "pure reason"; and since his time a host of philosophers and theologians have maintained that the "heart" can vouch for truth as truly as the logical intellect. William James maintained this thesis brilliantly in his essay on "Reflex Action and Theism": "Materialism and agnosticism, *even were they true*, could never gain universal and popular acceptance; for they both, alike, give a solution of things which is irrational to the practical third of our nature, and in which we can never feel volitionally at home. . . . Our volitional nature must then, till the end of time, exert a constant pressure upon the other departments of the mind to induce them to function to theistic conclusions. No contrary formulas can be more than provisionally held. . . . May you avert the formation of a narrow scientific tradition, and burst the bonds of any synthesis which would pretend to leave out of account *those forms of being, those relations of reality, to which at present our active and emotional tendencies are our only avenues of approach* . . . Infra-theistic conceptions, materialisms and

[1] McTaggart, *op. cit.*, pp. 65–66.

agnosticisms, are irrational because they are inadequate stimuli to man's practical nature." [1]

In the first clause which I have italicized, James seems to be saying only that, as a matter of fact, people *are* biased by their desires and needs, that they always have been and always will be affected in their beliefs by considerations beyond those of logic and evidence. And there are many pragmatists who are content to repeat that we are so made that we must cleave to satisfactory beliefs, true or not, and reject unsatisfactory ones, *even were they true*. But the stouter pragmatists follow the cue given in the latter part of the quotation, and insist that the demands of the heart constitute a means of ascertaining what *is* true. Schiller, for example, seems to be on the former ground when he declares " the real structure of the actual reason to be essentially pragmatical, and permeated through and through with acts of faith, desires to know and wills to believe, to disbelieve, and to make believe." To this we might reply that our minds are indeed usually so biased, but that they are usually untrustworthy for that very reason; only when a man succeeds in eliminating these disturbing factors and training his mind to be a disinterested recorder of facts and reasoner thereupon, does he become a safe guide.[2] But on that same page Schiller writes, "Common sense has always shown a certain sympathy with all such protests against the pretensions of what is called the pure intellect to dictate to man's whole complex nature. It has always felt that there are 'reasons of the heart of which the head knows nothing,' postulates of a faith that surpasses mere under-

---

[1] *The Will to Believe*, pp. 126–34.

[2] The pragmatist account of our mental processes is a singularly hopeless one. Professor Dewey's little book, *How We Think*, is typical. He does not consider how *to* think, how we *ought* to think to arrive at truth, but how stupid, prejudiced men *do*, and apparently always must, think. It is a substitution of observation for ideals, of psychology for logic.

standing, and that these possess a higher rationality which a bigoted intellectualism has failed to comprehend." [1]

To this argument we may reply: —

(1) It is proper for the heart to desire objects that shall gratify its longings, and to seek for such; the motive for truth-seeking may be practical, and the direction in which one looks may be determined by what one hopes to find. When Schiller writes, "In reality our knowing is driven and guided at every step by our subjective interests and preferences, our desires, our needs and our ends," [2] we may agree. But these interests and preferences cannot *answer* the questions they suggest; for that we must look to the evidence. The "heart" constructs hypotheses; but it cannot tell whether they are true. "All human needs have the same function in the discovery of factual truth: they constitute merely demands and incentives. It is the intellect which passes upon the validity of each proposition affirming, in the interest of any need, objective existence." [3]

[1] *Humanism*, p. 6. Cf. also G. Galloway, *Philosophy of Religion*, p. 265: "The truth of a religion will be decided by the way in which its conception of the world satisfies the reason, its practical ideal the will, and its presentation of the religious relation the feelings and emotions. The more fully the different elements support and supplement one another, the greater is the assurance of religious truth." And p. 269: "Only the mutual support of the theoretical and practical reason can give a sufficient assurance of religious truth." So Stratton, pp. 360–65: "There are several great activities, or interests, each with a claim to examine and report upon the character of reality — claiming, if not an exclusive power to reveal what is real, at least a power supplemental to that of its fellows. . . . Whatsoever is absolutely needed to make my experience morally intelligible I shall hold to, as having the solid reality of experience itself. . . . The intelligent thought of mankind will, in the end, regard as partial, and will attempt to correct, any view of the world that fails to satisfy this need."

[2] *Humanism*, p. 9.

[3] J. H. Leuba, in *Journal of Philosophy, Psychology, and Scientific Methods*, vol. 9, p. 409. Cf. Dickinson, *Religion, a Criticism and a Forecast*, p. 43: "The fact that [beliefs] afford a solution of the riddle of the world which to many minds is *satisfactory* does not in itself show anything about their truth or falsehood. It shows merely the tremendous bias under which criticism has to act."

(2) We may "trust our hearts" in matters of valuation: when they pronounce an object beautiful or good we may accept (after due criticism, of course) their verdict. For the beauty and goodness of objects consist precisely in their relation to our feelings; our knowledge of such beauty and goodness tells us really nothing of the nature of things save that they are so constituted as to affect us in certain ways. From a man's statement that a rose smells sweet to him, or that a certain conception of God is beautiful and inspiring to him, there is no appeal. His own feelings constitute the supreme court in such matters. But "the heart" has no right to make existential judgments, no means of ascertaining what facts do and what do not exist. Why does not some pragmatist adduce *reasons* for holding that "our active and emotional tendencies" are "avenues of approach" to reality? They are means of appraising such reality as they are confronted with by the senses or memory or imagination, but they do not add to our knowledge of what exists — except the knowledge of their own existence. "The intellect" and "the heart" are not two "faculties," each endowed with means of certifying to truth; there is but one means, observation, and inference therefrom, to be verified by further observation. To rail against a "bigoted intellectualism" is but bluster unless the critic can show what means "the heart" has at its disposal for ascertaining what lies beyond the ken of our senses, our introspective observation, and our logical inferences from these data.

(3) The argument rests, no doubt, on an unexpressed assumption that God would not allow us to have instincts that would deceive us, longings doomed to non-fulfillment. But this is, of course, to reason in a circle — deducing the trustworthiness of our instincts from the existence of God, and then deducing the existence of God from the trustworthiness of our instincts. We have no right to beg the

whole question in that way. Moreover, as a matter of fact, many of man's deep-rooted, instinctive beliefs have been proved false. To one who is familiar with the history and psychology of belief, the long persistence of a belief for which the "heart" vouches is no argument for its truth. Superstitions have extraordinary vitality. Man's instinctive notions are usually erroneous; and correct ideas have to win their way slowly. Especially slow in disappearing are beliefs which appeal to the emotions and the imagination, or affect conduct. But, for that matter, millions of human beings have longed for the oblivion of Nirvana; the great majority, since the dawn of history, have believed in many gods rather than in one God. If ever any beliefs were vouched for by the "heart," these were. No, our needs, our "demands," our hopes, are causes of our beliefs, but they cannot be held to be means of knowing that our beliefs are true. Unpleasant as the fact is, we have no guaranty that these passionate personal convictions of ours are not delusions, these hopes doomed to disappointment — except as we can discover evidence; and that evidence must be scrutinized impartially and criticized in accordance with the laws of logic.

(4) This is by no means to say that it is unlawful to retain these emotionally caused or instinctive beliefs, when we cannot find evidence to support them. The ethical problem involved, concerning the will or the right to believe when we cannot prove, will be discussed in chapter xxv. We may anticipate the outcome of that discussion by saying that such a will to believe is perfectly legitimate and highly desirable within certain bounds. But the admission that we may believe in spite of a lack of evidence must be sharply distinguished from the assertion that such a will, such an impulse of the heart, or push of the emotions, constitutes *evidence* that the belief is *true*.

III. Because it "works"? Another, and perhaps the commonest, form of the pragmatic argument, is that which insists that "what works best in practice is what in actual knowing we accept as true." [1] We have no means of ascertaining truth except by formulating hypotheses and seeing whether they "work"; and so, "When an idea leads to satisfactory results both in the individual life and the social medium, this dynamic efficiency constitutes a proper claim to truth." [2] If we demand any further evidence of religious truth, we are more exacting than in our attitude toward other matters. Why do we believe in atoms, in the heliocentric theory of the solar system, in the wave theory of light? We have no ocular evidence of these universally accepted truths; they were at first mere guesses, which have been tested and found to jibe with the fragmentary bits of our experience, and so satisfy our minds, which must formulate some generalization by which to unify and comprehend its observations. Why indeed does a man believe in the existence of other minds? In the nature of the case, they can never enter into his own experience. Does he not rest his belief upon the fact that his venture of faith in their reality is verified by a thousand daily experiences which fall out as if these other minds *were* real? Since, then, in the nature of the case we cannot directly experience God's mind, what further proof can we require of his existence beyond the fact that the belief in him, when tried, is similarly veri-

[1] Schiller, *Humanism*, p. 7.
[2] G. Galloway, *Philosophy of Religion*, p. 369. Cf. also A. P. Fitch, *The College Course and the Preparation for Life*, pp. 120, 107: "When men do thus accept the Christian Gospel on faith, they are able to prove it is true in their own experience by the marvelous things which it does to them." "Then a new power flows into his being, and then he begins to know the heavenly Father for himself. Then belief in God is no longer taking him entirely on faith; for then we have begun the verification by experience, and we know of ourselves and within ourselves that we are dealing with realities."

PRAGMATIC ARGUMENTS

fied? "On pragmatistic principles, if the hypothesis of God works satisfactorily, in the widest sense, it is true. Now, whatever its residual difficulties may be, experience shows that it certainly does work." [1]

(1) Superficially, this contention sounds plausible; and it is, of all contemporary arguments, perhaps the most widely welcomed. But its cogency rests upon a rather obvious confusion — an ambiguity, namely, in the word "work." The heliocentric theory "works" in the sense that it fits all observed facts. It is like an attempted reconstruction of a ruined temple; if the original plan has been rightly grasped, a place will be found for each fragment. Scientific theories have this sort of "verification in experience" — they lead us to expect, on a given occasion, a given phenomenon; if we find what we were led to expect, the theory is in so far verified. Whatever is observed to happen is in harmony with the theory, and no consequences logically deduced from the theory are found *not* to happen. But the theological beliefs supported by this argument do not "work" in that sense. They "work" in the sense that they console and inspire men — which is a very different matter. So, when Schiller writes, — "Religious postulates need confirmation as much as those of science. The true claim of religious experience is that they receive it after their kind; that, e.g., prayer 'works,' that it really uplifts and consoles," [2] we may reply that the uplifting and consoling power of prayer proves only — that prayer uplifts and consoles; a fact which was never in question. In such a case it is not the truth of the belief but the practical efficacy of the belief which is verified. If a man prays, believing that God hears him, his belief comforts him and his prayer inspires him, *whether his belief is true or an illusion.* [3]

[1] James, *Pragmatism*, p. 99.   [2] *Riddles of the Sphinx*, p. 468.
[3] Cf. Dickinson, *op. cit.*, p. 44: "The fact that a belief works is no proof

Granting, then, that the traditional Christian conception of God and a future life has been an enormous stimulus to morality, and has "worked well" in making men good and happy, what does that fact prove? Simply that it has been a fortunate thing for men that at a certain stage in their civilization they could believe such a world-conception. The fact that the belief has been inspiring is not in the slightest degree evidence that it is true. We have many instances of illusions and dreams that have helped men to be good and happy, that nevertheless turned out to be untrue.[1] If a lover believes in his sweetheart's fidelity, and is thereby quickened to do and be his best, those valuable results do in no wise prove that she *is* faithful, as many a lover has learned. Believing that the universe is friendly to us warms and kindles us; but it is the *belief* that has that beneficent effect, not the *fact* that the universe really is (if it is) friendly.[2]

of its validity, but only of its efficacy. Its validity can only be tested by the ordinary processes of criticism. And this is a fact which it will, I think, be increasingly impossible for the most religious and the most candid to deny. There is no general presumption that what is helpful and good is also true."

And Perry, *op. cit.*, p. 265: "A highly agreeable or inspiring idea, or a belief that disposes the mind to peace and contentment, may be of all ideas the least fitted to prepare the mind for what is to befall it. In other words, such emotional value is irrelevant to truth value, in the strict sense."

[1] How can such a statement as this be supported? — "It is surely a mistake to suppose that there are in the long run of history any beneficial illusions." "It is the truth in any idea that makes it useful." (D. S. Miller, professor of Apologetics in General Theological Seminary, in an address to the clergy of the diocese of Pennsylvania, December, 1914.) If the universe *is* indifferent to us, would it not be a beneficent illusion if men could always go on believing it to be at heart friendly? Precisely the good consequences which have followed from that belief would continue to follow from it, so long as men held it — even if, all the time, it has been an untrue belief.

[2] This simple discrimination takes the wind out of any number of contemporary arguments. For example, this of Carl Hilty, in his widely read little book on *Happiness*: "The mark by which the near presence of God's

(2) But leaving this popular and unscientific meaning of the term "works," let us grant that a theological belief works in the same sense in which the atomic theory works — namely, that it is a theory which actually does explain observed facts. We must then admit that our belief has only the status of a hypothesis, and that its probability is only that of the degree in which the observed facts accord with it. Scientific theories are frankly hypotheses, to be held provisionally and doubted or discarded as soon as they cease to explain phenomena. Moreover, if alternative hypotheses are suggested, each of which seems to explain some of the facts but to be belied by other facts, they are both regarded as only possibilities. A hypothesis is not proved true simply because it is a conceivable way of explaining certain facts. One must ask the further questions, Are there any facts that seem to disagree with it? and, Is there any other hypothesis which fits observed facts equally well? There are all degrees of probability for theories. Many a one long generally accepted, because it fitted known facts, has had to be discarded when new facts were learned; and one little ugly fact that refuses to harmonize with a theory is enough, if it is indisputable, to disprove it.

What, then, is the status, scientifically considered, of the

spirit is made irrefutably clear to those who have ever had the experience is the utterly incomparable feeling of happiness which is connected with the nearness, and which is therefore not only a possible and altogether proper feeling for us to have here below, but is the best and most indispensable proof of God's reality. No other proof is equally convincing, and therefore happiness is the point from which every efficacious new theology should start."

But how can the happiness which a belief gives be considered a proof of its truth? A comforting belief gives happiness in proportion to its *supposed* certainty, not in proportion to its *actual* truth. Just the fact of believing in the near presence of God, and being inspired by that belief to a deeper consecration and appreciation of life is the evident cause of the happiness. The further question, whether that sweet belief is a true belief or an illusion, must look elsewhere for its answer.

traditional theological beliefs? It must be confessed th it is very precarious. The average theologian needs training in scientific method. He finds facts that fit into his scheme, and at once considers it verified. But how about those unpleasant facts which refuse to fit into it? And has he candidly considered the various rival hypotheses which are in the field, and ascertained that his belief explains more facts than any other? Is he willing to admit that his cherished beliefs are but hypotheses, which stand, not by any means on a par with the theories of astronomy — from which the most intricate deductions can be made, and verified to a hair's breadth by subsequent happenings — but on a par with the belief, say, in the ether, or the electronic theory of matter?

The belief in the existence of other human minds is, strictly speaking, a mere hypothesis. But it is a hypothesis resting upon innumerable facts and contradicted by none. We see that our own movements, gestures, spoken words, facial expression, correspond to our mental states; then we see similar movements and hear similar words coming from bodies like our own. Those bodies have had the same genesis that ours have had; ours came indeed from one of them, and others have perhaps come from ours. The inference is irresistible that "behind" these other bodies live minds like our own. We try to deduce the workings of those minds, and predict from our past observations what acts those other beings will perform. Our predictions in general come true; where they do not, it is usually possible for us to see the flaw in our reasoning. There is no escape from the conviction that our experienced mind-body relation is paralleled in all human beings. . . . But is it so with the hypothesis of a divine mind? It is conceivable that we do see, in the stellar universe, a vast body "behind" which exists a vast mind, or that a divine mind exists without a visible body. It is conceivable that some of the saints and prophets have been right in thinking they heard an audible voice that was God's. A great number of arguments have been offered, the more important of which we have examined, which aim to deduce from observed facts the existence of such a Mind behind Nature.[1] But there is obviously no such evidence as for the existence of our fellow human minds. And there are facts — notably the existence of so much evil in the world — which do not seem to fit the hypothesis at all. Consequently, such beliefs as that in the personality or the creative function of God cannot be said to be at present, scientifically considered, more than highly interesting, but far from proved, working hypotheses.

(3) If, however, the argument is valid at all, it proves too much. There have been a great many, mutually contradictory, faiths that have "worked" successfully. Does that prove them all true? No faith ever worked more startlingly than Christian Science; does that prove its doctrine true? Schiller says to this, "If all religions work, all are true; and what is false is the rigidity of an idea which cannot tolerate such plural truth."[2] But is it necessary to come to such a conclusion? May it not be that there is "some truth in" all religions, and that none is true *Ueberhaupt*? Religions are complex; it may be only certain ele-

---

[1] Space limitations have made necessary the exclusion of the more technically metaphysical arguments. I especially regret the omission of the pantheistic and transcendental arguments. Good examples of the former may be found in Fechner's writings, and in F. Paulsen's *Introduction to Philosophy;* of the latter, in Josiah Royce's writings, and (briefly) in Galloway's *Philosophy of Religion*, chap. XI; or in *Foundations* (several authors, The Macmillan Co.), chap. IX.

Criticisms of arguments of this stripe may be found in Perry's *Present Philosophical Tendencies*, pt. III; W. James, *A Pluralistic Universe*, lects. II and V; F. C. S. Schiller, *Studies in Humanism*, chap. XII; W. H. Mallock, *Religion as a Credible Doctrine*, chap. X; A. Seth, *Hegelianism and Personality*.

[2] *Riddles of the Sphinx*, p. 469.

ments in the religion that were valuable; and those elements may not be contradictory of the valuable elements in the other faiths. Even, then, if it is not true, as argued above, that religions "work" successfully independently of their truth or falsehood, it would still be a difficult matter to show which element of a religious system was proved true by its success, in view of the marked success of so many irreconcilable systems.

(4) But all of this still does not touch the genuine pragmatist. For when one studies the pragmatic philosophy itself one finds that what it is, is precisely a new theory of the nature of truth. Truth, to the radical pragmatist, *is* successful working; that is all he *means* by truth, all, he asserts, that the term "truth" can mean.[1] Pragmatism rejects belief in everything beyond experience; it is really the most thorough skepticism. Schiller writes scornfully of "the traditional dogma of an absolute truth and ultimate reality existing for themselves apart from human agency."[2] For him "the truest religion is that which issues in and fosters the best life"[3] — simply because that is what he *calls* the "truest" religion. So James tells us that "the true is the name of whatever proves itself to be *good* in the way of be-

---

[1] Cf. James, *The Meaning of Truth*, and *Pragmatism;* and F. C. S. Schiller's, John Dewey's, A. W. Moore's writings, in a number of places. Professor D. C. Macintosh (in his *Problem of Knowledge*, p. 410), calls this *hyper-pragmatism*. The doctrine which I have just been opposing, that whatever "works" practically is thereby *proved* to be true (in contrast with this still more radical doctrine that the practical working is all we *mean* by its truth), he calls *pseudo-pragmatism*. Thus he reserves the name *pragmatism* itself for the mild doctrine that the test of truth is ultimately practical, residing in the consequences which follow from a hypothesis. I am quite willing to adopt this nomenclature, and to call the doctrines I attack distortions or excesses of pragmatism. But we must confess that these distortions of the true pragmatism have been voiced by the leaders of the movement, and constitute in the popular mind its very essence — and its attractiveness.

[2] *Humanism*, p. 9. [3] *Studies in Humanism*, p. 369.

lief."[1] "If theological ideas prove to have a value for concrete life, they will be true, for pragmatism, *in the sense of being good for so much*."[2] Of the doctrine of the Absolute, which he does his best to demolish, he tells us that, pragmatically considered, it is, after all, true; for it, in its way, "works," and that "working" constitutes its truth. But what then does the doctrine of the absolute *mean*, when pragmatically interpreted? It means simply "that we have a right ever and anon to take a moral holiday, to let the world wag in its own way.... If the absolute means this, and means no more than this, who can possibly deny the truth of it? To deny it would be to insist that men should never relax, and that holidays are never in order."[3] So with the belief in a Designer God. Since reality consists only of experience, "a vague confidence in the future is the sole pragmatic meaning at present discernible in the terms design and designer."[4]

Well and good, then. "Since the truth of an idea means merely the fact that the idea works, that fact is all you mean when you say the idea is true."[5] If you say that the belief in God is true, you mean only that the belief works well in human life. "Other than this practical significance, the words God, free-will, design, etc., have none."[6] All of which limitation of meaning is legitimate enough if one on principle refuses to admit the possibility of existences outside this present flux of "pure experience." But if one is interested in the possibility of a God who is a conscious Being, now living and working outside of our experience; if one is interested in finding out, not whether such a belief works well, but whether it is, in the usual sense of the word, *true*, a *bona fide* pragmatism has no comfort to offer.

[1] *Pragmatism*, p. 76.
[2] *Ibid.*, p. 73. My italics.
[3] *Ibid.*, pp. 74–75.
[4] *Ibid.*, p. 115.
[5] Pratt, *op. cit.*, p. 206.
[6] James, *op. cit.*, p. 121.

Pragmatic arguments: Kant, *Critique of Practical Reason,* bk. II, chap. II. W. James, *Pragmatism;* "Reflex Action and Theism" (in *The Will to Believe*). W. H. Mallock, *Religion as a Credible Doctrine,* chap. XII. E. H. Rowland, *Right to Believe,* chap. II. E. Boutroux, *Science and Religion in Contemporary Philosophy,* pt. II, chaps. III–IV. E. W. Lyman, *Theology and Human Problems* chap. IV. G. R. Montgomery, *The Unexplored Self.* F. C. S. Schiller, *Riddles of the Sphinx:* Appendix III; *Humanism,* I, XVIII. G. M. Stratton, *Psychology of the Religious Life,* chap. XXV.

Criticisms: J. M. E. McTaggart, *Some Dogmas of Religion,* chaps. II, VIII. R. B. Perry, *Present Philosophical Tendencies,* pt. IV. B. Russell, *Philosophical Essays,* IV–V. J. B. Pratt, *What is Pragmatism?* Lectures V–VI. W. Riley, *American Thought,* chap. IX. *Journal of Philosophy, Psychology, and Scientific Methods,* vol. 5, p. 90; vol. 9, p. 406.

CHAPTER XXII

THE COUNTER-ATTACK UPON SCIENCE

ONE of the most instinctive methods of self-defense is to say, "You're another!" And in recent years many a hard-pressed theologian, obliged to admit the flaws in his apologetic, has turned upon science with a *Tu quoque*. If theology has been built upon the sand, are the doctrines of natural science any better based? The defenders of tradition, so long fighting a losing battle, have turned upon their opponents with what would be called in military parlance an offensive-defensive; they have carried the war into Africa. A thoroughgoing attempt has been made to discredit human knowledge in general, in order in the universal shipwreck to assert that one belief is no freer from fallacy than another, and that therefore we need not hesitate to retain our theological beliefs, however riddled by objections they may be. The most skillful and influential, probably, of these counter-attacks upon science is Mr. Balfour's sensational book, *The Foundations of Belief*. But the point of view therein maintained has found expression in many contemporary essays. For example, in a widely read little book by an American college teacher, the opening argument is summed up in the words, "We are now apparently in the identical position from which we started. Nothing is proved, and we are prepared as before to believe one hypothesis as easily as the other." [1] If theological beliefs, when severely scrutinized, are found to be less certain than we had thought, no body of supposed truth is really in any better case; and to point out

[1] Rowland, *op. cit.*, p. 30.

this fact gives to many a theologian a particular and holy glee.[1] We must therefore consider the leading types of this radical skepticism.

Is reason untrustworthy because the product of blind forces?

Mr. Balfour writes as follows:[2] "On the naturalistic hypothesis, the whole premises of knowledge are clearly due to the blind operation of material causes, and in the last resort to these alone. . . . Reason itself is the result, like nerves or muscles, of physical antecedents. . . . [her] premises are settled for her by purely irrational forces, which she is powerless to control, or even to comprehend. . . . We are to suppose that powers which were evolved in primitive man and his animal progenitors in order that they might kill with success and marry in security, are on that account fitted to explain the secrets of the universe. We are to suppose that the fundamental beliefs on which these powers are to be exercised reflect with sufficient precision remote aspects of reality, though they were produced in the main by physiological processes which date from a stage of development when the only curiosities which had to be satisfied were those of fear and those of hunger. To say that instruments of research constructed solely for uses like these cannot be expected to supply us with a metaphysic or a theology, is to say far too little. They cannot be expected to give us any general views even of the phenomenal world, or to do more than guide us in comparative safety from the satisfaction of one useful appetite to the satisfaction of another." In short, our reasoning faculty, being the product of blind

---

[1] Cf. Perry, *op. cit.*, p. 85: "It is still generally assumed that the success of religion is conditioned by the failure of science. The major part of contemporary religious philosophy is devoted to a disproof of science."

[2] *The Foundations of Belief*, pp. 304–09.

forces, is not of guaranteed trustworthiness, and is far likelier to lead us astray than to conduct us safely to a knowledge of the truth.

(1) This argument, it may be noted in passing, can be answered in its own terms. For if Mr. Balfour's supposition is correct, and reason is untrustworthy, then his own reasoning is worthless, and his attack upon science, based upon it, has no cogency. While if Mr. Balfour's real belief is true, and reason is *not* the product of blind forces, but a God-given faculty, the argument has no force at all. As a recent writer puts it, "There must be some fallacy in any process of reasoning which ends by discrediting reason; for if reason is discredited, the reasoning which is supposed to prove it to be so is itself discredited in advance."[1]

(2) It is more profitable, however, to point out that although our reasoning powers have been evolved through a blind and thoroughly practical struggle for existence, and therefore could not be assumed *a priori* to be trustworthy; and though, as a matter of fact, no man can wholly trust his own particular reasoning powers; yet, by a long observation of the results of human reasoning, a method of using these powers has been discovered which, when accurately carried out, is shown by repeated experience actually to lead to trustworthy conclusions. This method is taught in the textbooks of logic. Whether or not it has been faithfully followed in any concrete piece of reasoning is to be decided only by the careful scrutiny of critics; but if it *has* been faithfully followed, our unbroken experience assures us that we can trust its results. However, then, we came into possession of the faculty of logical reason, our confidence in it depends not upon the causes that produced it but upon the observed accuracy of its working in all cases where we can test it by comparing its conclusions with actual facts. If,

[1] B. S. Streeter, *Restatement and Reunion*, p. 47.

for example, by the use of a complicated piece of reasoning we can predict an eclipse of the moon at 9.35 P.M. on December 1, ten years ahead; and if, when the time comes, that eclipse takes place at the moment predicted, no amount of dust-throwing at the faculty of reason will serve to discredit it in our eyes. Since, then, the method of logical reasoning has been verified by such subsequent observations in innumerable cases, and since wherever a concrete piece of reasoning has been belied by such observations it has been possible to discover some inadvertent disloyalty to the method, we have every reason for trusting the method in those cases where we are unable to test its results by observation.

Is science based upon unproved and self-contradictory postulates?

Trustworthy as the method of logic may be, however, the truth of any conclusion will be contingent upon the truth of the premises from which its proof starts; if these are merely assumed, the whole structure of supposed knowledge that rests upon them is, likewise, merely assumed; and if, in addition, those premises are found, upon examination, to be actually self-contradictory, the supposed body of knowledge has no validity at all. That such is the case with the traditional theological dogmas, Mr. Balfour admits; but he declares that it is also the case with our whole body of science. "All branches of knowledge would appear to stand very much upon an equality. In all of them conclusions seem more stable than premises, the superstructure more stable than the foundation." "One great metaphysician has described the system of another as 'shot out of a pistol,' meaning thereby that it was presented for acceptance without introductory proof. . . . The circumstance that all men are practically agreed to accept ['positive knowledge'] without demur, has blinded them to the fact that it, too, has been 'shot out of a pistol.'" [1]

Moreover, these underlying postulates of science can be shown to be full of inconceivabilities. "Space, time, matter, motion, force, and so forth, are each in turn shown to involve contradictions which it is beyond our power to solve, and obscurities which it is beyond our power to penetrate." [2] This supposed demonstration of the existence of hopeless dialectical difficulties in ultimate scientific ideas goes back to Kant's famous "Antinomies," Sir William Hamilton's paradoxes, and Spencer's ponderous argument at the threshold of his huge philosophical system. The net result, for these thinkers and their followers, is that we cannot conceive of space and time as finite or as infinite; we cannot conceive of force as material or immaterial; we cannot conceive how motion takes place, how one body acts upon another; in short, we can form no clear ideas of any of these ultimate realities, Science, then, resting as it does upon these concepts, is vitiated throughout by their obscurity. "As soon as the 'unthinkableness' of 'ultimate' scientific ideas is speculatively recognized, the fact must react upon our speculative attitudes towards 'proximate' scientific ideas. That which in the order of reason is dependent cannot be unaffected by the weaknesses and the obscurities of that on which it depends. If the one is unintelligible, the other can hardly be rationally established." [3]

---

[1] *The Foundations of Belief*, pp. 291, 293-94.   [2] *Ibid.*, p. 292.

[3] *Ibid.*, pp. 291, 93-94, 294-95. So Rowland, *op. cit.*, p. 27: "All thought must proceed on certain unproved and inconceivable assumptions." Mallock, *op. cit.*, p. 281: "If we allowed ourselves to believe in the existence of those things only which do not, when our intellect analyses them, confront us at last with contradictions, the plain truth is that we must content ourselves with believing in nothing." Schiller, *Riddles of the Sphinx*, p. 466: "No doubt it is true that science also ultimately rests on acts of faith"; and *Humanism*, p. 349: "The premise has to be assumed or conceded in every demonstration. The utmost we can do is to rest our

(1) But these supposed paradoxes concerning time, space, motion, and the other high abstractions of science, have been one by one patiently unraveled.[1] Messrs. Kant, Spencer, *et al.*, made themselves a lot of unnecessary and gratuitous trouble. These 'ultimate' ideas are *not* inconceivable. Some of them are, indeed, unpicturable; we cannot conceive infinite space, e.g., pictorially in full. But we can picture a part, and have the feeling that there is no boundary; we can so set our minds that it will reject the thought of a limit as incompatible with its conception. And this is all that is necessary. Conceptions do not need to be visualized at all, much less to be visualized in full; what is important is the disposition of the mind. Introspection will show that most of our abstract conceptions consist, psychologically considered, of unnameable mental stuff, tensions and releases, and vague associations. In this way our "ultimate scientific ideas" can be conceived as adequately as is necessary to serve their purpose.

Moreover, the fact that a suggested possibility was "inconceivable" would be no proof that the facts were not *so*. If our minds are incapable of conceiving certain aspects of the universe, we cannot set up our mental limitations as limiting outer existence. Self-contradiction in a conception is, indeed, enough to discredit it; for self-contradiction consists in unsaying what we are in the same breath saying, and its net result is a mutual cancellation of assertions that leaves nothing asserted. But except for this test, any

demostration on an assumption so fundamental that none will dare to question it; and this we here seem to have accomplished. For what could be more fundamental than the assumption on which the ethical argument rests — that the elements of our experience admit of being harmonized, that the world is truly a cosmos?" [i.e., as Schiller means, a moral order, an order arranged to satisfy our needs.]

[1] See, e.g., Mill's *Examination of Sir William Hamilton's Philosophy*, chap. VI. W. James, *Some Problems of Philosophy*, chaps. X–XI.

conception is valid as a conception; whether it is true or not can only be judged by observation of the facts. Time and space may be either finite or infinite, for all we know; the fact that men have difficulty in imagining either alternative reflects only upon the weakness of their imaginations.

(2) But however confused our ideas of time, space, and motion are, we at least have good reason to know that they correspond to some reality. To deny their existence because we cannot give an intelligible account of them would be on a par with denying my own existence because I do not understand the nature of consciousness. To doubt the existence of my life after death, on the other hand, or of a personal God now, is far less absurd; not because we have difficulty in conceiving those possibilities, but because we lack evidence of their existence at all. At least, we are not flatly confronted with their existence, as we are with the existence of time, space, and motion, or with our own conscious existence. So to assume that because all ultimate ideas are vague and dubious, the realities to which they correspond are equally dubious, and that therefore we may as well believe in any ultimate realities that it satisfies our souls to believe in, is to blur one of our most obvious and necessary distinctions, that between an inadequate idea of an indubitable fact and an inadequate idea of a doubtful fact.

(3) And after all, even if our notions of time, space, matter, ether, etc., are to be discredited, the great body of science is not discredited thereby. For these "ultimate" ideas are wrongly conceived as "postulates" upon which science "rests." They are rather its last and least certain generalizations. Science rests upon millions of concrete observations; its laws are shorthand summaries of those observations, a systematized account of experience. No inadequacy in our conception of space or time can vitiate the conclusions

of astronomy; eclipses of the moon do take place in accordance with predictions, the planets do appear at their appointed times. Thus the great body of truth that constitutes a science is not contingent upon those highest abstractions or remote deductions which are based upon it.[1]

So is it with the facts of religious experience. No doubt of the existence of a personal God can impugn the actual facts of conversion, or of the purity and peace to which the religious soul attains. The great structure of the religious life will not topple and go to pieces because "ultimate religious ideas" are dubious. Rather, it is the province of theology to take these concrete and indubitable facts as its foundation-stones; and only as the structure nears completion can it hope for a clear vision of those highest truths which rest, like the vaulted dome of a cathedral, upon the great masses of masonry patiently accumulated beneath.

Is science based upon purely subjective data?

A more radical criticism of science is that since it uses for its data our sensations, which are subjective and personal facts, its conclusions cannot be trusted as objectively true. Mr. Balfour writes: "We need only to consider carefully our perceptions regarded as psychological results, in order to see that, regarded as sources of information, they are not merely occasionally inaccurate, but habitually menda-

[1] Cf. Spencer, *First Principles*, chap. I, sec. 5: "Science is simply a higher development of common knowledge; if science is repudiated, all knowledge must be repudiated along with it. The extremest bigot will not suspect any harm in the observation that the sun rises earlier and sets later in the summer than in the winter. Well, astronomy is an organized body of similar observations, made with greater nicety, extended to a larger number of objects. And thus it is with all the sciences. They severally germinate out of the experiences of daily life; insensibly as they grow they draw in remoter, more numerous, and more complex experiences; and among these, they ascertain laws of dependence like those which make up our knowledge of the most familiar objects." (Abridged.)

cious. . . . Nine-tenths of our immediate experiences of objects are visual; and all visual experiences, without exception, are, according to science, erroneous. As everybody knows, colour is not a property of the thing seen; it is a sensation produced in us by that thing. . . . In what entanglements of contradiction do we not find ourselves involved by the attempt to rest science upon observations which science itself declares to be erroneous? . . . Can we by any possible treatment of sensations and feelings legitimately squeeze out of them trustworthy knowledge of the permanent and independent material universe of which, according to science, sensations and feelings are but transient and evanescent effects?" [1]

To take a familiar concrete case, one man sees a rose as a red object, another, whom we call "color-blind," sees it as a gray object; if a third man had optical organs somewhat differently made, he might see it blue or yellow or brown. Since, then, the color we see depends upon the nature of our eyes, how can we possibly tell what the rose is like in itself? Indeed, were the nerves running from our eyes to the visual centers in our brain to be cut and spliced with the nerves running from our ears to the auditory tracts, we should doubtless hear everything we now see and see when we now hear. In short, the data upon which we base our supposed knowledge of an outer world are all dependent, for their peculiar quality, upon the structure of our brains and sense-organs; and the knowledge we draw from them is knowledge rather of our own subjective experiences than of the nature of objective reality. Is not science then, after all, as subjective as theology?

(1) But knowledge of our own experiences is knowledge of the most valuable sort; and to enable us to predict what sensations we shall have under given circumstances is pre-

[1] *The Foundations of Belief*, pp. 111–19.

cisely the most important function of science. Except for slight individual variations, which can be allowed for, our sense-organs and brains are constructed alike; and the conclusions of one investigator hold good for all other men. If natural science is thought of merely as a detailed description of what we should see and hear and feel under all eventualities, it is not thereby proved "subjective" in any disparaging sense; it is still strictly determined by the facts as they are forced upon us, and not affected by our bias or desire. It is not fair to call our observations "mendacious," or "erroneous," because they are *our* observations, bits of our conscious experience, unless they mislead us. But — except for illusions and malobservations, which are checked by the coöperation of many observers — these experiences of ours do happen in accordance with regular and ascertainable laws of cause and effect; and the knowledge of those laws, which are for the most part independent of our volition, constitutes a highly trustworthy mass of scientific truth.

(2) Moreover, the fact that these sensations are, as it were, thrust upon us, intruding into our conscious life quite without relevance to our preceding mental states, suggests strongly that they are due to outer causes and not to a merely inward mental evolution. The strongest willing cannot exorcise these sensations; we are at their mercy. A great many other peculiarities of these sensation-experiences, of which space does not here permit even a summary, compel us to believe that they are the effects in us of an outer world of realities surrounding us. Subjective idealism, which would limit reality to the conscious experience of our several minds, and define science as merely an account of "permanent possibilities of sensation," is not only repugnant to our instinctive beliefs, but philosophically indefensible. Certainly the sight of a man killed by a bullet, or writhing from the effects of poison taken, should be enough

to convince any one that we are in the grip of a reality bigger than our own little streams of experience, a reality reflected, if not photographically pictured, by our sensations. And whatever the degree in which our sensations give us the qualitative nature of this outer world, they at least give us a good working knowledge of it. For they enable us to steer our way safely through its dangers and to avail ourselves of its resources. So we may have great confidence that science gives us not only truth concerning our own possible experiences, but in some sense truth concerning the objective world.[1]

Is science restricted in its scope?

If, then, we may accept scientific knowledge as valid, can we say with certain theologians that it is valid only within a restricted field or only of a certain aspect of reality — reserving a field for the exclusive domain of theology? It has long been the habit of religious philosophers to welcome the scientific method as applied to all facts except those of religion, but to put up a "No trespassing" sign about that sacred enclosure, using therein the time-honored and more satisfying methods of authority or *a priori* reasoning. But, as we saw in chapter XVI, this reservation is not warranted. If the scientific method gives such good results in the other fields, why not apply it to this field also? Why be content in these most important of all matters with a looser and less trustworthy method? "The field of science is unlimited; its material is endless, every group of natural phenomena, every phase of social life, every stage of past or present development is material for science.... The field of science is

---

[1] The present writer has dwelt at length upon this matter in the dissertation referred to, and in the following papers: *Journal of Philosophy, Psychology, and Scientific Methods*, vol. 8, p. 365; vol. 9, p. 149. *Mind* (N.S.), vol. 24, p. 29.

co-extensive with the whole life, physical and mental, of the universe. . . . To say that there are certain fields from which science is excluded, wherein its methods have no application, is merely to say that the rules of methodical observation and the laws of logical thought do not apply to the facts, if any, which lie within such fields. If there are facts, and sequences to be observed among those facts, then we have all the requisites of scientific classification and knowledge. If there are no facts, or no sequence to be observed among them, then the possibility of *all* knowledge disappears. . . . There is no short-cut to truth, no way to gain a knowledge of the universe except through the gateway of scientific method. The hard and stony path of classifying facts and reasoning upon them is the only way to ascertain truth." [1]

It is true that we commonly limit the name "science" to that body of truth which is a mere description and piecing out of the data of our experience. The question how far those truths hold good of a world beyond experience, and what the nature of that world is, in itself — including all other minds than our own — we leave to metaphysics. In so far, then, as theology concerns itself with an inquiry into the existence and nature of a personal God or gods, it may properly consider its task as lying beyond the frontiers of science. But the same spirit and method that have made science successful must be employed here also. Although no further observations can be made in these realms beyond our experience, whatever truth is to be ascertained must be based upon the facts offered by the various sciences; metaphysical and theological hypotheses can be granted no special indulgence, but must stand or fall according to the completeness and the exclusiveness with which they explain these verified facts.

[1] Pearson, *op. cit.*, chap. 1.

THE COUNTER-ATTACK UPON SCIENCE

A subtler way of limiting the scope of science is to permit it to invade all fields but to insist that it can everywhere only describe, and never explain. Paulsen writes, for example, "Let us not be deceived! Natural science will never again be decoyed from its path, which seeks a purely physical explanation of *all* natural phenomena. There may be a thousand things which it cannot explain now, but the fundamental axiom that these too have their natural causes and therefore a natural-scientific explanation, will never again be abandoned by science. . . . But would the completion of the natural-scientific explanation exhaust our theoretical interest in reality? I think not. For now a new question arises. What does it all *mean?* . . . Everything must occur and be explained physically; and everything must be considered and interpreted metaphysically."[1]

This word "meaning," as used by Paulsen and others, is ambiguous. If it means "plan," "purpose," "intention" — whether of God or man or any other conscious being — it lies within the realm of fact, and is to be ascertained by natural science, or philosophy, by the same method by which any facts are ascertained, or inferred. If it means "value," it lies within the domain of moral philosophy, or ethics — wherein a similar rigorously scientific method must also be used. Theology must deal, no doubt, with both facts and their values — or "meanings" — for human life; but in neither aspect of its inquiry is it absolved from the necessity of building its conclusions upon the concrete data of observation. So, whether or not we shall agree to restrict the scope of "science" is merely a matter of convenience of nomenclature; whether metaphysics and theology are to be regarded as a branch of science or as separate disciplines, they must, if they are really to add to our knowledge, come

[1] F. Paulsen, *Introduction to Philosophy*, pp. 161-62.

under the control of the scientific method. There is no other trustworthy avenue to truth.

Scientific men, of course, make mistakes. Sometimes the available evidence is slight, and it is not easy to decide between conflicting generalizations. Sometimes the investigator is insufficiently trained, or lacking in caution, or biased. There is always a borderland of science, near its farthest frontier, where all is uncertain, and where a theory viewed with favor to-day may be rejected to-morrow. But this region that is borderland to-day will be safely won to-morrow; and behind the frontier lies a vast region of thoroughly ascertained knowledge. Thus, while we must have no blind reverence for scientists, and should accept with caution the latest surmises they offer us, it is bad tactics to attack science in general in the interests of religion; the ensuing revulsion of feeling is bound to do more harm to the attacker. "The fact of human fallibility, since it may be urged against all knowledge, cannot be urged against any. It justifies a certain modesty and open-mindedness in all thinkers, but can never constitute ground for the rejection of any particular theory. Knowledge can only be disproved by better knowledge. If a specific scientific theory is doubtful, well and good; but it can justly be regarded as doubtful only *for scientific reasons*, and these had best be left to the scientist himself. It is scarcely necessary to add, that if variety and change of opinion are to be urged against any branch of knowledge, the philosopher of religion can least afford to urge them. For of all cognitive enterprises his is on this score the most in need of indulgence." [1]

It is, indeed, a poor pass for religion when she has to rest her claims on an attack upon the validity of science. For

[1] Perry, *op. cit.*, p. 92.

science is the most successful and splendid of human undertakings. Making its way at first against widespread and strongly entrenched opposition, it has gradually won general acceptance: and every day adds to its triumphant verification of its conclusions. Nothing is more needful for the future of theology than that it desist from its futile obscurantism, its impotent struggle against its now stronger brother, and accept openly and gladly whatever truths natural science has discovered. And if it too would win for man a permanent and unquestioned body of truth, it must espouse the same method, and become itself a branch of science, or of a scientific philosophy.

Attacks: I. Kant, *Critique of Pure Reason: Transcendental Dialectic*, bk. II, chap. II. H. Spencer, *First Principles*, pt. I. A. J. Balfour, *A Defence of Philosophic Doubt; The Foundations of Belief*. J. Ward, *Naturalism and Agnosticism*. G. P. Fisher, *Grounds of Theistic and Christian Belief*, chap. III. H. C. Sheldon, *Unbelief in the Nineteenth Century*, pt. I. E. Boutroux, *Science and Religion in Contemporary Philosophy*, pt. II, chap. II. W. H. Mallock, *Religion as a Credible Doctrine*, chaps. XI–XIII. E. H. Rowland, *Right to Believe*, chap. II. F. C. S. Schiller, *Humanism*, I, XVIII.

Defenses: W. James, *Pluralistic Universe*, Appendix A.; *Some Problems of Philosophy*, chaps. X–XI. K. Pearson, *Grammar of Science*, chap. I, secs. 5–8. J. S. Mill, *Examination of Sir William Hamilton's Philosophy*, chaps. I–VI. R. B. Perry, *Present Philosophical Tendencies*, pt. II. T. P. Nunn, *Aims of Scientific Method*. G. Santayana, *Reason in Science*. R. Poincaré, *Science and Hypothesis*. *New World*, vol. 5, p. 318. *Hibbert Journal*, vol. 3, p. 452. *Journal of Philosophy, Psychology, and Scientific Methods*, vol. 1.

CHAPTER XXIII

THE PROBLEM OF EVIL

WHEN we are well and light-hearted, when all goes prosperously with us, when

> "The year's at the spring
> And day's at the morn,"

it is natural for us to feel that

> "God's in his heaven,
> All's right with the world."

But when we see evil in some of its acuter forms — a helpless child writhing in the grip of unbearable pain, a youth of promise and eager ambition thrust by some accident or ill-fortune into weakness and failure, lovers separated by sudden death at the brink of their happiness, manhood lured by insidious temptation to shipwreck and sorrow, womanhood crushed by the drudgery of life into a sodden hopelessness — it is far easier to believe the universe indifferent to our human fortunes. There are, indeed, people to-day, in our advanced state of cilivization — bought by the blood and toil of countless generations — who know little of the pain and misery of the world. Well-fed, warmly dressed, snugly housed, they find nothing to disturb their assurance of the divine ordering of things. One wonders whether such people have really known pain — stinging, relentless, unendurable physical pain, that will not be stilled, that eats the very heart out of a man and leaves no thought but that of agony. Have they felt the "grisly, blood-freezing, heart-palsying sensation" of fear? Have they ever lost the one loved one that made life dear, or failed in the one endeavor the heart was set upon, and lived on and on, long, blank, bitterly reminiscent years? Have they eyes for the dull, patient endurance, the discouragement, the hopeless misery of millions of earth's poorer children even in this prosperous age?

Of course this is not the whole story. There are many good things in this world, so many that, with normal good fortune and reasonable wisdom in living, life can be made well worth while. To most men life even brings times of very deep and overflowing happiness. But there have been millions of human beings who have not had such normal good fortune. Did not God care for them too? If your wife or child were starving to death, pinned under the walls of an earthquake-shattered house, would the preponderance of pleasure over pain in the life of the average man be of any comfort? A good God must have a heart for the sufferings of each one of his creatures throughout the ages.

In any case we should face life with courage and with song. We should forget, as long as we can, the sick-rooms, the smell of ether, the faces of pale children and careworn women. And this optimism of attitude almost irresistibly leads to an optimistic world-view. To greet the days with good cheer, to respond to the wonder and beauty of the world — or rather *in* the world, to be filled with awe at its grandeur, rapture at its loveliness, and thankfulness at its opportunities, to declare life well worth living and go at it with shout and laughter, is to live it in the fullest and best way. And naturally, in such moods, we assent to the explanation our religion has offered of this beauty and grandeur and opportunity — the heavens declare the glory of God and the firmament showeth his handiwork! The inward emotion begets the outward belief; an optimistic frame of mind objectifies its emotion and calls the world good, believes it arranged and planned to evoke such emotions. Arguments fly to the four winds, the goodness of things is patent and obvious. More than that, the duty to be cheerful is generally taken to be a duty to believe the optimistic doctrine. In current opinion disbelief in the latter is invested with the meanness and ugliness of the pessimistic mood.

But though we should be loyal to our world, and love it all we can, we need not be blind to its grievous faults. However gaily we go to meet life, however bravely and buoyantly we take it, we cannot fail, if we are serious, to know that it is shot through and through with irredeemable pathos and tragedy. He who has no ideals may praise the world as it is; but for him who has conceived what life might be under more favorable conditions, the misery and sadness of which it so largely consists are not to be glossed over or condoned. Is it possible to square this recognition of the evil in the world with the belief in a benevolent Creator or Ruler thereof? The attempt to answer this question gives us the ancient and still unsolved "problem of evil."

Can evil be conceived as a partial view of the good?

The most radical solution offered is that of those who say that evil is merely "appearance," or "illusion," or — in Mrs. Eddy's language — "error." It seems evil to us merely because we have a shortsighted and partial view of it; could we see through God's eyes we should recognize that what we have taken to be evil is really a necessary part of the divine harmony. Just as a discord which, if taken alone, is displeasing, may add to the total excellence of a symphony; just as the catastrophes and the ugly characters may contribute to the interest and artistic effect of a novel or drama; so all that we call pain and defect, and even sin, may play its essential part in God's complete right. In one

THE PROBLEM OF EVIL

sense, then, it will still be evil; but in another and deeper sense it is good.

(1) But such speech, though comforting to those who are susceptible to the spell of unanalyzed ideas, amounts to nothing when examined. It is a merely verbal solution of the problem. Pain and suffering are real things, not to be made by words into anything else. If suffering is felt, it is suffering; for that is what suffering consists of, the feeling of it. To call it good is to call black white. Whatever it might be to God, it is suffering to us. And what help is it to the man who is in an agony of pain or sorrow to know that to God it is not evil? The fallacy in this easy solution lies in the word "seem"; for this is a case where "seeming" equals "being." The locus of suffering is consciousness; and if in our consciousness we find suffering, then it is undeniably there. To call it "illusion" or "appearance" is to give it a euphemistic name; but just as a rose by any name would smell as sweet, so pain by any name would feel as bad. Moreover, if what is good to God feels bad to us, that "appearance" or "illusion" is in itself an evil, and is as much in need of explanation and justification as it was before we so labelled it.

(2) The supposition springs, perhaps, from certain practical experiences. It is possible to learn to "transcend" evil, to take happily what once provoked our rebelliousness, and thus not only to cut out the worrying and fretting and repining, the fear and regret and despair, that form so large a part of our human misery, but to confront present failure and loss and actually physical pain itself without unhappiness. It is possible, that is, if men are taught how to do it, if a great emotion pushes them into it, if they have the strength of heart to carry it through. But, as a matter of observation, few men have realized that it can be done; few will ever, probably, have the perseverance and single-mind-

edness to do it. Poor, ignorant, helpless men and women, and still more children and animals, cannot find this difficult way, which means so sharp a transformation of human nature. And even could all sentient creatures attain to the inward poise and peace of the most successful of the Stoics or Christian Scientists, their lives would not be so rich and full and beautiful as they might have been if the instincts and desires that have been crushed and forgotten could have been fulfilled.

(3) We do not actually believe that the evil in the world is really good, for we fight hard to abate it. What mockery is all our struggle, our sacrifice, our effort, if the evils we are overcoming thereby are essential aspects of the universal harmony. No, "levity and mysticism may do all they can — and they can do much — to make men think moral distinctions unauthoritative, because moral distinctions may be either ignored or transcended. Yet the essential assertion that one thing is really better than another remains involved in every act of every living being. It is accordingly a moral truth which no subterfuge can elude, that some things are really better than others. In the daily course of affairs we are constantly in the presence of events which by turning out one way or the other produce a real, an irrevocable, increase of good or evil in the world." [1]

Variant forms of this doctrine, that evil is a necessary part of good, are to be found in the assertions that good always comes out of evil, or that it can exist only by contrast with evil. To the first statement it is sufficient to say that it is not borne out by observation; good sometimes can be seen to come out of evil, but just as often evil can be seen to come out of good; and more often good produces further good and evil further evil. Illness and poverty sometimes produce strength and resourcefulness and invention; but oftener

[1] G. Santayana, *Poetry and Religion*, p. 100.

they produce demoralization and ignorance and a host of other ills. Good and evil are so interwoven in life that what seemed hopelessly bad often proves to have its good side or consequences. But there remain multitudes of other cases where the opposite is the fact. And in any case, the good that "comes out of" evil is a justification of that evil only if it could have been attained in no other way. If human life is so planned that evils are a necessary precondition of some goods, here is a pretty problem of evil left unsolved.

The assertion that evil is necessary that good may exist, by contrast with it, is likewise contrary to observable facts. One kind of happy experience may contrast with another equally happy experience. Certain periods in the lives of the more fortunate of us bear witness to the possibility of a rich and vivid experience without a trace of pain. And the purest forms of happiness are those in which there is no hint of sorrow, glimpses of that ideal world which we construct in our imaginations, picture in art, and look forward to in some future heaven. But certainly, if our human nature were so formed that we could not be happy without a dose of pain, that sad fact would raise a problem of evil all its own. And it would effectually chill our faith in a better future by showing us the hopelessness of ever escaping from that odious law by which joy must always have its complement of sorrow.

Is evil necessary for character-building?

A much more plausible contention is that the evils in the world are necessary as obstacles and goads to prick us into energy, to cultivate in us patience, to transform us from creatures of impulse into men and women of fortitude and self-control. As a loving father may punish his child, or set him at an uncongenial task, so may God deal with us. We see many a man who has been tempered by pain, made wiser, stronger, better. Suffering is part of our education. It makes character; and character is worth much suffering.

(1) But this solution egregiously fails to cover a large part of the evil in life. There is the evil that *kills*. When a man starves to death, or is eaten by a tiger, or dies of a rattlesnake bite, is he being educated? When a shipload of children burn to death, as happened recently in New York harbor, is their character being formed? There is suffering of babies and of animals; they can hardly be thought to be learning moral lessons therefrom. There are the great catastrophes like the Messina earthquake and the Mont Pelée eruption; not only do they teach no salutary lessons to the thousands they kill, but they can hardly be supposed, except by a stretch of faith, to produce in the survivors a lift of character comparable to the suffering they cause. Pain is not tempered to human strength; if it sometimes has the power to inspire, it more often has power to depress. Sorrow that breaks men's hearts is worse than useless for discipline. And take the dull monotony of many lives, the withholding of opportunity, the bitter lacks that keep the mass of humanity ignorant and cramped and without hope. There is suffering that coarsens, that stupefies, that degrades; there is pain that breaks down a man's courage, crushes his will, drives him insane. The most ardent enthusiasms, the highest purposes, are checkmated, the purest and potentially greatest souls are tortured, limited, flung back from their aspirations. Any sensible person who had the control of nature, if he wished to use pain as a spur to character-building, could distribute and adjust it far more wisely and effectively.

(2) Again, is pain really necessary for the production of character? Do we grow in maturity and in virtue in proportion to the suffering we have to meet? On the contrary,

it may be plausibly maintained that we develop fastest when we find ourselves in the environment which is best suited to our needs, when we are happy and useful in it and free to exercise our faculties. Healthy children learn through happy play and happy study, through imitation of wise and loving elders, through contact with noble examples, through the persuasiveness of beautiful ideals. When a mother loses her child, she may attain through her patient suffering a saintly resignation that she would have acquired in no other way; but that gain is at the expense of other lessons that normal motherhood would have taught her. The withholding of opportunity may produce patience; the use of opportunity is the only way of reaching to a fully developed manhood or womanhood. Were there no pain in life, there would still be scope for action and energy in seeking positive goods, both for self and for others. There could still be altruism, sacrifice, renunciation, love, and self-control; and if there could no longer be (in the etymological sense of the term) sympathy, there could be more of that happier and equally noble virtue which the Germans call *Mitfreude*. For why is it not as beautiful to rejoice with others in their joys as to suffer with them in their sorrows?

(3) Are the virtues produced by pain of any value except to enable us better to bear further pain? What do we mean by "character" but the ability to react rightly to the conditions amid which we live, the proper adaptation of our impulses to our needs and situation? But were the world a pain-free one we should have no need of these particular virtues, so laboriously and painfully won. As it is, we rightly prize them, but only because we live in a world that makes them necessary. In an ideal world they would be out of place and loathsome. If there were no pain there would be no need of courage, longsuffering, endurance, resignation; these virtues have the taint of earth upon them, the shadow

of the primal curse. In a happier world we might be like light-hearted, care-free children, free to follow our impulses without sin or regret. And who can say that such a spontaneously happy life, filled with love of our fellows, contact with beauty, and innocent enjoyments, is not ideally as desirable as a life of saintly patience, heroic endurance of pain, and grim self-mastery?

(4) Granted that this sterner side of character is intrinsically desirable, why did not God create us with such a character to start with? Why should we have to remould ourselves, deny many of the sweetest impulses with which we were endowed, and cultivate new impulses? There may be some satisfaction in being in so far self-made, but who would not exchange that rather vainglorious pleasure for the sake of a strong character from the beginning — not to speak of escaping all the pain and agony of the process. If God could create all this complex and intricate world, create us with all our impulses and delicate adjustments, why could he not have adjusted our impulses a little more exactly, weakened our selfish passions, strengthened our love of purity, of honesty, of service, and thus saved us our stumbling and our sin! The loving human father, if he had the power to give his son better impulses, would be glad to spare the rod; if he could instantaneously give him wisdom and character without the dull routine of grammar and lexicon, without the mistakes and the pain, he would rejoice to do so. The father punishes his child only because of his powerlessness to endow him directly with virtue; it is an unhappy last resort. But is God equally limited in his power? Again we find our problem of evil confronting us, in a but slightly altered form.

Is evil necessary at a stage in the evolution of humanity?

If evil cannot be justified from the point of view of the individual life, can it be said to be a necessary accompaniment of the ascent of mankind from brutehood, to be finally forgiven when it disappears in the millenium to come? Certainly man is conquering, one by one, many of the evils that have plagued him; the individual, thanks to science, has now to suffer far less, on the average, than his ancestors, and another dozen centuries may find man freed from many other of the evils that have cursed his existence. This progress of the race is a legitimate source of pride and pleasure, and the proper goal of our effort; can it also serve as the basis for a satisfactory theodicy?

(1) We see at once that an omnipotent ruler of the universe could not be thus exonerated. For we must not make a fetish of the concept of "progress." The value of progress consists only in the goal attained; and if God is omnipotent, why should he bring men to that goal by a road that involves the suffering of the first few hundreds of billions of his human creatures? Why should he not have given them the fruits that only the later-born are to enjoy? Or at least have made them more intelligent, resourceful, able to progress faster? Think of the kind of life that most men have been vouchsafed! The vast majority of them, counting from the beginning, have grown up amid savage and harsh conditions, without comforts, without arts, with hardly a glimmer of reason or beauty or religion. Naked, half-brutish creatures, fighting one another, feasting gluttonously or starving, as chance offered, knowing no better, stupidly satisfied or dumbly miserable — what beings for an omnipotent God to create! No, the less desirable stages of evolution can only be excused if they were the only feasible way of attaining the higher stages; and to say that they were the only way, that God could not have endowed human nature at its first creation with the wisdom and skill and virtue and physical faculties necessary for a happy life, is very seriously to limit his omnipotence.

(2) Even were we to grant that the method of evolution is, for some reason, intrinsically desirable, is it fair to those who have been sacrificed on the way? Would the lucky generations of earth's hypothetically blissful future wish to buy their happiness, however exquisite, at the price of all the pain that their long line of ancestors will have endured? However great the ultimate balance of joy over sorrow may be, for humanity as a whole, would that overplus of happiness justify the suffering of those, even if they were but a few instead of millions, to whom life brought agony and fear and despair?

(3) Again, if an evolution, an unfolding of potentialities, a ripening of powers, is desirable in itself, there might conceivably have been such a development that should have been beautiful and happy in all its stages, like the growth of a rose from the bud, or the life of an exceptionally fortunate man from healthy childhood through ardent youth to mature age. Each stage might have had its peculiar sweetness, and all might have been free from pain. If animals had not been made carnivorous, if disease-germs and insect pests and poisonous reptiles had been eliminated, if sentient creatures had been made without pain-nerves, and withal had been made less fertile, so as to prevent overcrowding, the earlier stages of evolution might have been, although devoid of much that makes a developed civilization rich and joyous, yet in their own way interesting and pleasant, instead of full of tragedy and pain.

(4) Finally, unless human nature and its earthly environment can be made over far more radically than we can easily conceive possible, life on earth must always have its share of tragedy and pathos and suffering. Accidents will happen, earthquakes and thunderbolts and volcanic eruptions will continue to destroy and maim, fire will burn, falls will bruise; and even if man succeeds in taming his chaotic instincts and

impulses and in preventing physical death, there will remain inevitable forms of suffering and loss which would form a residue of evil still to be accounted for.

Is evil the result of man's perverse use of his free will?

But perhaps evil is due not to the Creator, but to the creatures themselves. Given free choice, they have perversely taken the wrong path, and plunged themselves into all their troubles. No doubt the Creator foresaw their perversity, but deemed it better to give them their freedom, at their own risk, than to endow them with impulses that would inevitably lead them in the ways of safety. There are those who assert that we should not wish a world in which we had no option to choose evil; the dignity that thus accrues to human nature is worth the cost. And if men have brought sorrow upon their own heads, they alone are to blame.

(1) But is this dubious gift of "free will" worth the pain that is thus charged to its account? Surely no humane man, witnessing the suffering of those he loves, would wish to keep his freedom to choose evil at such a price. Would we not really prefer, or *should* we not rationally prefer, to be so made that we could not help doing right, if we might thereby save all the suffering and degradation and sin in the world, satisfy all those longings which, as it is, are so largely destined not to be fulfilled, develop those capacities which have never been unfolded, attain to some measure of that wonderful happiness which we glimpse now only in a few rare and fleeting moments? [1]

[1] Cf. Ruskin, *Athena*, p. 114: "You will send your child, will you, into a room where the table is loaded with sweet wine and fruit — some poisoned, some not? — you will say to him, 'Choose freely, my little child! It is so good for you to have freedom of choice: it forms your character, your individuality! If you take the wrong cup, or the wrong berry, you will die before the day is over, but you will have acquired the dignity of a Free child!'"

(2) But granting "free will" to be a great desideratum, why need there have been any *evils* to choose? Why not simply a great variety of unequally desirable goods, amid which we could exercise our choice to any desired degree? Why need the results of wrong choices have been made so terrible? Or if the presence of potential pain adds a tang which is worth the danger, why should men not have been endowed with a stronger love of the good, a more insistent altruistic instinct, and less imperious impulses that lead to ruin? A world of free agents can be conceived in which all the dignity and satisfaction inhering in the making of choices could coexist with a freedom from suffering, a wrong choice involving at worst the loss of a possible joy.

(3) Whatever our belief may be with reference to the deterministic-indeterministic controversy, at least our conduct is to a very large degree determined by heredity and environment. We choose what we do because we have inherited certain instincts and been under the influence of certain educative and suggestive forces. Is it fair to give us such instincts and impulses, and then to punish us for following them? Not to attempt to answer the now discarded theory that we are involved in the punishment of Adam's primal sin, and supposing that our suffering is the result of our own misdeeds, those misdeeds are the direct result of the animal inheritance which persists in us, which we did not choose and cannot escape. If God created us with such instincts and desires, he is ultimately responsible for the acts into which they lead us.

(4) But after all, it is quite plain that only a small proportion of the suffering in the world can be laid to the door of "free will." It is not merely the wicked that suffer, or the foolish and imprudent. Much of our pain is thrust upon us independently of our volitions. The diseases that torture us, the wild animals that eat us, the lightning and flood and

drought, the drudgery we have to undergo to live at all, death that takes our loved ones from us and stares us all in the face — these evils and many others could not have been removed by the most conscientious exercise of free will. All this evil, and the suffering of the animal world, which must total an enormous amount, must be excused in some other way.

Is evil to be attributed to God at all?

If God is omnipotent, he is ultimately responsible for everything that happens. Since evils exist, it must be because he is willing that they should. Unless the existence of evil is not an evil — and that involves a contradiction in terms — he is content that the world should be less good than it might be. It is not enough to say that he prefers to tolerate these evils rather than involve the world in greater evil or deprive it of its present joys; for if he is omnipotent he can obviate those other evils and secure the joys without permitting these evils. But a God content to have a world with evil in it when he could make it free from evil would be a malevolent Being, unworthy of our worship, and not properly to be called by the sacred name "God." Hence, though we cannot disprove the existence of such a cruel omnipotent Being, it is a far more satisfying conception to believe in a God who is all-good, but unable, for one reason or another, to remove the evil in the world, or to remove it without bringing on greater evils; a God who could perhaps achieve any one good he pleased, but cannot attain an ideal combination of goods. Such a Being may still be so immensely superior in power to any other living being as to deserve a term approaching "omnipotence," especially if his power be great enough ultimately to overcome evil and bring in the millennium. And perhaps this faith in God's final victory is all that is really to be understood by the term.

But omnipotent in the literal sense of the word God cannot be without forfeiting his right to the epithet "good." For either he could not make a better world or he did not wish to. The former is the pleasanter alternative.

By thus giving up, in the literal sense, God's "omnipotence," we not only save his goodness, but we fall more into line with the actual belief of the great majority of Christians. Cling as they may to the comforting thought of his all-powerfulness, they have almost universally refused to attribute to him the bad in the world. Jesus, like the prophets before him, offered no solution of the problem of evil. But he evidently believed in a personal Devil, opposed to God; and popular Christianity has usually been more or less vaguely dualistic, regarding God not as the Principle of all nature, but as the Principle of the Good. If evil is not conceived to spring from the machinations of an Evil Spirit, it may be thought to be due to the obduracy of the material with which God has to work. Or, as in the Platonic-Aristotelian conception, God may be, not the Author of the universe, but its Saviour, not creating it, but drawing it toward his perfectness. The universe is certainly, in some sense, alive; it is acting and developing according to its own inner nature. God may be, instead of its begetter, a Great Power interpenetrating it, working in and through it, and bending its independent life toward we know not what glorious final consummation.

Some such conception has been the stay of many of the noblest souls. "The only admissible moral theory of Creation is that the Principle of Good cannot at once and altogether subdue the powers of evil, either physical or moral. . . . Of all the religious explanations of the order of nature, this alone is neither contradictory to itself or to the facts for which it attempts to account. According to it, man's duty would consist not in simply taking care of his own interests by obeying irresistible power, but in standing forward a not ineffectual auxiliary to a Being of perfect beneficence; a faith which seems much better adapted for nerving him to exertion than a vague and inconsistent reliance on an Author of Good who is supposed to be also the author of evil. And I venture to assert that such has really been, though often unconsciously, the faith of all who have drawn strength and support of any worthy kind from trust in a superintending Providence. There is no subject on which men's practical belief is more incorrectly indicated by the words they use to express it, than religion. . . . Those who have been strengthened in goodness by relying on the sympathizing support of a powerful and good Governor of the world, have, I am satisfied, never really believed that Governor to be, in the strict sense of the term, omnipotent. They have always saved his goodness at the expense of his power. They have believed, perhaps, that he could, if he willed, remove all the thorns from their individual path, but not without causing greater harm to some one else, or frustrating some purpose of greater importance to the general well-being."[1]

[1] J. S. Mill, *Nature* (in *Three Essays on Religion*). Cf. James, *Varieties of Religious Experience*, pp. 132-33: "The gospel of healthy-mindedness casts its vote distinctly for this pluralistic view. Whereas the monistic philosopher finds himself more or less bound to say, as Hegel said, that everything actual is rational, and that evil, as an element dialectically required, must be pinned in and kept and consecrated and have a function awarded to it in the final system of truth, healthy-mindedness refuses to say anything of the sort. Evil, it says, is emphatically irrational, and *not* to be pinned in, or preserved, or consecrated in any final system of truth. It is a pure abomination to the Lord, an alien unreality, a waste element, to be sloughed off and negated, and the very memory of it, if possible, wiped out and forgotten."

And cf. Samuel McChord Crothers (*Among Friends*, p. 235): "The conclusion of pseudo-optimism that 'whatever is is right,' is a dreary conclusion and a travesty on Faith. It is a way of saying that all the ills from which men suffer are irremediable, and that we might as well pretend that we like them. The contention of Ethics is that much that is is wrong, and that it is our privilege to make it right, and the sooner we go about our work the better."

At any rate, if we accept this view, we are absolved from the baffling task of justifying the existence of evil and apologizing for the world as it is. We are not to condone it, we are to hate it, as God hates it, and fight it, as God is fighting it. We are called to be co-workers with God, who needs our help. There will then be no more a problem of evil than there is a problem of good. Or rather, the only problem of evil will be the problem of how quickest to get rid of it, how so to work that future generations will have less of it to bear; and meanwhile, how to bear it ourselves with serenity and inward peace.

J. S. Mill, "Nature," in *Three Essays on Religion; Examination of Sir William Hamilton's Philosophy*, chap. VII. G. Galloway, *Philosophy of Religion*, chap. XIV. B. P. Bowne, *Theism*, pp. 262-86. G. Santayana, *Reason in Religion*, chap. IX. A. M. Fairbairn, *Philosophy of the Christian Religion*, bk. I, chaps. III-IV. Anon., *Evil and Evolution* (Macmillan, 1899). F. Paulsen, *System of Ethics*, bk. II, chaps. III, IV, VIII. G. A. Gordon, *Immortality and the New Theodicy*. E. H. Rowland, *Right to Believe*, chap. V. C. Gore, ed. *Lux Mundi*, chap. III. F. C. Wilm, *Problem of Religion*, chap. VI. J. M. E. McTaggart, *Some Dogmas of Religion*, secs. 171-215. G. T. Ladd, *Philosophy of Religion*, vol. 2, chap. XXXII. T. Caird, *Fundamental Ideas of Christianity*, lects. VIII-XI. A. K. Rogers, *Religious Conception of the World*, pp. 231-60. W. N. Clarke, *Christian Doctrine of God*, pp. 431-62. J. Wedgwood, *The Moral Ideal*, chap. VIII. *Harvard Theological Review*, vol. 7, p. 378. *Hibbert Journal*, vol. 1, p. 425; vol. 2, p. 767.

CHAPTER XXIV

IMMORTALITY

The evolution of the belief in a future life

So accustomed have we of Christian nurture become to faith in a future life, happier than the present, that we are apt to forget how few out of the billions that have lived on earth have shared that anticipation. Yet it is a recent one in man's history. Primitive man, to be sure, in his inability to realize the fact of death, commonly thought of his friends and foes as continuing to exist in some vague and shadowy fashion. Such a ghostly future existence has been believed in by most peoples. But it has been rather dreaded than longed for; it has been seldom thought of as a condition of bliss, as a reward or consolation, but usually as an unavoidable and dubious fate. Homer, for example, in a well-known passage,[1] makes one of his heroes declare that the humblest earthly life is to be preferred to the best estate in the underworld. Many of the more cultivated of the ancients, however, rejected the idea altogether, as a mere superstition, and looked forward calmly to their individual extinction. The hopefulness of Socrates in the matter stands out in sharp contrast to the unbelief of his friends, and evidently occasions them surprise. "'Are you not aware,'" Plato makes him say to Glaucon, "'that the soul is immortal and imperishable?' He looked at me in astonishment, and said: 'No, indeed; you do not mean to say that you are able to prove that.'"[2]

[1] *Odyssey*, bk. XI, 489–91.
[2] *Republic*, 608. Cf. *ibid.*, 330: "Let me tell you, Socrates, that when a

Among the Jews matters stood about the same, a general naïve belief in a pale and rather undesirable future existence in an underworld yielding among the more reflective to a skeptical attitude. King Hezekiah said, when facing death: "I shall go to the gates of the grave, I shall not see Jehovah in the land of the living. . . . The grave cannot praise thee: they that down go into the pit cannot hope for thy truth. The living, the living man alone shall praise thee, as I do this day." [1]

In similar vein the psalmist wrote: "I am counted with them that go down into the pit; I am as a man that hath no strength, free among the dead, like the slain that lie in the grave, whom thou rememberest no more; they are cut off from thy hand . . . Wilt thou show wonders to the dead? Can the dead arise and praise thee? Shall thy loving kindness be declared in the grave, or thy faithfulness in destruction? Shall thy wonders be known in the dark, and thy righteousness in the land of forgetfulness?" [2] And again: "In death there is no remembrance of thee; in the grave who shall give thee thanks?" [3]

The author of the Book of Job, in his vain endeavor to find a solution for the problem of evil, does not attempt to justify evil through its relation to a future and happier life. "There is hope of a tree, if it be cut down, that it will sprout again. But a man dieth, and wasteth away; yea, a man giveth up the ghost, and where is he? As the waters fail from the sea, and the flood decayeth and drieth up, so man lieth

man thinks himself to be near death he has fears and cares which never entered into his mind before; the tales of a life below and the punishment which is exacted there of deeds done here were a laughing matter to him once; but now he is haunted with the thought that they may be true." Cf. also the *Phædo*. It is true, however, that the Greek mystery religions taught a faith in a happy future life. And the Christian conception may owe a great deal to them. This point has not yet been cleared up satisfactorily.

[1] Isa. 38: 9–19.   [2] Ps. 88.   [3] Ps. 6: 5.

IMMORTALITY

down and riseth not; till the heavens be no more, they shall not awake, or be raised out of their sleep. . . . If a man die, shall he live again!"[1]

And in Ecclesiastes we read, "Whatsoever thy hand findeth to do, do it with thy might; for there is no work, nor device, nor knowledge, nor wisdom, in the grave whither thou goest."[2]

The Christian belief in heaven springs from neither the Jewish nor the pagan conception of the underworld-life of departed shades. It comes from a radically different source, namely, the late-Jewish hope in a coming Messianic Kingdom on earth. What the Jews had really thought of and longed for was simply long life on this earth, with children to inherit their name and preserve their memory. But as they lived generation after generation, oppressed, ground under foot by stronger races, they came more and more passionately to believe in an ultimate reversal of affairs, a time when Jehovah should manifest his power and love for them, smite their enemies, and establish an era of prosperity and peace. We have traced in an earlier chapter the rise of this belief, and then its transformation in Gentile minds into the belief in a future life in the skies, whither the faithful should go when the last trump sounded.[3] Gradually, as the expected New Age did not appear, and believers died without participation in it, it came to be held that their souls, separating themselves from the body at death, went at once to their reward in this heavenly region.

The conception of heaven has always been vague and unsatisfactory in Christian thought, but the belief in it remained hardly shaken until the more critical reflection of modern times turned its search-light upon all the traditional dogmas.

[1] Job 14: 7–14.   [2] Eccles. 9: 10.
[3] See pp. 60–62; 75–79; 93–95; 109–111.

What considerations make against the belief?

(1) It takes no critical acumen to perceive the *prima facie* case against immortality. In all our experience a man's conscious life is bound up with the fortunes of his body. We see men stunned by a blow, we see their minds enfeebled by bodily injury, we see their bodies killed and with that their mental life apparently ended. Consciousness seems to be dependent upon the body's supply of food, air, and sleep, and its safety from harm. To suppose that when the bodily mechanism stops entirely, consciousness, which has been so subject to its influence, gains a new lease of life on its own account, has always been difficult for reflective persons. And this explains, no doubt, the pale and impotent existence which the ancients almost universally attributed to the dead.

(2) The rise of modern physiological psychology, showing us, as it does, the intimate correlation of mind and brain, increases the difficulties of faith. We have discovered that thinking tires the brain; or, to put it the other way, the fatigue of brain-cells retards and inhibits thinking. The loss of memory, weakening of the will, increase in petulance of old age go hand in hand with a degeneration of brain-tissue. Certain kinds of consciousness are bound up with specific parts of the brain; when a certain portion of the brain is diseased or injured, the mind is affected in a definite manner. Whatever may be the relation between brain and consciousness, the study of the close parallelism between their activities makes it harder to resist the conviction that the disintegration of the one involves the disintegration of the other.

(3) Moreover, it is difficult to conceive what conscious life can be *like*, without a physical body, with its sense organs and organs of expression. If we cut out of our consciousness

the visual, auditory, tactile, motor, and other bodily produced images, what have we left? Very little if anything. Yet how could we have visual experiences without eyes, or touch-experiences without hands? And, setting aside the questions what sort of consciousness we could have, and how we could communicate with our friends, what would they *mean* to us apart from their bodies? Take away the *look* of your dear one, her facial expression, the light in her eyes, the sound of her voice, the grace of her movements, the touch of her hand, what have you remaining to attract and interest you?

(4) Modern psychology has no longer any use for the concept of "soul." But if there is a "soul," a something inhabiting the body as a tenant, and separable from it at death, where does it abide, how does it get into the body, *when* does it get into the body, when does it leave the body, and how? Do portions of the parents' souls separate themselves, join together with the joining of the germ plasms at conception, to form a new immortal soul? If so, does it remain immortal if the incipient fœtus is ejected from the woman's body, if miscarriage takes place, or the child is still-born? Or does a new soul come somewhence at the moment of birth, and enter the child when it first breathes? The more clearly we realize the continuity of the physical processes of conception, pregnancy, and birth, the more difficult it becomes to know where to interpolate a soul.

(5) A similar continuity is seen to pervade the course of evolution, whereby man has emerged from a brute ancestry. If man is immortal, must not his brute ancestors have been immortal, and their descendants in the diverging, non-human lines? A rather disagreeable alternative seems to be offered. On the one hand, you may say that at a certain point in his ascent, man acquired immortality. If so, there was a time, in the slow evolution of the human type, when

parents who, like all their ancestors, were doomed to die, gave birth to a child who was blessed with an immortal future. By what miracle was this momentous change effected? It seems unfair to the generations preceding. On the other hand, if you postulate no such moment of acquisition of an immortal soul, you must grant immortality to all the animals — and then perhaps to the plants too, for the vegetable and animal kingdoms merge gradually one into the other, just as brutehood grew insensibly into manhood. Many animals are, indeed, more intelligent and more affectionate than human babies, or underwitted men, idiots, and — doubtless — primitive savages; one would like to imagine one's pet dog immortal. But when it comes to tigers and snakes and mosquitoes and bedbugs and cholera microbes, our imagination halts!

(6) Where is the heaven to which souls go at death? It was easy enough for the ancients to picture a heavenly region up above the dome of the sky, easy enough for the evangelist to think of Jesus as having ascended into heaven and sitting there on the right hand of God. But we have long since learned the naïveté of that primitive world-view. We can no longer believe, with Dante, in an island in the Western sea, to which Ulysses could sail, where the mountain of purgatory reaches up to paradise. Nor can we believe that sulphur springs and volcanic steam bubble up from a hades under the earth where departed souls groan in torment. The stellar universe, as we scan it with our telescopes, offers indeed unlimited ports to which we may conceive of ourselves as going; but there seems something grotesque about the fancy of our winging our way to Sirius or the Pleiades. And whatever heaven may lie beyond the stars, millions of millions of miles away, we cannot easily feel so sure of it as the pre-Copernicans did of their paradise of God just above the ninth sphere.

All these skeptical reflections give us, however, nothing but a series of difficulties in the way of belief. They may be met by the reminder that we naturally cannot conceive our future life, because we have no experience thereof. We see only one side of the veil; and all we know is that the departed no longer figure in our earthly existence. In the nature of the case, we cannot disprove immortality; nor does the lack of evidence, in this case, constitute a presumption against it, since, if a future life is a reality, there is no reason to suppose that it is such as to be in contact with, and revealed to, this present life. The relation of mind to brain may be conceived in such a way as to make them separable; and it is easy to formulate answers to the other objections, which, if they have no positive evidence to support them, have equally no evidence against them. We may turn then with open minds to consider the leading arguments for the belief in immortality.

What are the leading arguments for the belief?

(1) The older Christian preaching based its argument for immortality upon the supposedly indubitable fact of the resurrection of Christ. But a critical study of the Gospel narratives has long since shown them to be late, confused, mutually contradictory, and in many respects obviously legendary; more than that, they are at odds with the earliest Christian preaching, as vouched for in the letters of Paul. Paul and the apostles undoubtedly believed themselves to have had revelations of the risen Lord; and that these were genuine revelations we may well believe. But just what their experiences were we shall never know; and that they were mistaken in taking them for revelations of the risen Christ must be admitted to be possible.[1] In any case, that the Messiah, a unique figure with a unique mis-

[1] See above, pp. 82–84 and 288.

sion, should have risen from the dead does not prove that ordinary men can do so. Christ's own words on the matter, and those of Paul and the other early Christian writers, are so sharply at variance with our modern conception of the future life that we cannot use them to support our own faith except by reading into them a meaning foreign to their original intention. For the future life anticipated by Christ, and all of his immediate predecessors, contemporaries, and followers, was a life on earth, with a renovated Jerusalem for its capital, to be preceded by the great Judgment Day, and inaugurated within that generation. Our modern hopes have grown so far away from that naïve conception that the faith of Christ in God and that of the disciples in Christ can hardly serve us as more than a stimulus to an equally daring though necessarily different and less tangible faith.

(2) Another Biblical support for faith, still often used, is Paul's analogy of the seed.[1] Briefly, the idea is this: as a seed seems to die when buried in the ground, but really gives birth to a new life, so may the human body, when dead and buried, pass into a new form of life. When read in the vague and sounding periods of the King James Bible, Paul's rhetoric easily wins assent from the unthinking. But a moment's thought suffices to show how empty it is. There is really no analogy between the buried seed and the buried body; the one, still living, and finding itself in an environment favorable to its growth, proceeds to develop into a plant; the other, which is really dead, disintegrates and returns to dust. The greater life that develops, by physical laws, out of the living seed is still a physical life, continuous with that which preceded; the new life postulated to succeed that of the human body is a non-physical life, invisible, intangible, utterly out of relation to the physical world, in

[1] 1 Cor. 15: 35–44.

which the germination of the seed is a natural and intelligible event. Moreover, at best, the plant produced from a seed is a different plant from that which bore the seed; there is no analogy here that points toward immortality of the individual. Every tree and herb dies in its time; it is only its descendants that survive. The human body has similarly its seed, buried in the mother's womb as the plant's seed is buried in the earth, there to give rise to a new life, which, however, has no continuity of memory or purpose with the parent life. This is the true analogy of the plant seed; there is an indefinitely continued life of the germ plasm, transmitted from body to body. But this is not personal immortality; the individual is only a transient by-product, surviving long enough to hand on the life force to its descendants.

(3) Perhaps the belief in immortality is oftenest held today as a corollary of the belief in God. Since God is good, it is felt, he cannot be so cruel as to deny us our deepest longing, to live on and to have our dear ones live. But the argument is over hasty. If God is not omnipotent, we cannot be sure that he can secure immortality for us. If he is omnipotent, we might suppose that he would not deny us immortality; but in view of the fact that we are denied so much that we should have supposed, *a priori*, that a good God would give us, we cannot be sure that he will not deny us this too. Many evils exist, in spite of God's existence; why not death too? If we were ignorant of the actual fact we might argue with equal cogency that since God is good, he could not be so cruel as to send suffering into the world, pain that crushes, agony that kills. Surely the parallelism of the two arguments should show that both are inconclusive. The fact is, we know as little about God's nature and power as we do about our own future; our trust in a personal Ruler of the universe, who is to triumph over evil,

is as much a venture of faith as our trust in our own immortality, and cannot be used to prove it.

(4) Another argument that figures prominently in current discussions is that which declares that we have an "instinct" or "instinctive longing" for immortality, and that instincts do not exist unless there are objects that can gratify them. In a moderate degree this is true. We have an instinctive wish to live, and we do have an object which can gratify it to some extent — we have some life. But few instinctive longings are gratified to the extent that we could wish; the instinctive longing for love, for power, for pleasure and freedom from pain — which of our longings is more than in slight measure fulfilled? Why may it not be so with our longing for life — we get some, but not nearly so much as we might desire. It is easy to see (to turn from dialectic to history) that those individuals that had some desire to live would be the only ones that would survive the long struggle for existence; this is the actual cause of the presence in us of the desire to live — this very transient earthly life called it forth, not necessarily any heavenly life beckoning from above.

(5) Certain scientific and philosophical speculations have frequently been invoked. The doctrines of the Conservation of Energy and the Persistence of Matter are held to show that nothing can possibly perish; when wood is burned, the same elements continue to exist in altered combinations, and when the body decays its constituents live on in other forms. And indeed, we need not question that the elements that go to make up our personalities persist into the indefinite future. But if those elements, like the body's cells, disintegrate and pass into other forms, would there be possible any continuity of memory or purpose? Consciousness, as the name implies, is an organic whole made up of many elements; only the persistence of this *combination* of elements would, apparently, constitute personal immortality. And

IMMORTALITY

such a continuity the doctrines above mentioned, even considering them proved, cannot guarantee.

Similarly, the "idealistic" metaphysics, which declares everything to be really "mind," or "spirit," and not "matter" at all, even if granted (and it is granted by but a minority of philosophers to-day), can bring us no farther toward a proof of the survival of the individual. To call the stuff of which the world is made "mental" instead of "material" is rhetorically suggestive; but a "mental" world may be as unconcerned with our personal fortunes as a "material" world. Let the universe be throughout a mass of mind stuff, or even a great consciousness, a World-Soul, or Absolute; grant the immortality of that universal life; and we are yet far from any evidence that you and I shall know each other in the future cycles of that Life, or that the ideals dear to us shall be attained.

(6) The only real attempt to bring forward evidence of a future life is that which has been made by the spiritualists and the societies for psychical research, in their investigations of automatic writing, table-turning, and the other trance phenomena, which are often so puzzling and often so uncanny. The study of these facts is still in its infancy; bulky volumes of "proceedings" have been published, and have convinced a few serious students of the reality of communications from departed spirits. But comparatively few scientifically trained men have been convinced by them, and this for several reasons. In the first place, it is by no means demonstrated that other explanations of the phenomena are untenable. The hypothesis of telepathic communication from living people is held by many to account for all the more puzzling facts. Others hold that they can be explained, so far as they are genuine, in terms of the subject's own subconsciousness. Certainly many of these phenomena that were once held to imply spirit-communica-

tion have been definitely relegated to the domain of the psychology of the subconscious, and the presumption is that other phenomena, now inexplicable, will be similarly interpreted as our psychological knowledge widens. A second reason for skepticism lies in the great amount of malobservation and superstition and actual fraud that has been discovered in these matters. Many students become so disgusted with the fraudulent practices in which some of the leading mediums have been caught that they will have nothing more to do with the whole business. In the third place, the sayings and doings of these rapping and squeaking ghosts are, for the most part, so trashy and silly and beneath the dignity of immortal souls, and withal so uncontributive to our knowledge, that serious investigators are apt to lose patience with them. Why do Alexander the Great and Edgar Allan Poe and an Indian Princess (to mention three "spirits" of whose presence, in succession, the writer was once assured) deliver themselves of such closely similar and equally paltry messages?

In reply to these criticisms, the spiritualists admit the existence of much malobservation, and of much fraud; they usually admit the applicability to many cases of the explanations by means of telepathy or the subconsciousness of the subject. But they insist that a residue of genuine phenomena remain, inexplicable save on the spiritistic hypothesis. If the words of the departed seem confused or absurd, it is perhaps because their intrusion into our world is abnormal, and they are unable to send through the veil that separates us more than these hardly articulate messages. It has even been suggested that what we get is their dream-life, which may be as chaotic and absurd as our own. At any rate, we must not reject this mass of unassimilated evidence simply because it is distasteful to us. And if the evidence should point toward a continued existence which is but brief, a gradual fading out of consciousness after death, perhaps, or a future life like that which the ancients imagined, pale, ineffectual, unhappy, at least the actual knowledge that death is not final, that the soul can survive the body's decay, would go far toward encouraging in us the faith toward which we yearn.

In the end, after all our argumentation, pro and con, we must, if we are candid and sincere, admit our ignorance. Eye hath not seen, nor ear heard, aught that takes place beyond the *flamantia mœnia mundi*. We are no better off than the Persian poet who wrote, —

> "Strange, is it not, that of the myriads who
> Before us pass'd the door of Darkness through
> Not one returns to tell us of the Road
> Which to discover we must travel too."

We cannot prove what is the end of all our hearts' desire. If any man think that he can prove it, he is (to echo Kant) just the man we want to see — until we have listened so long to alleged "proofs" that the hope long deferred maketh our hearts sick. Science gives us no evidence; and few philosophers have been able to construct systems that should include personal immortality. Nor is it necessary to believe; our duty is the same in any case. If we cannot believe in a future life, we can set to and make this life brave and glorious. Multitudes of men who have had not even hope in life beyond the grave have found this earthly life full of zest and savor, and have helped to make the lives of their fellows happier and better while they lasted. To sulk, to give way to depression or apathy, because this life were all, would be the part of cowardice and folly; while to give rein to lust and immorality because of a removal of fear of future retribution would be to expose the stupidity and selfishness of a soul that had never grasped the natural worth of virtue or learned to love what is most precious in this life.

But if faith in our future is not absolutely necessary, it yet adds immense vistas and a deep joy to life; it gives a great stimulus to moral endeavor; it brings a salve to sorrow; it takes away the sting from death. And if we cannot prove our faith, we may yet believe where we cannot prove. Cicero declared that he had rather be mistaken with Plato than be in the right with those who deny the life after death; and a noted American scholar, in a recent address, repeated that saying as his confession of faith.[1] Many of us have an almost irresistible feeling that this life cannot be all; that intuition may be right — many of us believe that it *is* right. It would seem that in cherishing that belief we have everything to gain and nothing to lose.

J. G. Frazer, *Belief in Immortality*. F. B. Jevons, *Immortality* (in *Introduction to the Study of Comparative Religion*). E. A. Crawley, *Idea of the Soul*. C. H. Toy, *Judaism and Christianity*, chap. VII. G. B. Cutten, *Psychological Phenomena of Christianity*, chap. XXXI. G. A. Gordon, *Witness to Immortality*. H. E. Fosdick, *Assurance of Immortality*. G. Galloway, *Philosophy of Religion*, pp. 562-74. C. C. Everett, *Theism and the Christian Faith*, chap. XXXIV. L. Abbott, *Theology of an Evolutionist*, chap. XI. J. Martineau, *Study of Religion*, bk. IV. S. D. F. Salmond, *Christian Doctrine of Immortality*. G. L. Dickinson, *Religion and Immortality*. J. S. Mill, *Theism*, pt. III (in *Three Essays on Religion*). J. M. E. McTaggart, *Some Dogmas of Religion*, chap. III. G. Santayana, *Reason in Religion*, chaps. XIII, XIV. *The Ingersoll Lecture Series* (Houghton Mifflin Co.): lectures on immortality by John Fiske, William James, William Osler, etc. W. H. Mallock, *Religion as a Credible Doctrine*, chap. IV. G. Forester, *Faith of an Agnostic*, chap. VI. G. T. Ladd, *Philosophy of Religion*, vol. 2, chaps. XLIV-XLV. A. K. Rogers, *Religious Conception of the World*, pp. 261-84. W. A. Brown, *The Christian Hope*. F. W. H. Myers, *Science and a Future Life*. F. C. S. Schiller, *Riddles of the Sphinx*, chap. XI; *Humanism*, XVII-XIX. *Harvard Theological Review*, vol. 8, p. 45. *Hibbert Journal*, vol. 10, p. 543; vol. 2, p. 722.

---

[1] William Osler, *Science and Immortality*.

CHAPTER XXV

THE VENTURE OF FAITH

THE venture of faith suggested at the close of the preceding chapter brings us to our final problem, which is the practical one concerning our right to believe where we cannot prove. This much debated issue can be divided into three distinct questions, which we will discuss in turn.

Which is the higher ideal, loyal belief or impartial investigation?

The Church has quite generally demanded loyalty to its tenets and branded unbelief as a sin. It has viewed free thought and criticism with distrust and alarm; it has called the spirit of suspended judgment infidelity, and insinuated that doubt is the fruit of an evil life. The desirable man is the "believer," the man who professes confident belief in the doctrines of the Church — which he has probably not investigated with any critical scrutiny and cannot defend with any show of reason — who refuses to harbor any critical reflections, who yields his intellect wholly to the Church's teaching, accepts whatever he is taught, and looks askance at the world of unbelievers outside. Men are urged to stifle any incipient doubts; and all sorts of emotional influences are brought to bear to keep their faith warm and living. Belief, in short, is viewed as a sort of loyalty; and unbelief, if not actual sin, is at least a sad obsession, to be exorcised by any means available.

In sharp contrast with this attitude is the ideal of modern science, the ideal of non-partisanship, of free inquiry and criticism, the temper that looks for evidence before avowing belief and seeks to follow it whithersoever it leads. This cooler-blooded attitude has not, of course, been unknown among theologians; Dr. Taylor, our New England divine, used to say, " Follow truth though it takes you over Niagara!" and Coleridge wrote, in a well-known passage, " He who begins by loving Christianity better than the truth, will proceed by loving his own sect or church better than Christianity and end in loving himself better than all." But on the whole, there has been little passion for truth in the Church, little willingness seriously to admit the possibility of delusion, little ability to look impartially at both sides of the great mooted questions. Its attitude of defense, of guarding the sacred deposit of faith, is only beginning to be discredited by the more judicial, unbiased spirit of science. The genuine scientist is ashamed to accept doctrines on the authority of past teachers who themselves were anything but critical in their temper, ashamed to yield his assent to articles supported by such slight and dubious evidence. Newton laid aside his theory of gravitation for fourteen years because of a discrepancy in his data for the moon's movements. Kepler, Faraday, Darwin, tried hypothesis after hypothesis, and kept their judgment in suspense for scores of years until the patient accumulation of facts seemed to them to warrant a safe conclusion. Does not our easy credulity and our cocksure dogmatism look pretty shallow and complacent by the side of such patient search and abstention?

It is clear that we cannot be really sure that we have the truth, and not illusion, unless we do freely and severely scrutinize the evidence for our beliefs. And if we really prefer the truth to comfort we shall refuse to prejudice our judgment prior to such an inquiry. But more than that. Beliefs affect conduct; and it is of the utmost importance that in adjusting ourselves to our situation in the world we should not let ourselves be blinded by our hopes or prevented by a false loyalty from looking facts squarely in the face. It is a realization of the vital importance of correct belief which led Huxley to speak of "the sin of faith" — "that form of credence which does not fulfil the duty of making a right use of reason, which prostitutes reason by giving assent to propositions which are neither self-evident nor adequately proved." [1] Similarly, Mill writes of "the great intellectual attainment of not believing without evidence." [2] And Clifford, even more emphatically, declares, "Belief . . . is not ours for ourselves, but for humanity. It is rightly used on truths which have been established by long experience and waiting toil, and which have stood in the fierce light of free and fearless questioning. . . . It is desecrated when given to unproved and unquestioned statements. . . . If a man, holding a belief which he was taught in childhood or persuaded of afterwards, keeps down and pushes away any doubts which arise about it in his mind, purposely avoids the reading of books and the company of men that call in question or discuss it, and regards as impious those questions which cannot easily be asked without disturbing it — the life of that man is one long sin against mankind." [3]

---

[1] *Life and Letters*, vol. II, p. 427. Cf. also this passage from a letter to Charles Kingsley (vol. I, p. 233), written after the death of his beloved son, in reply to Kingsley's plea for faith in immortality as a necessary comfort in such grief: "Had I lived a couple of centuries earlier I could have fancied a devil scoffing at me and them, and asking me what profit it was to have stripped myself of the hopes and consolations of the mass of mankind. To which my only reply was and is, O devil! truth is better than much profit. I have searched over the grounds of my belief; and if wife and child and name and fame were all to be lost to me one after the other as the penalty, still I will not lie."

[2] *Essay on Berkeley*.

[3] *The Ethics of Belief*, in *Lectures and Essays*, vol. II.

This rigorous self-restraint in belief is not a more intellectual feat, it is a moral victory. Facing as we do to-day political and social problems of the deepest importance, problems wrapped at best in perplexity, but made vastly more difficult through prejudice and passion, the habit of basing convictions on evidence, and not upon personal preference, or bias, or unquestioned authority, is an essential of good citizenship. Led this way by class interest, pulled that way by the easy hope that to most men so readily becomes belief, blinded by appeals to the emotions and duped by vague and superficial arguments, the man who has not accustomed himself to forming his judgments disinterestedly and accurately, as the facts point, will not be the man who will truly serve his country or the world. Not he who doubts and questions is the infidel, the unfaithful man, but he who lazily accepts what he is taught, or selfishly adopts a faith which pleases him, who makes his judgment blind, and lets himself be seduced by

"Sweet comforts false, worse than true wrongs."

Moreover, there is something absurd in the spectacle of a host of different churches, each demanding allegiance to its particular brand of doctrine, each seeking not the real facts in the case but the promulgation of its inherited and loyally espoused view of the facts. Not in any such way can Christian unity come, or any general knowledge of the real truth about our situation. Matters have indeed improved; but there is room for much further improvement. "A century ago we were all eyes for the errors of every religious body but our own; to-day we are recognizing the truth in one another's positions; but there is one more stage, and that is for each to awaken to the *errors* in his *own* views — and that is the hardest stage of all." [1] It is

[1] B. S. Streeter, *Restatement and Reunion*, p. 58.

necessary for us to realize that, however confident we may be in our accustomed views, we may be wrong. There are doubtless many facts we have not considered, many arguments to which we have never given a really fair hearing. We must not lazily assume the truth of inherited beliefs, or confine our reading to books that support our favorite notions. We must never consider any matter definitely settled so long as any doubt lingers in our minds. We must be willing to apply the same standards of evidence to our religion as to any other, the same methods of historical study to the Bible as to the Koran or the Zend-Avesta. We must be fair to all sides of a question, never shunning or suppressing evidence, never coloring our statements of the facts. We must not frown on the spirit of free inquiry in others, even when they question doctrines which to us are precious and beyond doubt. We must not fear for ourselves the leading of the evidence, or be unwilling to give up, if need be, whatever is most hallowed by old associations and most dearly cherished in our hearts. For there is no lasting safety in illusions, and no end of controversy or ultimate rest for the spirit of man but in the truth.

This does not mean that we should rudely thrust our doubts upon everybody we meet, or set atheistic literature before our boys and girls at every stage in their education. But it does mean that we should refuse to drug our own intellects and those of others over whom we have influence, or to prefer a stupid acquiescence to the pangs of growth. To him who has but just begun to doubt his creed the way back is usually still open, if the comfort and peace of his early faith weighs more with him than the pursuit of truth. Many a young man, beginning the study of life, finds the old assumptions tottering in his mind, and, unable to face the pain of losing what is so precious to him, runs away from the dangerous studies, devotes himself with renewed ardor to his espoused cause, and so encases himself in the shell of habit that he soon forgets the doubts that troubled him. He follows, in spirit, Pascal's cynical advice to the waverer, to take the holy water and say the masses; "that will stupefy you and make you believe again!" — *Ça vous abêtira et vous fera croire*. That stupefying of the intellect, that reducing it to the level of the beasts — *ça vous abêtira* — is a high price to pay for the consolation of the faith. Yet if it were impossible to make life strong and useful and full of cheer without it, we might well prefer, if we could do so, to sacrifice truth to happiness. But it is not impossible to be truly pious and yet scrupulous lovers of truth; it is not necessary to flinch from facts to make our religious life earnest and strong and devout. It is possible, while keeping our spiritual life aglow, to keep our intellectual integrity, to strip ourselves of irresponsible beliefs, and, however sure we may feel of this doctrine or that, to keep always a window open toward the light.

Should we accept or reject beliefs of whose evidence we are uncertain?

It seems hardly debatable that loyalty to the truth, or to whatever probability the evidence may seem to us individually to suggest, is to be set above loyalty to any authority of creed or dogma. But what are we to do in cases where there is no convincing evidence one way or the other, or where we are unable to satisfy ourselves of its leading? The more rigorous of the scientifically minded insist that in all such cases, where we have not found sufficient evidence to convince our reason, we must remain agnostic, keep our judgment in suspense, refuse to entertain any opinion. Clifford asserts roundly that "it is wrong always, everywhere, and for any one, to believe anything upon insufficient evidence. 'But,' says one, 'I am a busy man; I have no time for the long course of study which would be necessary to make me in any degree a competent judge of certain questions, or even able to understand the nature of the arguments.' Then he should have no time to believe."

But, declares the practical man, this limitation of belief is impracticable and undesirable. The beliefs which are so clearly evidenced as to be beyond doubt are not enough to live upon; we need to hold, at least provisionally, some belief concerning matters about which evidence is lacking one way or the other. To keep our minds a blank and refuse to decide at all would be to paralyze our action. Some choice is forced upon us: we have not only a right, but a duty, to adopt, at our own risk, one conjecture or the other, and act upon it. The youth has to ask himself the question, Will it be best for me to study this, or to study that? to enter this vocation, or that? He cannot have enough knowledge of his own powers and talents, or of the untried tasks into which his choice will lead him, to feel sure that he is judging aright. But decide one way or the other he must. His vocation is a venture of faith. So is his marriage, and parenthood, and a host of other undertakings. The man who should refuse to let faith have its way in any of these matters would amount to nothing, would lose his chance to count in the world. In the world of belief, as in the world of action — and, for that matter, the two are inseparably connected — it is, nothing venture nothing have.

Indeed, as William James pointed out in his now famous essay, we run as great a risk in not believing as in believing. "Believe truth? Shun error! — these are two materially different laws; and by choosing between them we may end by coloring differently our whole intellectual life. We may regard the chase for truth as paramount, and the avoidance of error as secondary; or we may, on the other hand, treat the avoidance of error as more imperative, and let truth take its chance. Clifford exhorts us to the latter course. Believe nothing, he tells us, keep your mind in suspense forever, rather than by closing it on insufficient evidence incur the awful risk of believing lies. You, on the other hand, may think that the risk of being in error is a very small matter when compared with the blessings of real knowledge, and be ready to be duped many times in your investigation rather than postpone indefinitely the chance of guessing true. . . . Dupery for dupery, what proof is there that dupery through hope is so much worse than dupery through fear? I, for one, can see no proof; and I simply refuse obedience to the scientist's command to imitate his kind of option, in a case where my own stake is important enough to give me the right to choose my own form of risk." [1]

No doubt we must discriminate between different types of situation. There are cases, where the decision has little or no practical bearing, where we may best keep our minds in the state of suspended judgment, in order not to bias our investigation or that of others. There are, further, cases of great importance, where we must check our belief from outrunning the evidence, because a hasty and ill-founded belief may be a wrong to some one. Clifford's shipowner should, indeed, have been especially slow to believe in the seaworthiness of his vessel, because that belief, if false, was pregnant with danger to those who might embark. A jury should be extra cautious about believing in the guilt of a man whom they have power to send to prison or the gallows. We should all hesitate long before believing a muckraker or a gossip, before believing in the guilt of a friend, or in the perfidy of a neighboring nation. Readiness to believe what it is to our material advantage, and some one else's disadvantage, that we believe, or what might

[1] *The Will to Believe*, pp. 18, 27.

involve us in a terrible and unnecessary war, is a grave fault and cannot be too severely rebuked.

On the other hand, there are cases where the risk in not believing seems to be greater than that in believing. Will this course of treatment cure my sickness? I may have little to go on in trusting it; but if I refuse my belief I lose that chance of being cured. Will the use of alcohol hurt me? I may not be convinced by the evidence shown me that it will; but unless I believe that it will, and avoid it, I run the risk of irreparable injury. Shall I believe in a personal God? The argument may seem to be weak; but the risk seems to be greater in losing the comfort of a belief that may be true than in enjoying a belief that may be false. The fact is that, in these matters, not to believe is, practically, to disbelieve. To refuse to believe in a personal God means to go without the sense of his companionship and care almost, if not quite, as much as if we flatly disbelieved. If the evidence is not strong, one way or the other, why should we not choose to avoid the greater danger, and accept, provisionally, some working belief, as we would use a temporary bridge or building, in order that our practical life may not be checked by a needlessly hesitating caution?

Certainly in such cases we should not forget that we are dealing with possibilities only, that we are making a venture of faith. We should be tentative and humble in our assertions of belief, always maintaining the distinction between working hypotheses and well-evidenced conclusions, never erecting our personal faith into dogma or thrusting it rudely upon others. For the sake of all clearness of thought, for the sake of freedom from discord and strife, above all, for the sake of the dignity and repute of our religion, we must cease from our cocksure assertion of these beliefs that we cannot prove, cease from using them as a requisite of piety. But with these cautions in mind, there seems to be no real reason why we should not allow our minds to run far beyond the little mass of observations and inferences that we have as yet accumulated, and adopt, as working hypotheses, any conjectures or hopes that can serve as a useful basis for our practical activity.

May non-evidential motives properly influence belief?

If we agree that belief may properly, on occasion, outstrip evidence, we have yet to consider whether these working hypotheses, these over-beliefs, may be influenced by non-evidential motives. In simpler phrase, may we let ourselves be guided by our desires? Is the "will to believe" legitimate?

Not a few, the Cliffords, the Huxleys, and other men of fine scruples, insist that to allow our wish to be father to belief is to corrupt our intellects. To refuse to face the fact of our actual ignorance, and let the mind dwell only upon the most palatable possibilities, is a sort of dreaming that is cowardly and demoralizing. Moreover, there is something childishly silly in thus dwelling in heavens of our own invention instead of recognizing our actual situation and making the best of it. "There is that to my own perception in honeyed theories of our place or prospects as men, in postulates of a golden solution of things, fetched from whatever heaven of invention, which are accredited because so eminently to our taste, — there is that in the sight of the constructive postulator, fancy-free, busy at his landscape-gardening in the infinite — which is not so noticeably immoral as ridiculous." [1]

To such asceticism of belief we must all give great honor. In a world where few question seriously the views which form their particular intellectual environment, and fewer still weigh impartially the evidence on matters that affect

[1] D. S. Miller, in *International Journal of Ethics*, vol. 9, p. 169.

their happiness, the refusal to be influenced by the congeniality of a conception is a very rare and admirable virtue. But is it necessary? The venture of faith in what is consoling and inspiring will not mean a tampering with the truth or vitiating our intellectual integrity, if we keep these over-beliefs as personal and provisional, clearly discriminating between them and those beliefs that rest upon evidence. It is not ridiculous, if these beliefs do really console and inspire us. In cases where we really do not know, to seek to deprive men of their conviction that their happiest hopes are well founded, is to diminish human happiness unwarrantably. It may be seriously urged, indeed, that it is our duty to cherish optimistic beliefs, of whatever sort are plausible to our particular minds, to "accept the richer of two unproved possibilities," since hopefulness is a great stimulant to energy and addition to the worth of life.

Certain cases, at least, seem clear. When believing in a desirable future fact may help to bring that fact about, it would be wrong to refuse to utilize this means. James gives us the case of the Alpine climber who must leap a chasm to extricate himself from an unlucky situation. A strict accounting of the evidence gained from his past experience might suggest grave doubts as to his ability to make the leap in safety. Must he then refuse to make the venture of faith? But precisely that faith is needed to nerve his powers and make its object actual. So in every man's life there are occasions when belief in one's self or in others may make a real difference in the outcome. Must a mother refuse to allow herself to believe in the morality of her son, in his abilities, and success? But many a son who, according to the evidence at hand, has seemed to others worthless, has been actually saved and made into a man by this blind belief of his mother. A lover's belief that he can win the girl of his desire, my belief that you like me, the patriot's belief that his country will be victorious in war, may help in the attaining of the object coveted. To abstain from faith, even in a forlorn hope, under such circumstances, might involve a practical loss for which the value of the intellectual scrupulousness could hardly compensate.

But in other cases also, where no practical consequences are involved, to let belief follow desire seems innocent. To believe in the safety of dear ones whom you know to be in danger, or in your own safe emergence from a dangerous situation, even though that belief can in no wise affect the outcome, seems clear gain. Why should we not live as long as we can in the presence of these more hopeful thoughts? Even if they turn out to be mistaken, we shall have been for so long the happier. So it seems to be with the beliefs in immortality, in the personality of God, and the other matters where evidence fails us. Our highest hopes may turn out to be true—*we believe they will*. Why should we then keep reminding ourselves that they are, after all, but hopes, and darkening our horizon by the reminder of our ignorance? We know, after all, so little; the uncharted is vastly greater than the little fragments of reality we understand. As regards all the infinite deeps beyond our gaze, let us be unashamed to trust our hopes.

We must, of course, hold all these over-beliefs open to revision when evidence appears; we must not let the "will to believe" deter us from the tedious and worrisome process of investigation and criticism; we must not pretend that our hopes are proved simply because we hold them personally with conviction; we must not suppose that our faiths are truths "above reason," or that their comforting power is a proof of their truth. Above all, we must not thrust them dogmatically upon others or make them a requirement of admission to our Church. We must not seek to *base* our religion upon our unproved hopes; Christianity has too much that is empirically verifiable for it to be rested upon foundations that may, even conceivably, be shaken. But we may well let our religion flower into these beautiful hopes as its sweetest development and consummation.

The legitimacy of a personal faith of this sort has been urged not only by theologians and churchmen but by many men of rationalistic temper and ideals. John Stuart Mill, keen critic and cautious reasoner, ends his very radical book, *Three Essays on Religion*, with this thought: "To me it seems that human life, small and confined as it is . . . stands greatly in need of any wider range of aspiration for itself and its destination, which the exercise of imagination can yield to it without running counter to the evidence of fact; and that it is a part of wisdom to make the most of any, even small, probabilities on this subject, which furnish imagination with any footing to support itself upon. And I am satisfied that the cultivation of such a tendency in the imagination, provided it goes on *pari passu* with the cultivation of severe reason, has no necessary tendency to pervert the judgment; but that it is possible to form a perfectly sober estimate of the evidence on both sides of a question and yet to let the imagination dwell by preference on those possibilities which are at once the most comforting and the most improving, without in the least degree overrating the solidity of the grounds for expecting that these rather than any others will be the possibilities actually realized. Though this is not in the number of the practical maxims handed down by tradition and recognized as rules for the conduct of life, a great part of the happiness of life depends upon the tacit observance of it. . . . On these principles it appears to me that the indulgence of hope with regard to the government of the universe and the destiny of man after death, while we recognize as a clear truth that we have no ground for more than a hope, is legitimate and philosophically defensible."

A more recent writer has phrased the same ideal as follows: "What I have wished to indicate is an attitude of what I may call active expectancy — the attitude of a man who, while candidly recognizing that he does not know, and faithfully pursuing or awaiting knowledge, and ready to accept it when it comes, yet centers meantime his emotional, and therefore his practical life about a possibility which he selects because of its value, its desirability. . . . When I speak here of faith, I speak of an attitude which is not primarily intellectual at all, and which is quite compatible with — nay, which depends upon — intellectual agnosticism; for it presupposes that, in the region to which it applies, we do not know. The attitude I would describe is one of the emotions and the will — the laying hold, in the midst of ignorance, of a possibility that may be true, and directing our feelings and our conduct in accordance with it. . . . [This] attitude is different in its origin and effect from an attitude based upon knowledge. It is more precarious, more adventurous, more exciting, more liable to ups and downs. But it may be equally and even more efficacious upon life; and it is not necessarily to be condemned as illegitimate."[1]

But can we not say even more than this? Such a faith in the meaning and destiny of life is not only legitimate, it is almost necessary, for most men, for the richest unfolding of their energies and the deepest dedication to their ideals. The men who have done great things are the men who have had faith in something, a faith held perhaps in spite of appearances or of ridicule, a faith that they followed like a guiding star through long years of patient labor and utmost sacrifice. Alexander, with his faith in the irresistible power

[1] G. L. Dickinson, *Religion, A Criticism and a Forecast*, pp. ix–x; 78–80. (Condensed.)

of his Hellenic phalanx; Paul, with his faith that his Gospel could redeem the world; Cecil Rhodes and the other empire-builders, with their faith in the future of the lands to which they gave their lives — such are the men who have pushed humanity along the path of progress. Can we not almost say that to be great is to cherish some such faith and let it dominate every hour? The patriot has faith in his country, the lover in his lady, the religious man in his God. Why should we not believe — earnestly, eagerly, as the patriot does, ardently, passionately, as the lover does? What if we should be mistaken? Even so, it will be better to have believed. But however mistaken the particular form of our hopes may be, nothing can shake our conviction that somehow good will triumph over evil, that some great destiny awaits us which will justify the patience and the passion of our faith.

W. K. Clifford, *Ethics of Belief, Ethics of Religion* (in *Lectures and Essays*, vol. II). W. James, *Will to Believe*, title essay; *Some Problems of Philosophy*, Appendix. *International Journal of Ethics*, vol. 9, p. 169; vol. 19, p. 212. E. H. Rowland, *Right to Believe*, chap. I. H. Sidgwick, *Ethics of Religion* (in *Practical Ethics*). G. L. Dickinson, *Religion, A Criticism and Forecast*, chap. IV; *Religion and Immortality*, chap. I. J. S. Mill, *Theism*, pt. v. L. Stephen, *An Agnostic's Apology*. T. H. Huxley, *Science and the Christian Tradition*, chaps. VII–IX. W. E. H. Lecky, *Map of Life*, chap. XI. A. H. Lloyd, *Will to Doubt*. G. S. Fullerton, *World We Live In*, chap. XVIII. B. W. Bode, *Outline of Logic*, chap. XV. *Harvard Theological Review*, vol. 3, p. 294.

SUMMARY OF PART III

What is the present status of theology?

WE have now passed in rapid review the leading arguments of contemporary religious philosophy. Much that was irrational and mistaken in the older tradition has long been exposed; on the whole, a far saner view of life and of religion prevails than among church-people of even a generation ago. But if we are candid, we must admit that upon its constructive side theology has less to show. We can raise far more problems than we can solve; and we know far less about the great enigmas than men once thought they knew. The situation is far from satisfactory: theology has been overhasty, unwisely dogmatic, and, for the most part, committed to an untenable method. But we need not despair. Already attempts at an empirical theology are appearing; the near future may show a great advance in this, the last field to be occupied by science. We await new philosophies. But in the meantime our duty is, in the main, clear; we are to serve and to work during the day. The ultimate outcome of our labors we cannot see; but perhaps it will be far greater than we dare to dream.

In any case, the religious experience rapidly surveyed in Part II of this volume remains unquestionable, however dubious the interpretations and inferences that have been based upon it. There is a way to transform life, to give it dignity and imperishable worth; religon has found that way, and remains the best thing in the world. And as for those beliefs that transcend experience, they may well be true, or adumbrations of something that is true, even if

SUMMARY OF PART III

the arguments by which they have usually been supported are weak and fallacious. We shall be told that men want something more definite, more sure. And with that want, that hunger of the heart, we can all sympathize. What would we not give to pierce the veil! But the trouble with the "definite" dogmas is that they are definitely assumptions, definitely presumptuous, surely unproved. The Church must be willing to acknowledge this; the world outside knows it, and discredits the Church for its blindness, or its unwillingness to admit the limitations of our present knowledge. The situation is not so soothing to our wistful wonderings as we should like, but it is vastly stimulating. The whole movement of theology, comparative failure as it has been, witnesses monumentally to man's indestructible sense that his ideals count in a greater world than here and now, that human life has a wider setting, that the struggle between good and evil has a cosmic significance and is but paving the way for a consummation of which our Christian hope has been, however inadequately, a symbol. This is the larger significance of the belief in God. That belief, in some form or other, man, whatever his future history may be, will never abandon. "A religion without a great hope is like an altar without a living fire." And Christianity, not only because of the insight and profundity of its ideals, but because of the splendid sweep of its cosmic hope, is probably destined to be, in some developed and rationalized form, the religion of the future.

In conclusion, the practical corollaries of the point of view from which this volume has been written may be gathered into a brief summary: We must be open-eyed and open-minded, keeping our intellectual integrity, never closing the window to new light, always ready to revise our beliefs when new evidence appears. We must recognize the difference between the assured conclusions of science and those personal over-beliefs, which, however passionately we may espouse them, stand upon a different level and cannot serve as bases for a universal religion. We must not delude ourselves into thinking that we know more than we do, or trouble ourselves over the limitations of our knowledge. We must be tolerant and sympathetic toward the beliefs of others, never thrusting our own beliefs dogmatically upon them, but sincerely seeking to learn from them as well as to win them to what seems to us good and true. We must learn to see God in human life, to love, fear, and seek God, as the guiding motive of our lives. We must cleave through all temptation to the way of life that Christ revealed, and that he lived, that we may find therein the joy and peace and power to serve that is our birthright. We must believe in prayer, and utilize this means, as well as the institution of the Church, for the deepening and purifying of our spiritual life. We must believe in and work for the coming of the Kingdom of God on earth, the time when righteousness shall reign and men shall live as brothers together. We must believe, so far as in us lies, in the power of the human soul to live beyond the grave, in the ultimate victory of good over evil, and the greatness of our destiny. We must seek to bring together the scattered forces of the Church, finding some common platform or covenant upon which men of good will the world over can unite for that age-long war with sin and suffering which it is the great mission of religion to wage. As a suggestion toward such a common covenant, and as an epitome of the spirit that has animated this volume, the writer would append this brief profession of his personal faith: —

I believe in God, the Eternal Power that makes for righteousness and all good: known to us in Nature, speaking to us as the Holy Spirit in our hearts, incarnate in the soul of Christ. I believe in the Way of Life taught by Christ, in the Bible as a revelation of God, and in the power of prayer unto Salvation. I pledge myself to live by the eternal laws of God, looking unto Christ for guidance and strength; to resist unto the end all sensuality, selfishness and sin; to work loyally with the Church of Christ for the coming of the Kingdom of God on earth; and to cherish the hope of eternal life.

INDEX

INDEX

Abelard, 176.
Abnormal experiences as a source of religious beliefs, 14, 171, 317, 319.
Absolute, the, 347, 349, 393.
Adam, J., 25.
Adams, G. P., 208.
Adler, Felix, 225.
Æneas, 32.
Æschylus, 25.
Ahriman, 46.
Allen, Grant, 14, 100.
Ahura-Mazda, 46.
Ambrose, 115, 199.
Amiel, H. F., 208.
Amos, 57.
Analogy, argument from, 303.
Angro-Mainyu, 46.
Animal-worship, 52.
Animism, 11, 22, 31, 37.
Anselm, 175.
Antioch, council of, 89.
A priori reasoning, 252, 255, 282.
Aquinas, Thomas, 111, 175, 252.
Aristides, 97.
Aristotle, 380.
Ark, the, 54, 155.
Arnold, Matthew, 4, 6, 60, 72, 141, 144, 146, 149, 159, 185, 193, 218, 223, 287, 293.
Aryan religion, 21, 26, 31, 36, 45, 49.
Ascension, 251, 287, 388.
Asceticism, 157.
Asoka, 44.
Atheism, 141, 146, 217, 332.
Athene, 30, 33, 130.
Atonement, the 104, 153, 174.
Augustine. *See* St. Augustine.
Aurelius, Marcus, 131, 201, 206, 209.
Authority, 249, 255, 275.
Aveling, F., 295, 299, 302, 321.
Avesta, 46.

Baals, 52, 130.
Bacon, B. W., 65, 88.

Bacon, Francis, 253.
Bahaism, 211, 231.
Balfour, Arthur, 351, 352, 354, 355, 358.
Baptism, 67, 167.
Beard, C., 119.
Bergson, H., 283.
Bible, editions of, 49, 66; value of, 57, 60, 273, 276; attitude of Protestants toward, 118, 121, 260, 274; dogma of its infallibility, 249, 260, 265; composition of, 264; criticism of, 267; authority of, 275. *See also* Old Testament, New Testament.
Bigg, C., 232.
Bishops, origin of, 113, of Rome, 114.
Bloomfield, M., 37.
Bode, B. W., 328.
Bousset, W., 75.
Boutroux, E., 255.
Bowen, C. R., 84.
Bowne, B. P., 298, 299.
Brahma, 37.
Brahmanism, 36, 130, 207, 314.
Bruno, 252, 261.
Buddha, 38, 130, 206.
Buddhism, 36, 131, 156, 203, 217.
Burgon, Dean, 267.
Burkitt, F. C., 66.
Burma, religion in, 42.
Butler, Bishop, 121.

Calkins, M. W., 190.
Calvin, 119, 130, 261, 276.
Calvinism, 119.
Campbell, R. J., 142.
Canon, origin of, 265.
Caritas, 93, 201.
Carlyle, T., 137, 221, 237, 280, 289.
Carpenter, J. E., 39, 66.
Carter, J. B., 32.
Carus, P., 110.
Case, S. J., 236.

INDEX

Catholic. *See* Roman Catholic.
Celibacy, 117, 158.
Channing, W. E., 120, 121, 122, 163.
Charles, R. H., 62.
Chesterton, G. K., 29.
Chivalry, 199.
Christ, his teaching, 39, 44, 75, 115, 171, 206, 231, 289, 293, 316; his life, 63; his healing, 67, 284, 287, 288, 289, 314, 325; meaning of the name, 68; his personality, 72, 143, 233, 239, 278; his resurrection, 72, 82, 84, 287, 288, 291; his genealogy, 75, 270; deification of, 106, 142; divinity of, 142, 236; his power to save, 167, 174, 186, 236; belief in, 238.
Christian Science, 38, 123, 183, 206, 209, 284, 313, 325, 347, 368, 370.
Christianity, contrasted with other religions, 1, 43, 229; primitive, 82, 97, 104, 239; causes of its triumph, 96, 131, 259, 325; modern, 119; its nature, 231, 244; its need of growth, 236; Christless, 238. *See also* Christ, Church, Protestantism, Reformation, etc.
Church, the, its present needs, 2, 4, 233, 258; its origin, 82, 113; its development, 98, 123, 236, 250; need of, 241; its opposition to free thought, 258, 397, 413. *See also* Christianity, Papacy, Sacraments, Reformation, Protestantism, Creeds, Dogma, Authority, Roman Catholic Church, Greek Orthodox Church, etc.
Cicero, 307, 396.
Clemens, S. L., 211.
Clifford, W. T., 399, 402.
Coe, G. A., 173.
Coleridge, S. T., 398.
Color-blindness, 359.
Comte, Auguste, 217, 334.
Confessional, 117.
Conscience, 16, 320.
Consciousness, 301, 386, 392.
Conservation of energy, 392.
Constantine, 99, 199.
Conversion, 167, 168, 244, 281, 284, 314, 322.
Cornill, C. H., 49.

Coulanges, F. de, 213.
Counter-Reformation, 116.
Covenant, 152, 240, 266.
Creation, 16, 270, 295, 303, 380.
Creeds, evolution of, 98; Athanasian, Nicene, Apostles', 102; relation of to religion, 215, 239.
Criticism, need of, 3, 401; meaning of, 267.
Crooker, T. H., 191.
Cross, preaching of the, 92, 231.
Crothers, S. M., 381.
Crusades, 199.
Cumont, F., 24.
Cutten, G. B., 207, 211.

Dante, 111, 130, 206.
Darwin, 198, 304, 398.
Decalogue, 51, 141.
Delahaye, H., 285.
Deliverance from sin, need of, 16, 41, 96, 105, 167.
Democritus, 304.
Design, 302, 349.
Deuteronomy, 55, 265.
Deva, 46.
Devil, 110, 174, 380.
Dewey, J., 338.
Dewey and Tufts, 185, 301.
Dickinson, G. L., 216, 257, 329, 339, 343, 410.
Dobschütz, E. von, 78.
Dogma, growth of, 98, 115, 239, 260; dangers of, 215, 250. *See also* Creeds, Orthodoxy, etc.
Dole, C. F., 238.
Dowie, John Alexander, 123.
Drake, Durant, 17, 18, 129, 158, 301, 361.
Dreams, significance for early religion, 13.
Driesch, H., 283.
Driver, Canon, 268.
Dualism, 46, 175.
Duty, 42, 140, 160, 224, 321, 335.
Dyaus, 22.

Ecclesiasticism. *See* Church, Creeds, Dogma, Sacraments, Authority, Priests, etc.
Eddy, Mary B. G., 210, 368.
Edghill, E. A., 97, 211.

INDEX

Edwards, Jonathan, 119, 120, 163.
Eleusis, 23.
Elijah, 57.
Elohim, 50.
Emerson, R. W., 20, 72, 138, 140, 163, 208, 212, 217, 219, 337.
Emotion in religion, 214, 341.
Empirical method in theology, 121.
Ennius, 32.
Ephesus, Council of, 109.
Epistles, 265, 266, 269.
Eugenics, 164.
Euripides, 28, 30.
Eusebius, 201.
Evangelism, 171, 173, 233.
Everett, C. C., 110, 121.
Evil, problem of, 210, 384; the war against, 233, 366, 382.
Evolution, 304, 306, 375, 387.
Exile, the, 55.
Ezekiel, 52.
Ezra, 265.

Fairweather, W., 62.
Faith, 180, 245, 396, 397; salvation by, 91, 105, 180, 245.
Faith-cures, 325. *See also* Faith, salvation by; Christian Science; Christ, his healing.
Fall, the, 164.
Farwell, L. R., 30.
Farquhar, J. N., 45.
Farrar, Dean, 5.
Fechner, G. T., 347.
First Cause, 295.
Fiske, John, 148.
Fitch, A. P., 220, 314, 342.
Fletcher, Horace, 211.
Foster, G. B., 255, 261.
Fourth Gospel, 64, 107, 144, 236, 239.
Free will, 377.
Friedlander, G., 100.
Fullerton, G. S., 299.
Future Life. *See* Immortality.

Galileo, 252, 261.
Galloway, G., 225, 314, 318, 329, 339, 342, 347.
Gautama. *See* Buddha.
George, H. B., 268.
Ghost-theory, 13.

Glossalalia. *See* Tongues, speaking with.
Gnosticism, 91.
God, historic conceptions of, 50, 56, 79, 106, 119, 120, 125, 175, 270; in nature, 135; nature of, 135, 145, 217, 291, 293, 316, 322, 327, 413; fear of, 140; in man, 142, 237; love of, 202; as Creator, 295, 303; pragmatic arguments for, 342, 346, 349; omnipotence of, 368, 379, 391.
Goethe, 227, 322.
Goodspeed, G. S., 61.
Gordon, G. A., 293.
Gospels, 65, 266, 269, 287. *See also* Fourth Gospel.
Gray, G. B., 66.
Greek Orthodox Church, 115, 154.
Greek philosophy, 24, 100, 103, 130, 223, 258.
Greek religion, 20, 284.
Green, T. H., 183, 232.

Hall, H. Fielding, 12, 43, 214.
Hall, J. J., 163.
Hannay, J. D., 159.
Harmony of the Gospels, 66, 287.
Harnack, A., 102, 109.
Harrison, J. E., 14, 24.
Hatch, E., 241.
Haupt, P., 49.
Heaven, 109, 130, 166, 285.
Hebrew religion, 49, 131, 265, 274. *See also* Prophets of Israel, Psalms, Messianic hope, etc.
Hell, 109, 130, 166, 176, 271.
Helmholz, 308.
Heresy, 259.
Hermits, 157.
Herodotus, 286.
Hesiod, 22.
Hierocles, Song of, 156.
Hilty, Carl, 344.
Höffding, H., 318.
Holley, H., 231.
Holmes, Edmond, 163.
Holtzmann, O., 66, 113, 114, 325.
Holy Spirit. *See* Spirit, Holy.
Homer, 22, 27, 383.
Horace, 34.
Hosea, 58.
Hume, David, 282.

Huss, 116.
Huxley, H., 257, 283, 399.
Hypatia, 260.

Idealism, objective, 347, 393.
Immortality, 109, 291, 383.
Incarnation, the, 100, 142, 237.
Inconceivability, 355.
India, religion in, 26, 36.
Infallibility of the Pope, 115; of the Bible, 249; of the Church, 250.
Inge, W. R., 185, 207.
Innocent III, 115.
Inspiration, 264, 272, 273.
Instincts, trustworthiness of, 340, 392.
Intuition, 330.
Isaiah, 58, 200, 269.
Isis, 34.
Israel. *See* Hebrew religions, Prophets of Israel, etc.

Jackson, H. L., 78.
Jahveh. *See* Jehovah.
James, William, 11, 28, 120, 160, 167, 168, 172, 182, 190, 207, 219, 224, 253, 309, 319, 323, 325, 329, 337, 343, 347, 348, 356, 381, 403.
Jefferies, R., 209, 217.
Jehovah, 51, 52, 56, 130.
Jesus. *See* Christ.
John the Baptist, 67.
John, Gospel of. *See* Fourth Gospel.
Jones, M., 78.
Jones, R. M., 119.
Josephus, 64.
Joshua, 52.
Josiah, reform of, 55.
Judaism. *See* Hebrew religion, Prophets of Israel, Psalms, Messianic hope, etc.
Judas, 70.
Judgment, the, 76, 88, 93, 109, 110, 385, 390.
Julian the "Apostate," 99, 156.
Jülicher, G. A., 66.
Jupiter, 22, 27, 32, 33.
Justification. *See* Salvation by faith.
Justin Martyr, 211.
Justinian, 260.

Kant, 337, 355.
Kennedy, H. A. A., 100.

Kent, C. F., 49, 61.
Khayyam, Omar, 395.
King, I., 11.
Kingdom of God, 50, 67, 76, 109, 232, 414.
Kingsley, Charles, 399.
Knox, G. W., 237.
Koran, 126.
Kuhns, O., 208.

Ladd, G. T., 225.
Lake, K., 84.
Lang, Andrew, 15, 16.
Lares and Penates, 32.
Last Supper, 103, 269.
Lazarus, 287, 288.
Lebreton, J., 109.
Leo III, 115.
Leuba, J. H., 16, 182, 185, 211, 323, 324, 339.
Lewis, E., 237, 238.
Liberal Christianity, 122.
Lindsay, T. M., 119.
Lobstein, P., 66.
Locke, John, 253.
Lodge, Sir Oliver, 156.
Logos, 65, 107.
Loisy, A., 105, 230.
Longfellow, H. W., 205.
LORD, the, origin of its substitution for Jahveh, 51.
Love, 79, 93, 97, 197.
Lucian, 97.
Lucretius, 9, 10, 34.
Luke, Gospel of, 65.
Luther, 116, 260, 267.

McConnell, Bishop, 173, 322.
MacFadyen, J. E., 49.
Macintosh, D. C., 237, 348.
McTaggart, J. M. E., 220, 334.
Madonna, worship of, 109, 117.
Magic, 10, 187.
Magna Mater, 34.
Mallock, W. H., 333.
Mana, 11.
Manes, 14, 52.
Manitou, 11.
Marett, R. R., 11.
Mark, Gospel of, 65.
Martineau, J., 216.
Mass, the, 117.

Mather, Cotton, 119.
Mathews, S., 109.
Matthew, Gospel of, 65.
Maximus of Tyre, 20.
Maya, 38.
Mazzini, 199.
Mechanism, 136, 282, 298, 300, 303.
Medical Materialism, 319.
Melancthon, 261.
Menzies, A., 214.
Messiah, meaning of the word, 61; Jesus' conception of the, 68, 78; Early Christian conception of, 106, 287. *See also* Messianic hope.
Messianic hope, 60, 67, 76, 93, 109, 385. *See also* Messiah.
Metempsychosis. *See* Transmigration.
Mill, J. S., 72, 233, 253, 308, 309, 318, 356, 381, 399, 409.
Miller, D. S., 344, 406.
Milton, 175.
Minds, belief in other, 327, 342, 346.
Miracles, 280.
Mithras, 24, 34, 97.
Modernism, 122.
Moffatt, J., 66.
Mohammed, 51, 124, 317, 318.
Mohammedanism, 124, 207.
Moody, D. L., 275.
Moore, A. W., 348.
Moore, G. F., 46.
Monasticism, 117, 204.
Monotheism, 37, 49, 107, 125, 130.
Montanism, 101.
Moral law, 17, 297.
Morality, contrasted with religion, 222, 335.
Morgan, J. V., 211.
Moses, 51, 53, 265, 268.
Mother of God, 109, 117.
Moulton, R. S., 50.
Müller, Max, 138.
Münsterberg, H., 285, 315, 316, 326.
Murray, Gilbert, 12, 20, 21, 26, 202.
Mycenæan religion, 21.
Mystery in religion, 214.
Mystery religions, 23, 384.
Mysticism, 137, 206, 320, 326.
Mythology, 23.

Natural law, 136, 281, 284.
Natural selection, 304, 392.

Nazarenes, 99.
Neo-Platonism, 103, 108.
Newman, J. H., 251.
New Testament, composition of, 64, 266; editions of, 66.
New Thought, 183, 211. *See also* Christian Science, Faith-cures.
Newton, Sir Isaac, 398.
Nirvana, 40, 341.
Numa, religion of, 31.

Observation, errors in, 312.
Odysseus, 29.
Oesterley, W. D. E., 61.
Old Testament, editions of, 49; introductions to, 49.
Olympian religion, 21, 26.
Optimism, 333, 367.
Organic life, 299.
Origen, 239.
Ormuzd, 46.
Orphic brotherhood, 23.
Orthodoxy, 238, 241, 267. *See also* Dogma, Creeds, etc.
Osiris, 34, 104.
Osler, William, 396.
Outer envelope, 66.

Paine, L. L., 109.
Paley, 303.
Palmer, G. H., 225.
Papacy, 114.
Parker, Theodore, 121, 276.
Parsees, 47.
Pascal, R., 402.
Paul, his life, 64, 85, 157, 171, 319; his vision of Christ, 83, 87, 269, 288, 292, 314, 317, 389; his teaching, 90, 104, 106, 162, 178, 180, 200, 231, 265, 272, 319, 332, 390.
Paulsen, F., 307, 309, 347, 363.
Peace, religious, 203, 244.
Peake, A. S., 66.
Pearson, K., 253, 255, 362.
Pentateuch, 268.
Perry, R. B., 299, 344, 352, 364.
Persecutions, 99, 199, 272.
Persephone, 27.
Persian religion, 45.
Pessimism, 40, 163, 203, 232, 368.
Peter, his "confession," 68; his vision of Christ, 82; his leadership, 84; as head of Roman Church, 114.

Pfleiderer, O., 66.
Pharisees, 69, 74.
Philo Judæus, 107.
Pinkham, H. W., 178.
Pitkin, W. B., 335.
Plato, 25, 137, 309, 380, 383.
Pliny, 64, 106.
Plotinus, 108.
Plutarch, 30.
Polybius, 32.
Polytheism, 11, 37, 46, 50, 106, 109, 130, 136.
Popes. *See* Papacy.
Poverty, cult of, 204.
Powell, L. P., 211.
Pragmatism, 332.
Pratt, J. B., 15.
Prayer, 187, 313, 343.
Predestination, 164, 272.
Presbyters, origin of, 113.
Priests, 113.
Progress, 375.
Prophets of Israel, 55, 155, 162, 200, 264, 313.
Protestantism, its origin, 116; its goal, 122, 130, 262.
Psalms, 59, 268, 271.
Psychical research, 317, 393.
Purgatory, 111, 117, 388.
Puritanism, 119, 221.
Purity, 80, 92, 97, 155, 197.

Rauschenbusch, W., 60, 231.
Reason, as the basis of belief, 121, 275, 352.
Redemption. *See* Salvation, Conversion.
Reformation, 115, 260.
Regeneration. *See* Salvation, Conversion.
Reinach, S., 214, 230.
Reincarnation. *See* Transmigration.
Religion, evolution of, 9, 128; nature of, 160, 202, 213, 239, 243; *vs.* theology, 215; *vs.* morality, 222, 335; *vs.* science, 258, 351. *See* also Christianity, etc.
Religious experience, interpretation of, 285, 312.
Religious sense, supposed, 329.
Remorse, 159.
Renan, E., 72.

Renunciation, 41, 161.
Repentance, 231, 241, 293.
Resurrection, the, 72, 82, 84, 287, 288, 291, 389.
Revelation, 249, 272; book of, 269.
Réville, A., 66, 84, 108.
Rhys-Davids, T. W., 41, 45.
Rice, W. N., 284.
Riehm, E. C. A., 61.
Righteousness, 57, 161.
Riley, Woodbridge, 211.
Rogers, A. K., 311.
Roman Catholic Church, 113.
Roman religion, 31, 114, 200.
Rousseau, 227.
Rowland, E. H., 351, 355.
Royce, J., 163, 230, 347.
Ruskin, John, 377.

Sabatier, A., 106, 176.
Sacraments, 67, 100, 103, 117, 167, 233, 235, 241.
Sacrifice, 151; human, 152; transformation of the conception of, 153.
St. Augustine, 120, 121, 163, 171, 175, 199, 250.
St. Francis, 38, 66, 198, 240.
St. Jerome, 113, 175, 267.
St. Simeon Stylites, 157.
St. Theresa, 318.
Saints, worship of, 109.
Salvation, 18, 96, 104, 117, 167, 168, 229; by faith, 91, 105, 172, 180, 245, 323; through Christ, 167, 174, 186, 236.
Santayana, G., 21, 23, 97, 98, 370.
Satan. *See* Devil.
Scapegoat, 152.
Schaub, E. L., 154.
Schiller, F. C. S., 332, 338, 339, 342, 343, 347, 348, 355.
Schools, closing of the, 260.
Schweitzer, A., 78.
Science *vs.* religion, 258, 351.
Scientific spirit, 254, 282, 345, 361, 397.
Scott, E. F., 65, 66, 67, 78, 103, 108, 113, 114.
Seeley, Sir J. R., 138, 139, 146, 256, 257.
Servetus, 261.
Service, spirit of. *See* Love.

INDEX

Seth, A., 347.
Shakespeare, 199.
Shamans, 15.
Shotwell, J. T., 100, 213, 214.
Showerman, Grant, 100.
Sin, 154; forgiveness of, 73, 79, 314; original, 162, 169, 175.
Smith, H. P., 49.
Smith, W. R., 19.
Socinus, 175.
Sōphrosynē, 29, 30.
Spear, R. E., 235.
Spencer, Herbert, 14, 214, 301, 355, 358.
Spinoza, 267.
Spirit, Holy, 106, 108, 139, 238, 314, 316.
Spiritualism, 285, 317, 393.
Spirituality, 244.
Soul, 387.
Stanton, V. H., 66.
Starbuck, E. D., 168, 169.
Stephen, 87.
Stoics, 25, 96, 201, 209.
Stokes, A. P., 145.
Stratton, G. M., 339.
Streeter, B. S., 353, 400.
Strong, C. A., 299.
Sturt, H., 231.
Suetonius, 64.
Sunderland, J. T., 289.
Supernatural. *See* Miracles.
Superstition, nature of, 217.
Synoptic Gospels, 65.

Taboo, 155.
Tacitus, 64, 83,
Taylor, Jeremy, 163.
Teleology. *See* Design.
Telepathy, 394.
Tennant, F. R., 163.
Tennyson, Alfred, 29.
Teraphim, 52.
Theodicy, 41, 306, 366.
Theology, its relation to religion, 215; its method, 249, 312, 332, 358; Scholastic, 252; origin of, 259; present status, 412.
Thompson, J. M., 66.
Tolstoy, L., 193.
Tongues, speaking with, 83, 317, 319.

Toy, C. H., 62.
Transcendentalism, 38, 347, 393.
Transmigration, 36, 37, 39.
Transubstantiation, 103.
Treves, 285, 325.
Trine, R. W., 211.
Trinity, the, 106, 109, 136, 145.
Tylor, E. B., 13.
Tyndall, 189.

Unworldliness, 80, 97, 117, 158, 204, 224, 232.
Uzzah, 155.

Vedas, 26, 36, 46, 156.
Vesta, 32.
Virgil, 34.
Virgin birth, 66, 142, 270, 286, 288.
Visions, 317. *See also under* Paul.
Vitalism, 283, 301.

Warner, C. D., 278.
Warschauer, J., 65.
Weber, A., 260.
Wedgwood, J., 37.
Wendell, Barrett, 121.
Wenley, R. M., 255.
Wernle, P., 66.
Wesley, John, 181,
Weymouth, R. F., 66.
White, Andrew D., 261.
Whitman, Walt, 161.
Wiggers, G. F., 163.
Will to believe, 406.
Witch of Endor, 15.
Worcester, Elwood, 185.
Word of God (= Logos), 107.
Wordsworth, W., 138, 208.
Workman, H. B., 159.
Wyclif, 116.

Xenophanes, 24.

Y.M.C.A., 123.
Yoga, 207.

Zend-Avesta, 46, 156.
Zeus, 22, 25, 33.
Zoroaster, 46.
Zoroastrianism, 42, 45, 131.

DATE DUE